D0731715

DEATH AND OTHER PENALTIES

Death and Other Penalties

Philosophy in a Time of Mass Incarceration

Edited by

GEOFFREY ADELSBERG, LISA GUENTHER,
AND SCOTT ZEMAN

FORDHAM UNIVERSITY PRESS

New York 2015

Copyright © 2015 Fordham University Press

All rights reserved. No part of this publication may be
reproduced, stored in a retrieval system, or transmitted
in any form or by any means—electronic, mechanical,
photocopy, recording, or any other—except for brief
quotations in printed reviews, without the prior permission
of the publisher.

Fordham University Press has no responsibility for the
persistence or accuracy of URLs for external or third-party
Internet websites referred to in this publication and does
not guarantee that any content on such websites is, or will
remain, accurate or appropriate.

Fordham University Press also publishes its books in a
variety of electronic formats. Some content that appears in
print may not be available in electronic books.

Visit us online at www.fordhampress.com.

Library of Congress Cataloging-in-Publication Data

Death and other penalties : philosophy in a time of mass
incarceration / edited by Geoffrey Adelsberg, Lisa
Guenther, and Scott Zeman. — First edition.
pages cm
Includes bibliographical references and index.
ISBN 978-0-8232-6529-9 (cloth : alk. paper) —
ISBN 978-0-8232-6530-5 (pbk. : alk. paper)
1. Capital punishment—United States.
2. Imprisonment—United States. 3. Punishment—
United States. 4. Criminal justice, Administration
of—United States. I. Adelsberg, Geoffrey, editor.
HV8699.U5D337 2015
365'.973—dc23
2014040671

Printed in the United States of America
17 16 15   5 4 3 2 1
First edition

CONTENTS

On the Inviolability of Human Life

Rethinking Power and Responsibility

Punishment, Desert, and Equality: A Levinasian Analysis
Prisons and Palliative Politics
Sovereignty, Community, and the Incarceration of Immigrants
Without the Right to Exist: Mass Incarceration
and National Security
Prison Abolition and a Culture of Sexual Difference

Isolation and Resistance

Statement on Solitary Confinement
The Violence of the Supermax: Toward a Phenomenological
Aesthetics of Prison Space
Prison and the Subject of Resistance: A Levinasian Inquiry
Critical Theory, Queer Resistance, and the Ends of Capture

FOREWORD:
LIFE AND OTHER RESPONSIBILITIES

Joy James

Pre- and postmortems attending U.S. society are intricately woven into histories of legal discourse and political hubris that oversee executions and penalties administered by the state. Official language seeks to shape our memories of what is right by law. The counterdiscourse prepares our minds for what is just.

On behalf of the United States and its society, an elite sector of the United States is allowed to kill and torture with impunity—while expecting gratitude for the safety it "ensures." A quick survey reveals death sentences meted out by state courts, federal courts, and military courts, and internationally by military drones that target both U.S. citizens and noncitizens. The extrajudicial killings by bureaucratic appendages of the state include police shootings, jail cell deaths, and deputized whiteness dispatching black teens. Physical deaths or killings coexist with devastating "penalties." Those other penalties are administered for deviance, mundane drug offenses, property theft, and tragic assaults. Finally, there are the punishments against rebellions. This last category, which encompasses rebels and revolutionaries with lives shaped by responsibilities to confront injustice, is often diminished in its importance; hence, its transformative acts disappear from print or are rendered less viable because of the asymmetrical warfare waged against it. One need only recall the 1971 suppression of New York's Attica Prison rebellion for human and civil rights.

State killings, the raw expression of state violence, are macroaggressions against life and community. Democracy's microaggressions, the "other penalties," are expressed in intimate state violence: the invasive incarceration practices that ravage the person without immediately killing his or her body. "Other penalties" is a synonym for trauma: "medical handcuffs" and drug stupors; captivity in mental and emotional wastelands; sterilization; vulnerability to (gang) rape while institutionalized; solitary confinement's evisceration of the soul and neurological stability. In the face of death and other penalties, life responsibilities have included resistance to human rights abuses, lethal injections, auction block transactions, and the caging and selling of human animals in the stock market of international commerce.

Life and other responsibilities embrace historical struggles against executioners and captors. Individual and shared lives are shaped by the political violence and terror we evade or witness, succumb to or survive. Our shared political memories of structural violence influence the political possibilities for a greater society. We would have to remember the power of resistance from the captive, not merely their victimization.

Captivity and victimization so commingle that one misses the nuanced political responses against injustice by those living lives of responsibility within and outside of formal prisons. A key responsibility is to the memory of resistance and the recall of agency among the wounded and dead despite the triumphal declaration of victory by those who administer the law.

Agency exists even in what is understood as defeat. Thus death and the other penalties never have the final word. Our history of rebellion against repression and captivity, where premature, violent death and torture are political phenomena designated for historically colonized or enslaved groups, is instructive.

Recall that the United States has, reportedly, engaged in only two mass executions. The first was in Mankato, Minnesota, during the 1862 Dakota war; there, the federal government and financial speculators vanquished indigenous fighters resisting starvation. President Abraham Lincoln shifted his attention from a very bloody killing field—a civil war fought for geographical integrity—to authorize the mass hanging of thirty-two indigenous fighters accused of murder (war) and rape (apparently fabricated to justify the executions). The government made a political point that enabled economic theft and profiteering to continue; its death sentences embodied both the immediate demise of resisters and the slow death by starvation of their families and kin. During the second mass execution in Houston, Texas, in 1917, the War Department deflected its attention from its newly declared war against Germany, and World War I, to exorcise black sovereign loyalty by hanging nineteen African American soldiers and imprisoning sixty-three with life sentences for rebelling against southern racial tyranny and causing the deaths of several whites who fought against black life.[1]

The historical ancestors in maroon camps, on reservations, in army camps seeking to either escape or belong to democracy's manifest destiny reappear among the contemporary captives. Their proximity to death and other penalties shaped and shapes our political imagination and responses today. Captives have always led, intellectually and politically, although some find it impractical to follow, or even publicly acknowledge this leadership. Nonetheless, it is important to hold accurate and responsible memories of the militancy that led to international or national trials and the public's growing knowledge of state abuses.

Death and Other Penalties exemplifies living with responsibilities and diverse agencies, including those from the prison. This anthology works to resuscitate western democracy as something other than imperial and deadly. Here we read analyses, philosophies, memoirs, and epitaphs as the chapters in this book code or reformulate codes for living with responsibilities.

Contributors, imprisoned for decades or executed, render historical resistance—1862 Dakota; 1917 Houston—in real time. Russell "Maroon" Shoatz recovers maroon camps as freedom sites at democracy's borders: "All that's missing is the *clarity* that tells us that such an effort is needed, and the *political will* to struggle to build such a movement. The same way that the historical maroons set their sights on being free from chattel slavery, then developing the will to run away and struggling to stay free."[2] Abu Ali Abdur'Rahman's grief illustrates our wounded capacity for healing and struggle: "We come from abusive and destitute environments. Our lives were built on anger, fear, hatred and lack of love."[3] Ezat Tabatabaeian's greeting at her execution reminds us of the transcendent ability to comfort in the face of physical, but not political, death: "Hello to all I have loved, I love and will love."[4]

Death and Other Penalties helps us to face responsibilities, not as burdens but as opportunities for steering democracy and our own lives beyond aggressions, manufactured death, and trauma toward new possibilities—toward life.

ACKNOWLEDGMENTS

This book project was inspired and motivated by a weekly discussion group called REACH Coalition. REACH is an organization for reciprocal education based on Tennessee's death row. We are committed to the idea that intellectual exchange can also become a site of ethical encounter, social transformation, and political resistance. Part and present members of REACH include Abu Ali Abdur'Rahman, Geoffrey Adelsberg, Rosalee Averin, Devin Banks, G'dongalay Berry, Kevin Burns, Ron Cauthern, Tyrone Chalmers, Natalie Cisneros, Gary Cone, LeMaricus Davidson, David Duncan, John Freeland, Lisa Guenther, Joshua Hall, Kennath Artez Henderson, Carmela Hill-Burke, Olen Hutchison, Akil Jahi, Don Johnson, Katie Kelly, Tatiana McInnis, Amy McKiernan, Donald Middlebrooks, Harold Wayne Nichols, Richard Odom, Pervis Payne, Andrea Pitts, Derrick Quintero, Donika Ross, Sandy Skene, Rebecca Tuvel, Sarah Tyson, and Scott Zeman.

Thanks to Derrick Quintero and Ann Catherine Carter for the cover art, and to Lara Giordano for preparing the index.

Thank you to Helen Tartar for her guidance and her support for this project. We will mourn her loss for many years to come. Thanks to Thomas Lay, who has upheld Helen's legacy and contributed his astute editorial vision and care to this project.

Introduction: Death and Other Penalties

Geoffrey Adelsberg, Lisa Guenther, and Scott Zeman

The United States incarcerates more of its own citizens than any other country in the world. A disproportionate number of these prisoners are people of color; today, a black man has a greater chance of going to prison than to college.[1] We are the only Western democracy to retain the death penalty, even though scholarship, statistics, and even legal decisions suggest that the system is deeply flawed and structured by racism and class oppression.[2] Sociologist Loïc Wacquant calls the United States "the first genuine prison society in history"; legal scholar Michelle Alexander calls mass incarceration a new, "colorblind" form of Jim Crow; and sociologist David Garland calls the death penalty a "peculiar institution," implying a continuity between state execution and slavery.[3] Clearly, the time has come for philosophers and radical intellectuals to rethink prisons and the death penalty.

Motivated by a growing sense that mass incarceration and state execution are among the most important ethical and political problems of our time, we have brought together a diverse group of scholars to offer their analysis of issues raised by the U.S. prison system. These scholars write from perspectives including deconstruction, psychoanalysis, phenomenology, and critical theory, as well as sociopolitical discourses such as critical race theory, feminism, queer theory, and disability studies. They engage with issues such as the hyperincarceration of people of color, the incomplete abolition of slavery, the exploitation of prisoners as workers and as "raw material" for the prison industrial complex, the intensive confinement of prisoners in supermax units, and the complexities of capital punishment in an age of abolition. They explore the parallels and interconnections between the prison, the university, the hospital, and the workplace, as well as the mutual reinforcement of carceral policies and immigration policies. They reveal the many ways in which prisons have failed to protect people or to address the harm of violent crime, functioning instead to manage and control populations that have been marginalized by poverty, racism, sexism, heterosexism, able-ism, and other forms of oppression. Finally, and most importantly, they develop strategies for intellectual and political resistance to the apparent inevitability of incarceration and state execution as responses to crime and social difference.

Death and Other Penalties includes the writing of incarcerated and non-incarcerated intellectuals, each of whom is situated differently in relation to carceral and academic institutions, to the discipline of philosophy, and to activist political practices. We hope that this volume will generate more sustained conversations across the boundaries of different disciplines, institutions, and social locations. The stakes are high for collaborative work on imprisonment and other forms of punishment, surveillance, and control, both for people behind bars and for those with the ambivalent privilege of being considered "free."

The first part, "Legacies of Slavery," takes as its point of departure the Thirteenth Amendment, which abolishes slavery and indentured servitude "except as a punishment for crime whereof the party shall have been duly convicted." This exception reinscribed slavery within the U.S. penal system in ways that are still being felt today. In the years immediately following the partial abolition of slavery in 1865, every former slave state passed "black codes" that made it possible to arrest newly freed slaves for vagrancy, unemployment, petty theft, and so forth and then lease them out for unpaid work clearing swamps, coal-mining, building roads and railways, and even picking cotton on former slave plantations. This was the convict leasing system, and by some accounts it was "worse than slavery" because the employer no longer had an incentive to maintain his workers as property.[4] The convict leasing system was quite literally a death penalty; most prisoners did not last longer than five years, and none lasted longer than ten. Convict leasing systems were in operation from 1865 to 1928, but their effects can still be felt today in the extremely low or nonexistent wages earned by prisoners across the United States and in the use of prison labor by private corporations as well as by federal or state-run prison employers.[5]

In his chapter, "Excavating the Sedimentations of Slavery: The Unfinished Project of American Abolition," Brady Heiner traces the desk in his office at California State University back to its production in California's Prison Industry Authority—a carceral manufacturing system that, at a rate of thirty to ninety-five cents per hour, employs a segment of the state's imprisoned population to provide goods and services to state agencies that the latter are legislatively mandated to purchase. He analyzes this hidden background of carceral production in terms of the prison industrial complex, the convict lease system, and other Reconstruction-era legal rituals that refashioned American prisons into receptacles that grant sanctuary to racialized forms of punishment prevalent during slavery. In the end, he advances a concept of *semiotic transfer* to explain how the institution of the prison became a functional substitute for the plantation, and how the discourse of "criminality" became racialized.

The incomplete abolition of slavery and the exploitation of convict labor raise conceptual and methodological questions about the political economy of crime and punishment. In "From Commodity Fetishism to Prison Fetishism: Slavery, Convict-leasing, and the Ideological Productions of Incarceration," James Manos argues that punishment is neither the effect of crime nor solely the effect of economic needs. Rather, he contends that punishment is an independent causal force that has shaped the economic organization of neoliberalism. To support this claim, Manos builds on the work of critical theorists Rusche and Kirchheimer, authors of *Punishment and Social Structure* (1935). Manos preserves their account of the centrality of the relationship between the dispossession of capital and punishment, while critiquing the primary role they assign to the modes of production in determining the modes of punishment. He argues that the rise of convict-leasing as a dominant mode of punishment was not just the *effect* of the modes of production but actually *restructured* those modes of production. Taking account of this shift demands that we examine the prison not from the framework of commodity fetishism but from a new framework of prison fetishism. This means, at the very least, moving our analysis of mass incarceration from the extraction of surplus value from the labor of the prisoners themselves to an understanding of how prisons produce convicts as not only a racialized and criminalized class but also a dispossessed class that has become a commodity in and of itself.

What forms of resistance are possible from within this social position, and what role might philosophical practices play in amplifying this resistance? The final chapter in this section, "Maroon Philosophy," presents a written exchange between incarcerated activist and scholar Russell "Maroon" Shoatz and philosophy professor Lisa Guenther. Shoatz draws on the history of fugitive slave (or "maroon") communities to address contemporary issues of poverty, violence, racism, sexism, environmental destruction, and the prison industrial complex. He was held in solitary confinement for more than twenty-two consecutive years before being released into the general population, thanks to the work of his family, supporters, and the Abolitionist Law Center. Mumia Abu-Jamal has called Shoatz "arguably the longest-held black political prisoner in America"; he has praised Shoatz's analysis of the Occupy Movement, social media, and grassroots political activism: "Although nearly 70 years old, his mind [is as] sharp as a cactus, informed, analytical, intuitive, acute."[6] In *Maroon the Implacable: The Collected Works of Russell Maroon Shoatz* (2013), Shoatz describes the decentralized structure of fugitive slave communities and connects this model to contemporary social movements. In the interview presented here, he reflects on the practical and theoretical implications of his analysis in conversation with Lisa Guenther, author of *Solitary Confinement: Social Death and its Afterlives* (2013). Shoatz's life and work attest to the legacy of not just slavery but also the *resistance* to slavery. He offers an alternative history of the Americas—one that does not begin with the "discovery" of a "new world" ready to be conquered but rather with networks of relation and resistance that go beyond the colonial project and offer concrete models of mutual empowerment.

The second part, "Death Penalties," offers critical perspectives on the practice of and discourses around the death penalty in the United States. All five authors seek expansive notions of the "death penalty." They not only consider the legal, moral, and political questions that surround state execution, but they contend with the death penalty's connection to mass incarceration, poverty, psychic investments in violence, state killing in war, extralegal racist violence, chattel slavery, neoliberal economics, and the expanding number of life-without-parole sentences. The breadth of the authors' engagement with the death penalty in this section signals a shared contention that the critique of the death penalty is inseparable from a critique of a jingoistic, racist, and classist U.S. carceral democracy.

In "In Reality—From the Row," Derrick Quintero proposes social democratic alternatives to present carceral and legal systems. Quintero is a writer, poet, and visual artist who has spent thirty-six years on Tennessee's death row. He brings his years of reflecting upon the legal system, the conditions of his incarceration, and his experience of building communities of support and resistance to the project of rethinking the death penalty. His social democratic vision is twofold: first, he proposes the institution of therapeutic resources to break cycles of violence and create conditions of community within prison walls. Secondly, he confronts the problem of poverty among death penalty defendants and proposes a redefinition of a "jury of peers" that would represent a diversity of race, class, political ideology, and spiritual beliefs.

In "Inheritances of the Death Penalty: American Racism and Derrida's Theological-Political Sovereignty," Geoffrey Adelsberg draws on the work of Jacques Derrida and Angela Y. Davis toward an examination of philosophical resistance to the death penalty, especially in the United States. He challenges the viability of Derrida's distinction between an unconditional death penalty abolitionism that abolishes state violence in all its forms and a conditional death penalty abolitionism that calls for the end of the practice of the state killing as punishment within a certain locality. Adelsberg looks to Davis's writings on slavery, racism, and the death penalty to show the ways in which an abolitionism that confronts a local practice of the death penalty can satisfy the reasons that motivate Derrida to call for an unconditional abolitionism. Adelsberg follows Davis in his claim that no confrontation with state violence in the United States can be considered without a confrontation with the history of U.S. racism and challenges Derrideans to interrogate this history more deeply.

In "Making Death a Penalty: Or, Making 'Good' Death a 'Good' Penalty," Kelly Oliver argues that juridical and public contentions that lethal injection protocols do not trespass prohibitions against cruel and unusual punishment rest on the fantasy of a clean, instantaneous, and painless death made possible by technological intervention. Oliver draws on resources in the work of Martin Heidegger and Jacques Derrida, as well as Supreme Court decisions, to put such a fantasy into question and to challenge the distinction between execution and murder, upon which ethical and political justifications for the death penalty depend.

Andrew Dilts's chapter, "Death Penalty Abolition in Neoliberal Times: The SAFE California Act and the Nexus of Savings and Economy," argues that recent death penalty "abolition" measures that have passed in states like Maryland and Connecticut and nearly passed in California exemplify a successful linkage between the logic of neoliberal austerity and public security rather than any categorical unacceptability of the death penalty. He focuses on the "SAFE California Act," whose supporters argued that the death penalty is too costly to maintain in the face of current economic conditions. To understand this particular discursive formation of security and savings, Dilts contends that we must pay attention to the theory of "human capital" developed in the mid-twentieth century by Chicago School economists. This discourse informs both criminological and popular conceptions of incarcerable persons as monstrous and incorrigible offenders who are nevertheless also fully responsible subjects. Through Foucault's 1979 analysis of "American" neoliberalism and the analysis of California exit polling data, Dilts reveals the underside of neoliberal death penalty abolition and its dangerous yet seemingly palatable replacement penalty of life without parole.

The part concludes with Julia Kristeva's meditation on the desire for a universal abolition of the death penalty, "On the Inviolability of Human Life." What motivates the desire for abolition, and what possibilities for a meaningful life—and a meaningful death—does this desire support? The desire for abolition affirms the singularity and inviolability of each and every human life. But what does this imply for the lives that have been destroyed by murder, or for the trauma of survivors? And what role does the death drive play in both the desire for abolition and the horror of murder?

The third part, "Rethinking Power and Responsibility," investigates the contemporary relationship between the U.S. judicial system as an institution of social control and the unexpectedly productive effects of that control on legal responsibility, social hierarchy, and "health" in and of prisons. Each of the chapters in this section points to the gap between ideals of justice and the state institutionalization of "justice" as an existing system.

In "Punishment, Desert, and Equality: A Levinasian Analysis," Benjamin Yost begins by defending the claim that the overincarceration of disadvantaged social groups is unjust. Many arguments for penal reform are based on the unequal distribution of punishment, most notably disproportionate punishment of the poor and people of color. However, some philosophers use a noncomparative conception of desert to argue that the justice of punishment is *independent* of its distribution. On this view, which has significant influence in Fourteenth-Amendment jurisprudence, unequal punishment is *not* unjust. After detailing the "noncomparativist challenge," this chapter argues that Levinasian conceptions of desert enable a theory of penal justice according to which comparative considerations are essential. In so doing, it shows that the noncomparativist challenge can be met. The chapter concludes by considering whether Levinasian conceptions of desert and responsibility show members of socially advantaged groups to be more blameworthy for their wrongdoing than members of disadvantaged groups.

In "Prisons and Palliative Politics," Ami Harbin examines the experiences of ailing and terminally ill prison inmates as well as those of the inmate volunteers in prison hospice and palliative care programs to suggest that we critically reorient our understanding of what "health" might mean in circumstances of carceral death. Against the backdrop of bioethical research into prison palliative care, Harbin reflects on how the relationships between dying inmates and inmate hospice volunteers are both allowed for and strategically constrained by prisons. And by analyzing and employing Judith Butler's concept of grief as "livability," she considers how such relationships function to support all those involved *beyond* what is typically foreseen in the hospice training programs. She thus initiates a broader discussion about what a palliative ethics informed by grief and mortality could and should offer for a social critique of imprisonment: to the degree that prisoners' palliative work redeploys their experiences in prison as significant and relational, it highlights grief as a form of resistance of those imprisoned to crushing isolation. Thus, according to Harbin, palliative ethics for prisoners needs to move beyond traditional bioethical questions about the rights of the dying to comfort (e.g., to palliative sedation) and final wishes (e.g., about where to die) into a critique of the very institution of imprisonment. As she puts it, palliative ethics must become palliative politics.

In "Sovereignty, Community, and the Incarceration of Immigrants," Matt Whitt examines how the United States increasingly employs its network of jails and prisons as a form of border control. Since the mid-1990s, the United States has shifted its border control strategy from immediate expulsion to punitive detention, and then deportation, of undocumented immigrants. Concurrently, the United States has criminalized immigration, treating undocumented entry and residence as threats to the social order. In this chapter, Whitt argues that the criminalization of immigrants is an unacknowledged strategy by which the United States exercises the fundamental prerogative of state sovereignty—namely, the ability to reconstitute the political community by deciding upon issues of membership. This reconstitution operates not only demographically, by distinguishing full members from nonmembers and partial members, but also ideologically. By opposing the figure of the "criminal alien" to that of the presumptively law-abiding citizen, U.S. law and political discourse stage an opposition between those who purportedly have not "earned" their place in the community and those who are presumed, merely by contrast, to "deserve" the benefits of residence and membership. This opposition is the hallmark of modern sovereignty. Although some observers have suggested that state sovereignty is waning in a globalized world, Whitt argues that the criminalization of immigration shows how sovereignty might persist, but adapt, to new material conditions.

In "Without the Right to Exist: Mass Incarceration and National Security," Andrea Smith critiques the debate over national security and civil liberties from a prison abolitionist perspective. She argues that both sides of that debate make invidious assumptions. National security arguments claim that extrajuridical means are necessary to secure U.S. democracy. Smith shows how this argument assumes the foundational sacrificial logic of the U.S. nation-state: it once again calls for the sacrifice of the lives of people of color for the sake of the nation-state. Civil libertarians critique the extrajuridical measures of the Bush and Obama administrations, but they offer the U.S. criminal justice system as the proper channel of redress for suspected terrorists. As such, they assume the integrity of institutions of criminal justice and, by extension, institutions of mass incarceration that create disproportionate levels of social, political, and physical death within communities of color. For Smith, the failure of both sides of the debate generates the necessity of a third position: a nation-state that does not rely upon the continual deaths of racialized others. Smith shows how opposition to mass incarceration in the United States necessitates this rethinking.

In "Prison Abolition and a Culture of Sexual Difference," Sarah Tyson contends with the complex relationship between feminism and prisons. She looks to the often-conflicted relationships between feminist groups like Communities Against Rape and Abuse (CARA) and policy changes meant to address feminist issues, including sexual assault and domestic abuse, that have been directly involved in the unprecedented growth of prison populations since the 1970s. Against the silence and calls for harsher sentencing that characterize many feminist responses to the question of what should happen to perpetrators of sexual abuse, Tyson argues that feminists ought to see mass incarceration *as* violence against women. She engages with prisoners' writings on sexual abuse in prison and shows how prisons reinforce and are reinforced by violence against women—as well as men. She concludes by extending Luce Irigaray's critical work to show the depth of transformation that a world without prisons *and* without violence against women will require.

The fourth part, "Isolation and Resistance," addresses both the violence of solitary confinement and other forms of isolation in carceral systems and the possibilities for resistance within and beyond these systems. While each of the authors approach isolation and resistance through a different lens, each suggests a relationship between sociality and its elaboration as central to developing effective forms of resistance. What is needed to resist torture of this or that form of isolation is the work of sociality. The strength of these chapters, in this respect, is not confined to their own lenses. Read together, they point to the reproductive relationship not just between torture and isolation but also between sociality and growth. Thus what resistance to isolation and torture requires is simply a place, albeit one saturated with common social difficulties, where social others can begin to hear and understand the claims of the otherwise isolated and tortured.

In his "Statement on Solitary Confinement," Abu Ali Abdur'Rahman testifies against the use of solitary confinement from the perspective of someone who has spent many of his teenage and adult years—reproducing some experiences as a child—in solitary. Submitted to the June 2012 Senate Subcommittee on Solitary Confinement, this statement describes the damaging effects of his confinements as well as the link between confinement and the institutional failure to address sexual abuse in prison. Acknowledging his and others' injuries and failures, he argues for the need for a social space to heal and grow. Further, he argues against the "criminalization of mental illness" and for a transformation of the prison into a psychologically and socially aware space offering direction to those who have suffered confinement, poverty, racism, and class oppression.

In "The Violence of the Supermax: Toward a Phenomenological Aesthetics of Prison Space," Adrian Switzer addresses the problem of violence in Supermax prisons from a dual phenomenological and aesthetic perspective. A review of the sociological evidence on the relationship between maximum-security prisons and violence reveals several inconsistencies: a facility originally designed and built in the name of reducing prison violence instead has been a site of persistent and increased violence. Prompted by the incongruities in the empirical evidence on Supermax violence and by the sense that those incongruities stem from the assumption that prison violence is a matter of prisoner violence, this chapter approaches the same problem from a transcendental phenomenological perspective. Switzer follows Husserl's directive that empirical and pure psychology require, first, a transcendental phenomenology. By working through Husserl's remarks on space and spatiality, and by appealing to Bachelard's *Poetics of Space*, Switzer argues that there is a basic "mode" to space-in-itself, namely, a hostility that constitutes from a nonsubjective perspective the inhospitability of the bare spaces of the Supermax prison. The chapter concludes with an aesthetic supplement that *shows* the "hostility" of bare space in a way that a theoretical phenomenology, even at its best, can merely *state*.

In "Prison and the Subject of Resistance: A Levinasian Inquiry," Shokoufeh Sakhi examines isolation and torture from the perspective of political prisoners within totalitarian systems. By elucidating a dialectic of capitulation under torture and the threat of death, this chapter explores the meaning of ethical resistance and shows how this meaning may both embody a praxis of resistance beyond the grasp of coercive systems and also point toward a theory of ethical engagement as such. While the interrogation of the ethical meaning of resistance may be informed by theory, its meaning is, of course, lived. With reference to experiences of resistance and capitulation in the context of various political prison systems, Sakhi draws on Emmanuel Levinas's ethical philosophy to articulate what she calls a "resistance beyond resistance," a resistance of humanity itself, that may represent an absolute limit to the reach of coercive practices, and a site from which to conceive an *effective* resistance.

Finally, in "Critical Theory, Queer Resistance, and the Ends of Capture," Liat Ben-Moshe, Che Gossett, Nick Mitchell, and Eric A. Stanley hold a roundtable discussion on the intersections, divergences, and collisions between trans/queer politics and critical theory in service of abolishing the prison industrial complex. Working from recent interventions in critical prison studies that focus on the specificity of dis/ability, sexuality, and gender, they discuss the ways in which Derrida, Fanon, and Foucault push our analysis beyond legal comfort, prison reform, and constitutional fetishism. The discussants consider a wide range of questions from the viability of contemporary formations of "queerness as anti-normativity" for the project of prison abolition, to the innocent/guilty binary as it appears in current mainstream political immigration debates and AIDS Action Now! and ACT UP HIV/AIDS activism, to the questions that arise with "neoliberal queer inclusion" in the carceral state. The responses pay careful attention to the perceived and possibly real antagonism between deconstruction and the materiality of prison, and they consider the moments when deconstruction can work in the interest of queer/trans, disability, race, and gender prison abolition activists.

Legacies of Slavery

Excavating the Sedimentations of Slavery: The Unfinished Project of American Abolition

Brady Heiner

> The futility of severe punishment and cruel treatment may be proven
> a thousand times, but so long as society is unable to solve its social
> problems, repression, the easy way out, will always be accepted.
> It provides the illusion of security by covering the symptoms of
> social disease with a system of legal and moral value judgments.
>
> —GEORG RUSCHE AND OTTO KIRCHHEIMER,
> *Punishment and Social Structure* (1939)

Mass incarceration is arguably the most pressing and protracted social crisis of postindustrial America. The imprisoned population in the United States has exploded from 200,000 people in the early 1970s to 2.3 million people in the first decade of the twenty-first century, including 95,000 youths under the age of eighteen. To accommodate this colossal movement toward confinement, close to one thousand prisons have been built throughout the United States since 1973. "Short of major wars," writes criminologist Elliot Currie, "mass incarceration has been the most thoroughly implemented government social program of our time."[1] U.S. criminal justice policy and imprisonment practices are drastically out of line with international human rights norms and those of comparably developed democracies across the globe—so much so that America's peculiar institution of penality has been branded as "American penal exceptionalism."[2] The United States incarcerates the largest population in the history of the world.[3] A mere 5 percent of the global population, we maintain 25 percent of the world's incarcerated population. Incarcerated persons are disproportionately from racialized groups[4] (nearly 70 percent of the imprisoned population are people of African, Native American, or Latino/Chicano ancestry);[5] they are disproportionately from economically disadvantaged backgrounds (e.g., 11 percent of those incarcerated were homeless in the year before their confinement, and 63 percent had incomes of less than $1,000 in the month prior to arrest);[6] and at the time of their arrest, they are disproportionately less educated than their counterparts in the general population (e.g., 43 percent of the imprisoned population had not completed high school or its equivalent prior to their confinement, compared to 18 percent of the general population over the age of eighteen).[7]

The crisis proportions of U.S. mass incarceration have generated myriad forms of critique, proposal, and resistance at the academic, policy, and grassroots levels; they have led analysts to refer to contemporary American democracy as a "penal state,"[8] "penal democracy,"[9] or "carceral state."[10] This chapter argues that the policy, practice, and discourse of mass incarceration are animated by a prison industrial complex that reactivates social sedimentations of American slavery. I am thus a part of a growing collective of philosophers, social and legal theorists (e.g., Angela Y. Davis,[11] Saidiya Hartman,[12] Joy James,[13] Dorothy Roberts,[14] Michelle Alexander,[15] Loïc Wacquant,[16] Colin Dayan,[17] Lisa Guenther,[18] Frank Wilderson,[19] Patricia Ocen,[20] and Michael Hallett[21]) who advance accounts that variously articulate the *functional continuum* linking contemporary mass incarceration to past regimes of racial domination such as slavery, the convict lease system, and Jim Crow.[22]

The chapter begins with a phenomenological exploration of the desk in my university office at California State University, bracketing its everyday familiarity as an instrumentally available background of scholastic and pedagogic activity in order to trace its social conditions of emergence in the transpersonal horizons of California's Prison Industry Authority—a carceral manufacturing system that, at a rate of thirty to ninety-five cents per hour, employs a segment of the state's massive and largely racialized imprisoned population to provide goods and services to state agencies that the latter are legislatively mandated to purchase.

Analyzing this hidden background of carceral production in terms of the prison industrial complex, I draw on critical race theory and analytical history to argue that the contemporary American prison system operates as a repository for sedimentations of sense whose historical genesis is traceable to the postbellum convict lease system and other Reconstruction-era legal rituals that refashioned American prisons into receptacles that grant sanctuary to racialized forms of punishment prevalent during slavery. I refine this genealogy by advancing a concept of *semiotic transfer* to explain how the institution of the prison became a functional substitute for the plantation and how the discourse of "criminality" became racialized. I argue that the antebellum positionality of the "slave" and the postbellum positionality of the "criminal" come to be *semiotically and associatively paired* and are thus genealogically linked through postbellum legal rituals and everyday practices. I conclude by outlining a two-sided account of abolition involving intertwining movements aimed at mass *decarceration* and socioeconomic and political *reconstruction*.

From the Philosopher's Desk to the Prison: Becoming Oriented through/to the Sedimentations of Slavery

The form of wood, for instance, is altered if a table is made out of it.
Nevertheless the table continues to be wood, an ordinary, sensuous
thing. But as soon as it emerges as a commodity, it changes into a
thing which transcends sensuousness. It not only stands on its legs
on the ground, but, in relation to all other commodities, it stands
on its head, and evolves out of its wooden brain grotesque ideas, far
more wonderful than if it were to begin dancing of its own free will.

KARL MARX (1867)[23]

Let us start with an example. Constantly seeing this table and
meanwhile walking around it, changing my position in space in
whatever way, I have continually the consciousness of this one
identical table as factually existing 'in person' and remaining
quite unchanged. The table-perception, however, is a continually
changing one; it is a continuity of changing perceptions. I close
my eyes. My other senses have no relation to the table. Now I
have no perception of it. I open my eyes; and I have the perception
again. *The* perception? Let us be more precise. Returning, it is not,
under any circumstances, individually the same. Only the table is
the same, intended to as the same in the synthetical consciousness
which connects the new perception with the memory.

EDMUND HUSSERL (1913)[24]

What is there in *the* room there at home is *the* table (not 'a'
table among many other tables in other rooms and houses) at
which one sits *in order to* write, have a meal, sew, play. Everyone
sees this right away, e.g., during a visit: it is a writing table,
a dining table, a sewing table—such is the primary way in

which it is being encountered in itself. This characteristic of 'in
order to do something' is not merely imposed on the table by
relating and assimilating it to something else which it is not.

MARTIN HEIDEGGER (1923)[25]

If I stand in front of my desk and lean on it with both
hands, only my hands are accentuated and my whole
body trails behind them like a comet's tail.

MAURICE MERLEAU-PONTY (1945)[26]

Tables abound in the texts of philosophy. This is not surprising, since
tables are among the objects nearest to the bodies of philosophers. The
table, specifically the writing table or desk, is part of the philosopher's
equipment—part of the instrumentally available background of her or his
scholastic and pedagogical activity. Desks are what philosophy is written
upon. They function as the (often unreflected upon) support not only for
philosophical reading, writing, and reflection but also for the individual
and communal articulation of philosophical problems. The activities of
questioning and critique often take place, are shared with, and cultivated
in others on and around tables: the seminar or conference table, the professor's desk during office hours, the lectern.

Each of the famous philosophical passages just quoted explicitly invokes
a table as an example and employs it as an orientation device to light up a
region of analysis that is typically overlooked or forgotten. Marx's dancing
table functions to orient the reader's attention to the fetish character of
commodities—the way that commodities, as embodiments or repositories
of social labor, conceal that social labor and obscure the exploitative relations and conditions of production that are responsible for the production
of objects as commodities (as distinct from simply objects of utility). As an
illustration of commodity fetishism, Marx's table is intended as the simplest and most universal example of the ways in which the economic forms
of capitalism (e.g., capital, wages) conceal underlying social relations (e.g.,
surplus value, exploitation).

Husserl's table serves to orient the reader's attention to the intentional
and temporal structure of consciousness. Through his description of the
perception of the table, he seeks to loosen the intentional threads that
tendentially tie us to objects in order to catch sight of the way that the
objects that we perceive, in their seeming stability and identity, are not
just ready-made impingements of the material world but the products and

accomplishments of an intricate process of sense-constitution, which he later calls passive synthesis. In an expressly critical but unnamed evocation of Husserl's table, the table that Heidegger describes in the lectures that would ultimately generate *Being and Time* is intended to orient his students' regard to the everydayness of being-in-the-world, through which the ontological difference between being (*das Sein*) and entities (*das Seiende*) can be discerned.

The desk in Merleau-Ponty's vivid account, which is also an unnamed evocation of one of Husserl's later descriptions of a table,[27] functions as an orientation device to the conceptual difference between the physical body and the lived body (*le corps vécu* or *le corps propre*)—in other words, between the body as an object among other objects in the world and the body as "our general medium for having a world," not an object of which one has an internal image or representation but that which "is polarized by its tasks, insofar as it *exists toward* them, insofar as it coils up upon itself in order to reach its goal."[28]

In these passages, phenomenology, like Marx's critical theory, turns toward an object proximate to the body of the philosopher—a table, something that appears self-evident, fully formed, or ready-made (whether in its objective presence, its readiness-to-hand, or its status as a commodity). Philosophy then employs the table as a "support" for reflections that point to a set of horizons and histories that condition the sensuous presentation of the table: the history of expropriated social labor (Marx), the sense-constituting accomplishments of consciousness (Husserl), the ontological conditions on the basis of which entities show up as intelligible to us (Heidegger), the sense-constituting accomplishments of the lived body (Merleau-Ponty). Each distinct history of arrival or condition of appearance must be philosophically unpacked in order to release it from its concealment in the object (or in the naïve or scientific manner of regarding the object). This is because in each case, however distinct, the philosopher's mode of relating to the table is situated within forgotten or ideologically mystified horizons that structure that relation and its results. Philosophy then, whether phenomenological or critical, seeks to "reactivate" these forgotten horizons, to conjure them for analytical articulation and critical consideration.

The aim of this chapter is to critically disclose, through regressive procedure and commodity chain analysis, the hidden and predominantly overlooked *carceral background* that conditions and makes possible institutionalized philosophical practice in the United States. Interrogating this hidden background of carceral production makes it possible to delineate sedimentations of sense whose historical genesis is traceable to American regimes of slavery and to articulate the way that these sedimentations continue to at once undergird and undercut contemporary higher education and academic inquiry. Like the philosophers cited earlier, I will begin with a desk. Unlike them, my line of questioning is animated in advance by a critical concern for the way that contemporary philosophical practice, including my own, is at once supported and undermined by mass incarceration.

As a professor of philosophy, one of the places in my work-world is my office in the humanities building at California State University, Fullerton. The office is an unremarkable exemplar of a faculty office at a large state university that relies upon (consistently diminishing) public funding: a windowless cinderblock box furnished with the relevant tools of the trade, including a desk, chair, computer, bookshelves, table, and filing cabinet. The manner in which I've inhabited the space is typical for a professor: books, articles, and sundry documents line shelves, fill filing cabinets, and often form stacks that colonize unoccupied horizontal surfaces. There is a stack of framed credentials and artwork intended for display but relegated to a pile, since more than a year of the responsibilities of becoming oriented to a new academic institution and to the demands of parenthood have prevented me from yet hanging them on the walls. Perhaps the most essential thing that my office contains is the chair opposite my desk, which is meant for students whom I regularly receive and dialogue at great length with, not only about philosophy and other regions of inquiry but also about contemporary social and political issues and activism, their interests, ambitions, projects, and their existential situations. My desk and chair and the chair for visitors that faces them form a triad that is essential to my academic and pedagogical work; it constitutes an instrumentally available and supportive background, typically taken for granted, that upholds and facilitates philosophical praxis.

This desk, at which I now sit as I write, and which was purchased by the university office of procurement and contracts at some point in a past that predates my arrival, was built by men incarcerated in California state prison (Figure 1). Not only my desk ($860) but the entirety of the pedagogical triad that "upholds" my philosophical practice and every other item of furniture in my office—my desk chair ($520), receiving chair ($320), two bookshelves ($609 each), work table ($251), and filing cabinet ($419)—were all manufactured by the laboring capacities of confined people employed by the California Prison Industry Authority (CalPIA).[29] CalPIA is a "semi-autonomous state agency" created in 1982 "to operate California's prison industries in a manner similar to private industry."[30] It operates over sixty service, manufacturing, and agricultural industries at twenty-two prisons

Figure 1. The desk in my California State University faculty office featured in the online catalogue of the California Prison Industry Authority, which employs state prisoners for wages of thirty to ninety-five cents per hour. (Source: http://catalog.pia.ca.gov [accessed 29 May 2014].)

throughout California, producing over eighteen hundred goods and services, including, besides office furniture: clothing, food products and packaging (e.g., meat, maple syrup, almonds, coffee, peanut butter, jelly, bread, milk, and cookies), bedding, shoes, stationary and printing services (e.g., binders, business cards, conference folios), municipal and highway signs, U.S. and California state flags, prescription and safety eyewear, work and firefighter gloves, license plates, modular buildings, lockers, and even my students' diploma covers (Figure 2).

Prior to the economic recession, CalPIA recorded $234.2 million in revenue for the 2008/09 fiscal year, with gross profits of $47.9 million.[31] This is modest considering the conditions under which it operates. Ninety-eight percent of CalPIA's revenue is derived from sales to state agencies—such as the University of California and California State University systems, the Department of Motor Vehicles, Department of Health Services, Department of State Hospitals, and the Department of Corrections—that are legislatively mandated to purchase CalPIA products and services at all costs.[32] And as the catalogue prices of my austere office furniture illus-

CALPIA Enterprises
& Career Technical Education Locations (CTE)*

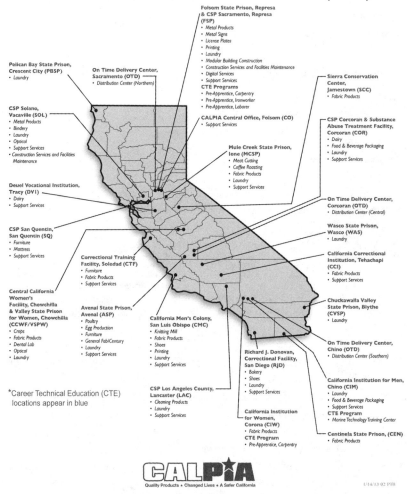

Figure 2. Map of California Prison Industry Authority enterprises in prisons across the state. (Source: http://pia.ca.gov/About_PIA/InstitutionMap.aspx [accessed 29 May 2014].)

trate, that cost is quite high. As one state auditor put it: "With few exceptions, the PIA establishes prices in a monopoly environment with a captive customer base."[33] The California Legislative Analyst's Office found that "state agencies could save $12 million annually if they were free to make purchases from other sources instead of the PIA."[34] And a state performance review reports that "[o]ne of California's college systems estimates it could save more than $400,000 annually if not required to buy PIA products."[35]

CalPIA's relationship to the state university systems evidences my claim about mass incarceration at once undergirding and undercutting contemporary higher education and academic inquiry. Though few students, faculty, or staff are even aware, all of the state's collegiate facilities are literally furnished with the commodities of prison labor; our daily scholarly work is materially upheld and supported by the backs of captive populations. At the same time, my own university and others across the state are not only beneficiaries but also themselves captives of the prison industrial complex. Since 1980, state general fund expenditures for higher education in California have fallen by 13 percent in inflation adjusted dollars, whereas spending on prisons has skyrocketed 436 percent.[36] During that same period, the state built two public universities and a staggering twenty-two new prisons, including the nation's largest prison medical facility recently constructed for $1 billion. California currently operates the third largest prison system in the world, following China and the United States as a whole. Despite the carceral construction explosion, overcrowding reached such heights (187 percent of capacity) that the U.S. Supreme Court ruled in 2011 that the state was subjecting imprisoned persons to cruel and unusual punishment and ordered the state to reduce overcrowding to 137 percent—a court order that has yet to be satisfied.

California now spends substantially more each year—nearly $1 billion more—on its prisons than it does on its public universities (UC and CSU combined), and with the amount that noncarceral state agencies are required to pay CalPIA for its inflated commodities, that differential is even sharper than the official state budget reflects.[37] I have students who are hungry and homeless and many more living below the poverty line, and I rarely meet a student who isn't stretched thinly between work, class, and study schedules exceeding sixty hours a week, as students' share of UC and CSU tuition and fees more than doubled since 2007. Students know they're not paying more for better education; course offerings have been reduced, faculty-student ratios have decreased, and the percentage of courses taught by part-time faculty has gone up exponentially. What they may or may not know is that they're paying for prisons.[38]

In addition to having a captive consumer market, CalPIA's captive labor force, which consists of nearly 7,000 prisoners, works thirty to thirty-five hours per week and receives wages between $0.30 to $0.90 per hour, an average of 40 percent of which is automatically deducted to pay court-ordered restitution and fees.[39] CalPIA also does not pay incarcerated workers benefits such as health insurance or social security taxes. The profits gleaned from the labors of CalPIA's imprisoned workforce not only pay the salaries of its 620 civilian employees (e.g., in administration, legal, marketing, management)—employees who, unlike imprisoned employees, do receive state employee health and retirement benefits. That revenue also extends beyond the prison industries proper, as a 2010 study funded by CalPIA reported that CalPIA's 2008/09 sales and in-state expenditures put $497 million back into the state economy, producing an estimated 2,400 jobs and adding $132 million to Californians' household incomes.[40] Nor is California exceptional in this regard. The largest network of prison labor is run by the Federal Bureau of Prisons' manufacturing corporation, the Federal Prison Industries/UNICOR, which in 2011 employed over 14,000 prisoners, paid between $0.23 to $1.15 per hour, in eighty-eight factories. With net sales (primarily to the Department of Defense) in 2011 of $745 million—3 percent of which went to inmate pay, 19 percent to civil staff salaries, and 78 percent toward purchases of materials and supplies from private sector vendors—federal prison labor injected $640 million into the private sector through the manufacture and sale of military equipment like missile launchers, Kevlar helmets, camouflage uniforms, body armor, protective goggles, night-vision eyewear, microphone headsets, parachutes, chemical gas detection devices, and bomb components.[41] The normative orientation of the Federal Prison Industries is illustrated by a UNICOR-authored history of the government-owned corporation, *Factories with Fences,* which periodizes its history from the "Rehabilitative Years: 1963–1976" to the "Growth Years: 1977–1989" and the "Customer Outreach Years: 1990–2004."[42]

California prison labor not only produces wealth for nonstate agencies through indirection; it is also a direct source of profit for private companies through the Joint Venture and Free Venture Programs. By means of these programs, established through the Prison Inmate Labor Initiative of 1990, private businesses can set up operations inside California prisons and juvenile detention centers and hire inmates with substantial state subsidization. The websites of both state programs advertise to prospective businesses: "long-term leases at below market rates ($0.02/sq. ft.), a 50% discount on Workers' Compensation Insurance, no employee benefit packages required (medical, vacation, sick leave, etc.), state tax credits, a reliable, motivated labor force ready to work immediately, available space in locations throughout California," and remind companies that they can feature a "Made in the USA" label on their products.[43]

Although prison work assignments are voluntary, those who refuse or are unable to work suffer significant consequences. They are only allowed to be outside of their cells for two hours per day; they are restricted from spending more than $35 per month; and they are ineligible for earning "half-time conduct credit," which is a sentence reduction granted to those who maintain "good" conduct.[44] (The fact that laboring—effectively unpaid—for the profit of the prison industrial complex is constitutive of the penal definition of "good" conduct is further indicative of the racial genealogies and exploitative underpinnings of American mass incarceration: a constitutive feature of "good" conduct is to conduct oneself as one of the prison industry's "goods.") Some prisoners and their advocates claim that prison staff use work programs as a punitive device, meeting refusal to perform with threats of physical abuse or solitary confinement.[45] Moreover, contrary to the prevailing ideological justification of prison labor (i.e., that it provides imprisoned workers with valuable vocational skills), UNICOR's and CalPIA's confined labor force uses obsolete equipment and outdated techniques, thus acquiring job skills that are unmarketable in the present-day economy.[46]

Prison labor, however, is only the most obvious (if largely concealed) form of the commodification of prisoners. Here is a sampling of other ways through which contemporary imprisonment policies and practices have generated a renewed conception of prisoners as sources of economic and political profit.

PRISONERS AS CAPTIVE CONSUMERS

Incarcerated populations generate exaggerated profits for corporations through the goods and services they consume. For example, the national phone market in state and private prison systems is worth an estimated $1.2 billion annually in gross revenue.[47] The industry is highly profitable because prison phone companies have state-sanctioned monopolistic control over the state prison markets. State and private prison systems award corporations these monopolistic contracts in exchange for "commissions" or kickbacks averaging 42 percent or $143 million a year.[48] State prison systems are thus economically incentivized to award contracts not to the telephone company that offers inmates the lowest rates but to the one that provides the highest commission. Consequently, in many states, someone behind bars must pay as much as $17 for a fifteen-minute phone call.[49] The known social and rehabilitative benefits of maintaining prisoners' relationships with their families are sacrificed in exchange for profitable phone revenues that deepen the excommunication of the incarcerated.[50]

Prison Construction and Operation

Every time a prison or jail goes into construction, lucrative contracts are made with private industry (e.g., investment bankers, architects, building contractors, and consultants), and every time a prison or jail is constructed, thousands of annually renewable outside service contracts and civil service jobs are created.[51] At least 750,000 people are directly employed by U.S. prisons, which does not include the people who build and maintain prisons and jails, and those who supply goods and services for the everyday operation of prisons.[52] Having been born and raised in California's Central Valley—known by many as "prison alley" because of the twenty-five state and federal prisons and community correctional facilities clustered there—I grew accustomed at an early age to hearing official and mainstream media discourses frame mass-scale prison construction as a strictly economic issue. Across the country, rural communities like mine struggling from the deindustrialization of capital and corporate consolidation of agriculture were motivated by official promises of economic stimulus and job creation to compete for state prison construction projects— what critical geographer Ruth Gilmore calls "the search for a prison fix."[53] Tip Kindel, a California Department of Corrections and Rehabilitation spokesman, exemplified this promotional rhetoric when he stated: "Prisons not only stabilize a local economy but can in fact rejuvenate it. There are no seasonal fluctuations, it is a nonpolluting industry, and in many circumstances it is virtually invisible."[54] Sound bites such as these, which construct prisoners as commodities in constant, ready supply, and capable of being conveniently "disappeared" to economically bolster rural communities, helped swell California's debt for prison construction projects from $763 million to $4.9 billion in less than a decade between 1985 and 1993.[55] They also assisted the state in enlarging its incarcerated population from 20,000 to over 160,000 in less than twenty-five years.[56]

Prisoners as Commodities of the Private Prison Industry

Mass incarceration, and the attendant overcrowding of government-run prisons and jails, also constitutes a business opportunity for private prison corporations, which have amply expanded and profited in the last twenty-five years.[57] In private prisons, prisoners serve as immediate sources of profit—not solely for their labor but for their bodily ability to generate per diem payments for their private keepers. In 1987 the number of people incarcerated in privately operated prisons worldwide was 3,100.[58] Today, the state of California alone pays Corrections Corporation of America $415 million a year to detain 12,500 of its state prison population in out-of-state private prisons in Arizona, Oklahoma, and Mississippi.[59] California is not alone in this regard. At the end of 2010, a total of 130,000 people were detained in private prisons across the United States—a population growth of 4,000 percent in just over twenty years.[60] The Corrections Corporation of America (CCA), the largest for-profit prison company in the United States, employed nearly 17,000 workers nationwide in 2010 and reported revenues of $1.67 billion.[61] The company is one of the hundred largest employers in the country and was ranked number one in *Forbes* magazine's "Business Services and Supplies" category and named as a "Top 50 Military-Friendly Employer" by G.I. Jobs magazine. The recruitment feedback-loop between American military and corrections is just one of the facets of what Angela Y. Davis aptly names the "symbiotic relationship" between the military and prison industrial complexes.[62]

There is a comparable symbiosis between "tough on crime" and anti-immigrant lawmakers and the private prison industry. For example, thanks to a National Public Radio story exposé, we now know that the controversial Arizona law, SB1070, which significantly (and unconstitutionally) augmented law enforcement's authority to criminalize, racially profile, and detain Latino communities, was literally written by CCA.[63] The same company constructed prisons in and was awarded contracts by the state to warehouse those detained for immigration violations.

In 2012 CCA sent a letter to forty-eight state governors offering to buy their public prisons and informing them of "the full economic development benefits of the public-private partnership that accompanies a CCA-owned facility, including the payment of property and sales taxes, potential for further job growth, and vitality to the local economy."[64] CCA offered to purchase and operate state prisons in exchange for a twenty-year contract that included a guarantee from the governors that the prisons would be at least 90 percent filled for the entire term. While no state has yet taken CCA up on its offer, occupancy guarantee provisions or "lockup quotas" are a standard feature of for-profit prison contracts. In 2013, In the Public Interest, a resource center "committed to equipping citizens, public officials, advocacy groups, and researchers with the information . . . they need to ensure that public contracts with private entities are transparent, fair, well-managed, and effectively monitored, and that those contracts meet the long-term needs of communities," released a study finding that 65 percent of private prison contracts with state governments included "lockup quotas" of between 80 and 100 percent. States that decline or otherwise do not meet that carceral quota are required to pay fines or "decarceration taxes" for empty prison cells. Private prison lockup quotas and decarceration taxes effectively "put taxpayers on the hook for guaranteeing profits for private corporations" by requiring them to pay for empty, corporate-owned prison cells.[65]

PRISONER DISENFRANCHISEMENT AND PRISON GERRYMANDERING

Forty-eight states and the District of Columbia prohibit inmates from voting while incarcerated for a felony offense (Maine and Vermont are the sole exceptions). Thirty-five states prohibit persons on parole from voting and thirty of these states exclude persons on probation as well. Eleven states continue to deny voting rights to ex-felons even after they have successfully fulfilled their prison, probation, and parole sentences—four disenfranchise ex-felons for life. Because of these policies, the Sentencing Project estimates that 5.85 million Americans (40 percent of whom have completed their sentences) have currently or permanently lost their voting rights, resulting in one of every thirteen African Americans (one of seven African American men) of voting age being disenfranchised. American penal exceptionalism again displays itself to be out of step with comparable liberal democracies in this regard, as at least twenty democracies, including Canada and Israel, allow current prisoners to vote.[66]

In light of widespread felon disenfranchisement, the practice of prison gerrymandering is all the more disturbing. The U.S. Census Bureau counts incarcerated people as residents of the (predominantly rural and white) locales in which they are confined, rather than the (predominantly urban and nonwhite) cities where they resided prior to their imprisonment. Prison gerrymandering is the practice of using this data (uncorrected) when drawing voting districts. This practice results in the creation of districts with large percentages of incarcerated "phantom constituents," who, unable to vote, merely pad the population of rural counties. Prison gerrymandering exploits the civically dead bodies of incarcerated people to artificially inflate the political representation and the state and federal funding of districts with prisons. It thus constitutes the contemporary functional analogue of the three-fifths compromise of 1787, according to which disenfranchised slaves in southern voting districts were counted as three-fifths of a person, aggrandizing southern electoral representation. "In both cases," as Christopher Muller argues, "a constituency bolsters its political influence with body counts of the disenfranchised."[67] The rehabilitative benefits of civic reintegration that enfranchising incarcerated communities would produce—not to mention the democratic commitment to universal suffrage—are here sacrificed in order to enhance the local budgets and political representation of the predominantly rural and white communities in which American prisons are located.[68]

Whether as fungible commodities, captive laborers, consumers or debtors, or phantom constituents, the prison industrial complex transforms imprisoned and criminalized populations into sources of profit while simultaneously subjecting them to social and civil death. As such, contemporary penal practices are undergirded by sedimentations of sense the historical genesis of which are traceable to past regimes of racial dominance, specifically to the southern convict lease system and other Reconstruction-era legal rituals that refashioned American prisons into technologies that grant sanctuary to racialized forms of punishment prevalent during slavery. These sedimentations structure the treatment of *all* people within carceral spaces.

The Semiotic Transfer of Social Death

The bond, transparent or not, that is supposed to exist
between crime and punishment prevents any insight
into the independent significance of the history of penal
systems. It must be broken. Punishment is neither a simple
consequence of crime, nor the reverse side of crime, nor a
mere means which is determined by the end to be achieved.
Punishment must be understood as a social phenomenon
freed from both its juristic concept and its social ends. We
do not deny that punishment has specific ends, but we do
deny that it can be understood from its ends alone.

GEORG RUSCHE AND OTTO KIRCHHEIMER (1939)[69]

[A]ll prejudices—in the literal sense, pre-judgments—
are obscurities arising out of a sedimentation of tradition.

EDMUND HUSSERL (1936)[70]

[E]yes beaten out, arms, backs, skulls branded, a left
jaw, a right ankle, punctured; teeth missing, as the
calculated work of iron, whips, chains, knives, the canine
patrol, the bullet. These undecipherable markings on the
captive body render a kind of hieroglyphics of the flesh

> whose severe disjunctures come to be hidden to the
> cultural seeing by skin color. We might well ask if this
> phenomenon of marking and branding actually
> "transfers" from one generation to another, finding
> its various *symbolic substitutions* in an efficacy of
> meanings that repeat the initiating moments.
>
> HORTENSE SPILLERS (1987)[71]

Jacob D. Green was born into bondage in Maryland in 1813 and enslaved for thirty-five years of his life before succeeding, after two prior attempts, to escape to Canada and then England. In his 1864 autobiography, he recounts a flogging he received when he was fourteen years old. His master's son had gotten ahold of one his master's pistols and accidentally broke it. When asked about the damaged firearm, the boy lied to his father, telling him that he had seen Green with the gun in his possession. When Green denied the accusation, his master tied him up by his thumbs, gave him sixty lashes, and made him confess to the offense before he would release him. The wounds Green suffered on his back were so severe, and the labor to which he was subsequently subjected so grueling, that the coarse tow linen shirt he wore in the field became fastened to his back, baked onto his body by the sun. "For four weeks I wore that shirt, unable to pull it off, and when I did pull it off, it brought with it much of my flesh."[72]

Green subsequently discovered that his master had later learned the truth about the incident. "[W]hen I saw that he did not offer me an apology for the beating he had given me, and the lie he had made me confess, I went to him and said—now, master, you see that you beat me unjustly about that pistol, and made me confess to a lie."[73] To this his master replied: "[C]lear out, you black rascal; I never struck a blow amiss in my life, except when I struck at you and happened to miss you; *there are plenty of other crimes you have committed and did not let me catch you at them, so that flogging will do for the lot.*"[74]

The purpose of this section is to trace the sedimentations of sense that genealogically link the desk in my university office to the shirt baked onto Jacob Green's lacerated back. In addition to locating my desk within the prison industrial complex from which it was produced, it must now be asked: What genealogical ties could exist between the antebellum scene of violence that Green describes and the contemporary prison industrial complex? In other words, what inglorious concatenation of events and enunciations draw together a gratuitous and unaccountable punishment meted out and justified in a prior era on the basis of a semiotic identification of blackness with criminality, with the web of political conjunctions, socioeconomic relations, and legal and cultural mediations that, 150 years after Green's *Narrative*, articulates America's prison system to a symbiotic circuit of corporate profiteering, public and private economic development, and the careerism of elected politicians, judges, criminal prosecutors, and nonelected governmental corrections employees? The answer to this question resides in the transmogrifications of punishment that begin to take place between 1866 and 1928 (i.e., with formal Emancipation).

The fundamental tenet of slavery was that the slave be subject to the master's will in all things and at all times. As one southern slave owner remarked, "I have ever maintained the doctrine that my negroes have no time whatever; that they are always liable to my call without questioning for a moment the propriety of it; and I adhere to this on the grounds of expediency and right."[75] Against this background, performances of black autonomy and intentionality were dominantly construed in terms of defiance, dangerousness, and lawlessness. "Breach of law," writes Saidiya Hartman, "provides the only possibility for the emergence of the subject, since criminality is the only form of slave agency recognized by law."[76] The agency of the enslaved (i.e., any exercise of autonomy or appropriation of the self) was only intelligible or recognizable, was always already encoded, as crime.[77]

The regime of slavery produced two separate systems of punishment. Penal reforms during the Jacksonian era (1820–1850) largely displaced corporal punishment as the dominant mode of punishment, ushering in an era of increasing incarceration and the dramatic invention and dissemination of disciplinary techniques throughout the social body.[78] However, disciplinary codes and carceral punishments, which aimed at reforming delinquents and disappearing disorder, were massively and predominantly intended for white folks alone.[79] "[P]enitentiaries in a republican society simply were not for slaves. Slaves had no rights to respect, no civic virtue or character to restore, no freedom to abridge. As Thomas R. R. Cobb, an expert on the law of slavery, put it, the slave 'can be reached only through his body.'"[80] "Punishment of death and stripes—these form the whole penal code for the slave," wrote Gustave de Beaumont and Alexis de Tocqueville in their 1833 analysis of the American prison system. "There are no prisons to shut up slaves: imprisonment would cost too much! Death, the whips, exile, cost nothing! Moreover, in order to exile slaves, they are sold, which yields profit."[81]

Imprisonment was typically considered unsuitable for slaves also because it deprived slave owners of labor. "The very idea of imprisonment as a punishment for crimes committed by slaves was a contradiction. The African slave was already a prisoner. Whereas the white felon was punished for violating the norms of freedom, slaves were punished for rejecting the rules of bondage."[82] As a result, each plantation was a law unto itself, where masters sought to impose an absolute system of authority over, while extracting a maximum amount of labor from, their captives.[83] Conversely, the prison system, especially in the south, confined a population well-nigh entirely white (Figure 3).

Angela Y. Davis articulates how the plantation, and the slave law that governed it, served as a receptacle of exclusion during America's nascent democracy.

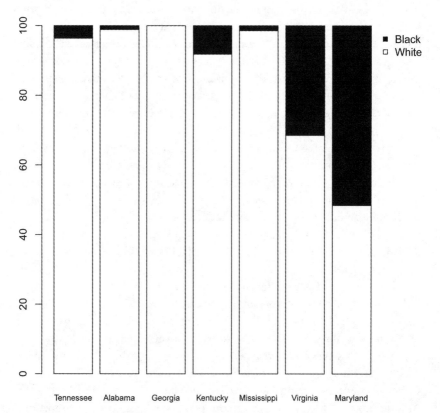

Figure 3. Average percentage of incarcerated population in southern states by race, 1817–1860 (various years). (Source: Edward Ayers, *Vengeance and Justice: Crime and Punishment in the Nineteenth-Century American South* [New York: Oxford University Press, 1984], 61, 279n57.)

[S]lavery as an institution, during the end of the eighteenth century and throughout the nineteenth century . . . managed to become a receptacle for all those forms of punishment that were considered to be barbaric by the developing [American] democracy. So rather than abolish the death penalty outright, it was offered refuge within slave law. This meant that white people were eventually released from the threat of death for most offenses, with murder remaining as the usual offense leading to a white's execution. Black slaves, on the other hand, were subject to the death penalty in some states for as many as seventy different offenses. One might say that the institution of slavery served as a receptacle for those forms of punishment considered too uncivilized to be inflicted on white citizens within a democratic society.[84]

Emancipation and Reconstruction failed to dismantle this receptacle of exclusion; rather than abolish it, the Thirteenth Amendment (1865) to the U.S. Constitution recodified and relocated it: "Neither slavery nor involuntary servitude, *except as a punishment for crime whereof the party shall have been duly convicted,* shall exist within the United States, or any place subject to their jurisdiction." At the legal dawn of abolition, slavery and crime are thus explicitly linked in the foundational document of U.S. democracy. In fact, as Davis elsewhere points out, "there was no reference to imprisonment in the U.S. Constitution until the passage of the Thirteenth Amendment declared chattel slavery unconstitutional."[85] In a dual motion, the Thirteenth Amendment extends formal political freedom to blacks at the same time as it withholds such freedom; it "refigured subjection"[86] and "rebranded the captive"[87] by *restricting* rather than abolishing the operation of slavery. Employing Orlando Patterson's definition of slavery as a form of social death, Joy James writes that "Congress resurrected social death as a permanent legal category in U.S. life, yet no longer registered the socially dead with the traditional racial markings. Breaking with a two-hundred-year-old tradition, the government ostensibly permitted the enslavement of nonblacks. Now not the ontological status of 'nigger' but the ontological status of 'criminal' renders one a slave. Yet, as became apparent in the convict prison lease system, blackness remained the signifier of social death, although now all those relegated to prisons would be imbued with that pariah race status."[88]

The legal loophole of the Thirteenth Amendment is the inaugural inscription of what Saidiya Hartman calls "the complicity of slavery and freedom." "The ways in which [slavery and freedom] assumed, presupposed, and mirrored one another . . . troubled, if not elided, any absolute and definitive marker between slavery and its aftermath. . . . Emancipation announced the end of chattel slavery; however, it by no means marked the end of bondage."[89] The fragile and formal "as if equal" of liberal discourse fashioned an abstract equality that, in Hartman's words, "is utterly enmeshed in the narrative of black subjection, . . . defined so as to sanction subordination and segregation."[90] As within the regime of slavery, where performances of black subjectivity were coded as criminal insubordination, in the postbellum period the dominant social meanings attached to black responsibility were fundamentally those of obligation and culpability. "[Blacks'] exercise of free will, quite literally, was inextricable from guilty infractions, criminal misdeeds, punishable transgressions, and an elaborate micropenality of everyday life."[91]

Hartman's breathtaking exposition in *Scenes of Subjection* of "the tragic continuities in antebellum and postbellum constitutions of blackness"[92] foreshadows the increasing number of philosophers and critical historians of the last two decades who follow W. E. B. Du Bois in recognizing that, though the practice and justification of forced labor and racialized punishment were adapted to the new set of social relations inaugurated by formal emancipation, there is a *functional and semiotic continuity* between the systems of slavery and postbellum penality.[93] The functional continuity is marked by the coercive extremes through which the two regimes served to control and exploit black labor and bolster white supremacy. Semiotic continuities persist in the social construction of blackness, through which ideas of racial inferiority and criminality are fastened to black subjectivity.[94]

The principle argument I would like to advance here, the conceptual framework that I seek to build around the genealogies provided by other critical theorists and analytical historians, is that the process through which the institution of the prison became a functional substitute for the plantation was buoyed by a process of *semiotic transfer*. By *semiotic transfer*, I refer to a process of sense-transference that involves a transposition of an already-instituted system of predicates and prepredicative investments to a new semiotic object. Through postbellum legal rituals and other extralegal discursive practices—what Du Bois in 1935 called a "succession of political expedients by which the South sought to evade the consequences of abolition"[95]—the "criminal," a racially fashioned postbellum object of knowledge, comes to be constituted (or ought we say "reconstructed") in a way that semiotically conjoins it to an antebellum system of predicates and investments that had previously constituted the "slave" as a socially dead person. The antebellum positionality of the "slave" and the postbellum positionality of the "criminal" come to be *semiotically and associatively paired* and are thus genealogically linked through a fund of figures, "corrosive prescriptions,"[96] and "controlling images"[97] of criminality that tethers African Americans to an orbit of oppression functionally analogous to slavery.[98]

The postbellum semiotic transfer of the predicates of social death from the enslaved to the incarcerated is juridically enacted first in the Thirteenth Amendment and subsequently in a multiplicity of legal rituals that include the southern Black Codes, *Ruffin v. Commonwealth*, and other judicial decisions. This *semiotic* transfer has its co-constitutional correlate in the *visible* transfer carried out by the executive penal apparatus. As Angela Y. Davis writes, racialized policing practices and the southern system of convict leasing "transferred symbolically significant numbers of black people from the prison of slavery to the slavery of prison. Through this transference, ideological and institutional carryovers from slavery began to fortify the equation of blackness and criminality in U.S. society."[99] The institutional carryovers or sedimentations of this postbellum semiotic pairing persist in the present and continue to functionally commingle with the machinations of capitalism through the prison industrial complex.

After the Thirteenth Amendment, the next prevalent set of postbellum legal rituals to participate in, and act as sovereign anchorage for, a generalized process of semiotic transfer were the formulation and vigorous enforcement of the Black Codes. These laws, originally passed in Mississippi but copied, sometimes word for word, by legislators in South Carolina, Georgia, Florida, Alabama, Louisiana, and Texas, improvised racially coded crimes that "deliberately multiplied"[100] young black vagrants and criminals, literally transforming the color of southern prisons almost overnight (Figure 4). As Du Bois remarked in his pioneering work *Black Reconstruction*: "Since 1867, Negroes have been arrested on the slightest provocation and given long sentences or fines that they were compelled to work for as if they were slaves or indentured servants again. The resulting peonage of criminals extended into every Southern state and led to the most revolting situations."[101]

The Black Codes established imprisonable offenses specified solely for the "free negro," including "mischief" and "insulting gestures." Vagrancy laws were at the center of these codes. The Vagrancy Act provided that "all free negroes and mulattoes over the age of eighteen" must have written proof of a job at the beginning of the year. Those found "with no lawful employment . . . *shall be deemed vagrants*, and on conviction . . . fined a sum

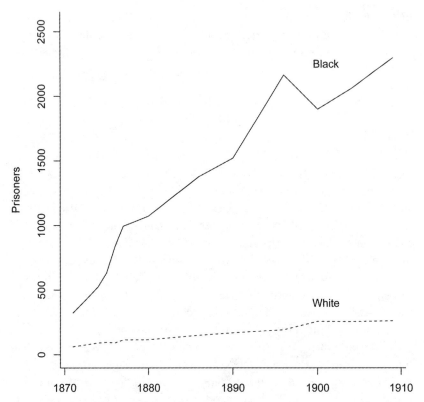

Figure 4. Number of prisoners in Georgia Penitentiary by race, 1870–1909. (Source: Alex Lichtenstein, *Twice the Work of Free Labor: The Political Economy of Convict Labor in the New South* [New York: Verso, 1996], 60.)

not exceeding . . . fifty dollars." As historian David Oshinsky writes, "If the vagrant did not have fifty dollars to pay his fine—a safe bet—he could be hired out to any white man willing to pay for him."[102]

The symbiotic relationship between southern penality and capital was axiomatic. For example, in 1906 the Georgia-Florida Sawmill Association, seeking to solve its labor shortage, passed a resolution calling on those states' legislatures to "make the vagrancy laws of Georgia and Florida more effective." Florida's legislature complied by expanding the definition of vagrancy to encompass:

> rogues, vagabonds, idle or dissolute persons who go about begging,
> common gamblers, persons who use juggling or unlawful games or
> plays, common pipers and fiddlers, common drunkards, common night-

walkers, thieves, pilferers, traders in stolen property, lewd, wanton and lascivious persons in speech or behavior, keepers of gambling places, common railers and brawlers, persons who neglect their calling of employment and misspend what they earn, . . . idle and disorderly persons including therein those who neglect all lawful business and habitually spend their time by frequenting houses of ill fame, gaming houses or tippling shops, persons [who are] able to work but are habitually idle and live upon the earnings of their wives or minor children, and all able-bodied male persons over eighteen years of age who are without means of support.[103]

As southern labor historian Alex Lichtenstein observes, "The convict lease was a method of labor 'recruitment' and control."[104] The postbellum legal containment of blacks aimed to defuse the perceived threat of black equality, reassert white supremacy, "protect" free(d) blacks from their own "vices," and reharness recently emancipated black labor power within a revised, and in many ways more violent, system of coercive constraints.[105]

Indeed, as can be gleaned from the titles of major historical works on postbellum southern criminal justice—*Worse Than Slavery* (Oshinsky), *One Dies, Get Another* (Mancini), *Twice the Work of Free Labor* (Lichtenstein)—the convict lease system, which was constitutionally legitimized by the exceptional clause of the Thirteenth Amendment and legally enabled at the state and local levels by Black Codes, was in many ways worse than slavery, often working laborers to death as it established "a racism no longer mitigated by paternalism."[106] The intensification of the violation and exploitation of black southerners by a racism untethered by the property interest of paternalism is illustrated by the remarks of a southern delegate to an 1883 convention of the National Prison Association, who said: "Before the war, we owned negroes. If a man had a good negro, he could afford to keep him. . . . But these convicts, we don't own 'em. One dies, get another."[107] Observing the steadily mounting deaths in the postbellum Georgia convict lease system, principle keeper John T. Brown wrote in his annual report to the state legislature: "Casualties would have been fewer if the colored convicts were property, having a value to preserve."[108] In contrast to traditional chattel slaves, who, while *fungible* and subjected to profligate violations, were not typically considered *expendable*, as they represented a valuable investment, convict laborers were dominantly constructed as both fungible and expendable. The imprisoned population, which suddenly in the postbellum era became overwhelmingly black, was legally (re)constructed as slaves of the state.

A wealth of juridical discourses performatively reenacted the logic of exclusion ensconced in the Thirteenth Amendment, generalizing and stabilizing the semiotic transfer that the latter had inaugurated. Exemplary among them was *Ruffin v. Commonwealth of Virginia* (1871), in which justices were called upon to consider the applicability of the Virginia constitution's bill of rights to Woody Ruffin, a black convict leased by the state to work for the Ohio Railroad. Ruffin was sentenced to death when, in the course of attempting to escape from captivity and involuntary penal servitude, he killed Louis Swats, whom the railroad company had hired as a guard. Justice Joseph Christian of the Virginia Appellate Court, dismissing Ruffin's appeal, moved afield of the immediate issue before the court to express in his ruling a broader judgment concerning the relation of prisoners to the law.

> A convicted felon, whom *the law in its humanity* punishes by confinement instead of with death, is subject while undergoing that punishment, to all the laws which *the Legislature in its wisdom* may enact for the government of that institution and the control of its inmates. For the time being, during his term of service in the penitentiary, he is in a state of *penal servitude to the State*. He has, as a consequence of his crime, not only forfeited his liberty, but all his personal rights except those that *the law in its humanity* accords him. He is for the time being *the slave of the State*. He is *civiliter mortuus* [i.e., in a condition of civil death]; and his estate, if he has any, is administered like that of a dead man. The bill of rights is a declaration of general principles to govern a society of freemen, and not of convicted felons and men civilly dead. Such men have some rights it is true, such as *the law in its benignity* accords them, but not the rights of freemen. They are *the slaves of the State*.[109]

The ruling repeatedly reinscribes a demarcation between the law, on the one side, and the convicted felon, on the other, constructing a series of semantic alignments that fasten the law to "wisdom," "humanity," and "benignity," and the outlaw to "slavery," "servitude," and "civil death." Rendered just six years after the Civil War and the passage of the Reconstruction Amendments, the ruling exhibits a not-so-subtle racial subtext; it exudes an animus that in its ostentatious performance of self-certain authority betrays a fundamental instability in the racial order of postbellum subjectivity and political organization. This anxiety manifests in the defensiveness through which Judge Christian fashions the law's humanity over against the civilly dead and implicitly inhuman otherness of the racialized felon. Through a semiotic process of criminal marking, animated by what Derrida terms a "logic of supplementarity," the convicted felon is represented as external to the humanity of the law—a representation that scarcely conceals the law's attempt to refashion white supremacy's tenuous unity by reconstructing a constitutive alterity, a reconstituted racialized other.[110]

What Hartman incisively argues about the antebellum regime of slavery applies equally to postbellum practices of racialized penality. "In positing the black as criminal, the state obfuscated its instrumental role in terror by projecting all culpability and wrongdoing onto the enslaved. The black body was simply the site on which the 'crimes' of the dominant class and of the state were externalized in the form of a threat. The criminality imputed to blacks disavowed white violence as a necessary response to the threatening agency of blackness. . . . White culpability was displaced as black criminality, and violence was legitimated as the ruling principle of the social relations of slavery."[111] The postbellum semiotic transfer of social death obfuscated the state's responsibility for racial violence by discharging all culpability onto free(d) blacks; it occasioned what Frederick Douglass referred to as "the general disposition in this country of imputing crime to color";[112] and it fashioned color as a "proxy for dangerousness,"[113] fastening notions of deviance, depravity, and culpability to the dominant construction of free black subjectivity. As the Georgia state penal system's principle keeper during Reconstruction, John T. Brown, wrote, reiterating the logic of Jacob D. Green's master from half a century prior, "The only difference existing between the colored convicts and the colored population at large" was that "the former have been caught in the commission of crimes, while the latter have not."[114] This tendency to impute crime to color persists, as demonstrated, for example, by recent psychological studies revealing that subjects mutually associate blackness and crime in visual perception.[115]

The semiotic transfer of social death, as Du Bois pointed out over a century ago, also "linked crime and slavery indissolubly in [the] minds [of freed blacks] as simply forms of the white man's oppression, which depleted any faith they might otherwise have had in the integrity of the courts and the fairness of the criminal justice system."[116] It restored the familiar conviction among blacks that their collective welfare and survival are inseparable from the violation of the law, that the breach of law offers the only possibility for the emergence of black subjectivity.

By fashioning the punishment of crime as the exception to abolition, postbellum legal rituals established the "criminal justice system" as the institutional inheritor of the regime of slavery, as the receptacle of slavery's racialized forms of punishment. Just as the regime of slavery served as a racially fashioned receptacle for those forms of punishment deemed to be too violent to be inflicted on white citizens within a democratic society, in the century since formal abolition, the prison system, as Angela Y. Davis argues, "has become a receptacle for all those human beings who bear the inheritance of the failure to create abolition democracy in the aftermath of slavery. And this inheritance is not only born by black prisoners, but by poor Latino, Native American, Asian, and white prisoners."[117]

The Sedimentation of Social Death

How might we explain the persistence of the semiotic transfer of social death across contexts from the postbellum period to the present practices of mass incarceration, which predominantly and disproportionately target black and other people of color (Figure 5)? In his genealogical analysis of punishment, Nietzsche argues that one must distinguish punishment as a practice (*Brauch*), act, or strict series of procedures, on the one hand, from the sense (*Sinn*), purpose, and expectation that are linked to the performance of such procedures (i.e., from the particular interpretations put on the configurations of practice).[118] The practices of punishment, Nietzsche claims, are, like all practices and institutions, older and more enduring than the meanings or purposes that are fleetingly, contingently, and retroactively (*nachträglich*) inserted into (*hineingelegt*) and read into (*hineingedeutet*) those practices.[119] The meaning attributed to the practice of punishment is much more fluid, unstable, and haphazard than the practice itself, which predates its employment in a particular historical regime of punishment.[120]

Nietzsche maintains that any existing moral institution is the reinterpretation of a preexisting institution, which the current institution has subdued, reshaped, reinterpreted, and redirected (*umgerichtet*) to new purposes or intentions (*Absichten*).[121] When new interpretative enterprises take over a preexisting practice, they adapt its sense in such a way that necessarily obscures (*verdunkeln*) or expunges (*auslöschen*) the meanings and purposes that had been previously attached to it.[122] However, no matter how comprehensively a new interpretation may seek to abolish earlier meanings deposited into a set of practices, Nietzsche thinks that such attempts to take over or reinterpret an existing set of practices will not in general be so completely successful that *nothing* remains of the earlier meanings. Some elements of those antecedent meanings are inevitably incorporated into new interpretations; although, as extensively as possible, they are shed, ex-

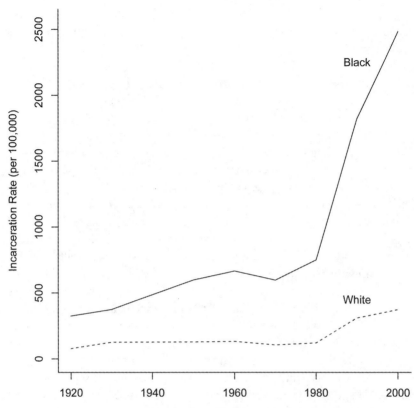

Figure 5. Incarceration in state and federal prisons and local jails per 100,000 by race, 1920–2000. (Source: Allen J. Beck and Jennifer C. Karberg, "Prison and Jail Inmates at Midyear 2000," *Bureau of Justice Statistics* [Washington: U.S. Department of Justice, 2001].)

punged (*ausgelegt*). Historically, then, as feminist philosopher Alison Stone writes in a discussion of Nietzschean genealogy, successive layers of such meanings will be, as it were, sedimented in the practice, as "pre-existing meanings that succumb to reinterpretation have already taken shape as re-interpretations of still earlier layers of meaning, from which, in turn, they preserve some elements, while transforming or erasing others."[123] Over time, therefore, there will be some gradual change in the actual practices and a rather more mercurial shift in the dominant "interpretation" given to the practice, as earlier layers of meaning eventually get eroded away through successive waves of reinterpretation. But even the dominant inter-pretation won't have been able to utterly eradicate the sedimented mean-ings that previously accumulated (i.e., that were imposed upon the practice by a series of past agencies).[124] As Nietzsche concludes, "The whole history of a 'thing,' an organ, a practice can to this extent be a continuous chain of signs [*Zeichen-Kette*], continually revealing new interpretations and adaptations."[125]

In light of this shifting and unstable history of reinterpretation, Nietzsche makes the argument at the end of the nineteenth century that "[t]oday it is impossible to say precisely *why* people are actually punished"—an idea that Foucault reactivates nearly a century later in 1983: "I believe that one must . . . recall what Nietzsche said over a century ago, . . . that in our contemporary societies we no longer know exactly what we are doing when we punish and what at bottom, in principle, can justify punishment. Everything happens as if we carry out a punishment by allowing a certain number of heterogeneous ideas—at different layers of sedimentation and stemming from different histories, distinct movements and divergent rationalities—to prevail."[126] Insofar as it has a history, Nietzsche writes, punishment defies definition, for "an entire process is semiotically concentrated or condensed (*semiotisch zusammenfasst*)" in it.[127]

The racialized moral codes, modes of commodification, and practices of domination of American slavery semiotically sedimented themselves in American penal practice. Once these codes have penetrated American penal practice, modified it, given it a certain direction and a particular kind of coherence, successive attempts to impose a new interpretation on American penality (thus constituted) do not encounter a set of practical institutions, instruments, and procedures that have, as it were, a kind of grammatical tabula rasa. Rather, reformative initiatives and transformative movements confront a set of actively structured and deeply sedimented forces and meanings that resist, at least by inertia and evasion if not by more active measures, attempts to turn them into other directions, impose new functions and significations upon them, and so forth. It is precisely this intransigent persistence of the vestiges of slavery in the prison system that gives contemporary *abolitionism* its historical resonance and radical philosophical content.[128]

Conclusion: The Philosophical Scope of Abolitionism

The contemporary project of abolition aims at reanimating and carrying forward the unfinished project of American abolition by advancing a two-pronged commitment to *decarceration* and *reconstruction*. Decarceration is the negative aspect of abolition—a project that does not simply signify a reduction in the number of confined persons but aims to dislodge incarceration and the retributive, adversarial criminal justice apparatus to which it is attached as the dominant modes of addressing social conflict, disorder, and disparity. This undertaking involves a thoroughgoing excavation and deactivation of deeply sedimented historical, psychological, and sociopolitical structures. It is a project of tearing down and dismantling that extends not only to the prison industrial complex and the vestiges of slavery sedimented within it but also to the retributive tendencies toward ethical violence within each one of us and the processes of socialization through which those tendencies are cultivated.[129]

Reconstruction is the affirmative, constructive facet of abolition—a broad and creative social process of fashioning new radically democratic institutions, constructing participatory economies that are sustaining and sustainable, cultivating restorative communities, and fostering subjects capable of harmoniously, yet critically, inhabiting them.[130] Like the two heads of Janus, the Roman god of beginnings and transitions, facing, like portals, in opposite directions—past and future—the two sides of abolition, though conceptually distinct, are materially inseparable. The movements of decarceration intrinsically solicit and entail reconstruction, and reconstructive processes deepen the work of decarceration. The contemporary abolitionist project of reconstruction involves building, refashioning, and investing in institutions, such as public health, housing, and education, and community-based practices, such as community accountability and restorative justice, that aim to substantively resolve the plethora of social, economic, and political problems for which mass incarceration currently serves as a one-dimensionally punitive panacea—a panacea that, by devouring the public resources needed to ameliorate those problems, in actuality exacerbates, deepens, and protracts the very problems that have led to spiraling numbers of prisoners.[131]

Abolitionism is thus a far-reaching social project of restructuring existing institutions, cultivating restorative communities, and fashioning civic subjects capable of inhabiting them. Prison abolitionists and activists from the community accountability, restorative justice, and nonviolent conflict resolution movements have argued for years that modern policing, prosecution, and imprisonment practices have *deskilled* individuals and communities in peacefully and autonomously resolving disputes.[132] The normalization of the modern criminal justice system, including the formation of professional policing agencies and adversarial court systems—all centered on retributive and incapacitative confinement—has produced subjects that are no longer actively capable of resolving their own disputes. The adversarial criminal justice system, as Norwegian sociologist and penal abolitionist Nils Christie argues, systematically "robs" individuals and communities of their own conflicts.[133] Of course, this process of *conflict sequestration* is not a unilateral phenomenon. As individuals' and communities' autonomous skills of social and interpersonal mediation become eroded, we become increasingly reliant upon professionals (whether criminal justice or social workers) to resolve the conflicts in which we invariably become involved. Deskilled subjects do not help a victim when they see a harm being committed; when immediately involved in a conflict, they do not attempt, or in some cases even desire, to directly participate in its resolution. They call upon or simply wait for the police, as has become dominant and deeply ingrained custom. Or in racialized and overpoliced communities that, because of histories and experiences of police abuse, avoid police intervention at all costs, people often just find themselves, despite often valiant struggles of survival and resistance, entrapped by interlocking schemes of oppression, which constitute, in Beth Richie's words, a "more fundamental sense of confinement."[134]

Social conflicts, as Christie points out, are potentialities for activity, participation, and norm clarification. The system of mass incarceration not only commodifies racialized communities, but it also transforms social conflicts into the exclusive professional province and economic livelihood of criminal justice professionals (e.g., police officers, lawyers, judges, social workers, and probation and parole officers).[135] To use the categories of Aristotelian metaphysics, as the activity of conflict resolution becomes more thoroughly sequestered by the disciplinary apparatuses of the state, our communities' capacity for autonomous, peaceful conflict resolution degrades from an active potentiality, which can be activated at will, to a passive potentiality. It becomes like a foreign language in which we are able to become fluent only after great effort, practice, and social immersion.

Abolitionism entails a mass-scale disinvestment in the opportunistic and exploitative armaments of the prison industrial complex, and a removal of them from our communities so that we may more capably invest in participatory, sustaining, and sustainable economies, and more adequately engage in the reconstructive labor of cultivating restorative justice skills in ourselves and instituting such practices in our communities. These efforts aim to comprehensively abolish the sedimentations of slavery, to construct the possibilities of what Angela Y. Davis, following W. E. B. Du Bois, calls an "abolition democracy."

From Commodity Fetishism to Prison Fetishism: Slavery, Convict-leasing, and the Ideological Productions of Incarceration

James A. Manos

It must be remembered and never forgotten that the civil war in the South which overthrew Reconstruction was a determined effort to reduce black labor as nearly as possible to a condition of unlimited exploitation and build a new class of capitalists on its foundation.

—W. E. B. DU BOIS, *Black Reconstruction in America: 1860–1880*

Over the past thirty years, the United States has undergone a prison boom. Since 1980, incarceration has increased from a little fewer than 500,000 inmates to more than 2 million.[1] If we extend these statistics to those on probation or parole, this number jumps to over 7 million. This means, as a recent Pew Center report indicates, one in every thirty-four adults is monitored and controlled by the legal apparatus in the United States.[2] One might expect this drastic increase in incarceration to be the result of a simultaneous increase in the rate of criminal activity. However, the crime rate has remained stable during the same period. Indeed, one cannot help but question the validity of the assumed causal relationship between crime and incarceration rates when the breathtaking increase in incarceration is contrasted to a stable rate of crime. For this reason, contemporary scholarship broadly agrees that there is no causal relationship between crime and punishment, especially during the rise of the neoliberal "prison-industrial-complex."[3] When confronted with this exponential increase in incarceration, one cannot help but recall Max Horkheimer's concern from *Eclipse of Reason* that machine of rationality, like the prison today, has "dropped the driver; it is racing blindly into space."[4] If there is no causal connection between crime and punishment, then what, if anything, is driving this growth in incarceration?

When scholars delink punishment from crime, they normally explain its function through the rubric of economics and commodity fetishism. This is best exemplified in the fields of radical criminology and the political economy of punishment. Scholarship on the political economy of punishment is largely inspired by the work of the Frankfurt School thinkers Georg Rusche and Otto Kirchheimer. They argue in their seminal text *Punishment and Social Structure* that the causal relationship between crime and punishment is ideological. Rusche and Kirchheimer claim that the labor needs of capital indexed against the available quantity of surplus labor is the causal influence upon punishment, rather than the result of criminal activity. This is a compelling and important argument. However, Rusche and Kirchheimer assume that punishment is a secondary social effect without considering its independent causal force. Indeed, as they shift the locus of punishment from crime to the modes of production, they also obfuscate the independent, yet interrelated, function of the modes of punishment within the capitalist organization of society. Moreover, this argument fails to integrate the complicated impact of New World slavery on both the modes of production and the modes of punishment.

Some scholars have approached breaking the ideological connection between crime and punishment by articulating the impact of slavery on the prison in the United States.[5] Not only was slavery the economic ballast securing the rise of the bourgeoisie in both Europe and America, but its "abolition" also marked a distinct shift in the function of incarceration. After the abolition of slavery and the corresponding development of convict-leasing as a new mode of punishment, incarceration would no longer serve the modes of production alone. Instead, it would begin to shape the organization of society. I would like to suggest that we cannot fully understand the implications of separating crime from punishment, or even the relationship between economy and prisons, until we have accounted for the transformation of slavery into a form of punishment and its after-effects.

In this chapter, I argue that punishment is tied by necessity to neither crime nor the modes of production. To support this claim, I first turn to Rusche and Kirchheimer's attempt to investigate the independent status of the modes of punishment in *Punishment and Society*. By placing their argument within the framework of Marx's discussion of the inherent relationship between primitive accumulation and incarceration, I rescue and critique parts of their argument. Specifically, I preserve their account of the centrality of the relationship between the dispossession of capital and punishment, while critiquing the primary role they assign the modes of production in determining the modes of punishment. After setting up the framework of dispossession and punishment, I then turn to slavery's effect on the modes of punishment in the postbellum South to argue that, with the rise of convict-leasing as a dominant mode of punishment, we see punishment as *restructuring* the modes of production and not as the *effect* of the modes of production. Taking account of this shift, I conclude, demands that we examine the prison not from the metaphysical framework of commodity fetishism but from the framework of prison fetishism. This means moving our analysis of the growth in incarceration from the extraction of surplus value from prisoners' labor to an understanding of how prisons produce convicts as a stigmatized and dispossessed class.

Prisons and Economy

If we want to understand the impact of slavery on the modes of punishment, and thus how the modes of punishment consequently shaped the modes of production, then it is necessary first to go back to Rusche and Kirchheimer's argument for unbinding the causal connection between crime and punishment in *Punishment and Social Structure*. As we will see in the next section, part of the story of slavery's impact on the modes of punishment involves an analysis of the relationship between the modes of production and the modes of punishment. In returning to Rusche and Kirchheimer, we can see the prison's administrative role in producing and managing the class dispossessed by capitalism's need for primitive accumulation. And while I will claim that this argument restricts our understanding of the function of the prison for the economy, thus concealing the truly independent role of the modes of punishment, the link they articulate between prisons and primitive accumulation is essential, I believe, in understanding both the prison's contemporary form and its skyrocketing rates of incarceration.

Rusche and Kirchheimer's argument that the modes of punishment correspond to the labor needs of capitalism is indebted to Marx's account of primitive accumulation in volume 1 of *Capital*.[6] Marx's description of the link between capitalism's rise and economic and political incarceration plays a central role. It secures the dispossession driving capitalism forward both at its origin and in its mature form.[7] With an eye toward unfolding Rusche and Kirchheimer's argument, it is thus helpful to return for a moment to Marx's description of the relationship between prisons and capitalism.

For Marx, imprisonment becomes the dominant model of punishment at the same time capitalism emerges as the dominant economic model. This shift in the form of punishment reflects the central role of primitive accumulation in capitalism. To understand the role of primitive accumulation, one must understand how law and punishment institute capitalism's dispossession. Law and punishment are, as I will show, central to the economic system of capitalism and its reproduction for Marx, an insight that directly informs Rusche and Kirchheimer's work.

To understand the complex of primitive accumulation, one only has to turn to the legal developments that slowly destroyed common property and dispossessed the masses, which transformed the nature of labor.[8] In the shift to capitalism, the emerging bourgeoisie enacted a host of laws by fiat. These laws were designed to undermine the economic relationships bolstering feudalism. The legal struggle over the status of common land held particular significance. Indeed, commonly held land was torn asunder using the emergent legal category of private property. Further, private property transformed the nature of labor. For Marx, the erasure of common property was nothing more than the process that "divorces the worker from the ownership of the conditions of his own labor."[9] After common land was enclosed as private land, the labor of the worker, and the products of that labor, belonged to and benefited the owner of the means of production. Thus, primitive accumulation describes a double split: first, severing the worker from the means of production and second, divorcing the worker from the products of his or her labor. And indeed, as Marx writes, as capital progresses, "it not only maintains this separation, but reproduces it on a continually extending scale."[10] Thus, capital must preserve this double split and incessantly perpetuate the alienation that primitive accumulation generates.[11]

Primitive accumulation, thus, results in an ever-increasing dispossession of the masses. In response to this dispossession, the modes of production call into service the modes of punishment to discipline and warehouse surplus "free laborers." The newly created proletariat turned into "beggars, robbers and vagabonds, partly from inclination [and] in most cases from force of circumstances."[12] Dispossessed en masse, the "free and rightless proletariat could not possibly be absorbed by the nascent manufactures as fast as it was thrown upon the world."[13] In short, the dispossessed masses could not earn a living under the new conditions of labor and property. And in their activities, to secure a living outside of the new conditions of labors became criminalized. Thus, in the process, the surplus population became criminalized as it was forced outside of the labor market and into an illegal economy in order to survive.[14] This class was in turn "whipped, branded and tortured by laws grotesquely terrible, into the discipline necessary for the wage system."[15] Imprisonment became the necessary release valve of surplus labor resulting from the disappearance of the commons by legal fiat. As such, it is the material mechanism, for Marx, securing the dispossession of the masses.

Significantly, in Marx's account, imprisonment spatially segregated the dispossessed surplus population; in this segregation, imprisonment protected the boundaries of private property. The surplus population was put to work in the prison and disciplined into their new status as dispossessed and alienated "free-laborers." Imprisonment thus regulates the refugees created by primitive accumulation through spatial segregation and work-discipline. Prisons produced and maintained the new conditions of alienation wrought by the legal transformation of the status of property. They, in turn, became the corresponding form of punishment to the legal structures that put capitalism in motion. And in this sense, one can only say that for Marx, imprisonment is central to both the historical development of capitalism and its continual reproduction. It is the metaphysical motor both disciplining the workforce and simultaneously organizing the space for capital to flow through.

Georg Rusche and Otto Kirchheimer's argument in *Punishment and Social Structure* begins from the function of the prison outlined in Marx's account of primitive accumulation. For they, too, claim that the "bond, transparent or not, that is supposed to exist between crime and punishment . . . must be broken."[16] They, like Marx, examine the development of bourgeois law, the dispossession grounding it, and the attendant punishments meant to secure these laws and manage the human debris of capitalist economy. Yet, as Michel Foucault claims in *Discipline and Punish*, Kirchheimer and Rusche demonstrate that "punitive measures are not simply 'negative' mechanisms" but are also "linked to a whole series of positive and useful effects which it is their task to support."[17] Their text is distinct because it shows the productive nature of the intricate relationship between law and punishment in constructing and preserving new forms of class dominance. In other words, the discussion of punishment in their text seeks the "independent significance of the history of penal systems" by examining its productive status as a causal agent.[18] And although they seek the active and causal status of the modes of punishment in their analysis, it is not until we examine the role of convict-leasing in the next section that we will truly see the independence of the modes of punishment.

In *Punishment and Social Structure*, Rusche and Kirchheimer argue that law reproduces class structure by criminalizing poverty. The assault on the commons was not the only legal maneuver deployed by the emerging bourgeoisie in their ascendency into economic and political dominance; they also criminalized the survival activities of the dispossessed. Laws prohibiting begging and vagrancy, for example, emerged in concert with the laws transforming the nature of property. These laws both served to round up the surplus dispossessed population and produced new forms of criminality that collapsed the categories of poverty and crime. By collapsing poverty and criminality, the newly formed legal schema constructed the poor as criminals. The criminalized poor now found themselves subject to a structure of punishment that shaped their class status and adjusted them to the needs of capital. Imprisonment supplemented the failure of the ideology surrounding surplus value and alienated labor. When ideology failed to motivate workers to take on longer hours and to receive less than the value they created, the state relied on imprisonment to either ideologically reorient these workers or brand them as outlaws. As Rusche and Kirchheimer argue, this gives rise to "the houses of correction, where those who were unwilling were forced to make their everyday practice conform to the needs of industry."[19] Imprisonment was designed specifically for the criminalized poor. From its beginnings in the workhouse, where the dispossessed were trained in the skills needed to enter the new workforce, to its modern iteration where the poor are warehoused, imprisonment is capitalism's administrative response to regulating and exploiting the surplus dispossession it creates. Punishment, for Kirchheimer and Rusche, is not concerned with "humanitarian considerations" but rather with exploiting "the potential value of a mass of human material."[20]

Kirchheimer and Rusche rely on Marx's account of punishment's role in primitive accumulation. Both arguments break the assumed causal relationship between crime and punishment, and in doing so demonstrate capitalism's inherent need for incarceration. For Marx, this happens by understanding incarceration through the paradigm of capitalist economy in the shift from feudalism to capitalism. Incarceration, in this argument, becomes the reactive effect of the necessary dispossession driving the accumulation of capital. For Kirchheimer and Rusche, it is necessary to separate punishment from crime to illuminate its administrative function of subjugating society to the labor needs of capital. Here, punishment becomes not only the negative force sweeping up the human fallout of capital's rapacious search for profit but also a positive force shaping, managing, and producing subjects in response to the needs of capital. Thus, we have seen that the modes of punishment under capital serve two functions. First, they regulate the surplus dispossession affecting the masses as the trajectory of accumulation continuously exacerbates the separation of the worker from the means of production. Second, they productively harness the labor potential of the refugees of capital through a game of capture and stigmatization: containing, exploiting, and branding the criminalized poor.

Although these arguments demythologize the ideological connection between crime and punishment in pointing out the productive forces of punishment, they still subjugate the function of prisons to the organizational needs of capital. As both arguments demonstrate, law and punishment are central to the logic of alienation, displacement, and dispossession propelling capital's primitive accumulation. Nonetheless, questions remain: Is incarceration a secondary effect of capital, a tool it deploys to create the conditions of its own survival? Or, is incarceration a co-conditioning agent of capital that at times can direct how capital organizes the modes of production? In order to address these questions, I argue that it is necessary to integrate the history of New World slavery into the discussion of the development of incarceration as the dominant model of punishment. Once we account for the impact slavery had on the trajectory of the prison, specifically in light of the development of convict-leasing after the abolition of slavery in the United States, we will see that punishment and race are not just co-conditioning factors of capitalism but perhaps even the driving motors of capitalism.

Prisons and Slavery

Nothing affected the development of the capitalist modes of production more than chattel slavery. The human trafficking and brutal extraction of surplus value formed the backbone not only of American industry but also that of Europe.[21] Furthermore, nothing affected the modes of punishment in the United States more than slavery's abolition in the ratification of the Thirteenth Amendment.[22] The Thirteenth Amendment abolished chattel slavery "except as a punishment for a crime whereof the party shall have been duly convicted." Contrary to popular sentiment, this amendment simultaneously abolished and preserved chattel slavery in the United States. It took slavery out of private hands and restricted it to a function of the state. In practice, as Angela Davis argues, after the passage of the Thirteenth Amendment, "what during slavery had been the particular repressive power of the master became the far more devastating universal power of the state."[23] This surreptitious displacement of chattel slavery left its impression in the development of law and changed the function of incarceration. This is left out of both Marx's and Rusche and Kirchheimer's narratives concerning primitive accumulation. Although the relationship of New World slavery to primitive accumulation is a necessary augmentation to their arguments, for the sake of my own argument, I will restrict myself to New World slavery's impact on the modes of punishment. When slavery became a form of punishment, I will argue, it transformed the modes of production, thus demonstrating the co-conditioning status of punishment in relation to the modes of production.

Before the abolition of slavery, Southern states left the management and discipline of the slave population to the loose network of slave masters. The state was relegated to arbitrating disputes among slaveholders in accordance with the slave codes. These codes ensured slaves could not "bear witness" in a court of law,[24] could not "meet" with other slaves;[25] they set standards for rounding up and returning runaway slaves,[26] and regulated the movement of the slave population.[27] After the abolition of slavery, the South rapidly developed new laws to deal with the influx of former slaves.[28] Where these new laws almost universally included the capacity of the newly freed black population to "sue and be sued" in court, the majority of them were only slightly rewritten slave codes known as the black codes. Changing the words "master" and "slave" to "employer" and "apprentice" was often the only difference between the two sets of law.[29] Just as Rusche and Kirchheimer describe the process by which poverty and criminality collapsed to criminalize poverty, in the postbellum South the black codes collapsed blackness and criminality so that it could contain, manage, and exploit criminalized ex-slaves.[30]

The black codes ensured that the labor power of the former slave population would remain within the purview of either former slaveholders or the state. Just as the bourgeoisie's usurpation of law simultaneously dispossessed the masses and criminalized the poor in Marx's account, after the abolition of slavery a new set of laws emerged ensuring the dispossession and criminalization of the newly freed slaves. Not only did these laws cordon off the commons according to the matrix of racial domination,[31] but they also made it illegal for newly freed black citizens to be unemployed, unruly, lazy, or just insubordinate at work.[32] Breaking these laws was "punishable by incarceration and forced labor, sometimes on the very plantations that previously had thrived on slave labor."[33] The institution of the black codes left an indelible impression in the construction of law, an impression that remains and drives the grossly disproportionate incarceration rates among African Americans today.[34] In other words, when slavery becomes punishment, the law becomes racialized and the function of imprisonment alters, as evidenced by the convict-leasing system that developed in the postbellum South.

Convict-leasing resulted from slavery's transformation into a state-codified form of punishment in the postbellum South. It was, in essence, state-codified slavery, producing new conditions of labor and a new relationship between private industry and the state.[35] Where the state could not keep black labor under the control of its former slave masters,[36] it rounded up, imprisoned, and rented out black labor to the burgeoning southern industrialists under the convict-leasing program. At first glance, convict-leasing appears as an attempt to maintain the antebellum system of chattel slavery. Yet, as Alex Lichtenstein argues in *Twice the Work of Free Labor*, convict-leasing was not a "symbol of southern backwardness," an attempt to hold onto slavery despite its abolition, but rather represented "the embodiment of the Progressive ideals of southern modernization, penal reform, and racial moderation."[37] When slavery became a form of punishment, incarceration—specifically in this case, convict-leasing—began to shape the modes of production.

The South was economically devastated after the Civil War. Factories and cities were destroyed. The labor pool was drastically reduced. The states were drained of their economic base and could not support the spatially segregated institution of prison. Convict-leasing was an answer to the bankruptcy of Southern states and helped to shape the development of private industry. Almost all of the Southern states contracted out the function of incarceration to private industry, thus dispersing the function of imprisonment to various companies. The counties and states were paid a lump sum for each prisoner they provided for industry. By allocating the carceral function of the state to private industry, the state became the manager of a new form of slavery aimed at the production of profit for both the state and private industry. As W. E. B. Du Bois notes in "The Spawn of Slavery": "The innocent, the guilty, and the depraved were herded together, children and adults, men and women, given into the complete control of practically irresponsible men, whose sole object was to make the most money possible."[38] States quickly became dependent on this new income, forming the kernel of what Angela Davis identifies as the "prison industrial complex."[39] As Du Bois would note, in light of this new income for the state, "it was almost impossible to remove the clutches of this vicious system from the state."[40] With the seemingly endless supply of black convict labor provided by the enforcement of the black codes, companies often extracted surplus value at the expense of the health of its workers, something not economically viable under slavery.

Because the cost of convicts was so cheap, convict-leasing, in some respects, was worse than slavery. While many of the punishments used to control convict labor were similar to those used on the plantations of the antebellum South, convict-leasing intensified and transformed them. Punishment under these conditions still operated on the racist ontological assumption that the prisoners were no more than chattel, yet they framed this assumption through the lens of the continual drive of capital to seek ever-increasing profit. In this way, the alienation of capitalism's primitive accumulation expanded beyond the limit of life itself. Convicts were divorced not only from the land and the value of their labor but also their lives. One only needs to look to Pratt Mines in Alabama as an example. As Douglas Blackmon recounts in *Slavery by Another Name*, convicts were controlled by an unsupervised gang of "overseers" who often hung "men by their thumbs or ankles" as punishments for minor offenses.[41] When the convicts committed major offenses, such as failing to "work at the rate demanded by their overseers," they received "as many as sixty or seventy lashes"—so many that the "skin literally fell from their backs."[42] One should keep in mind that most slave codes protected against the malicious harming of slaves and often regulated the amount of lashes one could inflict at not more than twenty.[43] This is absent when the slave codes become the black codes. These punishments were meant to harness the full labor power of the convicts. When not punished, the prisoners were often worked to death. In many instances, large unmarked mass graves were used to dispose of the bodies at long-term work sites.[44]

The divorce between the worker and the means of production at the heart of primitive accumulation was grossly exaggerated when slavery became a form of punishment. The dispossession propelling the logic of primitive accumulation accelerated to such an extent that the reproduction of the life of the worker became unnecessary in the face of the total extraction of surplus value. In other words, as Davis argues, under the convict-leasing system in the postbellum South, a "small but significant number of black men and women were condemned to live out the worst nightmares of what slavery might have been had the cost of purchasing slaves been low enough to justify conditions of genocide."[45] When the Thirteenth Amendment transformed slavery into a state form of punishment, convicts became a disposable commodity. It was more profitable to work convicts to death than to take care of their biological needs. Most importantly, through this incorporation the economic relation between private industry and state no longer reflected the old practices of antebellum slavery. Rather, these new relations formed what Du Bois called "a new slavery and slave-trade," in which convicts became commodities, temporarily leased to corporations for the rapid production of profit and industrial development during times of what today we could call austerity.[46]

When we consider chattel slavery's impact on the modes of punishment, we find the exact opposite of either Marx's or Kirchheimer and Rusche's account. Convict-leasing shows how incarceration affected the modes of production. As we have seen, both Marx and Rusche and Kirchheimer demonstrate the central role of prisons in the development of capitalism. For them, the prison secures the dispossession of primitive accumulation and produces and stigmatizes the proletariat as it disciplines them to their new status as "free" workers. Indeed, prison is an active, creative force in both of their arguments. It spatially segregates the dispossessed masses. This spatial segregation preserves the boundaries of private property and allows for the architectural design of disciplining, as well as concentrating the dispossessed in several sites.

Convict-leasing is based on spatial desegregation. No longer able to maintain these sites of spatial segregation, the state dispersed its convicts into many different corporate work sites. Like commodities thrown onto the market, there was no stable site housing convicts. More often than not, they lived in mobile camps and sometimes would be leased to multiple companies during their sentences—if they were able to survive the horrific conditions. Thus, convict-leasing practically demanded different spatial conditions of labor than did the model of the state institution. Discipline enforced by walls was no longer the order of the day; rather, fragmented mobility aimed solely toward the production of profit at the expense of the workers' life became the organizing feature of the modes of punishment. It is this difference that allows us to view the modes of punishment as the vanguard of the modes of production and not merely their effect.

Post–Thirteenth Amendment incarceration disciplined the human debris of capital and formed new exploitative labor relations organized to sustain racial domination. Indeed, punishment captured the newly freed and newly criminalized slaves and harnessed their labor power. In doing so, they collapsed blackness and criminality while simultaneously producing new labor relations.

The schema of labor forged by the convict-lease system has the same characteristics of modern post-Fordist workforce: flexibility, mobility, and fragmentation.[47] This connection makes sense, of course, only if we understand convict-leasing, as Alex Lichtenstein has argued, as the "triumph of the modern state's version of the social and economic benefits to be reaped from bound labor, in the name of developing a more healthy, less dependent, 'progressive' economy."[48] Like convict-leasing, neoliberalism demands the mobility and flexibility of its workers as they are exchanged among different companies. Each company pays less and less, giving fewer and fewer benefits. In other words, just like the labor relations of convict-leasing, they spend less and less on the reproduction of the necessary life conditions of the worker. Neoliberalism, just like the laws of the postbellum South, creates a mass of dispossessed workers who are both criminalized and racialized. In other words, our contemporary organization of capitalism, like convict-leasing, intensifies its need for surplus value by intensifying the incarceration of a racialized and criminalized class.

Once we wrest punishment away from the modes of production in this way, we can begin to see that incarceration is an organizing metaphysical principle of capitalism more broadly. Moreover, when we place it within the historical narrative of New World slavery, we can see that the criminalization of the poor resulting from this principle also relies on the ontological assumptions of racial dominance. Punishment creates a disposable population whose dispossession is racially distributed.

From Commodity Fetishism to Prison Fetishism

While punishment is bound to the modes of production, its function does not merely respond to and reflect the modes of production. Marx and Kirchheimer and Rusche are correct to note the simultaneous rise of the prison as the dominant form of punishment during the ascendancy of capitalism. Moreover, their insight that this is rooted in how law and punishment produce and manage the dispossession inherent in capitalism's primitive accumulation is instructive as to the function of prison once we have dismantled the ideological connection between crime and punishment. Nonetheless, without incorporating the narrative of convict-leasing, we fail to see two things: how the modes of punishment shape the modes of production and how they concentrate and reproduce the ever-increasing dispossession of capitalism as a form of racist domination. Taking these two factors into account forces us to note that the primary feature of capitalism may not be its economic organization but rather its organization and distribution of racialized punishment. In accounting for the centrality of punishment to the capitalist organization of society, I would like to argue in this final section that we should reorient the metaphysics of capitalism from commodity fetishism to prison fetishism.

When we view the rise of incarceration through the lens of commodity fetishism, it appears to institute and manage the double split producing surplus value, as well as the ideological function of concealing the exploitative fracture from which profit appears. Commodity fetishism is the abstracted and displaced fracture spurred by capitalism's ongoing primitive accumulation. As such, it is normally taken to be not only the metaphysical motor of capital's exploitation but also the heart of its ideological illusion.[49] For Marx, the result of primitive accumulation's separation of the worker from the means of production is alienated labor. Marx argues in "Wage Labour and Capital" that because the worker is alienated from the means of production, the worker must sell his or her life, his or her "real" laboring activity in the world "piecemeal," to the owners of the means of production for a price less than what the labor itself produces.[50] Because capital seeks to dispossess the worker on an ever-extending scale, it makes sense that the more the worker produces, the less value he or she receives back from that production. Alienation culminates in the worker being severed from the conditions of his or her life process, the practical activity of labor. If we were to understand the function of the prison through this separation alone, then we would conclude, like Marx and Rusche and Kirchheimer, that prisons ensure this extensive extraction of surplus value while harnessing the productive labor power of those who have been totally dispossessed by capital. Thus, if we were to read the ideological function of the prison in terms of this framework, then it becomes clear that once the rate of incarceration has been divorced from the rate of crime, prisons would conceal the dispossession of workers producing surplus value that characterizes the secret of the commodity.

For Marx, commodity fetishism structures the form of ideology. The difference between exchange-value and use-value, a difference born of the double split of primitive accumulation, forms the heart of ideological deception. As Marx writes in *Capital*, the "value of labour-power, and the value which that labour-power valorizes [*verwetet*] in the labour-process, are two entirely different magnitudes."[51] The value of reproducing the power of labor is less than the exchange value obtained by the products of labor on the market. When the product becomes valuated by its symbolic relationship to other commodities in exchange, the value produced in this exchange conceals the material conditions, and thus labor, of the product itself. In other words, once the product "emerges *as a commodity*, it changes itself into a sensuously supersensible thing [*sinnlich übersinnliches Ding*]."[52] The secret of the commodity, the condition of its possibility, is the labor and primitive accumulation hiding behind its symbolic valuation in exchange. In other words, the commodity erases any recognition of the primary and necessary coercive relations of primitive accumulation and alienated labor that give rise to it. Due to its primary orientation toward commodity fetishism, a capitalist mode of production depends upon a structure of appearance that conceals material forms of exploitation. If the prisons, too, were oriented by this framework, then their ideological function would supplement, as Rusche and Kirchheimer demonstrate, the failure of this ideology by rounding up and disciplining the poor to capital's demand for dispossession.

Moreover, if we were to view convict-leasing from the paradigm of commodity fetishism, our analysis would restrict its function to securing the intensification of the divorce between the worker and the products he or she produces, and supplementing the failure of this ideological drive. Of course, this is part of the story. Yet, this part of the story only posits the prison as replicating and reproducing the organizing logic of the modes of production as they are governed by the metaphysics of commodity fetishism. And as we have seen, the introduction of convict-leasing to the modes of punishment does more than reproduce and intensify the ideological fracture between the worker and the product; it also radically reshapes this relationship. And in light of the centrality of punishment to capitalism, perhaps we might also reorient the metaphysical frame used to approach it. In other words, if prisons are a central organizing feature of capitalist society, then might we not speak of prison fetishism?

We can abstract several features from slavery's impact on the modes of punishment in order to articulate a metaphysics of prison fetishism and its ideological consequences. Roughly these features would include: (1) the economic function of punishment and social control, (2) the valuation of the reproduction of capital over the reproduction of labor power, (3) the disinvestment from the reproduction of life by both the state and private industry, and (4) the total objectification and profitable exchange of a racialized and criminalized class who have been excluded from the labor market.

First, the labor relations created by the modes of punishment in the postbellum South appear similar to the post-Fordist labor relations marking the era of neoliberalism. One need only track the difference in form between the antebellum prison and postbellum convict-leasing. Whereas the antebellum prison concentrated its disciplinary function in spatially segregated state institutions based on the model of the workhouse,[53] post-bellum prisons were spatially dispersed in the various work camps of private industry. Both models represent different organizations of labor, and most importantly convict-leasing seems to herald the conditions of the post-Fordist workforce. As Alessandro de Giorgi describes it in *Re-Thinking the Political Economy of Punishment*, "the rigid organisation of the labour process" no longer seems to apply to the modern workforce; rather, "mobility, flexibility and decentralization replace the fixity, rigidity and centralization of the Fordist factory."[54] As such, the conditions under which the extraction of surplus value and the dispossession of primitive accumulation have also shifted.

Second, the labor relationships of punishment ground the growing interdependence between the functions of the state and private industry. This relationship sets the standard for valuing the production and reproduction of capital over the value of labor power. On the one hand, the state becomes reliant on private industry to fulfill the roles of the programs and institutions it can no longer maintain. On the other hand, the reorganization of the modes of punishment in response to this crisis comes to determine a new organization of labor and spurs the dream of private industry to free the flow of capital from the regulation of the state. Specifically, the advent of convict-leasing created a flexible and mobile workforce for which neither the state nor private industry was responsible. This allowed the state to fill its coffers with the money gained from renting out this labor while simultaneously allowing private industry to derive the maximum amount of surplus value from its cheap flow of laborers. In both cases, we see the extraction of surplus value based on the exchange value of the convict as commodity. In both cases, this proto-version of post-Fordist labor relations involves the reversal of both the paternalistic corporation and the state.

Third, given this reorganization of labor and the total extraction of surplus value, there is a rapid disinvestment of the state and private industry from sustaining life. Whereas, in both Marx and Rusche and Kircheimer, the modes of punishment control, discipline, and harness the labor power of the dispossessed poor, with convict-leasing the aim is not the harnessing of labor power through techniques of discipline but rather a double disinvestment. On the one hand, the state cuts its social programs and institutions. On the other hand, private industry no longer sets its wage in accordance with what it takes to reproduce the life of the worker. Since the worker is temporary, private industry balances the extraction of surplus value against the lump sum paid for the convict and not against the cost of maintaining the life of the convict. This double disinvestment reemerges in the economy of austerity, where not only are the masses divorced from the means of production, but also the price for their labor is so greatly depreciated that they can no longer rely on the value of their labor alone. Loïc Wacquant calls this the shift from the welfare state to the "workfare" or "prisonfare."[55]

Finally, the culmination of measuring the impact of the modes of punishment on the modes of production lies in the complete objectification of subjectivity. The model of commodity fetishism posits the worker as a subject in as much as it considers the worker as the possible producer of value through his or her labor. Even though commodity fetishism describes the frame of the exploitation of the worker and in some sense objectifies the worker, it still posits the worker as a laboring being. When slavery becomes a mode of punishment, and when slavery's iteration of convict-leasing impacts the modes of production, we find set in motion the total dehumanization of subjectivity. Neither the convict nor the worker is viewed as a laboring being whose value lies in their labor but as commodities to be rented and reproduced. As Michael Hallett observes, the "nature of prisoner's commodity-value has changed somewhat in modern times—prisoners are no longer profitable solely for their labor, but also now for their bodily ability to generate per diem payments for their private keepers."[56] Convicts have become commodities who are exchanged among various corporations and what remains of state institutions. We thus see, as Hallett has noted, "the historical pattern of racially distinct *commerce* in imprisoned human beings, most of whom are poor, nonviolent, minority offenders, has returned."[57] In other words, it is no longer the human capacity to labor that becomes objectified in the processes of production, as we see in commodity fetishism, but rather the human itself becomes a commodity. This is nowhere more evident than in current exchange of bodies occurring between impoverished communities and prisons.[58]

Taking these characteristics of prison fetishism, we can draw out its ideological implications. Unlike commodity fetishism, prison fetishism does not conceal an exploitative fracture at the heart of capitalism. Rather, it conceals the state and private industry's rapid disinvestment in life itself. Whereas the ideological function of the prison, for Rusche and Kirchheimer, was to discipline and extract surplus value from those dispossessed by capitalism, under prison fetishism we observe the warehousing and exchange of the surplus population as commodities with exchange value. There is still extraction of value, but now it happens at the level of commodification and exchange. This process totally reifies the racialized and criminalized poor because it does not read this population through the rubric of subjectivity. This framework reflects Loïc Wacquant's claim in *Punishing the Poor* that incarceration provides "punitive containment," offering a form of "poor relief," a "relief not *to* the poor but *from* the poor, by forcibly 'disappearing'" them in the machinery of objectification and exchange that marks neoliberalism's penal policies.[59]

In moving toward a model of prison fetishism, not only do we account for its central role in organizing the modes of production, but we also begin to account for its ideological correlates, which I believe differ greatly from the framework of commodity fetishism. Only when we address slavery's impact on the shape of punishment can we trace punishment's impact on the modes of production. From this vantage point, we can observe the perverse shift devaluing life in its commodification, propelling the most extensive instance we have seen to date of the severance instituted by capital's rapacious process of primitive accumulation. This extensive separation is not supported by the modes of punishment but rather propelled by it. Now the machinery of punishment has rocked loose from its economic principles and is speeding into space, without driver, leaving nothing but human wreckage and despair in its wake.

Maroon Philosophy: An Interview with Russell "Maroon" Shoatz

Russell "Maroon" Shoatz and Lisa Guenther

Russell "Maroon" Shoatz is an activist, a political theorist, a father, and a political prisoner. He was held in solitary confinement for twenty-one consecutive years at State Correctional Institution Greene in Pennsylvania. He was first locked up in 1972—just a year after I was born. In the 1960s Shoatz became active in black radical politics. He was a founding member of the Black Unity Council in Philadelphia, which later merged with the Black Panther Party. And like so many black radical activists in the era of police repression and FBI surveillance—an era that has not, in any obvious way, come to an end—Shoatz was falsely accused and convicted of murder. He was sentenced to spend the rest of his natural life in prison. But from behind bars, and even from his current isolation unit, Shoatz continues to analyze and resist the interlocking systems of racism, capitalism, patriarchy, and state violence that affected his community in the 1960s and that continue to affect us today in the age of mass incarceration, or what Michelle Alexander has called *The New Jim Crow*.

I first encountered Shoatz through Facebook—which seems ironic, given both his isolation from technologies like the Internet and his commitment to decentralized networks (like the Internet). An organization called Occupy the Hood had posted a video interview with his daughter, Theresa, and I followed the threads to Shoatz's website and a written interview about democracy, matriarchy, the Occupy movement, and food security. I wondered: How could a person in solitary confinement be so tuned in to the issues and political movements of today? I had to know more, so I wrote to him.

A week later, a package arrived in the mail. It contained a wonderful letter, which began by wishing me a "Happy International Womyn's Day!" as well as two of his essays, "The Dragon and the Hydra" and "The Real Resistance to Slavery." Both essays describe the social and political structure of maroon communities in the Americas—places where fugitive slaves joined forces with indigenous people and disenfranchised whites to form communities of resistance to colonial domination and capitalism. These essays offer an alternative history of the Americas, one that does not begin with the "discovery" of a "new world" ready to be conquered but rather with networks of relation and resistance that go beyond the colonial project and offer different models of power and community.

Shoatz has an amazing capacity to connect the past and the present in a way that opens new possibilities for the future. He draws connections between the decentralized activist networks of the Arab Spring and the Occupy Movement, and the decentralized political structures of fugitive slave communities and the Underground Railroad. He links the desire for independence and self-reliance, which are so central to U.S. culture, to grassroots urban farming movements such as Will Allen's *Good Food Revolution*, where people in inner-city neighborhoods are reclaiming vacant lots to grow food, create jobs, and strengthen their own communities. And he sees feminism, especially ecofeminism, as a key component in any democracy or liberation movement, because without the full participation of women, the movement will be blocked by an internal struggle to uphold patriarchy by centralizing power in the hands of men.

In every situation—theoretical or practical—Shoatz looks for the "escape routes," or what the philosopher Deleuze would call "lines of flight," which allow people to move through systems of oppression and create new ways of thinking, acting, speaking, and living in solidarity with others. The main insight I have learned from Shoatz is that we must all collaborate in creating networks of escape and resistance. *We must all become maroons.* For some of us, this means resisting the prison industrial complex from within, or supporting family members in prison, or working with others to resist domination as activists in a global network. For others, it means resisting our own privilege and complicity in systems of racism, sexism, economic exploitation, and other forms of domination—and investing the resources that our privilege has granted us in collective projects to dismantle those systems. Whatever your escape route may be, Russell "Maroon" Shoatz has something to teach us about the importance of building and maintaining networks of mutual support, so that everyone is empowered to seek the meaning of freedom in connection with others.

LG: What does "maroon" mean to you?

SHOATZ: Historically, a maroon was a fugitive slave of the sixteenth, seventeenth, and eighteenth centuries Americas—and even on the west coast of Africa, where most enslaved Africans were shipped from. In Latin America, they were generally referred to as *cimarrones* in the Spanish speaking colonies, *marrons* in the French colonies, the Dutch word for Bush Negroes in their colonies, and in the British colonies of the Caribbean and the southern areas of what would become the USA, either outliers or maroons. Yet maroon is an accepted generic name for *all* of these fugitives. The word is sometimes capitalized when it's used to identify an ethnically adopted designation: like the Jamaican Maroons or the Boni Maroons. Usually, it's assumed that all maroons were of African origin. In fact, for centuries all over the Americas there were many, many maroons of *both* European and indigenous/Amerindian origin.

Maroons differed from the runaway slaves who tried to blend in or fully integrate themselves within the otherwise "free" societies. And that's where the true distinction lies between maroons and the other fugitives! Whether the maroons term their communities *quilombos, ladeiras, palenques, cumbes*, Nanny Town, Trelawny Town, or one of the scores of other designations we know of, they *all* were clear on the fact that direct integration into the surrounding oppressive settler colonial communities was something they did not desire. One could argue that their fugitive status militated toward making that choice. Yet the historical record clearly shows that for centuries, thousands of runaway slaves and indentured servants successfully integrated themselves within the free communities. Among those of European origin, untold numbers blended in to join the periodic expeditions that were mounted to explore, exploit the riches of, conquer, or settle vast areas that had previously only been inhabited by Amerindians. Among the Amerindian runaways, they most often could find refuge and protection among kindred or other sympathetic Amerindian ethnic groups.

Those fugitives of African origin could at times find "free black" communities—who themselves were in league with sympathetic antislavery abolitionists—who would offer them a certain amount of refuge and protection. And it's known that these things were generally known and understood by the maroon communities in their regions. And by definition, a rejection of these attempts to integrate oneself within the mainstream of either of these free communities—while establishing one's own maroon communities—meant that such maroon efforts accepted the idea that their former owners would *aggressively* seek to return them to enslavement, or kill them if that failed. This was primarily because *all* maroon communities represented a direct threat to the idea and practices of slave and indentured labor, in other words, a threat to the *engine* that made the colonies in the Americas exploitable and fantastically profitable for the ruling elites.

Thus, in essence, all maroon communities—men, wimmin, and children—were communities at war with their former masters. We know this to be true because for centuries various settler colonial regimes sought to violently stamp out numerous maroon communities all over the Americas. Even going so far as to sign *peace treaties*—which came with autonomy and land grants and material subsidies—in return for these maroon communities' promises to reject any further acceptance of new fugitives into their ranks, as well as their aiding the slavers in capturing the latter (a stipulation that was not always followed through on). The direct descendents of some of these maroon societies in South America (Surinam), the Caribbean (Jamaica), and the United States (among the Negro Seminoles of Texas and along the Mexican border, and in Oklahoma, and the Amerindian Seminoles in Florida) still stubbornly cling to the remnants of their ancestral ways and speech.

So it must be recognized that—in spirit—a maroon was one who not only rejected oppression but also went further to help establish an alternative, even though such an effort could have been avoided by simply removing themselves from the direct effects of that oppression. They were fully conscious that seeking to establish such an alternative would bring about attacks from those who benefited from the rejected oppressive arrangements.

LG: How can we learn from the history of maroon communities to "escape" from the prison industrial complex? This must be a different process for prisoners, their families, and others who have no personal connection to prisons. I'm interested in sketching out a kind of "escape manual" for those who want to build on this tradition of resistance.

SHOATZ: The Prison Industrial Complex (PIC) is *a modern-day form of slavery*! Michelle Alexander says it's a part of "the New Jim Crow," and she's correct in saying that. Yet we must recall that the original Jim Crow itself was simply a way to continue to derive the benefits from the exploitation of a segment of society that chattel slavery earlier provided. Similarly, the PIC serves to benefit segments of today's society at the expense of others. It's held up by those who derive these benefits as a necessary social mechanism to control the criminal elements in society: so much of the "tough on crime" posturing can be found here.

When one gets past that *scare tactic* and simply *follows the money trail*, it's easily recognized as the *giant con game* that it is. A tool that helps the economic and social elites—the "one percent" (if you will)—to use the PIC to serve as a lid to keep the most volatile economic and social elements from boiling over in reaction to the dysfunctional and exploitative policies the one percent have set in motion and oversee. At the same time, using the police power associated with this drive to construct a—not so subtle—*terroristic police state* in order to keep in check the other "ninety-nine percent" who do not find themselves to be direct victims of the PIC, but are, nevertheless, *indirectly terrorized* into feeling they too must accept the economic, political, and social policies put forth by the one percenter's advocates. If not, they too will fall victim to the terrifying specter of themselves becoming prey to the paramilitary police and spy agencies: the unaffordable legal system and the dreaded jail/prison archipelago that they've all seen on reality TV shows, which is fodder for pop-culture comedians.

The ninety-nine percent are living in a *fool's paradise*. One that cons them into subsidizing their own oppression by allowing the one percent to spend billions upon billions of *their tax dollars* yearly to support this police state and its PIC. Most will object to my terming the United States a police state for one simple reason: They periodically get a chance to vote for whichever politician the one percent's massive outlay of money propels to the front of the—otherwise—easily recognized *millionaires voting club*. . . . The giveaway is that whoever is voted into office, the one percenter's interests are always given preference over the ninety-nine percenter's.

Still, there is hope of using the "maroon spirit" to help us find our way forward. Even so, as Michelle Alexander points out in her "New Jim Crow" book, such an effort demands a collective type of energy and creativity to form a *movement* that is capable of getting the job done. And any process to accomplish this must be launched, refined, protected, and sustained simultaneously among the prisoners within the PIC, the paroles and probationers, their collective families and loved ones, and by other members of the ninety-nine percent who are not personally (bodily) connected to the PIC and its supporting police, spy, and court arms—an effort consciously directed toward building on the maroon tradition of resistance to oppression and exploitation.

Ironically, the segment of the population that presently has the most potential to effect change in the PIC is those who usually have no direct—bodily—connection to this system. That is, the *taxpayers* among the ninety-nine percent. Without their massive yearly outlays of billions in taxes—taxes they've been bamboozled into believing serve a good purpose but instead serve [to] keep active a police state machine—the whole house of cards would collapse!

These taxpayers have allowed themselves to be painted into a corner—as already pointed out—and must be broadly encouraged to join an effort to construct a national campaign to vote out of office any and all politicians who will not pledge to help us abolish the PIC and its supporting police state terror arms, while simultaneously using their tax dollars to prepare the millions of prisoners, parolees, probationers, prison staffs, police/spy, and court arms for *new lives*.

Such an effort will help educate these taxpayers on the extortion con game that the "tough on crime" political hucksters have been playing [with] them, as well [as] help reign in the out-of-control police/spy state apparatus, which will allow this taxpaying public to feel *less* terrorized in order to *more* aggressively pursue all of the other pressing problems the one percenter's policies have allowed to collect in their living rooms.

At the same time, the prisoners, parolees, and probationers must spearhead a campaign to educate their peers on the fact that their pursuit of the *gangsta lifestyle* and its petty crimes must be abandoned, for the simple reason that they're being played for fools when they kill and are killed to make money and gain status, only to lose the money, their freedom, and all too often their families as well—while going in and out of the PIC. Their only hope rests with organizing themselves and using their time and creativity to develop intelligent ways to get the taxpaying citizens to recognize that they must demand that their tax dollars be used to prepare them to fully join their communities as productive individuals—in a win-win situation for both groups.

The families and loved ones of prisoners, parolees, and probationers are ready to become a part of such an effort, as already laid out. Moreover, the adult members of these families are themselves voters and taxpayers. As such, they will form the nucleus and backbone of a nationwide effort to get other taxpaying voters to force the politicians to pledge to work on abolishing the PIC, while initially channeling their tax dollars into programs designed to *really* prepare prisoners, parolees, probationers, prison staffs, police/spy, and courthouse workers for their new lives.

Here the academic community must be brought into this undertaking. We must get them to see that it's also in their interest—as taxpayers and voters—to forcefully interject themselves into such a movement because colleges and universities nationwide are progressively being sidelined and hollowed out in favor of the neoliberal *education for profit* model; one that most administrators will be forced to pursue, because they are being starved of tax dollars that presently are being shoveled into the PIC. Where else will the prisoners, parolees, probationers, prison staffs, police/spy, and court workers find individuals who are able to perform such a Herculean task?

Further, it's abundantly rational to fight for such an initiative, seeing how the material aspects are already in place: the archipelago of jails and prisons can serve as learning quarters. There are millions of people who need to be prepared for new productive lives—or else they will remain tax burdens. This includes tens of thousands of unemployed or underemployed college and university graduates. This work can be accomplished by intelligently using the billions of tax dollars that today are being wasted on prisons, jails, parole, probation, police/spy, and court activities that only serve to terrorize and keep in check the ninety-nine percent. All that's missing is the clarity that tells us that such an effort is needed and the political will to struggle to build such a movement—the same way that the historical maroons set theirs sights on being free from chattel slavery, then developed the will to run away and struggled to stay free.

LG: One of the things I love about your work is that it reveals another history of the Americas underneath the story of "discovery" and colonization. This is a history of struggle and resistance, which is as old as—if not older than—colonial domination. What can we learn about political resistance from our own history, read "against the grain" in this way?

SHOATZ: One cannot fully appreciate the history of the maroons without first taking the time to read about them. Even then, one cannot gain this knowledge by reading only a single book on them. For myself, i began to seriously study them after escaping from a Pennsylvania prison and living in the surrounding mountains and forest in 1977. After a month, i slipped up and was captured and returned to prison. It was at that time I was given the nickname "Maroon" by an older prisoner who had studied maroon history. Up until that point, all i knew was that the "maroons were escaped slaves in Jamaica. . . ." Nothing more.

Nowadays, i can say that i've read many books about the maroons, even though it took a bit of an effort to locate the material, since i had no access to the Internet and was in prisons that restricted the books that i could get. Yet i'm still learning more about them as enterprising scholars and researchers are making that history available. Jane Landers, a professor at Vanderbilt University in Nashville, Tennessee, recently provided me with some fascinating original research and publications surrounding the maroons. Further supporting what i've discovered long ago: The various maroon communities and a number of Amerindian communities stand *alone* as the only peoples who've withstood the crushing and absorbing effects of the colonial, "manifest destiny" imperialist, and genocidal movements that have overwhelmed most of the rest of the Western hemisphere.

Though considered "backward" by most people, it's becoming clearer every day that such elements—like the maroons and Amerindians spoken of—people who've learned to live alongside the environment without destroying it, show the rest of our civilization as those "who are backwards!" Moreover, the remnants of these Amerindian and maroon communities steadfastly resist efforts by outsiders to co-opt or submerge their communities within the complexities of the modern state.

Even though the jury is still out on their choices in that matter, it's also becoming crystal clear that the huge and complex undertakings like the old Soviet Union, the European Union, the United States, China, and India are in for some truly rough sailing, as their ruling elites lose more and more of their ability to use the state to exploit and oppress/repress. This level of resistance was almost impossible to accomplish prior to modern technological wizardry, which is serving to demystify the "why's" and "how's" of what being done to the global ninety-nine percent by this elite minority. Indeed, i believe there are things that can be learned by studying how the maroons and certain Amerindian societies have been able to navigate their way forward until now. That knowledge and wisdom is sorely needed because we've allowed the global-ruling elites to place us on a runaway train, which if not arrested will present a clear threat to our existence!

LG: What's the relationship, in your view, between anarchism and the decentralized structure of maroon communities?

SHOATZ: Historical maroons and anarchists have many things in common. Both also have many variations that have to be studied to prevent any errors in addressing this question. Nonetheless, they all share a deep-seated rejection of oppression/repression emanating from any state structure. That said, the maroons differed from most anarchists—at least during their classical "fighting maroon" stage—because unlike most anarchists, *they lived their ideal of rejection.* Most anarchists, on the other hand, aspire to protect that ideal—short of what's needed to realize it on a higher level. Of course, much of that has to do with the extreme level of oppression/repression the maroons had to confront. That's usually missing in the case of the anarchists, the notable exceptions being the anarchists involved with struggles during the period of czarist/ revolutionary Russia and during the Spanish Revolution and Civil War of the 1930s. There, one cannot distinguish any difference between those anarchists and the earlier fighting maroons.

Those instances also highlight another striking difference between the two camps—other than during the Russian Revolution and with Spain during its own struggles—and that is the premium the fighting maroons placed on always developing and maintaining a high level of organization! They were forms of organization that were usually highly decentralized, creative, and organically connected to those served, yet sophisticated enough to be able to coordinate various decentralized formations in order to give the coordinated collective a critical mass when needed. Sort of like a swarm of bees. Usually anarchists have not been confronted with the level of threat that the fighting maroons *always* had to live with and that has hindered them in developing a need or desire to organize on such a high level.

LG: In "Black Maroons in War and Peace," Eugene Genovese writes about the difficult relationship between maroons and slaves, and the many examples of betrayal and complicity, where slaves were used as pawns by both the colonizers and the maroons.[1] What can we learn from these struggles about the possibilities for solidarity and community-building today?

SHOATZ: I've read a lot in this area but am hard-pressed to recall
any instances of fighting maroons betraying other slaves. In fact, take
Surinam; there they even had a "Code of the Forest" that strictly
militated against such betrayals. And in the fighting maroon formations in
Jamaica, Mexico, Haiti, and the United States (Southern colonial areas),
we see the same practices. Such betrayals were *not* in their interests,
seeing as how solidarity with all slaves generally served to increase their
numbers and ability to avoid capture and death. That's not to say that the
fighting maroons always got along with each other. They didn't. But that
was usually settled by agreeing to go their separate ways.

The treaty maroons were the parties that indulged in such betrayals! Such
treachery was the fruit that their co-option by their former enslavers
yielded. The European imperial and colonial enslavers discovered after
generations of all but useless wars designed to capture or kill maroons
that the most sophisticated fighting maroons could not be overcome by
warfare. They therefore settled on a broad strategy of co-optation, a more
subtle way to both neutralize the fighting of the maroons and turn them
into another auxiliary to help their other forces hunt, capture, and kill
new runaways. In Mexico, the Spanish slavers successfully implemented
the co-option of the famed and feared Yanga and his followers among
the fighting maroons; and even today, "Yanga the African rebel slave" is
lauded in Southern Mexico. In both Jamaica and Surinam, the British
and Dutch slavers (respectively) also came to adopt the same methods
and had success doing that. In each case, the co-option of the most
sophisticated and powerful fighting maroons worked to the detriment of
those still-fighting maroons and the new runaways as well.

One lesson we can draw from that is a need to be more vigilant in our
efforts to both identify and struggle against co-option. And we know
from the maroons' experiences as well as more contemporary experiences
brought about by struggles within the global anticolonial struggles, the
U.S. Civil Rights Movement and the Women's Liberation Movement
of the 1970s (in particular), that those in power will resort to co-option
against strong movements they cannot defeat otherwise. One rule of
thumb is that we must continue to struggle as long as the most adversely
affected have not been relieved of the causes of oppression and repression
they suffer under.

LG: In *The Wretched of the Earth*, Fanon writes: "The party must be
decentralized to the limit. This is the only way to revive regions that are
dead, the regions that have not yet woken up."[2] This made me think of

your hydra model. What is the influence of Fanon on your thought and practice?

SHOATZ: Franz Fanon had for decades been one of my guiding lights. His writings that highlight both his "revolutionary" theories and practice still hold much truth. Yet i've come to learn that Fanon also was in need of a worldview that was not shaped by the patriarchal fixation on a malignant ego-based form of violence, a type of violence that he conflated with the otherwise necessary *defensive revolutionary violence* that the best of his theories and practice uphold. This is a shortcoming that i outline in an essay in an upcoming anthology of my writings.[3] The essay entitled "The Question of Violence" and a subsection labeled "Towards a Matriarchal Prefigurative Praxis in Controlling Male Violence" contain my thesis that separates ego-based violence from defensive revolutionary violence, and how and why Fanon and others have conflated the two, as well as my theory about how to arrest that shortcoming.

LG: The connection between prisons and capitalism is clear. But can you spell out the connection between prisons, capitalism, and environmental issues such as food security, climate change, respect for animals, and so forth?

SHOATZ: As was pointed out in my answer to your second question, the ruling one percent has constructed a police state—with prisons at its core. Thus, it follows that *without that* and the threat of the paramilitary police/spy networks—backed up by an awesome array of weapons, military vehicles, helicopters, drones, reality police, and jail TV shows, which daily sow terror in the minds of the ninety-nine percent—the bulk of the citizenry would more seriously question *all* of those things. But they fear that if they go beyond voting (where that is allowed), or peacefully demonstrating (where that is allowed), they could easily wind up in a prison hellhole or be gunned down in the streets!

In the United States, a huge segment of the ninety-nine percent own firearms—allegedly for hunting or to simply exercise their rights to do that. In reality, so many millions owning these weapons is itself a testament to the fear felt by them; a fear that they cannot rationally understand is grounded in their inability to understand the complexities of a society that otherwise points to the bankruptcy of the one percent's accumulation mania and the ninety-nine percent's inability to stay afloat in that game. Thus, the owning of weapons is a way to achieve a small amount of *psychosocial relief* from the everyday fears and terrors that torment them. Periodically, one of these tormented individuals will snap under the strain and shoot and kill another one of the ninety-nine percent over a minor dispute or, more dramatically, shoot and kill as many as possible—before the feared paramilitary police SWAT team shows up . . .

The global ninety-nine percent would also act in a similar fashion—being subjected to similar pressures—but mostly weapons are not as [readily] available, unless you are willing to be cannon fodder in some drug or resource warlord's army . . .

LG: You write about matriarchy and suggest that it is a better word than "feminism" to describe your own approach, which you share with Fred Ho and Stan Goff. Could you explain what matriarchy means to you? I must admit, the word makes me uneasy for a number of reasons. For example, it is possible to admire and even worship mothers without actually granting them social or political power. Mothers are often romanticized as wonderfully caring, responsible, even self-sacrificing people—which creates an impossible standard for most women to live up to. And not every woman wants to become a mother; feminists have worked hard to distinguish between being a woman and having to be a mother, so it seems like we risk backsliding if we suddenly replace feminism with matriarchy. But at the same time, much of the history of feminism has been dominated by white, middle-class straight women who still have a lot to learn about the many different ways of being a woman, being powerful, and working with others in solidarity. For these reasons and more, I prefer to focus on the promise of "global feminisms" rather than matriarchy. But I'm interested to hear more about why this term appeals to you.

SHOATZ: My outlook on this is a work in progress. For most of my life, i was a male supremacist, faithfully following the patriarchal paradigm that permeated all areas of my life, even *after* becoming what i thought was a "revolutionary," someone struggling to achieve an egalitarian social order. Then about eight years ago i was introduced to radical feminist writings by another former male supremacist. And since that time, radical feminist ideas and practice have turned my worldview upside-down! Nowadays, i too consider myself a radical feminist, but one who believes our worldview and practices are better served by drawing a line in the sand by opposing everything that patriarchy champions! In the words of Fred Ho, "The goal is not gender equality, but the abolition of gender as a social differential completely, and the restoration of Mother Right:

procreation and nurturance of humans and Nature, not ownership and domination of people and the earth for private property."

The use of the much-misunderstood and maligned word *matriarchy* is a way to present that revolutionary challenge to the age-old ruling patriarchal order. A clear line in the sand! The word *feminism* is also maligned, misunderstood, and attacked, but i believe—in the long run—it would serve us to do the hard work of returning to the source of the birth of both words (matriarchy and patriarchy) to better grasp the essence and ramifications surrounding the need to do battle on this front—something we're much less likely to do by shying away from a word (matriarchy) that has a lineage and pedigree that cannot be fully or properly understood without such an intense struggle.

My use of the word *matriarchy* is no attempt to either directly or indirectly romanticize mothers, set any "impossible standards for most women to live up to," or demand that all wimmin become mothers. All of which are *patriarchal ideas*, which a struggle over these words will make clear—ideals that were introduced in order to help defeat the then-prevailing matriarchal order during what Frederick Engels wrote was the era of "the overthrow of mother right, [which] was the world-historic defeat of the female sex" in his neglected and little-studied *The Origin of the Family, Private Property, and the State.* This work has stood the test of time.

Though a work in progress, like all "new believers" i too am zealous about confronting, struggling with, and ultimately helping to defeat the patriarchal worldview, which i've termed "the father of oppression." So i ask you to bear with me as you weigh and examine my positions.

LG: In "Liberation or Gangsterism," you explain how the black radical resistance of the 1960s and 1970s gave way, under the pressure of police oppression and programs like COINTELPRO, to gang violence in which young black men fight each other for power and money rather than joining together in resistance to the system that oppresses them. What do you think of the growing movement within prisons to put aside racial differences and gang affiliations in order to increase pressure on prison administrators through hunger strikes (as in California) and labor strikes (as in Georgia)? Are we witnessing a rebirth of radical political resistance within prison? How might this affect possibilities for addressing street violence within communities and creating alternatives to police surveillance through policies such as Stop and Frisk?

SHOATZ: i'm thrilled to know that the prisoners in Georgia, California, and elsewhere have been taking steps to end the monstrous conditions they face. For them to overcome the decades of bloody violence between the various ethnic, racial, and regional affiliations—violence that was provoked and sanctioned by prison staff—is truly historic, and it points to the potential to move forward. That said, i fear that the prisoners' overseers will take steps to derail this growing movement by reducing the potential for the prisoners to continue providing much-needed direction on their end. The way the prison staff usually does that is by separating and transferring the most sophisticated thinkers among the prisoners to other prisons—replacing them with a new, younger, less savvy group of prisoners—while allowing most of the prisoners a measure of relief from their present harsh conditions and not initially making the mistake of treating the new prisoners too badly until they too come to grips with the primary contradiction, which is: the PIC and the prisoners "gangsta culture" are two sides of the same coin; a giant con game that ultimately serves the one percent's accumulation pursuits, as i've already pointed out.

Consequently, we must return to my previous comments. My view is that the "manual" you would like to produce is something that would be very valuable in helping prevent the prison staff in places like Georgia and California (and elsewhere) from continuing to use the PIC as a tool of repression. Your use of the word "escape" in such a manual, however, will certainly guarantee that it will *not* reach most prisoners! Think along the lines of producing something free of inflammatory anti-PIC catchwords but that still drives home the organizing points i suggested in my answer to question #2. You first must make direct contact with a savvy prisoner or two in each state's isolation units to solicit their advice on how to fine-tune your message to their area, as well as for advice on the best way to circulate such a manual in their area and region.

More importantly, such a manual must be small, free, and mass-produced (seeing how they will have to flood the prisons in order to assure enough of them reach their destinations!). Such an effort will benefit prisoners throughout the United States, but the prisoners in isolation in California and Georgia should have priority because they are the most advanced in their broad-based organizing and resistance at the present time. Things have the potential to develop into "a rebirth of radical political resistance within the prisons" and into "possibilities for addressing street violence within communities," and so forth. My view, however, is that the main obstacle here will *not be* the resistance that comes from the prison staff and their supporting police/spy/court arms but will be from *our own* continued failure to adopt to a worldview and practices that are capable of fully unleashing the wimmin and girl half of the ninety-nine percenters that the bulk of even the most committed and advanced males on our side don't realize they're holding back—primarily because these males are still wedded to the patriarchal worldview, which leads to patriarchal thinking, planning, actions, and results. All of which—sooner or later—will (again) alienate the wimmin and girl half of the ninety-nine percent, who will *not* benefit from such an arrangement, except for a minority of co-opted individuals.

In order to overcome that problem, along with everything else we must do to immediately combat the PIC, we must also introduce the male prisoners and the males in the streets to our radical feminist/matriarchal views, literature, and ideas—along with also introducing it to the wimmin and girls they're associated with . . . in case the latter are not already familiar with it. There is no other way I can imagine that we can fully tap into the necessary creativity and energy needed to tackle this problem.

LG: How have you managed to stay sane and clearheaded after twenty-one consecutive years of solitary confinement?

SHOATZ: Perhaps my ego will not allow me to be destroyed by this experience (smile). In the sense that my captors can kill my body, as long as i breathe air they'll never kill what all i've learned about the nature of oppression and repression and why i must stand against both.

Death Penalties

In Reality—
From the Row

Derrick Quintero

Spiraling down the silent corridors of the halls of injustice scream the tormented souls of those lost to the caring eyes of society. Once loved, twice forgotten are the multitude. Where are the families and friends who knew these people? Lost in a world that finds no compassion, no love, and where friendships are draped with proverbial strings. The heart hardens, and the light of the eyes become ruby red from examining the back trails of each and every day for enemies with scathing tongues and honed scraps of steel and plexiglas. Today's prison regimes fail because they are not designed to help prisoners understand their value as human beings. Instead of correcting behavior, they warehouse prisoners for years in prisons that are more akin to gladiator pits. As the years pass into decades, the prisoner's scars of conflict become so deep that it is virtually impossible to find the remnants of humanity buried beneath. But there is always a hope of reclaiming their humanity. This hope resides within the individual prisoner in spite of the prison regime, not because of it.

The current American prison regime compounds violence rather than prevents it. This is because the psychological and social aspects of violence are not addressed by prison administrators. Violent as well as nonviolent responses are learned behaviors, by and large. It is my contention that violent responses are directly associated with a lack of respect for authority figures. And this lack of respect for authority starts with the forms of discipline used on the child, specifically corporal punishment. Often one's childhood has a direct relation to one's actions as an adult. Not addressing these childhood issues while a person is imprisoned is socially irresponsible. Based on my exhaustive conversations with fellow prisoners these past thirty-two years, I have come to the conclusion that prisons are filled almost exclusively with those who were spanked and beaten. A healthy respect for authority is undermined when people use violence to teach others to obey societal rules and to respect all authority without question. It's hypocrisy to think that violence can lead one to respect the peace and dignity of others. A person can be beaten into submission but not beaten into respect. The proof of this is found in the failure of current carceral policies and practices.

It is my belief that prisons, in general, fail to rehabilitate prisoners because they do not effectively, if at all, address the psychological and social aspects of past and present violence. It is my experience that when violence erupts in prisons, the administrative response is suppression, containment, and separation of the individual(s). These responses have some logic in the overall security plan; however, nothing is learned by anyone regarding how to evolve one's response to stressors in a nonviolent manner. What typically occurs is that these prisoners are placed in segregated units where the conditions are so restrictive they border on inhumane. And they are housed with prisoners who are placed there specifically because of mental disorders. Even the guards who normally preside over these punitive segregation units tend to have the most oppressive and even sadistic attitudes of all the rank and file. Being placed in these restrictive conditions understandably elicits further violent responses from the prisoners, all of whom display a slow but sometimes irreversible mental decline.

Nothing positive is gained by the current carceral practice of punitively oriented management. The issue of violence needs to be addressed in a different way. When a person enters the prison, a treatment plan should be developed that is inclusive of past and present episodes of violence. This would include treatment as a victim and/or as a perpetrator of violence. It is my contention that all unsolicited acts against the peace and dignity of another person are necessarily acts of violence. It is not a leap to believe that crime rates can be reduced by treating the individual prisoner's use of violence as a response to the stressors of life. This is probably the most critical function that society should demand of its carceral regime.

Responses to violence are taught to the individual one incident at a time in a series of incidents too many to count. Therefore, to change systemic social practices of violence as a response mechanism and to develop teaching tools for peace, dignity, and respect for (legitimate) authority, you have to treat and heal on the individual level. This individual treatment has to begin within the context of prisons at the structural levels of policy and practice. All prison employees have to be on board with a stance of nonviolent interaction with prisoners unless it is to prevent actual physical harm to other prisoners, to staff, or to prisoners themselves. An effective carceral system must address the root causes of violence in oppression and tyranny. Structural oppression is found in practices that discriminate by race, religion, gender, sexual orientation, culture, and class. Oppression attacks the right of individuality through patterns that isolate, label, and exaggerate differences between people. It is made acceptable by standardizing these patterns and making them seem natural and inevitable.

The reality of the current American carceral regime is that the prisoners must find transformation in prisons that tend to destroy both individualism and community. Prison administrators must allow the advancement of both to triangulate with security needs. It takes individual tenacity within a group dynamic to effectively transform oneself. If there is no effective support group, the prisoner must either develop an appropriate model or seek help doing so. It is my contention that it is possible to transform oneself without help, but the spirit of community makes this process more successful. There are many prisoners who honestly seek to heal and rehabilitate their minds and spirits. Each individual prisoner has to make the first step. It has been my experience that sincere efforts will find the support of fellow prisoners, prison officials, and outside volunteers. The multitude of programs that are currently being offered at Riverbend Maximum Security Institution in Nashville, Tennessee, is proof that even in the most restrictive prisons, the sincere efforts of prisoners are being recognized.

If we do not change the dominant punitive model of incarceration and build on rehabilitative models to address the structural violence of oppression, we cannot expect those who are warehoused in these hellholes of inhumanity to come out better people. What we can expect is for these people to come out with a deep-seated rage, combined with a predatory attitude. Only a few will return from these emotional and physical mazes of terror with their lives centered on love and caring for humanity as a whole. This is not because of the current penal regime but despite it.

Crime cannot be completely eradicated from any society. What *can* be achieved is a reduction of crime by providing resources for people to live in equality. Social democracies seem to have lower rates of crime and punishment than the United States. And, for those naysayers out there, social welfare already exists in the United States through tax shelters for the middle and upper classes, minimal health care for mothers and their children, food stamps for the poorest, and in the escalating cost of imprisoning the poorest of the poor (whether in state-operated prisons or in the increasing numbers of for-profit prisons). The majority of those who are imprisoned arrive with inadequate education to maintain jobs that would support them and their families. I find it suspect that the same people who point to decreasing crime rates as proof that mass imprisonment policies work are also the people who own large shares in either the for-profit prisons or in the for-profit businesses that are increasingly utilized to provide prisons with services such as food, medical care, telephones, and hygiene items sold to prisoners. And everyone in the know understands that anything sold to prisoners by these businesses is mostly paid for by the prisoners' impoverished loved ones. The present carceral regime should be scrapped and reformed to provide for the psychological, educational, and vocational needs of those imprisoned.

The problem with the current carceral regime is fourfold: First, prisons compound the violence of crime rather than creating meaningful alternatives to violence. Secondly, poverty and inadequate education leave some people with fewer options for making a decent living without resorting to some form of criminal activity. Third, with no "legitimate" job skills, prisoners cannot find the employment necessary to support themselves, let alone a family. This will inevitably lead them back into the very same spheres of conflict that caused them to be imprisoned in the first place. The fourth problem is even more clear. Even if the ex-prisoner has the skills necessary to obtain adequate employment, it is almost impossible to find a job with a criminal record. It is easier to say that our society believes in giving a person a second chance than it is in reality. The reality is that ex-prisoners will always be imprisoned, even after they are released. By not directly addressing the reasons why a person ends up in prison in the first place, we find ourselves facing higher taxes to build more prisons. This takes away from the money needed to prepare children in the free society for their future, and it perpetuates the revolving doors of prison that we witness presently.

The best place to see what a lack of education and a dysfunctional family can create is on any state's death row. Death row is filled to capacity, almost exclusively with borderline illiterates, people with varying degrees of mental deficits, and those from poor, working-class, and dysfunctional families. Rarely is one of the rich segments of society found on death row. This does not mean that any of these wealthy murderers are less mentally screwed up than their poorer counterparts. It only means that they had the financial wherewithal to hire adequate legal counsel. Plain and simple: prisons are teeming with poor people. Rich people receive treatment for their problems, while the poor are targeted for punishment. As such, more children in poverty grow up without both parents . . . and the cycle continues.

I look around me and see people on death row who have been victims of extreme child abuse in all its ignominious forms. I see Vietnam veterans who are still fighting the ghosts of their wartime experiences. And I see disproportionate numbers of people who come from poor and working-class families with very inadequate education levels. It makes me wonder if any of those people sitting on death row could have received a fair trial, because they were not really judged by a jury of their peers. There are exceptions to these, but they are few and far between.

The jury selection process contributes to this problem. The financial hardship of participating as a jury member in a long, complex trial negatively impacts the ability of working-class people to participate. There needs to be a living wage paid to all jurors. Without this, most juries will continue to be comprised of middle- and upper-class people, especially in trials of lengthy duration. The poorer people cannot afford to miss the paychecks necessary to their families' survival to participate in jury duty. And since most people in prison come from poor families, they cannot possibly be judged by a jury of their peers, as is mandated by both state and federal law.

This is more clearly evident on death rows strewn across the lands. When a person goes on trial on a capital case, she/he is faced not only with the burden of proving his/her innocence (even though the laws dictate that the prosecutor has the burden to prove one's guilt) but also with having to overcome the stereotype of their race and class designation. These two factors cannot ever be stripped from the individual jurors' minds, no matter what promises or oaths they swear to the contrary. In essence, if the present criminal justice process worked, the jury would represent a fair proportion of race, class, and spiritual beliefs of that particular society; potential jurors would not be excluded from sitting upon the jury based on their belief that the death penalty is wrong, which is how the present legal process works, and which is contrary to federal and state constitutions; the defendant would be given the exact same quality of resources to prove his/her innocence as the state attorneys are given to prove the defendant's guilt; and people with mental problems would not face the death penalty in the first place, as they presently do, even though various state prosecuting attorneys would say otherwise. The prosecutor points to charts and expert witnesses for proof, just as the defendant's attorney points to his/her own charts and expert witnesses, which dictate the exact opposite interpretation. Who to believe?

The death penalty should be abolished not only because it is inhumane but also because the legal process used to achieve the guilty verdict can never overcome the individual jurors' prejudices regarding race, religion, and class, any of which would undermine the constitutional mandate of a fair and impartial trial by a jury of one's peers. Naturally, this critique could apply to all jury trials, but due to the finalized nature of the death penalty, the stakes are much higher. The first corrective step must be the elimination of the death penalty. Sentences of life should also be eliminated. Any sentence that does not take into consideration the possibility of redemption and forgiveness—a person's ability to change—should not be allowed. I am calling for a radical transformation of the legal process used to convict, imprison, and execute people in the United States. True justice demands that we examine the root causes of violence and the current legal practices that create unjust and unreliable convictions and sentences.

U.S. Racism and Derrida's
Theologico-Political Sovereignty

Geoffrey Adelsberg

The connection between theology and the death penalty is central to Derrida's study of capital punishment. As Michael Naas, a participant in the Derrida Seminar Translation Project, states: "In the two years he devotes to the death penalty . . . Derrida seems to want to show how the concepts, rhetoric, symbolism, images, and imaginary of the death penalty are all determined and *marked* by a Christian or Judeo-Christian theologico-political heritage."[1] This chapter aims first to provide a working definition of this relation among religion, politics, and the death penalty. Second, I will offer an interpretation of Derrida's methodology, asking: Why does Derrida focus his analysis on the rarefied realms of sovereignty and religion qua Western European sovereignty rather than focusing on the particular histories of the death penalty in the countries where it is/was practiced? I contend that Derrida's methodological avoidance of the history of the death penalty is premised upon the thought that abolitionist movements are at their strongest when they conceive of the death penalty as central to the state rather than an instrument of its criminal law.

I will contend that Derrida's focus on the death penalty's connection to religion and politics requires supplement by a historical analysis, and

I argue that this is possible without falling into a conditional abolition-ism. I will interpret Angela Y. Davis's account of the connection between slavery, the death penalty, and prisons as that critical supplement to Der-rida's theologico-political analysis of the death penalty. I contend that the death penalty during slavery and the prisons that thrived in the wake of U.S. post–Emancipation Reconstruction reveals a continuing differential exposure of Black and Brown people to sovereign decision. I conclude with preliminary speculation that this differential exposure of Black and Brown people to sovereign decision is a structural feature of European sovereignty. Reading Derrida together with Davis provides ground for thinking about the particular histories and people that are exposed to the death penalty alongside the death penalty's theologico-political grounding.

In the first session of the *Death Penalty Seminars*, Derrida identifies a pattern in the executions of Socrates, Christ, Al-Hallaj, and Joan of Arc, which he deems classical cases of Judeo-Islamicate-Christian tradition: the religious authority prosecutes heresy by giving the state the right to en-force the will of a punishing god.[2] Derrida conceives of the death penalty as the foundational alliance between religious authority and sovereign au-thority. Insofar as the state becomes the enforcer of sacred law, it is also the judge of whether the religious claim ought to be upheld. The state becomes the judge of whether the heretic defendant ought to live or die. Insofar as it decides the life or death of the subject, the state takes on the power of the divine judge. In this judgment, the sovereign decides who is sacred and deserving of protection and what is profane and deserving of death or the indifference of exile.

In *For What Tomorrow*, Derrida claims that in order for a sovereign to be a sovereign, she/he must have the power over life and death. Derrida writes, "State sovereignty thus defines itself by the power of life and death over subjects. And therefore by this right of exception, by the right to raise itself . . . above the law."[3] The self-definition of the sovereign is at stake in the sovereign power over life and death. Without the power over life and death, the sovereign would be unable to define her/himself as sover-eign. For Derrida, as for Schmitt, the sovereign's self-definition in power over life and death is at once self-definition by a decision on the exception that raises the sovereign beyond the law. There are a great deal of ways to think of exception, but for the purposes of this chapter, I suggest that the sovereign right to power of exception is the right to decide on the sacred and profane without reference to previously existing law. In other words, the sovereign's self-definition is the power over life and death unrestricted by law. No matter how many international organizations a nation joins, no matter how much one sovereign state submits to the strictures of the laws of these institutions, the sovereign only retains her/his sovereignty if she/ he holds the right of exception, the right to put these laws aside and decide over life and death.

In Derrida's conception of a sovereign state, the sovereign both makes the law and is exempt from the law. The laws of the sovereign state establish the distinctions between sacred and profane, but the sovereign always has the power to redefine the sacred and profane for the sake of upholding the state's law and stability. I would resist reading sovereign decision too literally. It need not refer to a sovereign in a throne or a head of state receiving a call from the death chamber; it does refer to a power that the state must reserve for itself in order to remain a state.

The death penalty, for Derrida, is the exemplary moment of the establishment of theological-political sovereignty because it instantiates the sovereign power over life and death. I have followed Derrida previously in his contention that the death penalty arises from the foundational alliance between religious authority and sovereign authority. In each of the "classical" cases of the death penalty, the religious authority prosecutes heresy by giving the state the right to take the place of god. The sovereign decides whether the god's law has been broken, thereby taking the place of god in the decision of life and death. If the decision over life and death is at the foundation of the sovereign's power, we can make sense of Derrida's claim that he "does not rely on an *already available* theologico-political concept that it would suffice to apply to the death penalty as one of its 'cases' or examples."[4] For Derrida, it is not enough to think of the death penalty as an effect of sovereignty. It is not enough to think of the death penalty as a moment when the sovereign exercises her/his power over life and death. It is not enough to think of the death penalty as one mode of punishment among others. For Derrida, the sovereign practice of the death penalty is the moment that constitutes sovereignty. It is only in the decision to put the heretic to death that the sovereign raises himself to the godly decision over life and death. It is only in the capacity to exercise the death penalty that the sovereign becomes the sovereign. Derrida affirms the death penalty as the primary moment of sovereignty: "I would be tempted to say that one cannot begin to think the theologico-political, except from this phenomenon of criminal law that is called the death penalty."[5] The death penalty instantiates sovereignty's power over life and death.

Now that we have a working definition of the relation between religion, politics, and the death penalty—death penalty as sovereign power over life and death—I will offer an interpretation of Derrida's methodology.

As Derrida writes, and as I quoted earlier, "One cannot begin to think the theologico-political, except from this phenomenon of criminal law that is called the death penalty." I take phenomenon to refer to both the existence of the death penalty in legal code of a particular country as well as the concrete instances of people being put to death by the law of that country. When we, as philosophers, take the death penalty to be a phenomenon, we find ourselves in a particular sovereign's legal code; we find ourselves in a particular history of the exercise of that legal code. When the phenomenon of the death penalty is the object of our study, we can speak of its history and the people that come under its decision. Derrida does not take the phenomenon itself as the object of his study. The phenomenon of the death penalty, for Derrida, points the way to theologico-political sovereignty. Derrida is concerned with the formal structure of sovereignty; his sovereign governs no specific state. Rather than borders, Derrida's concept of sovereignty is tied to an intellectual Judeo-Christo-humanist tradition. Indeed, he does not devote his intellectual attention to particular histories of the death penalty in the United States, even when the U.S. death penalty is at stake in his analysis.

The question for Derrida is: Why move immediately from the phenomenon of the death penalty to sovereignty and its intellectual religious background? Why this restlessness? Why not a fuller analysis of the particular history of the U.S. death penalty? My contention is that Derrida moves swiftly from the phenomenon of the death penalty to questions of sovereignty because he does not believe that we can gain an adequate abolitionist discourse from the phenomenon or the history of the death penalty alone.

If we follow Derrida and say that the death penalty is the condition without which the state could not be, the abolitionist demand for the state to end its practice of the death penalty would be the equivalent of asking the state to abolish itself. Although this is a strong claim, seeming to verge on hyperbole, we can make this claim intelligible by following Derrida's strict definition of the death penalty. If the death penalty attests to the state's capacity to decide over life and death, then when we ask the state to give up this right, we are asking for a great deal. We are asking for the state to give up its right to decide, unconditionally, when and whom to kill. Without this right, the state would lose its justification for defensive and offensive war in addition to law. Following Derrida's definition of the state, we would be asking the sovereign state to give up the terms of its founding: the violence with which it enforces its law and protects its perpetuity.

If we were to study the phenomenon of the death penalty as an instrument of the state rather than its founding condition, then we might see the spectacle of the death penalty as one way among many that the state enforces its law. On those grounds, we would be led to request that the state enforce the law without killing. As in European Union countries, we might find this demand successfully implemented by the U.S. state. But this abolition will be unsatisfactory for Derrida because the stakes of his abolition are deeper. For Derrida, the demand of abolition must be an unconditional abstinence from the sovereign's decision over life and death. For Derrida's theologico-political state, that is unintelligible. It calls for the end of the theologico-political state as such.[6]

For Derrida, historical and present-day death penalty abolitionists will be limited as long as they fail to recognize that the stakes of abolitionism are more radical than ending the death penalty as a form of punishment. It is here that I distinguish between calls for abstinence from the death penalty as punishment, which I will call phenomenal abolitionism, and Derrida's call for the opposition to all sovereign decision over life and death, which I will call sovereign abolitionism. Phenomenal abolitionism aims to civilize and improve the rule of law by ridding it of its recourse to the death penalty. It therefore assumes an already-standing rule of law. Phenomenal abolitionism asks the sovereign to refrain from using the death penalty as an instrument of punishment. Sovereign abolitionism considers the death penalty as the condition upon which the rule of law can exist in the first place. Against phenomenal abolitionism and its desire to civilize the rule of law, sovereign abolitionism stakes its opposition against all instances of the sovereign power over life and death. The sovereign abolitionist therefore stakes her/his abolition against the sovereign itself.

Derrida motivates the move from phenomenal to sovereign abolition by showing the limits and conditionality of Cesare Beccaria's phenomenal abolitionism. For Beccaria, the death penalty is one of many weapons in the sovereign's arsenal of punishment. He argues that the death penalty ought to be largely removed on grounds of limited effectiveness: deterrence from wrongdoing requires prolonged suffering, the death penalty is too quick a punishment, and therefore it fails to deter.[7] Beccaria claims that his abolitionism is valid only for a well-ordered society under the rule of sovereign law.[8] Beccaria thus distinguishes between the death penalty in a stable, well-ordered state and the death penalty when the stability of the state itself is threatened. For Beccaria, we must allow the death penalty in the latter case. On grounds of securing the safety and stability of the state, the sovereign can justify the death penalty.

For Beccaria, as well as for everyday phenomenal abolitionists, there is a distinction between the punishments within a society ruled by law and punishments meted out to secure and defend that society. For Beccaria, as well as for many abolitionists who are focused on the abolition of the death penalty as an instrument of lawful punishment, the only death penalty their abolitionism opposes is within a stable society under the rule of law. Derrida argues that this is insufficient. In his criticism of Beccaria, Derrida writes: "In other words—here we touch on one of the more obscure stakes of the problem, insofar as one has not clearly defined the concept of war, the strict difference between civil war, national war, partisan war, 'terrorism' whether domestic or not, etc. (so many concepts that have always been and are still more problematic, obscure, dogmatic, manipulable than ever)—the abolition of the death penalty within the secure borders of a prosperous and peaceful nation will remain something seriously limited, convenient, provisional, conditional—which is to say, not principled."[9]

Beccaria assumes a clear distinction between the death penalty that takes place under the rule of sovereign law and the death penalty that secures and defends that state's stable existence. Derrida calls into question this distinction between that which is internal to rule of law and that which is external to it by pointing to the lack of definite criteria and limits for the acts of violence that are supposedly justified for the sake of preserving the state. Insofar as death penalty abolitionists leave war and terrorism outside their purview, they allow the sovereign exercise of the death penalty to return under a different name. As we have too often seen in the last decade of U.S. foreign policy, the supposed threat of terrorism to the stability of U.S. sovereignty as such can justify unlimited death penalties in the Middle East.

As long as our focus on the death penalty is limited to the instances of lawful execution, our abolitionism remains conditional. We only deny the sovereign the right to decide over life and death in one domain without confronting the need to deny the sovereign the right to decide over life and death in all domains. Our abolitionism will be conditional upon the stable functioning of the rule of law. If this is the limit of our abolitionism, the sovereign can too easily reinstate the death penalty by justification on grounds of protection of the state itself. The conditionality of this abolitionism is unsatisfactory insofar as we also want an abolition that denies the sovereign right to exercise arbitrary violence whenever that sovereign can spin a yarn justifying violence on grounds of the preservation of the state. Sovereign abolition aims to remove this power itself from the sovereign; it challenges every instance of the sovereign's decision over life and death.

With Derrida, we can endorse sovereign abolitionism above phenomenal abolitionism on two grounds: (1) The death penalty is a foundation upon which sovereignty is built because it establishes the sovereign's power of life and death. Phenomenal abolitionism is inadequate to this insight because its view of the sovereign's relation to the death penalty is too narrow: it takes the death penalty as an instrument of sovereign power rather than the moment when the sovereign capacity to decide over life and death is established. The phenomenal abolitionist is limited to questioning the death penalty as *practice* rather than death penalty as sovereign *capacity* to decide over life and death. As such, phenomenal abolition can only speak to one instantiation of the sovereign violence rather than the condition upon which the sovereign violence can happen in the first place. (2) A principled abolitionism can only attack the sovereign capacity to decide over life and death if it stakes its opposition against all instances of the sovereign decision over life and death. When we oppose the death penalty as an instrument of punishment only, our abolition becomes conditional upon the stability of the state and the rule of sovereign law. The sovereign may lose her/his capacity to decide on the life and death of citizens in the realm of criminal law, but she/he will retain it as recourse when the stability of society and law itself is supposedly at stake. This leads to a partial, merely conditional abolition that leaves the sovereign power of decision over life and death violently intact. It allows the decision over life and death to be justified in terms of the security and stability of the state.

Derrida's opposition to a phenomenal analysis of the death penalty is due to the impossibility of building an adequate abolitionism on phenomenal grounds. He wants to move away from grounding abolition on phenomenal analysis, but this still leaves room for interpreting the phenomenon of the death penalty in light of theologico-political analysis. In the rest of this chapter, I will read the most pressing insights of phenomenal analysis in light of Derrida's unconditional sovereign abolitionism. Derrida gestures toward phenomenal insights regarding representations of the U.S. death penalty in the media, the death penalty as colonial war in Algeria, and the continuing legacies of racism in the United States. Even here, his phenomenal analysis is not rich enough. The history of racism in Europe and the United States is gestured to without changing the central terms of analysis. If Derrida were to wade more deeply into this phenomenal analysis, I believe that the sufficiency of Derrida's conception of theologico-political sovereignty would be challenged: that he would see that European sovereign violence is not violence as such but violence that threatens Black and Brown people to a much greater extent than people of white European descent.

In contrast to Derrida's claim that the phenomenon of the death penalty persists in the United States due to its status as the most Christian country in the world, Angela Y. Davis claims that "the most compelling explanation for the routine continuation of the death penalty in the United States . . . is the racism that links the death penalty to slavery."[10] Derrida's claim follows from his theologico-political analysis: where there is the death penalty in a European nation, there is a religious inheritance of the theologico-political. Insofar as the death penalty remains practiced in the United States, the United States will bear the mark of its Christian inheritance more outwardly than its European counterparts. Davis's claim that the death penalty remains in the United States due to its racist history follows from her phenomenal analysis: the death penalty is analyzed in terms of *who* was killed by the state. Davis also asks *why* they were subject to this punishment and under what historical, political, and legal conditions they were executed. Bringing the two analyses together, we can ask: What can the history of those who have been subject to the death penalty reveal about the structure of the sovereign decision over life and death? Responding to this question enriches our conception of sovereignty and its subjects without formulating abolition on limited, phenomenal grounds.

Davis is attentive to the intersections of slavery and the death penalty that continue to inform capital punishment and its attendant prisons. She offers an account of the death penalty in the United States beginning with its near abolition with the emergence of prisons at the end of the eighteenth century. Davis explains, "What is interesting is that slavery as an institution . . . managed to become a receptacle for all those forms of punishment that were considered barbaric by the developing democracy. So rather than abolish the death penalty outright, it was offered refuge within slave law."[11]

The "humanization" of punishment, as in the late eighteenth century's talk of inalienable rights of citizens, referred only to white male citizens.[12] Hardly erased from the law, barbaric punishments were simply displaced from white males to slaves. Insofar as slaves were exposed to barbaric treatment while "humane" punishment was reserved for white males, the stage of American theologico-political sovereignty was set: the white man's dignity would be sacred under the law while the African-descended slave would be subject to punishment unmitigated by the Enlightenment.

Slave law establishes the exposure of Black and Brown people before U.S. law: White citizens were released from the threat of death for most crimes while "Black slaves . . . were subject to the death penalty in some states for as many as seventy different offenses."[13] Davis's explication of slave law shows that punishment in the United States is founded upon an unequal exposure to sovereign decision. The possibility of sovereign decision threatens the slave to a much greater extent than the white male citizen. After the abolition of slavery, the death penalty "was incorporated into the legal system with its overt racism gradually concealed."[14] Although free and equal before the law, the death penalty remained a much greater threat to African-descended people before the law than white people. Today, the claim is that we can rid the death penalty of racism by assuring proportionality, by assuring that equal crimes receive equal punishment. This is an impulse to equalize the protection of all people under the law.

I have so far used the language of differential exposure to punishment to capture the phenomenon of European and European-descended countries punishing Black and Brown people to a much greater extent than white people. My usage is meant to invoke a phenomenon of quantitative overrepresentation of African-descended people in penal systems in those countries. But, I wish to make the notion of differential exposure to punishment speak to injustice beyond the fact that people of color are vastly overrepresented in penal systems and subject to harsher punishment than white people when they commit similar crimes. Davis offers the resources to show how the history of Black and Brown institutions of enslavement and colonization shape the qualitative features of contemporary penal structures in the United States.

One way to explicate Davis's claim that slave law was incorporated into post-Emancipation U.S. penal codes is to say that those who are punished by post-Emancipation penal codes inherit the legacy of subpersonhood from those punished under slave code. The criminal under slave code is one whose discipline depends on the infliction (or at least the threat) of great violence and whose self-defense is prohibited. That criminal is one whose educative and cultural life outside of uncompensated productive labor is considered a threat to the extant social and political order. The analogy between the framing of subpersonhood during slavery and the civil death of U.S. prisoners today is inexact. Nonetheless, the overcrowded warehouse prisons, the denial of educational/therapeutic opportunities to incarcerated people due to governmental divestment, and the preventable continued violence faced by incarcerated people speaks to inheritances of subpersonhood in the contemporary U.S. penal code. Davis's analysis shows that the continuing differential exposure of Black and Brown people to punishment is not only about quantitative overrepresentation but also about the notion of who the criminal is and what they deserve. Such racialized notions of personhood have concrete implications for life within contemporary prisons. Equalizing the racial distribution of who is subject to the suffering and disenfranchisement of contemporary penal systems does not erase ways that that very suffering and disenfranchisement is constituted by racist conceptions of personhood and subpersonhood.

Davis's insistence on the connection between the death penalty and the civil death of prisons reveals another point at which Derrida's abolitionism must stretch. Derrida insists on the opposition to all forms of sovereign decision over life and death, but it is also necessary to be explicit in the expansion of what it means to be subject to sovereign decision. To be killed by the state is the literal incarnation of the sovereign decision, but being sent to the civil death of imprisonment where every minute is regulated and managed, one's civil rights are stripped, and one is subject to arbitrary punishment and pain must also fall under the sovereign decision over life and death. In condemning its subjects to prison, the sovereign is subjecting life to violence unmediated by sovereign protection. Solitary confinement, medical neglect, exploitation of prisoners' labor, and sexual coercion in women's and men's prisons demonstrate the extent of the exposure to violence in the civil death that is imprisonment.

Davis's research also shows that the death penalty in slave law and contemporary practices of imprisonment are coextensive insofar as they expose Black and Brown people to punishment of a much greater extent than their white counterparts. Engagement with differential exposure to punishment means engaging with thoroughly racialized notions of criminality and disposability that support European sovereignty. I believe the racist U.S. history and present illustrates this clearly, but we can widen our scope and examine imprisonment within the larger community of theologico-political states. European nations show a similar inequality of exposure to sovereign decision over civil life and death. Although European nation-states are not as strict in their accounting of the ethnicity of their prison population, theorist Lucia Re claims that "the average percentage of foreigners detained in European prisons exceeds 30% of the prison population, as compared with a presence of foreigners on the European territory that is around 7% of the population."[15] The inequality of exposure of immigrants to punishment in France, England, and Italy speaks to a larger problematic debated and developed among decolonial and postcolonial intellectuals that Derrida should have engaged with: how does the analysis of legal violence transform when we consider colonialism, enslavement, and racism to be essential rather than accidental features of political sovereignty?

This is a question that goes beyond the scope of this chapter, but toward a conclusion, I will offer preliminary speculation. Recalling the Derridean and Schmittean thesis, the sovereign's power is predicated on her/his capacity to decide on the life and death of its subjects. We should extend this thesis: the sovereign not only must establish her/his power by killing but must *re*establish power by killing on a continual basis.[16] For sovereignty to remain sovereign, the potency of the sovereign decision over life and death must be practiced.

We can think of the punishment in its current racialized form as sustaining a political "economy of sacrifice." This is in contrast with potentially revolutionary practices of mourning. If those killed by the state are of a privileged sociopolitical status, their death can be mourned in such a way that the legitimacy of the sovereign is put into question.[17] As martyr, the executed is a cause against the sovereign. Those killed in Tahrir Square in 2011, for instance, had the effect of delegitimizing the sovereign decision. In these cases, the sovereign's decision to punish was stripped bare. Hosni Mubarak had no recourse to justification outside the furtherance of his tyrannical rule.[18] To both kill and retain legitimacy, the sovereign decision to kill must be justified and accepted by a substantial majority (or a strategically placed minority) as justified killing, killing that maintains or otherwise protects the body politic.

For Derrida, the economy of sacrifice creates viciously successful mourning.[19] He says, "In successful mourning, I incorporate the one who has died, I assimilate him to myself, I reconcile myself with his death, and consequently, I deny death and the alterity of the dead other and of death as other."[20] White supremacist sovereignties and populations view the deaths of Black and Brown people sent to death row or "accidently murdered" in a foreign airstrike as justifiable insofar as they are an unfortunate consequence of an otherwise justifiable military action. Incorporation is the (tacit) acceptance that this death is necessary for the security of the community or the state. Death is accepted as "for a purpose" rather than the end of a life, which overwhelms the political community's capacity to incorporate it.

The differential exposure of Black and Brown people to punishment in U.S. history is also a differential exposure to the logic of sacrifice and incorporation. In order for sovereignty at once to maintain its decision over life and death and to hold the consent of certain constituents, the sovereign repurposes the white imaginary of Black and Brown criminality to frame certain people as always already a threat and thus deserving of sacrifice for the sake of protecting the polity. Such language of protection in European (and European-descended) sovereignties has always been code for protecting those racial and sexual groups deemed innocent and therefore protected from sovereign violence.

Reading the phenomenal history of the American death penalty together with Derrida's notion of the death penalty as a constitutive moment of political theology deepens our conception of what is at stake in the structure of sovereignty as well as what is at stake in its abolition. The differential exposure of Black and Brown people to sovereign violence reveals that the effects of sovereignty are going to be distinct across populations. We must then begin speaking of sovereignty's effects in a way that captures its inequality of decision and moves toward an analysis adequate to the ways that this differential exposure is endemic to sovereignty as such.

My gratitude to Darla Migan, Lisa Guenther, and Kelly Oliver for their critical comments on drafts of this chapter. Thanks also to the organizers of the Philosophy Born of Struggle Conference at Texas A&M University in October 2012 for offering me a space to present a version of this paper.

Making Death a Penalty: Or, Making "Good" Death a "Good" Penalty

Kelly Oliver

Currently, the United States is the only country in the so-called developed Western world that continues to execute prisoners.[1] Since 2008, in order to avoid construing the death penalty as "cruel and unusual" punishment, which would violate the Eighth Amendment, the Supreme Court has upheld the use of a tripartite lethal injection protocol as more "humane" than other methods of execution: the first drug renders the condemned unconscious, the second paralyzes his muscles, and the third kills him by stopping his heart. In *Baze v. Rees* (2008), the Supreme Court upheld Kentucky's lethal injection protocol and ruled that there is no cruelty in execution as long as the prisoner is unconscious at the time of death, particularly since use of the drug that stops the heart is excruciatingly painful.[2]

One of the drugs in the court-approved, three-drug "cocktail," however, is no longer being made and states have had to halt executions because they don't have legally sanctioned means to carry them out. European pharmaceutical companies will no longer sell drugs if they are to be used in executions.[3] The shortage of sodium thiopental, an anesthetic that renders prisoners unconscious, and other drugs used more recently in lethal injections, has done more to stop the death penalty in the United

States than centuries of protests. It is noteworthy that many states are now considering using one injection of pentobarbital, the drug most commonly used by veterinarians to euthanize animals.[4] In fact, this was the drug used in the recent executions of Troy Davis in Georgia (2012) and Lawrence Brewer in Texas (2012).[5] As they did with sodium thiopental, however, European manufacturers of pentobarbital refuse to sell the drug to be used in executions. Still, states that use the death penalty continue to try to find lethal injection drugs that can meet the Supreme Court standard prohibiting cruel and unusual punishment.

States like Tennessee, which have tried to use suppliers not approved by the FDA, have had their supplies of the drug seized by the federal government; in Tennessee, scores of prisoners are now waiting on death row for execution, which has been halted for years because of issues with the lethal injection protocols caused by the shortage of sanctioned and tested drugs.[6] In addition, attorneys for several Tennessee death row inmates temporarily succeeded in challenging the state's method of determining whether inmates are unconscious before being put to death, which is the purpose of the discontinued drug.[7] Along with other states, executions in Tennessee were on hold for almost four years as a result of the unavailability of drugs sanctioned by the Supreme Court for use in lethal injection. Recently, however, Tennessee has adopted a new drug protocol and plans to resume executions using what they call "consciousness checks" to ensure that the condemned is unconscious before the paralytic drug is administered.[8] Other states have instituted so-called consciousness checks, which usually consist of wardens calling the name of the condemned, brushing his eyelashes, or pinching him.[9]

In this chapter, I examine the issue of consciousness as it relates to death and the death penalty. I argue that the Supreme Court's justification for the three-drug protocol, along with recent attempts to provide a "humane" and painless death by first rendering the condemned unconscious, circumvent the ability to determine whether the method of execution meets the criteria for avoiding cruel and unusual punishment. Because the condemned is rendered unconscious and his muscles are paralyzed, he cannot testify to his own suffering; furthermore, medical science cannot guarantee unconsciousness, particularly in terms of "consciousness of death." In *Baze v Rees*, the Supreme Court sanctioned lethal injection because, as the reasoning goes, if the condemned is unconscious, then he will not suffer. This raises the complicated question of what it means to suffer. In this chapter, my focus is slightly different. Here, I analyze the notion of unconsciousness at the time of death, both in terms of whether medical science can ever guarantee it and philosophically in terms of what it might mean to be conscious or unconscious of death.

I argue that this notion is a fantasy, since we cannot ensure that the condemned is not conscious at the time of death and therefore does not suffer. I contend that the fantasy of the "good" or clean and painless death not only covers over the ways in which the death penalty itself is cruel and unusual punishment but also perpetuates the practice of capital punishment. I argue that this fantasy of the "good" death is necessary in order to distinguish lawful execution from unlawful murder. In other words, the state justifies the death penalty as humane by distinguishing it from the barbarity of murder. So, even while some proponents of capital punishment may think that lethal injection is "too good" for brutal murderers, the state must maintain a distinction between clean, high-tech, civilized killing and brutal murder. Finally, I analyze the concept of death as a penalty in order to show a tension inherent in the very notion of the death penalty, or death as a penalty.

Consciousness of Suffering or Consciousness of Death

One of the first executions of 2014 took place in Ohio, using an untested combination of drugs, and took twenty-five minutes; the condemned, Dennis McGuire, was heard making gasping, snorting, and choking sounds.[10] McGuire's children plan on bringing a lawsuit charging the state with violating the Eighth Amendment against cruel and unusual punishment. But, given that McGuire cannot testify that he suffered, legal authorities speculate that it will be difficult to prove.[11] One of the questions is whether McGuire was conscious at the time of his death. Witnesses say that he "went unconscious" and then a few minutes later started moving and gasping. In order to prove suffering, McGuire would have to have been conscious at the time of his death. But, how can we determine whether, and with certainty, that McGuire, or any condemned, is conscious at the time of death? The question of what constitutes consciousness is not just an empirical question but also a philosophical one.[12] In fact, the question of what constitutes consciousness is a fundamental philosophical issue and has been, and continues to be, the topic of much philosophical debate.

As the McGuire case makes evident, consciousness is always in excess of what can be witnessed. No one has, or can, testify to his own death, or whether that death resulted in suffering. That testimony can only come from external witnesses; and yet, they can never witness to—or in any case "see"—consciousness itself. Even expert testimony is always a supplement to, and substitute for, the experience of death itself, which cannot be seen by witnesses or testified to by the condemned.[13] The question of consciousness necessarily troubles the fantasy of instant "clean" death imagined in the latest death penalty protocols involving lethal injection as a humane way to kill.

The "standards" or protocols upheld by the Supreme Court for humane execution skirt the issue of whether the death penalty itself may be cruel and unusual punishment by focusing on the method of killing. When the Supreme Court effectively abolished the death penalty from 1972 to 1976, it wasn't because the penalty itself was cruel and unusual but rather because its application was. In *Furman v. Georgia* (1972), the Supreme Court ruled that the application of the death penalty was inconsistent in terms of when and how it was used.[14] Abolitionists have argued that the application of the death penalty is discriminatory and used disproportionately against Blacks; that innocent men are executed; and that various methods of execution constitute cruel and unusual punishment. All of these arguments, however, allow that although the practice is flawed, the principle may be sound; if only we improve and perfect the practice, then we authorize the principle. The fantasy of humane, painless, instant death, technologically administered, contributes not only to the idea of the perfection of the means of death in order to justify the principle of the death penalty but also to the fantasy of death itself as an absolute, in this case, the absolute end of suffering and pain.

The Supreme Court's 2008 decision upholding the use of tripartite lethal injection—the first rendering unconscious, the second paralyzing the muscles, and the third stopping the heart—ruled that there is no cruelty in execution as long as the prisoner is unconscious while being killed.[15] This so-called "clean death" sterilized with high-tech medical apparatus, including IVs, syringes, and hospital gurneys, supposedly sanitizes death; and like the surgical strike in high-tech warfare, it focuses death into an imagined instant, but only by dividing into the three stages of lethal injection that ensure that the prisoner will look dead before he actually is dead. The look of death, then, is a necessary supplement to the real thing.

This is why the Supreme Court insists on the use of the second injection to paralyze the muscles. This supplementary injection can only be for the sake of the witnesses. Writing for the plurality, Chief Justice Roberts contends that the state adequately proved that the second paralyzing injection "serves two purposes: (1) preventing involuntary convulsions or seizures during unconsciousness, thereby preserving the procedure's dignity, and (2) hastening death."[16] Yet, the preservation of dignity and quick death can be ensured only if the body is made to look dead before it actually is. Paradoxically, the very characteristic that makes the condemned sane and sound enough to stand trial—consciousness—is taken away.

In her dissenting opinion, Justice Ginsberg argues that once the second drug is injected, "further monitoring of the inmate's consciousness becomes impractical without sophisticated equipment and training. Even if the inmate were conscious and in excruciating pain, there would be no visible indication."[17] Indeed, the petitioner's expert witness testified that "a layperson could not tell from visual observation if a paralyzed inmate was conscious and that doing so would be difficult for even a professional."[18] And yet, in states that have subsequently instituted so-called "consciousness checks," many rely not on medical experts but rather on prison wardens who, in the realm of determining consciousness, are laypeople. Of course, all of these claims assume that medical personnel and/or sophisticated equipment can always distinguish consciousness from unconsciousness. Moreover, the concern over consciousness or unconsciousness does not address the problematic issue of whether an unconscious person, as medically defined, can experience pain and suffering, or, more to the point here, whether they can experience death. Again, this raises the question of what it means to be conscious of death.

The question of consciousness of death reveals an assumption at work in various discourses around execution and more humane applications of the death penalty: namely, that death happens in an instant and that we can determine the moment of death. The idea seems to be that as long as we can provide an instant death, then not only is it painless and therefore more humane, but also it reduces the risk of consciousness of death. In other words, the fantasy is that death happens in an instant, and if we can condense dying and death to the same moment, we have achieved the goal of painless, humane death rendered in a split second so as to avoid consciousness. It is as though if we kill fast enough, we can outrun consciousness. If only we can separate dying from death and give death without also a prolonged dying.

Certainly, the number of botched hangings, electrocutions, and even lethal injections indicates that even advanced technologies cannot insure a pain-free instant death or guarantee that the victim is unconscious at the time of death. In fact, a study of postmortem examinations on prisoners executed by lethal injection concludes that given blood levels of anesthetic, "prisoners may have been capable of feeling pain in almost 90% of cases and may have actually been conscious when they were put to death . . . Because a muscle relaxant was used to paralyze them, however, inmates would have been unable to indicate any pain."[19] This is not, however, merely a practical problem but also and moreover a philosophical one: because we cannot be certain, from a phenomenological perspective, what counts as "the time of death," or as "consciousness of death."

The three-drug protocol circumvents the very possibility of establishing whether the condemned man is suffering or in pain, whether he is conscious at the moment of death, and therefore whether the punishment is cruel and unusual as defined by the Court. Because the second drug paralyzes the condemned, he cannot indicate whether he is suffering. He cannot testify to his own pain and suffering. As in the recent case of Dennis McGuire, executed in Ohio with a lethal injection that first rendered him "unconscious," the drugs make it impossible for the condemned to indicate whether he is suffering, even when his body is gasping and choking. Furthermore, this fabulous fantasy of painless death disavows the reality that we don't know how to define what constitutes consciousness of death because firsthand testimony is impossible. As long as Lawrence Brewer, executed in Texas, goes out snoring as if in a sound sleep (which he apparently did), at some level we can reassure ourselves that his death is the least cruel, most usual, and perhaps even the most desired, namely dying in his sleep.

Natural Death versus Death as Punishment

Ironically, even a painful natural death does not satisfy those seeking the death penalty because the death must be explicitly exercised as a penalty by the state. For example, on November 1, 2013, Paul Dennis Reid Jr. died, "not strapped to a gurney by lethal injection but in a bed at Nashville General Hospital," and some of his victims' families were "furious" that he died a "peaceful death," "a natural death," "a normal death like everyone else."[20] It is not enough that the condemned died after spending sixteen years on death row, presumably because his death was not a punishment. Some suggest that the recent push by Tennessee officials to execute prisoners on death row is to avoid the possibility that any more of them might escape execution by dying.[21]

Obviously, the death penalty, then, is not just about death but rather about death rendered as punishment. Indeed, if some people are "offended" when a condemned man dies before he can be executed, then it is clear that death itself is not the issue.[22] As we have seen, in terms of the Supreme Court rulings, death itself is not the issue but rather how death is given: how it is administered, the means of application, how it is distributed, the policies governing it, its consistency and maintenance. In terms of the Supreme Court's interpretation of the Eighth Amendment, death is to be given without excessive pain and suffering, wherein the moment or instant of death is seen as the end of pain and suffering. So, for example, in the case of Pedro Medina, whose head caught on fire during his electrocution in Florida in 1997, the Florida Supreme Court concluded: "Medina's brain was instantly and massively depolarized within milliseconds of the initial surge of electricity. He suffered no conscious pain."[23]

Cruelty, then, has been reduced to the duration of death. Within this logic, cruelty can be measured in milliseconds. A "good" death is one that happens instantly. Paradoxically, this "good," instantaneous, painless death is to be given as a penalty. The death sanctioned by the Supreme Court must be given without undue pain and suffering, and yet it must be given as a punishment. As the case of Medina shows, within this logic, the question of cruelty has been reduced to the question of how many minutes of dying constitute cruelty. Does it matter whether the condemned is conscious during those minutes? Does it matter whether he suffers? And more to the point, how do we measure that pain and suffering, let alone the question of how we measure consciousness or unconscious of it, or, more problematically, consciousness or unconsciousness of death?[24]

Indeed, Martin Heidegger maintains that what distinguishes the human way of being in the world from other living beings is consciousness of death as a being-towards-death. This is not consciousness of the moment of death but rather of the inevitability of death. This is not consciousness of the instant of death but rather of finitude. The fact of our consciousness of finitude, and of the inevitability of death—the human relation to death— complicates any easy notion of the moment or instant of death, just as it complicates the idea of consciousness of death. In an important sense, for Heidegger, and for Derrida following him, what it means to be finite is to be subject to both birth and death, both of which are out of our control. This means that essential to finitude and thus to human existence is that we do not deny that we are not the sovereigns of death. In other words, by giving death the sovereign state claims a power that calls into question what it means to be human.[25] There is much more to be said about this line of reasoning, but that will have to wait for another context.

It is significant, then, that death can be a punishment properly speaking only for those who realize that they are going to die. If it is true that other animals do not have a sense of their impending deaths (which is debatable), then while they can be punished by pain or even shame, they cannot be punished by death. Only a being with the consciousness of death can be punished by death. In this case, however, it is not the death itself, that moment or instant of death, that is the punishment; rather, the punishment can only be awaiting death. The punishment is precisely consciousness of death in the sense of knowing that you face the death penalty. This is a strange aspect of the death penalty, namely, that the condemned are not just sentenced to death but sentenced to await death on death row, sometimes for most of their lives. That is to say, the death sentence brings with it a life defined by waiting for death. But this waiting is not like the "natural" waiting for death that accompanies human life. Indeed, the law requires that it be unnatural. Neither the law nor the families of most victims wants the condemned to die a natural death. Rather, his death must be unnatural. His death is given by the state.

As the Reid case makes apparent, death is considered a punishment only when it is given by the state, even if the condemned spends decades on death row and dies a "natural death" as a result of inadequate health care. The condemned is not allowed a "natural death," "a normal death like everyone else," and that is his punishment. And, by this logic—the logic of the death penalty—the state has an obligation to make sure that the condemned neither dies of natural causes nor takes his own life before he can be executed. Before the death penalty was abolished in France in 1981, "a condemned man was revived and snatched back from the brink of suicide so that he could undergo his capital punishment in full lucidity."[26] The state must levy the punishment of death. It cannot be given by nature or suicide. Rather, it must be authorized as a punishment by the penal institutions that carry out the sentences handed down by the courts. As reactions to the "natural death" of Tennessee death row inmate Paul Dennis Reid Jr. indicate, anything "less" is "offensive" to some people, presumably because the condemned is "getting off" without facing his punishment.

What becomes clear, however, is that his punishment is not death per se. Rather, it is the fact that he is not allowed to die like "everyone else." His death must be extraordinary, an execution. Furthermore, in the case of Reid, it was pointed out that he died in a bed and not strapped to a gurney; he died in "a hospital surrounded by family" and not in a prison behind a glass wall.[27] In other words, he was not rendered motionless by physical restraints and drugs such that he could not indicate whether he was suffering. He was not separated from his family and held down by force. Presumably, he could testify to his experience, his suffering, and his illness, to those close to him.

The presumption is that unlike McGuire's children, who could only watch in horror at a distance as their father was strapped down and "suffered" the effects of the lethal injection drugs for twenty-five minutes, or the witnesses to the two hours that Ohio officials tried to execute Romell Broom before they gave up,[28] Reid and his family "enjoyed" the intimacy of a natural, normal death.[29] Of course, given that Reid was under guard, and that he lacked what many would consider "normal" medical care while on death row, and that we don't know whether his family—if he had any— were present in the hospital, the "testimony" from the victim's family member is as much her own fantasy as the reality.

And that is exactly my point. The death penalty is surrounded by conflicting fantasies of painless death delivered humanely through pharmaceuticals and high-tech medical devices to insure that is it not cruel, while at the same time, dying a natural or normal death is imagined as "cheating" insofar as it is not a punishment. The death given by the death penalty must be at once humane and punishing. Certainly, as a form of discipline, capital punishment makes no sense since the condemned is not expected to be rehabilitated or to learn from such punishment.[30] Rather, the principle of *lex talionis*, based on a death for a death and a life for a life, or retaliation demands death as a penalty.

Although lex talionis takes us back to the Judeo-Christian doctrine of an eye for an eye and a tooth for a tooth found in the Old Testament, one of its most forceful advocates as political philosophy is Immanuel Kant. Kant, however, is clear that the retaliation or retribution required by the law of talionis cannot be based on revenge but, rather, must be based on equality. To be fair, the punishment must fit the crime in the sense of like for like. For Kant, the ultimate test for the strict principle of talionis, or like for like, is the death penalty. The strictness of Kant's concept of equality is related to his insistence that retribution must be devoid of vengeance to ensure an equality that does not unjustly favor those we love and torture those we hate. Kant produces his most powerful articulations of the metaphysics of morals through a strict moral bookkeeping based on the principle of equality contained in the notion of lex talionis, wherein justification for the death penalty becomes his prime example. Rather than interpret the death penalty as exchanging one life for another—life for life—Kant sees *giving death* as the necessary demand of the principle of talionis.[31] This distinction is significant insofar as it is how Kant justifies death over, say, a life of hard labor. For Kant, no two lives are the same, but death equalizes. So, following this logic, even if the life of a murder victim is not equal to the life of the condemned, in death they are equal and therefore the principle of lex talionis is satisfied.

The spirit of this Kantian legacy is evident in current capital punishment practices in the United States. Although families of the victims are often motivated by revenge and express sentiments that even lethal injection is "too good" for the condemned—let alone dying a natural death—the law requires a humane punishment. To ensure that the principle of "like for like" is not contaminated by vengeful feelings, the Supreme Court has insisted on not only limiting the suffering of the condemned but also protecting the dignity of the condemned, as voiced by Justice Roberts. Following Austin Sarat, we could say that the court demands a civilized execution to distinguish its killing practices from the barbaric murder committed by the condemned: "Law imposes on sovereignty the requirement that no matter how heinous the crime, or how reprehensible the criminal, that we do not do death as death has been done by those we punish. We give them a kinder, gentler death than they deserve to mark a boundary between the 'civilized' and the 'savage.'"[32]

Thus, in order to be a punishment, as sanctioned by law, rather than merely revenge, the death penalty must appear to be practiced in a humane way, not for the sake of the condemned but rather for the sake of maintaining the legitimacy of the law. On the one hand, legal punishment requires reducing suffering as much as possible and giving a "clean," dignified death in order to separate state killing from murder. On the other hand, to be punishment, death must be given by the state. This is implicit in Kant's insistence that in terms of capital punishment, lex talionis requires a death for a death and not a life for a life. Within this logic, whoever gives death to another must be given death by the state. And this is why dying a natural death satisfies neither the law nor the vengeful families of victims.

Giving Death

One of the ways that Jacques Derrida challenges the death penalty is by challenging the state's right to give death. What does it mean to have the right to give death? And how is a death that is given different from a natural death? Derrida suggests that within the history of Western thought, only animals die natural deaths. That is to say, insofar as we are animals, we too die natural deaths. And obviously living beings, by nature, die. And yet, insofar as we give ourselves, or claim, the right to give death, then, we claim to be unnatural in our relationship to death. Unlike other animals, we do not merely die or perish. Rather, we can give ourselves or others death. And the fact that we can supposedly demonstrates not only that we have free will—we can choose to live or die—but also that our social contract gives us the right to kill those who break it, which is another sign of our freedom. In other words, when someone freely breaks the law, the law can take away their freedom even absolutely as in the case of capital punishment.

Derrida makes the stronger argument that law requires the right to give death: "Between law and death, between penal law and death penalty, there is a structural indissociability, a mutual, a priori dependence that is inscribed in the concept of law or right, human right, human law, as much as in the concept of death, of *non-natural death*, thus of death decided by a universal reason, a death that is given or that one gives oneself sovereignly."[33] While there is much more to say about the link between law and death, for our purposes, suffice it to say that the law requires nonnatural death, and the ability to give it and the right to give it are bound up with what we take to be our capacities and rights as human beings, that is to say, beings that have transcended our "natural" animal bodies.

It is noteworthy, then, that the word *cruel* comes from the Latin root *crudus*, which means *rough*, *raw*, or *bloody*, and shares its root with the word *crude*, meaning "in its natural state" or not changed by any processing or technology. The crude or cruel death, then, is one that is raw and bloody, while the human death is sterile and clean. The cruel death is the one of animals or nature, while the humane death is the one of humans or technology. Technology renders death "cooked"—sometimes even fried—rather than raw, bloody, and crude. After all, scientific, medical, and technological intervention has been crucial in the court's upholding of lethal injection as a humane mode of execution.

As long as the condemned is not conscious at the moment of death, then, capital punishment meets the Eighth Amendment requirement that it is not cruel and unusual. As long as we maintain this "standard" of rendering the condemned unconscious (or just paralyzed), we prevent any possible testimony to pain and suffering, and thereby legitimate lethal injection as humane. As long as we maintain the fantasy of bloodless, painless death, promised by technologies that make it as easy as flipping a switch, pushing the plunger, or pulling the plug, we maintain the reason for our commitment to a more humane death penalty. High-tech medicalized executions involving machines that administer carefully measured lethal drugs at regulated intervals create the illusion of a "clean" or "good" death. Paradoxically, this good or clean death is also an "unnatural" death, an "abnormal" death, which can be rendered a punishment because it is not like the death of "everyone else."

Death Penalty "Abolition" in Neoliberal Times: The SAFE California Act and the Nexus of Savings and Security

Andrew Dilts

> Accomplishing [death penalty] abolition is pretty good but
> also easy; now the essential thing to do is get rid of prisons.
>
> —MICHEL FOUCAULT, 1981[1]

> If one were forced for the sake of clarity to define [fascism]
> in a word simple enough for all to understand, that word
> would be "reform." We can make our definition more precise
> by adding the word "economic." "Economic reform" comes
> very close to a working definition of fascist motive forces.
>
> —GEORGE JACKSON, 1971[2]

Introduction

On November 6, 2012, the state of California was poised to become the eighteenth state in the United States to abolish the death penalty, replacing it with a sentence of life imprisonment without the possibility of parole (commonly referred to as LWOP). The Savings, Accountability, and Full Enforcement for California Act (The SAFE California Act) appeared on the statewide ballot as Proposition 34 and would have overturned a previous 1978 ballot initiative that restored the death penalty in California following the U.S. Supreme Court's 1976 ruling in *Gregg v. Georgia*.[3] When the votes were counted, Prop. 34 lost by a margin of four percentage points, leaving the California existing death penalty statute in place.[4]

The prospect for passage looked promising leading up to the vote.[5] Not only has there been an emerging national trend in support of death penalty abolition but there has also been increasing support for ending the death penalty in California during the previous decade.[6] Prop. 34 had the backing of supporters of the previous 1978 initiative, insisting that it had been a "terrible mistake" to reinstitute state executions following *Gregg*.[7]

But perhaps the best reason to think that California would move into the "abolitionist" column was because the state faces one of the worst fiscal crises in the nation.

Prop. 34's supporters seized on this fact, centering their argument on the high cost of the death penalty and California's fiscal austerity. Even the title of the bill behind Prop. 34 succinctly stated the central argument proffered by supporters of the ballot initiative: a tight linking of "savings" and "full enforcement" of the law. The text of the bill itself and the $2 million statewide advertising campaign launched by supporters insisted that death penalty abolition was both necessary and justifiable because the state's citizens would be more secure through savings realized by closing death row.[8] "Killers and rapists," the bill declared, "walk our streets and threaten our safety, while we spend hundreds of millions of taxpayer dollars on a select few who are already behind bars forever on death row."[9]

Compared to other "western" nations, the end of capital punishment in the United States appears long overdue. As Michel Foucault noted in a 1977 interview discussing French capital punishment, the death penalty appears increasingly "absurd" in the world of the prison and its modern reinvention as a form of punitive correction and reformation. It is only "possible," Foucault stated, to "condemn someone to death" under a "justice that functions only according to a code. . . . But if justice is concerned with correcting an individual, of gripping the depth of his soul in order to transform him, then everything is different."[10] The persistence of the death penalty in the United States, thus, can be read as an archaic manifestation of an older technique of power, invested in a likewise archaic notion of sovereignty and a rejection of the rehabilitative ideal and its technique of indeterminate sentencing and criminological knowledge. "Today," Foucault continues, "two systems are superimposed on one another."[11] To abolish the death penalty in favor of incarceration (as the proponents of Prop. 34 sought) would be to finally render the penal system consistent with its own rationality and dominant form: the prison.

Had Prop. 34 succeeded, however, it would arguably have not been out of concern about the absurdity or contradictory nature of capital punishment in the modern period but rather because of the ascendency of neoliberal governmentality, a political system that, as Bernard Harcourt has recently argued, attempts to "displace political conflict, contestation, and struggle . . . by extending an idea of orderliness from the economic realm to other spheres of human existence and practice."[12]

In this chapter, I take up the case of Prop. 34 to question the meaning of death penalty abolition at the nexus of neoliberalism and penality, reading the failure of the referendum's passage as part of the way in which sovereign modes of power function within and possibly against neoliberalism. I am less interested in the specific reasons for the failure of Prop. 34 than in understanding how "abolition" of the death penalty appears most possible when its form is not an abolition at all but rather the substitution of one kind of death for another: of "death-in-prison" rather than execution.[13] Part of the puzzle of current death penalty abolition, of course, is that LWOP sentences appear "absurd" in much the same way as the death penalty.

As critics of Foucault have rightly noted, however, his account of the death penalty (as well as his genealogy of the prison) largely ignores the particularity of the U.S. carceral regime and its pernicious cultural and racial dimensions.[14] There is truth in these critiques, yet they should not lead us to reject Foucault's relevance to understanding death penalty abolition in our current moment. Foucault's account of the analytics of power, his engagement with "American" neoliberalism, and his own statements on the death penalty and its abolition are both relevant and helpful for conducting new genealogical investigations of the death penalty and its abolition, especially given the decidedly neoliberal turn in U.S. penality over the last forty years.[15] While it is indeed possible to read Foucault's accounts of the death penalty in *Discipline and Punish* and the first volume of the *History of Sexuality* as *necessarily* connected to sovereign or juridical exercises of power, Foucault's own analysis complicates such a reading. By looking at the case of the death penalty and its abolition through the specific instance of the SAFE California Act, we can better understand Foucault's own insistence that power may be exercised through multiple discourses in mutually supporting and interlocking ways, and, more importantly, we can better identify the dangerous form that mainstream death penalty abolition has taken in the current moment.

The first section of this chapter details Prop. 34, reading the text of the SAFE California Act as an instance of a "neoliberal bargain," trading in the death penalty for LWOP in order to secure greater security through savings. The following section focuses on the key condition of possibility of this bargain—the commensurability of "death" for "life"—and shows how this condition functions through a productive contradiction or *aporia* between these two terms, ultimately displacing the lives of those being "exchanged." The next section shows how the language of neoliberalism informs both criminological and popular conceptions of permanently incarcerable persons as nevertheless monstrous and incorrigible offenders who are also fully responsible subjects, allowing for neoliberalism to coexist with "earlier" modes of power. Finally, the last section returns to the question of what we mean by abolition itself, its potential limits, and the necessary task of constant self-reflection and transformation we face as a result.

The Neoliberal Bargain of Security through Savings

The "abolition" of California's death penalty statute proposed in the SAFE California Act had four key legislative components. First, it would have eliminated the punishment of "death" as a sentencing option and would have replaced any "death" sentence in the state's criminal code with the sentence of "imprisonment in the state prison for life without the possibility of parole." Second, any prisoner found guilty of first-degree murder and sentenced to imprisonment (of any duration) would be required to "work within a high-security prison as many hours of faithful labor in each day and every day during his or her term of imprisonment" with wages subject to deduction for victim restoration funds. Third, it would have established a $100 million fund for law enforcement, specifically for the investigation of homicide and sex offense cases. Lastly, it would have automatically converted all standing death penalty sentences to a sentence of LWOP, effectively prohibiting all pending executions in the state while also suspending all litigation by current death row inmates.

As with most ballot measures, the text of the provision included preliminary statements of "findings and declarations" and "purpose and intent," spelling out the justifications for the proposed legal changes. These sections lay out the rhetorical argument for the legislative changes, tightly linking together the discourses of public safety and fiscal austerity. More than half of these statements make claims about both the direct fiscal costs of the death penalty and the indirect costs imposed by trade-offs being made in terms of law enforcement. Directly, the provision claims that in "replacing the death penalty with life in prison without the possibility of parole, California taxpayers would save well over $100 million every year," and "$1 billion in five years without releasing a single prisoner." The majority of these savings would be realized by the wholesale elimination of the appeals process available to death row inmates and additionally through savings in prison housing (e.g., the proponents note that former death row inmates would no longer receive "private" cells).[16]

In addition to these direct costs, there are indirect opportunity "costs" of the death penalty in the form of unsolved rapes and murders. "Murders and rapists," the first finding declares, "need to be stopped, brought to justice, and punished. . . . Our limited law enforcement resources should be used to solve more crimes, to get more criminals off our streets, and to protect our families." The second finding echoes this claim: "Police, sheriffs, and district attorneys now lack the funding they need to quickly process evidence in rape and murder cases . . . Law enforcement should have the resources needed for full enforcement of the law. By solving more rape and murder cases and bringing more criminals to justice, we keep our families and communities safer." Throughout the relatively short text of the bill, its authors insist that these "killers and rapists" go free *because* the death penalty saps resources away from investigating those crimes. By saving money through repealing the "costly" and "ineffective" death penalty, the state will "free up law enforcement resources to keep our families safe."

If there is a moral argument in the bill, it is made in classically utilitarian terms of cost-benefit analysis: the positive good of public safety (under conditions of limited resources and fiscal austerity) *requires* the abolition of the death penalty. Absent such limited fiscal conditions, the bill offers only two other reasons to end the death penalty: (1) to reduce the "risk" of executing an innocent person and (2) to offer relief to families that must endure "the more than 25-year-long process of review in death penalty cases." Yet even these claims are framed in actuarial language of risk and economistic concerns about inefficiency, respectively. Moreover, these remaining two justifications are arguably in tension, given that one way to reduce the "risk" of a wrongful execution is through an extensive review and appeals process in capital cases.

The rhetoric of the public campaign in support of Prop. 34 was broader but still echoed this central argument. Television, print, and web advertising relied heavily on personal narratives to convey the message of increased public safety through fiscal savings. Television and radio ads in particular featured the family members of unsolved murder victims and law enforcement officials (including former wardens, district attorneys, judges, and police officers, all attesting to the fiscal costs of the death penalty litigation at the expense of other investigations). The campaign's widest-reaching advertisements highlighted the case of Franky Carrillo, who was wrongly convicted of murder at age sixteen and served twenty years before finally being exonerated and released.[17] In one advertisement, Carrillo looks into the camera and states: "Even today people make mistakes. In my case, it was false eyewitness testimony. A 'yes' on Prop. 34 means we will never execute an innocent person. Life without parole is justice that works for everyone. We can't afford to take chances; the costs are just too high."[18] In just a few sentences, the Carrillo ad deftly frames questions of fallible judgment, corrupt police practices, and justice as questions of costs and risk.

While the advertisement may not have proved effective at the ballot box, the *Los Angeles Times* directly pointed to the Carrillo ad in their endorsement of the ballot measure, writing, "[T]here is no knowing whether all 725 [death row inmates] . . . are guilty. That's why the appeals process is so long, burdensome and expensive, and it's why voters should end the risk that California will execute an innocent person."[19] Other papers followed more closely to the script of safety through savings, such as the *San Jose Mercury News*' endorsement of Prop. 34, in which the editorial board wrote, "*Never mind moral arguments;* the death penalty simply doesn't work. Since it was reinstated in 1978, California has spent $4 billion on just thirteen executions. We are no safer."[20] This language very nearly echoed the words of one web ad released by the supporters, in which a former warden of San Quentin prison (where death row is housed) is heard speaking over a series of visuals of police lights, city streets, chain-link fencing, and a long, slow pan across a pile of $100 bills. Jeanne Woodford states,

> Working in criminal justice and understanding what really works, knowing that what makes us safer is solving crimes, . . . knowing that we have so many unsolved homicides and rapes in the State of California, and that local communities are having to take police off the streets, and rape kits still sit on shelves and aren't tested because some communities don't have the money to do that, knowing that when you use your criminal justice dollars in a much more strategic way, that's what makes us safer, that's really why I'm here and passionate about replacing the death penalty, because we can use our dollars and cents in a much more strategic way that improves criminal justice.[21]

Through the consistent linking of savings with security, the campaign for Prop. 34 masterfully brought together a host of public policy concerns (unsolved rapes and murders, wrongful executions, fiscal austerity, etc.) into a single narrative, picking up on what has become the dominant neoliberal analysis of crime and punishment, which has effectively shifted the elite discourse (if not actual policy) toward "smart on crime" frameworks that rely on statistical analysis and economistic reasoning about policy.[22]

The "neoliberal bargain" of Prop. 34 promises both "security" and "savings" in the face of fiscal austerity, itself a broader manifestation of the meeting of the "penal" and "fiscal" crises in California.[23] This instance of the "bargain" works through a series of trade-offs. The California voter is asked to give up punishing criminals with the death penalty in exchange for the punishment of life imprisonment without the possibility of parole. The "costs" of the repeal will more than pay for themselves in financial terms, and the voters themselves will be "paid" with both material and symbolic benefits: increased spending on law enforcement, catching more "killers and rapists," forcing previously "idle" inmates to work, to share cells, punitively degrading their conditions and forcing them to be fully "responsible" laborers, and, finally, the promise that "no innocent person" will be killed by the state. There are moral claims present, but they become subsumed under the logic of exchange, transforming the "abolition" of capital punishment into a straightforward series of exchanges. The puzzle, however, is how exactly this vision of "abolition" became possible. Or rather, how could this series of exchanges be rightly called "abolitionist" at all when the replacement penalty, LWOP, *promises and assures* that inmates will die in jail?

"'For life' or 'for death,' the two expressions are the same"

The heart of the "neoliberal bargain" is really a trading of "life" for "death," such that a life sentence without parole can be both substitutable for a death sentence and also qualitatively *not* a death sentence. This trade, in turn, depends on the fabrication and reification of a specific conception of the sentenced criminal as fundamentally incorrigible, monstrous, and yet also deeply responsible for their actions. More narrowly, the *legal* condition of possibility for such a trade has been well established in the widespread adoption of LWOP sentences throughout the United States, beginning in the early 1970s and dramatically expanding since the 1990s.[24] As such, the otherwise thorny question of proposing a replacement for the death penalty is relatively simple.[25] The greater difficulty appears to be the question of popular support, as, even despite a general decline, the death penalty continues to have overall high levels of popular support in the United States and in California.[26]

For anti–death penalty activists in California, building high popular support for "abolition" is a political necessity because the existing death penalty statute was passed through a ballot initiative, and as such, that statute can only be altered in the same manner.[27] This has been a difficult task given that support for capital punishment in the state has remained strong since the 1970s, with a steady two-thirds majority of voters supporting it. In November 2011, however, for the first time, a plurality of voters polled stated a preference for LWOP over the death penalty.[28] This opening in public opinion goes partway to explaining the strategy employed by the proponents of Prop. 34, in that they would need to capitalize not only on this shift in public opinion but also build a relatively broad coalition to do so. That is, death penalty abolition appears to become more possible if it is reframed rhetorically and substantively as death penalty *replacement.*

Of course, the same poll that identified this political opening also demonstrated that many voters did not prefer LWOP to "death," refusing their substitutability. This position echoes the nearly cliché principle enshrined in U.S. jurisprudence and political activism that death is "different" and "unique" as a form of punishment. This principle is so powerful and so taken for granted that it grounded both the Court's 1972 moratorium on the death penalty and its reinstatement four years later. For pro– and anti–death penalty activists, it likewise grounds both abolitionist and retentionist positions: because "death" is a final and absolute punishment, abolitionists can claim it is outside the domain of civil society and "barbaric." And likewise, because it is final, absolute, and represents the high-water mark of punishment, it serves as an *ultimate* punishment, and thus, as retentionists claim, it demonstrates the sanctity of human life in a way no other punishment can.

At the same time, however, what distinguishes life sentences without parole or executive clemency is that they, as Jessica Henry succinctly notes, "can only be fulfilled by the death of the offender."[29] As such, "life" sentences should rightly be called "death-in-prison" (DIP) sentences.[30] As Henry argues, LWOP in particular, and all "death-in-prison" sentences more generally, easily meet the Court's description in *Furman* of capital punishment as the "ultimate" punishment, distinct in its *kind* rather than its *severity:* it is an irrevocable punishment, rejecting the possibility of rehabilitation, and is an "absolute renunciation of all that is embodied in our concept of humanity."[31] Or, as put by the proponents of Prop. 34, LWOP provides a "justice that works for everyone." It can do so, only insofar as it is an "ultimate" punishment, taking the possibility of rehabilitation as a justification off the table, marking the offender as a permanent prisoner, fundamentally irredeemable.[32] But perhaps most bluntly, LWOP is still *effectively* a kind of death sentence. As put by Jeanne Woodford, the former death row warden at San Quentin quoted earlier, "We are spending millions and billions of dollars on a handful of inmates, when we could give them a sentence of life without the possibility of parole, *which would ensure that they would die in prison.*"[33]

At the same time, for LWOP to count as "abolition," it must also be sufficiently a different *kind* of punishment than death. Tellingly, perhaps, the case made for the SAFE California Act almost entirely avoided the question of its reality as a "death-in-prison" sentence and instead relies on an unarticulated yet seemingly "obvious" distinction between life and death, and between a "natural" death and an "execution." This is in part because the majority of both popular and legal debate over capital punishment has focused specifically on the execution itself, and its manner, to almost fetishistic levels.[34] Legal debates in particular have focused almost entirely on getting execution "right" in constitutional terms. While both the method and meaning of "execution" have dramatically shifted over the course of U.S. history, there remains a presumption that an execution is qualitatively distinct from a "natural" death, even when that death occurs in prison, or when death can be linked to the pernicious racial history of capital punishment, to its persistent racially disproportionate application, or to the striking historical similarities between state executions and extrajudicial lynchings in the United States.[35] Yet because the public attention to the death penalty, its jurisprudence, and its activist attention have focused primarily on the moment, method, and meaning of *execution*, the adoption of LWOP and other DIP sentences effectively deflects attention away from the moment of death, even though death is necessarily a part of the sentence.[36] Being able to avoid a specific moment or technique of "execution," such sentences become capable of appeasing the moral concerns of many abolitionists and, at the very least, offer incremental satisfaction, even for those who are deeply troubled by LWOP sentences as well.[37]

A side effect of this *aporia* between "life" and "death" has been that the same qualities that allow for the exchange of death in prison for death by execution also have allowed for their similarities to be selectively ignored. Because "death is different," the Court requires strict review of offender qualifications, strict procedural guidelines, extended appeals processes, and additional standards of heightened scrutiny. The same procedural and substantive protections are simply not applied to DIP sentences at this time. This dramatic reduction of appellate rights was not at all lost on the supporters of Prop. 34 but rather was central to their "cost-savings" argument: the high cost of the death penalty stems primarily from the cost of litigating the appeals of inmates. Nor has this act been lost on death row inmates themselves. As explained by California death row inmate Correll Thomas:

> The authors of [Prop. 34] know that . . . the courthouse doors will be
> slammed forever. They are attempting to force us condemned men
> and women to accept another death penalty without any habeas corpus

review of our sentences. And the few condemned men and women who currently have representation today, unless they have the funds to retain counsel for representation, would automatically be sentenced to life without the possibility of parole and lose their representation.[38]

Yet underlying these difficulties is a deeper connection between the death penalty and all prison sentences: the seemingly overdetermined notion that death is different. This is not to say that death is not, in fact, a final or ultimate punishment but to resist the distinction from the other side and account for how the prison system itself functions through the specter of death. In 1972, at the same time that the Supreme Court of the United States was considering its temporary moratorium on the death penalty, France was embroiled in debate over its own death penalty, prompted in part by the high-profile executions of two inmates at Clairvaux Prison in France. Writing in *Le Nouvelle Observateur*, Foucault responded to these executions with a scathing indictment not simply of the executions but of the entire French prison system. "The whole penal system," he wrote, "is essentially pointed toward and governed by death. A verdict of conviction does not lead, as people think, to a sentence of prison *or* death; if it prescribes prison, this is always with a possible added bonus: death."[39] Foucault's involvement at the time with the *Group d'information sur les prisons* (GIP) had lead him, along with other intellectuals and activists, to question not only the practice of punishment in France but moreover the logics by which punishment through prisons operated. In a precursor to his genealogy of the prison in *Discipline and Punish*, Foucault argued in the pages of the French press that the question of the death penalty and its particular application necessarily implied that the prison be questioned as well.

"'For life,' or 'for death,'" Foucault writes, "the two expressions mean the same thing. When a person is sure that he will never get out, what is there left to do? What else but to risk death to save one's life, to risk one's very life at the possible cost of death."[40] For Foucault, separating the question of the death penalty from the question of the prison—given the work that the GIP had been doing during the previous two years and a rash of inmate suicides that had occurred throughout 1972—was to ignore the material conditions of confinement that refused so neat a separation, a "choice," as it were, between "life" and "death." The public interest in the death penalty sparked by the Clairvaux case in France came at the expense of attending to the brutality and the constant presence of death within the prison walls. "Prison is not the alternative to death," Foucault writes, "it carries death along with it. The same red thread runs through the whole length of that penal institution which is supposed to apply the law but which, in reality, suspends it."[41]

Other scholars have built on Foucault's analysis here, and in turning to the U.S. context they note the central role the death penalty plays in the broader schemes of disciplinary power and governmentality.[42] The current practice of the death penalty in the United States, Timothy Kaufman-Osborn argues, "is a logical extension of certain strategies of disciplinary control that are part and parcel of the political economy of the late liberal state."[43] For Kauffman-Osborn and others, any account of the death penalty or its abolition in the United States must grapple with its intimate connection to the broader carceral regime.[44] What they point to, along with critiques of the actual material conditions of imprisonment, is the fact that the trade-off between LWOP and the death penalty functions because of a displacement of analysis from the broader carceral system and the modalities of power that structure that system.

Under the current conditions of incarceration in the United States—violent, overcrowded, lacking oversight—a sentence of "life" and one of "death" are both distinct from each other and yet also commensurable. The conceptual and material *aporias* between "life" and "death" are perhaps contradictory but nevertheless productive of an abolitionist strategy that can embrace LWOP as a replacement for the death penalty. The punishment of death establishes the limits of the carceral system, at the same time functions through and with it, and nevertheless displaces our attention away from the specific conditions of that system. Put differently, if what we mean by the "abolition" of the death penalty is its replacement with LWOP, then we find ourselves confronting the challenge issued by Foucault's statement that "for life" and "for death" express the same thing under the carceral form. And such a confrontation should necessarily call our attention to the specific and material practices of the carceral system and the rationalities that both underpin and are produced by those practices. Specifically, we must attend to the way in which incarcerated persons have been rendered entirely responsible for their actions and at the same time treated as radically irresponsible (and irrepressible) "killers and rapists" who will necessarily offend again.

After all, what is the common denominator or the common factor that can let us establish an exchange value (to borrow Marx's language in the analysis of the commodity form) between life and death? Quite simply: the body of the condemned. What is the body of the condemned, the "lifer," the prisoner being exchanged for? What underlying conceptions of criminality and subjectivity allow for this exchange to be "successful"? Who is this permanently incarcerable subject who takes the place of the executable subject and is still distinct from the more generally (and temporarily) incarcerable subject?

Given the terms of this neoliberal bargain, the permanently incarcerable subject is a strange mix of things. First, they must be a person worthy of punishment, deserving retribution for a specific crime. But they must also be deserving of "ultimate" and "irrevocable" punishment, by virtue not only of the severity of their crime but also because they are ultimately irredeemable (otherwise, parole should be an option). Additionally, they appear to be such dangerous creatures that they are not worth the risk; they are not simply irredeemable but incorrigible.[45] Yet, as stipulated in the SAFE California Act, they must also be forced to labor like other prisoners to repay financial debts to their victims and not allowed to remain "idle" in private cells. They must be treated just like other prisoners, stripped of the privileges currently afforded to them on death row. Such a figure is obviously a self-contradictory one, and my analysis of the SAFE California Act could simply end here, noting the inherent contradictions between retributivist and utilitarian frameworks at the core of the bill. But this would be to miss the figure that has emerged from this neoliberal criminology: a kind of fully responsible monster that is radically dangerous, deserving of the worst, and yet always also alike enough to other prisoners to be treated equally. And it wrongly assumes that this contradictory mess of fully responsible monsters undermines rather than sustains our contemporary criminal punishment system.

Neoliberal Criminology *and* homo œconomicus

On Foucault's account, the emergence of the prison as a definitive form of penal practice and the incumbent development of disciplinary techniques of power reaching far outside the prison carried with them the specter of death at every turn. The "ultimate" punishment was never completely buried, forgotten, or entirely displaced. Once the public torture of the condemned criminal gave way to the simplicity, economy, and egalitarianism of the guillotine, the penitentiary technique quickly completed the "humane" transformation of punishment throughout the nineteenth century (at least in France). The prison had a "'self-evident' character" as a form of punishment, Foucault notes, "based first of all on the simple form of 'deprivation of liberty.' How could prison not be the penalty *par excellence* in a society in which liberty is a good that belongs to all in the same way and to which each individual is attached . . . by a 'universal and constant' feeling?"[46] A single punitive form (detention) could be imposed in nearly infinite degrees of severity as a quantification of time, making it both a universal and particular form of punishment. Moreover, at the heart of Foucault's analysis is the claim that the twin principles of this apparatus— isolation and work—provided not simply a powerful form of social control but a subject of disciplinary power "transformed" into a docile body.[47]

According to this logic, the punishment of death *should* have faded away entirely, and not simply out of sight. If the prison gives birth to a mode of knowledge (the human science of crime, i.e., criminology) and an account of the criminal subject (the prison's "twin," i.e., the delinquent), then the finality of death by execution seems to work directly against these ends. Moreover, from the point of view of the eighteenth- and nineteenth-century reformers and proponents of the prison, a punishment of death appeared as an archaic if not barbaric form of punishment, a seeming throwback to a conception of the nation that is invested not in a people but in the sovereign body of the king.

That the "absurd" persistence of the death penalty is nevertheless a reality, however, makes it useful to track not simply the overlaps between regimes of power but also the ways in which power changes its justification and shifts its exercise over time and place, complicating simplistic readings of Foucault's analysis of power. In the first volume of the *History of Sexuality*, Foucault famously argues for an analytics of power that moves beyond the limits of its sovereign conception linked to juridical power and enshrined in the language of law, prohibition, and, more generally, its "juridico-discursive" representation.[48] In its place, Foucault insists, we must make sure our accounts of power reflect a "strategical model" that emphasizes the "multiple and mobile field of force relations."[49] Foucault turns to the "example" of the death penalty to illustrate how force relations have changed in the West: "Together with war it [the death penalty] was for a long time the other form of the right of the sword; it constituted the reply of the sovereign to those who attacked his will, his law, or his person."[50] But while sovereignty had traditionally been defined in Hobbesian terms as that body (collective or singular) that possesses an exclusive right over life and death—to "take life or let live"—the "very profound transformation" of force relations in the West means that "the right of the sovereign is now manifested as simply the reverse of the right of the social body to ensure, maintain, or develop its life."[51]

The effect of this transformation is observable, Foucault argues, in the corresponding change in the logic behind the death penalty: "As soon as power gave itself the function of administering life, its reason for being and the logic of its exercise . . . made it more and more difficult to apply the death penalty. How could power exercise its highest prerogatives by putting people to death, when its main role was to ensure, sustain, and multiply life, to put this life in order?"[52] While the death penalty of the classical age operated through a public execution and the spectacle of the scaffold, under the disciplinary system the death penalty signaled a failure to reform a delinquent. As an exercise of biopower, the death penalty appears as an open contradiction of the "new" *raison d'etat:* a taking of life rather than a making live. The necessary transformation would be to both shun the death penalty and, at the same time, to give it a new justification: "For such a power, execution was at the same time a limit, a scandal, and a contradiction. Hence capital punishment could not be maintained except by invoking less the enormity of the crime itself than the monstrosity of the criminal, his incorrigibility, and the safeguard of society. One had the right to kill those who represented a kind of biological danger to others."[53] This transformation, which does not ban the death penalty but reconfigures it as a technique for the promotion of (some) life at the necessary expense of some others, provides the conceptual footing for the bloodiest, most deadly, and most horrific executions of the twentieth century. In his 1976 lectures at the Collège de France, *Society Must be Defended*, Foucault succinctly notes that this cut between who may live and who must die is drawn expressly through the appearance of modern racism.[54] For Foucault, modern racism itself is "a way of introducing a break into the domain of life that is under power's control: the break between what must live and what must die."[55] Such an exercise of biopower by the modern state, he insists, is twofold: first it draws distinctions within the human species that appear to be biological in character, and, second, it establishes a form of death for those marked as biologically dangerous, abnormal, and unhealthy that will *directly* promote the life of the biological population to be preserved in a more purified and healthier form. "The fact that the other dies," Foucault states, "does not mean simply that I live in the sense that his death guarantees my safety; the death of the other, the death of the bad race, of the inferior race (or the degenerate, or the abnormal), is something that will make life in general healthier: healthier and purer."[56]

This conceptual footing—both rejecting and also justifying the death penalty for the good of the greater population—continues to drive current abolitionist legislation and mainstream death penalty activism, even as legislative language and campaigns appear to be racially "neutral" and "colorblind." The death penalty must be rejected, as expressed in the SAFE California Act, because under the conditions of austerity and the requirements of due process, executing criminals fails to protect the population. And at the same time, a different form of death—the living death in prison assured by LWOP—can ensure that existing threats will be contained because they will nevertheless die in prison, cheaper primarily because these prisoners are refused the same legal protections afforded to death row inmates. That is, what LWOP *as abolition* represents is not the end of the death penalty but a recent (and politically seductive) form, expressed as an economistic replacement that stands not outside or against the power of the state to take life but entirely within it and subsumed by it. In this case, part and parcel with the death in prison, comes the prohibition on suicide implicit (and strictly enforced) as part of the LWOP sentence. Inseparable from the harsh treatment of extended confinement itself in LWOP, *life itself* has become a part of punishment, and those lives are discursively identified as pathologically abnormal, deviant, and incorrigible.[57] In part, what makes understanding Prop. 34 difficult is how it simultaneously invokes juridico-legal/sovereign techniques of power, disciplinary assumptions of the subject and an attachment to the prison, and, above all, the powerfully economistic logic of biopower.

To understand this strange hybrid requires two additional theoretical contributions from Foucault's lectures that followed the introduction of the terms of biopower and his account of modern racism. First, we must finally dispense with the notion that these different modalities of power described by Foucault (juridico-legal/sovereign, disciplinary, mechanisms of security/biopower) are exclusive. To analyze a practice or discourse from the point of view of a Foucauldian analytics of power is not to identify the "correct" modality of power and move on. Rather, as Foucault makes clear in his 1978 lectures, *Security, Territory, Population*, each of these modalities can appear simultaneously throughout history, mutually supporting one another. What gives them a "kind of historical schema," and which might mislead our analyses, is that each modality can rightly be said to become dominant in different epochs (ancient, modern, contemporary).[58] Foucault states, "There is not the legal age, the disciplinary age, and then the age of security. Mechanisms of security do not replace disciplinary mechanisms, which would have replaced juridico-legal mechanisms. In reality you have a series of complex edifices in which . . . the techniques themselves change and are perfected . . . in which what above all changes is the dominant characteristic . . . the system of correlation between juridico-legal mechanisms, disciplinary mechanisms, and mechanisms of security. In other words, there is a history of the actual techniques themselves."[59]

Foucault gives special attention to the "mechanisms of security" of neo-liberal governmentality not simply because they have become dominant in the contemporary period but also because the history of punitive practices leads us in this direction, as the latter half of the twentieth century saw a revolution in criminological practice and the emergence of mass incarceration in the United States. As Foucault puts it, "For some time now, for a good dozen years at least [i.e., since the mid-1960s], it has been clear that the essential question in the development of the problematic of the penal domain, in the way in which it is reflected as well as in the way it is practiced, is one of security. Basically, the fundamental question is economics and the economic relation between the cost of repression and the cost of delinquency."[60] What characterizes the late twentieth century, especially in penal practices, is a heightened attention to costs, risks, and a way of knowing the subject that seeks to radically evacuate the subject of the pathologies of previous eras, in particular, the "disciplinary" era in which the rehabilitative ideal was dominant.

The second important contribution from Foucault's lectures is found in his genealogy of liberalism in the 1979 course *Birth of Biopolitics* and its account of the distinctly "American" form of neoliberalism that attempts to redescribe criminal subjectivity on strong assumptions of rationality and responsiveness, what can be called neoliberal subjectivity.[61] This understanding of the subject is in turn predicated on the theory of human capital and its redescription of all of one's actions and activities as investments in the self, what Foucault identifies as the critical redescription and ascendency of *homo œconomicus*.[62] Foucault's interest in the "American" neoliberal theorists' account of economic rationality and subjectivity stems from the ascendancy of biopolitical governance, in which techniques of power operate primarily at the level of the "population" and function primarily through "mechanisms of security."[63] The new figure of *homo œconomicus* that emerges out of human capital theory developed by the "Chicago-school" economic theorists—in particular, Gary Becker and Theodore Schultz—insisted that all actions, all activities, are coincident with one's person.[64] From the point of view of this economic analysis, an individual is reduced to one's market choices, and these choices are figured as investments in the self, in the manner of capital investments. The fundamental axiom of neoliberal human capital theory is that all consumption choices are also investment choices, that is, that one *is* what one *does* insofar as all actions are subsumable to the logic of consumption.[65]

An effect of this account of rationality, pioneered by Becker and Schultz along with other behavioral economists such as George Stigler and Isaac

Ehrlich, is the production of a neoliberal criminology that insists that there is no biographical or anthropological distinction between criminals and other persons. This view rejects traditional notions of criminal anthropology or of inherent criminality, and it actively resists the racist, classist, ableist, and sexist assumptions that permeated previous traditional criminological assumptions. As Becker puts it in his influential 1968 article "Crime and Punishment: An Economic Approach": "The approach taken here follows the economists' usual analysis of choice and assumes that a person commits an offense if the expected utility to him exceeds the utility he could get by using his time and other resources at other activities. Some persons become 'criminals,' therefore, not because their basic motivation differs from that of other persons, but because their benefits and costs differ."[66] In contrast to the contradictions and pathologies of nineteenth- and early-twentieth-century criminology, this is arguably a progressive position, seeking to be rid of the very model of "delinquency" Foucault diagnosed in *Discipline and Punish*.

But at its core, this neoliberal criminology is in effect not a criminology at all but rather the rejection of criminology itself in favor of economics. From the perspective of neoliberal human capital theory, Foucault glosses, "the criminal is not distinguished in any way by or interrogated on the basis of moral or anthropological traits. The criminal is nothing other than absolutely anyone whomsoever."[67] Under these terms, criminal law sets the "price" for crime by modulating the quantity (and quality) of punishment issued to produce a socially efficient level of crime. Gone is the assumption that the purpose of the law is to eradicate all crime (which would be inefficient), and gone, Foucault notes, are the figures of *homo legalis*, *homo penalis*, and *homo criminalis*. In their place is the singular figure of *homo œconomicus*.[68]

Foucault points to Ehrlich's analysis of the death penalty to underscore this point of the analysis: that this approach results in the "anthropological erasure of the criminal."[69] All that an economic analysis of crime requires is "responsiveness" to sanction, an ability to react to the "price" imposed by punishment.[70] Foucault glosses Ehrlich, stating, "The abhorrent, cruel, or pathological nature of the crime is of absolutely no importance."[71] Ehrlich's specific claim is importantly not this strong; he writes, "The abhorrent, cruel, and occasionally pathological nature of murder not withstanding . . ."[72] Nevertheless, Foucault is generally correct that Ehrlich's analysis of the death penalty seeks to remove notions of deep criminal differences (in keeping with Becker's assumptions about rational behavior), but Foucault's gloss misses the more interesting fact that Ehrlich does this *while nevertheless assuming* that pathological and other "nonrational" motivations might influence the decision to murder. A more careful reading of Ehrlich's analysis demonstrates that the economic reading *includes* nonrational action under the rubric of rationality through the idea of responsiveness. Even monsters, we must conclude following Ehrlich, are *responsive* to stimuli and therefore can have their behavior altered by increasing the "price" of murder with criminal punishment. Foucault does note that what matters from the point of view of neoliberal criminology is not that pathological or anthropological monsters might cease to actually exist but that even such monsters can be held responsible for their decisions *as if* they were rational actors. As Ehrlich himself puts it (and which Foucault quotes), "There is no reason a priori to expect that persons who hate or love others are less responsive to changes in costs and gains associated with activities they may wish to pursue than persons indifferent toward the well-being of others."[73]

This is to say that the primary outcome of neoliberal criminology is not the complete or successful elimination of practices that discriminate between *kinds* of criminals but only one that purports to do so. This is even clear in Becker's germinal 1968 article. The crimes of rape and murder are almost always mentioned in tandem and appear throughout Becker's analysis as limit cases of the economic approach. While he argues that most punishments should be replaced with a system of monetary fines, he nevertheless notes that

> another argument made against fines is that certain crimes, like murder or rape, are so heinous that no amount of money could compensate for the harm inflicted. This argument has obvious merit and is a special case of the more general principle that fines cannot be relied on exclusively whenever the harm exceeds the resources of offenders. For then victims could not be fully compensated by offenders, and fines would have to be supplemented with prison terms or other punishments in order to discourage offenses optimally. This explains why imprisonments, probation, and parole are major punishments for the more serious felonies; considerable harm is inflicted, and felonious offenders lack sufficient resources to compensate. Since fines are preferable, it also suggests the need for a flexible system of installment fines to enable offenders to pay fines more readily and thus avoid other punishments.[74]

When confronted with the hardest set of cases, Becker tempers his otherwise radical economic approach (and the replacement of most criminal law with tort law) with the continued presence of the prison, bodily punishment (of confinement), and the spectre of death carried along with them. The central move Becker makes is to insist on the strict separation between acts and identities. There are, strictly speaking, no "criminals" for Becker but only actions that are criminal, defined "fundamentally not by the nature of the action but by the inability of a person to compensate for the 'harm' that he caused. Thus an action would be 'criminal' precisely because it results in uncompensated 'harm' to others."[75] Thus, the quality that distinguishes rape and murder from other crimes, for Becker, is that the harms they cause are quantitatively greater than any individual could afford to repay. They are only "special cases" of where society must still rely on nonfinancial compensation (i.e., bodily punishment) for indigent individuals who commit crimes for which they cannot afford to pay. In this sense, Becker's own argument reverts back to disciplinary forms of punishment such as "imprisonment, probation, and parole."

Within the neoliberal approach to punishment generally, and with capital punishment specifically, disciplinary and juridical techniques and rationalities of power *remain and reemerge*. While neoliberal human capital theory enables and supports penological and criminological practices that might otherwise resist anthropological assumptions of criminality, they do so only by shifting attention to other points of contact and levels of analysis and by displacing questions such as "why might some persons be *systematically* less able to compensate for harms they have caused?" As Wendy Brown puts it more generally about neoliberalism as a political rationality, "[Neoliberalism] erases the discrepancy between economic and moral behavior by configuring morality entirely as a matter of rational deliberation about costs, benefits, and consequences. But in so doing, it carries responsibility for the self to new heights: the rationally calculating individual bears full responsibility for the consequences of his or her action no matter how severe the constraints on this action."[76]

In the penal domain, however, this full responsibility in fact goes further, rendering "criminals" fully responsible for their actions but without actually displacing the categories of monstrous criminality. We are left, especially in cases like "murder or rape," with individuals who are held fully responsible for their monstrosity, for a harm that cannot be repaid, and therefore subject to permanent punishment. Neoliberal criminology in practice has not brought about an end of the rehabilitative idea nor juridical forms of retributive punishment. Rather, what characterizes neoliberalism is, on the one hand, a reintroduction of these principles under what Pat O'Malley has called the "sign of risk" and, on the other hand, an intensification of these techniques under those terms.[77] Moreover, the neo-liberal shift in attention to crime rates (focusing on the population rather than the individual) and a renewed attention to "bad acts" rather than "bad actors" both actively hide (and possibly disavow) continued assumptions of classical liberal subjectivity. While these shifts may seem less caught up in the pathologies of disciplinary criminology (at least compared to nineteenth-century figures like the delinquent), they nevertheless belie the way in which the interpretation of one's actions relies upon existing modes of interpretation that often refuse to identify some actors' actions as ever being "bad" ones. The categorization of one's acts as good or bad continues to depend on the existing norms and frames that guide our perception.

One is often marked as deviant and delinquent by virtue of racial and sexual identification rather than through a judgment of one's actions inde-pendently (as if such a thing were possible). This is demonstrably the case in the United States, where the creation of criminal law, the very defini-tions of "harm," and the boundaries of normality and deviance have been fully inflected by white supremacy, patriarchy, heteronormativity, and ab-lism (to give an obviously incomplete list).[78] Insofar as biopower, Foucault argues, operates through state racism, its neoliberal operation produces a cover story or alibi for contemporary white supremacy by reducing all "bad acts" to "poor investments." That is, this outcome is not simply a fail-ure to be sufficiently "colorblind" or properly "liberal" but rather reflects how forms of difference *have always* been integral to the establishment of "universal" categories that refuse to acknowledge difference. As Marx fa-mously warned in "On the Jewish Question," the abolition of social and political distinctions does not, in fact, end those distinctions but presup-poses and requires them to operate in their own fashion, outside the reach of political redress.[79]

Through neoliberalism's ability to deeply responsibilitize all behavior and identify new forms of dangerousness (even if they are actuarial in their mode) while still clinging to older forms and figures (even as they continue to be racialized), in a refusal to attend to the multiplicity of theoretical and empirical discourses that shape reality, and above all in its claims to "optimize" difference, neoliberalism (in practice if not in theory) supports incarceration rather than works as a force to suppress it.[80] Neoliberalism in practice relies on harsh punitive sanction to govern poverty (and poor people) and to paternalistically police a racialized underclass.[81] Yet it has managed to do so under the rhetorical masks of equality, universality, and objectivity. As such, it remains subject to a basic critique: neoliberalism posits a universalism that presupposes the various forms of political difference (race, sex, gender, etc.) that it then displaces to the economic margins as evidence of failed "investments" in human capital.

We are left with a form of criminal responsibility that is more pernicious than nineteenth- or early-twentieth-century notions of a criminal anthropology. This form of neoliberal subjectivity produces deeply responsible monsters and at the same time offers a plausible liberal deniability of such an anthropology. It pervades both left and right adoptions of neoliberal concerns over fiscal responsibility and the "crisis" of mass incarceration. And we should not, therefore, be surprised that a pervading fear of "killers and rapists left on the streets" runs throughout the abolitionist discourse of the SAFE California Act. Written into the earliest applications of human capital theory to the question of crime and punishment are its remainders, leftovers, uncompensatable harms, and *political* questions that return even in the face of the radical displacement of politics attendant to neoliberalism. But it is important to recognize the power of the neoliberal discourse: these are exceptions that do not challenge the rule, but which prove it.

Reform, Resistance, and the Limits of Abolition

The failure of the SAFE California Act to pass as Prop. 34 was bemoaned by death penalty abolitionists and explained by pointing to a deep attachment to the death penalty, a general skepticism in the fiscal claims made by supporters of the measure, and (for more radical critics) a concern for the sake of death row inmates themselves who stood to lose access to the courts. Despite this setback, the abolitionist strategy of replacing the death penalty with LWOP continues in other states. In May 2013 Maryland repealed its death penalty statute. Under the Maryland repeal, death row inmates are to be resentenced, with an LWOP sentence available for capital murder cases.[82] As in California, proponents of the bill noted substantial cost savings to the state that would come from eliminating the appeals process reserved for death row inmates. Even in the face of defeat at the ballot box, the "road to abolition" continues to be paved in part by the neoliberal bargain: in these times of massive fiscal constraints, both supporters and opponents of state execution can be mollified by the promise of increased security through savings and the replacement of "death" with "life." The editorial endorsement of the Maryland repeal made by the *Baltimore Sun* echoed the Prop. 34 campaign in California: "Replacing the death penalty with a maximum sentence of life without the possibility of parole serves to protect society and render severe punishment on those who commit the worst crimes. It is cost-effective, and it provides finality for the families of murder victims in a way that the death penalty does not."[83] Or as the Democratic Governor of Maryland Martin O'Malley put it more bluntly shortly before signing the repeal into law, capital punishment is "expensive and does not work."[84]

Under current conditions, it appears that abolition of this sort is the only kind that is even possible (and in the case of Prop. 34, even this form of "abolition" continues to be out of reach in California). From one perspective, this can be regarded as the increasingly contracting space of political disagreement not subsumed to market rationality and a narrowing of possible sites of resistance outside of neoliberalism. This contraction should not be surprising to readers of Foucault, and his account of power refuses to think of power as a spatial topology or object to be held but instead as a set of force relations, situated practices, and ways of knowing that shift and move over time and across space. As such, we should not think that there is some ideal or pure form of "abolition" either, outside of a specific context or history. But we should remain cautious of the reach of "reform," especially when it so clearly operates on the terms of "replacement" rather than a rethinking of the conditions of possibility of the practice in question. Reform is clearly not impossible, but an abolition of the death penalty that replaces it with LWOP and expands the reach of the carceral system is not an abolition worthy of the name.

The contemporary practice of execution *and its abolition* identify a location at which multiple modalities of power intersect and interact. In this way, both the failure of Prop. 34 and the success of Maryland's repeal reflect the persistence of juridical power: a state that kills in a multitude of ways, each exposing the racial psychodramas of the "American" experience and its penal history. Additionally, the persistence of the death penalty in law (if not in practice, as actual executions continue to be under a de facto moratorium in California) might be read as a kind of popular resistance itself. The difficulty of neoliberalism is that the identifiable spaces of "resistance" appear smaller and more impossible to carve out. Insofar as the contemporary "abolitionists" have taken on a distinctively neoliberal and actuarial form, they also remain powerfully attached to disciplinary techniques and a retrenchment of confinement, forced labor, and death, even if it is now under the "sign of risk" and appears as a resistance to the state's power to kill. Perhaps neoliberalism's distinctive feature is its ability not simply to displace other strategies but to intensify them and to harmonize even contradictory and heterogeneous strategies. Even more than its reliance on an economistic language that depoliticizes contemporary death penalty "abolition" campaigns, we should be concerned by the ease with which that language *includes* rather than sets aside demands for permanent exclusion, forced labor, more police, more punishment, and more prisons. Neoliberalism, in this sense, is "neo" primarily in its reach: everything—all discourses, all practices, all persons—are professed to be subject to market rationalities. And as such, abolition itself, as a practice of resistance, can become "completely correlated to the systems of power that were designed to stifle it."[85]

Shortly before France ended capital punishment in 1981, Foucault noted "the way in which the death penalty is done away with is at least as important as the doing-away. The roots are deep. And many things will depend on how they are cleared out."[86] What France was in danger of doing in 1981, Foucault insisted, is precisely what neoliberal abolitionist strategies are in danger of doing today: failing to question the relation of the death penalty to broader systems of incarceration and the logics that support it. Once the death penalty is gone, Foucault asked:

> Will there be a radical departure from a penal practice that asserts that it is for the purpose of correction but maintains that certain individuals cannot be corrected, ever, because of their nature, their character, or a bio-psychological defect, or because they are, in sum, intrinsically dangerous? . . . [T]here is a danger that will perhaps not be evoked—that of a society that will not be constantly concerned about its code and its laws, its penal institutions and its punitive practices. By maintaining, in one form or another, the category of individuals to be definitively eliminated (through death or imprisonment), one easily gives oneself the illusion of solving the most difficult problems: correct if one can; if not, no need to worry, no need to ask oneself whether it might be necessary to reconsider all the ways of punishing: the trap door through which the 'incorrigible' will disappear is ready.[87]

In the case of California, this danger was expressly written into Prop. 34 in multiple ways. And as death penalty abolition appears to be solidly on the track of reconfiguring and intensifying the carceral system but without questioning penal policy more generally, the danger continues to loom in future cases. If we are to go further, pushing against simplistic distinctions between life and death and the reigning "death is different" jurisprudence, it becomes clear that abolishing the death penalty requires that we question not only LWOP sentences but the prison itself, the entire carceral network, and also the basic grounds and practices of punishment. It may already be much too late, considering that the fastest growing populations of incarcerated persons in the United States have not even been convicted of crimes but are persons languishing in immigration detention centers. When pressed to identify what a "model" prison would look like, Foucault noted that such a thing did not exist. The question of the prison would have to give way to the question of marginalization in all its forms: "The problem is not a model prison or the abolition of prisons. Currently, in our system, marginalization is effected by prisons. This marginalization will not automatically disappear by abolishing the prison. Society would quite simply institute another means. The problem is the following: to offer a critique of the system that explains the process by which contemporary society pushes a portion of the population to the margins. Voilà."[88]

This challenge of continued analysis must be applied to the idea of abolition itself. In the "American" tradition, the practice of "abolition" must never be separated from its historical roots in the abolition of chattel slavery, lynching, and legal segregation. As Angela Davis notes, the idea of prison abolition necessarily takes these projects as models, recalling that each of these institutions were, within recent history, understood to be defendable if not permanent features of American society.[89] The work of groups like Critical Resistance, the Sylvia Rivera Law Project, and Against Equality draws on the increasingly large body of abolitionist theory and practice in fields such as critical race theory and queer theory and points to possibilities for such permanent self-reflection.[90] Yet the costs are visible as well. It is well worth remembering that the abolition of slavery in the Thirteenth Amendment contains a provision allowing for its continuance as "punishment for a crime," allowing for the widespread growth of the convict-lease system following the Civil War; that the extension of voting rights in the Fourteenth Amendment likewise contained provisions allowing states to bar convicted criminals from the ballot box; that the death penalty in practice is so racially skewed as to resemble a legal version of lynching; and that schools are statistically more racially segregated today than at the time of *Brown v. Board of Education*. There can, on such an account, be no "end" to the analysis of penal practice, but rather it would become what Foucault called "a locus of constant reflection, research, and experience, of transformation."[91]

On the Inviolability of Human Life

Julia Kristeva

October 10, 2012: Tenth World Day for the Abolition of the Death Penalty. Mobilization, ignorance, hostility, incomprehension, solemnity, and gravity suspend the time of global crisis, the time of hyperconnected acceleration and diverse threats of destruction. And we are called to contemplate, invited to meditate and to question: what does a project for the universal abolition of the death penalty mean?

I am neither a jurist nor a specialist on abolitionism. I've never been to an execution, nor has anyone close to me ever been a victim of murder, sexual abuse, torture, or degrading violence. I won't read you the medical reports detailing the tortures of the guillotine, the ones recopied by Camus himself to communicate his nausea to us. Nor have I ever felt the romantic empathy that carries Hugo away when he compares the suffering of exile to the suffering of a man condemned to die. I find that experiences of suffering are incommensurable, more or less incommunicable, and the death drive that inhabits us threatens us all . . . singularly.

I hear my analysands confide the suffering they've endured at the hands of executioners in Latin American prisons, or their inconsolable suffering after their parents have been exterminated in concentration camps. I come undone along with them, and I will not venture to say that evil is without a why in the way a mystic affirms that the rose is without one. Because I search for them, with them: Why? In order that meaning might be restored, because meaning is what brings us back to life.

Abolishing the death penalty: What wish, what project are we putting forth here? And what, then, is its meaning?

Abolishing the death penalty means that we are positing as the foundation of twenty-first-century humanism what Victor Hugo was already calling "the inviolability of human life" more than 150 years ago in 1848.[1]

Since the beginning of time, men have feared death. They have given death, however, in order to better safeguard life, to attempt to save the *good* by inflicting the supreme *evil*. For the first time in history, however, we realize that it's not enough to replace the old values with new ones, because the new ones will in their turn congeal and become potentially totalitarian dogma and impasses.

And we realize that life is not a "value" like any other, nor even *the* value. What's more, for the past two centuries, and particularly today, life is not only a line of questioning: What is a life? Does it have a meaning? If so, what meaning? But from now on, life is an exigency. We must preserve it and prevent its destruction—because the destruction of life is radical evil. While everything seems to be falling apart, while wars, the threat of ecological disaster, and the mindless enthusiasm for virtual economies and consumer societies permanently remind us of our fragility and our vanity, *the inviolability of human life* invites us to think about the meaning of our existence: it is the bedrock of humanism.

What *life* are we talking about? The abolitionist responds: *all life*, regardless of what kind, to the point even of "taking responsibility for the lives of those who horrify us" (lunatics, criminals . . .), as Robert Badinter proclaimed in his 1981 testimony before the French Parliament in support of his proposed law to abolish the death penalty.[2] Can contemporary humanity test itself, and prove itself (*s'éprouver, et se prouver*), to the point of "taking responsibility for the lives of those who horrify us"? Abolitionists, we say: Yes. But even if 141 out of 192 members of the United Nations have already abolished the death penalty, 60 percent of the human population lives in a country where it's still applied since it's still in force in four of the most populated countries on the planet: China, India, the United States, and Indonesia.

Fortified by its plural heritage—Greek, Jewish, and Christian—Europe chose secularization, thereby bringing about an emancipatory mutation unique in the world. But its history was also marked by its too-long procession of horrors: wars, exterminations, colonialism, totalitarianisms. This philosophy and this history impose a moral and political conviction on us whereby no state, no power, no man can usurp another man's rights or have the legal power to take his life. No matter whom the man or woman we condemn, no justice should be a justice that kills.

Making a plea for the abolition of the death penalty in the name of *the inviolability of human life* does not, therefore, stem from naivety or an irresponsible, blissful idealism. It is not a question of forgetting the victims and their loved ones' suffering. *No!* I do not believe in human perfection, or even in absolute perfectability through the grace of compassion or education. I'm only betting on our capacity to understand human passions better and to accompany them to their limits, because experience teaches us that it is impossible (unthinkable) to respond to a crime with a crime.

I repeat: a human's greatest fear is to see his life taken, and this fear founds the social pact. The oldest jurisprudence treatises we possess bear witness to this. Take the Hammurabi Babylonian Code (1792–1750 before our era), and yet again with Plato and Aristotle's Greek philosophy, but also with the Romans, and also the sacred texts of Christians and Jews. All societies have advocated and practiced putting criminals to death in order to defend, protect, and dissuade.

Voices against execution have, however, been raised: contemporary abolitionists return to them and listen to them to support their struggle. Thus, already, Ezekiel: "I have no pleasure in the death of the wicked; but that the wicked turn from his way and live" (Ez. 33:11). But above all, Saint Paul: "O death, where is your victory? O death, where is your sting? The sting of death is sin, and the power of sin is the law. But thanks be to God, he gives us victory over sin and death" (through the Resurrection) (1 Corinthians 15:55–57). Or again, after them, Maimonides: "It is better and more satisfactory to acquit a thousand guilty persons than to put a single innocent one to death."[3]

Religion and politics rarely make pronouncements against the death penalty: Tibetan Buddhism forbade it in the seventh century, and in 747 the first abolition was proclaimed in China. Moreover, Montesquieu points this out, praising these Chinese authors according to whom "the more severe the punishments, the nearer, the revolution. This is the case because punishments increased in severity to the extent that mores were lost."[4] Maybe we should remind the Chinese authorities. China abolished the death penalty in 2011 for thirteen nonviolent crimes, but executions for corruption continue and multiply. As for Islam, there is absolutely no question of challenging the death penalty.

In France, the abolitionist movement began after the torture of Damiens, who had tried to assassinate Louis V. While Diderot advocates the death penalty for its dissuasive power, Voltaire is one of the few to support the work of Cesare Beccaria who, from 1764, asks: "By what right can men presume to slaughter their fellows?"[5] In the spirit of the Enlightenment and libertarian humanism, abolitionism develops throughout the nineteenth century: I'm thinking of Clémenceau, Gambetta, and of Jean Jaurès's lucid words, proclaiming that the death penalty "is contrary to both the spirit of Christianity and the spirit of the Republic."[6] Or, closer to us, Camus states that "one can only write about capital punishment in a low voice" because "this new murder, far from making amends for the harm done to the social body, adds a new blot to the first one[7]. . . . Capital judgment upsets the only indispensable human solidarity, the solidarity against death."[8]

Abolitionists advance three main arguments against the death penalty: the inefficiency of vengeance and dissuasion, the fallibility of justice, and the suffering of elimination.

In the first place, nothing proves that the death penalty works in countering human destructiveness: there is no correlation between maintaining the legality of the death penalty and the criminality curve. Furthermore, the perspective of death, far from annihilating criminal passions, to the contrary, exalts them. He who sows terror and transcends it through his own death is not seeking expiation. In reality, the stigmatization of his acts and the sacrifice itself have no other end but to inflame martyrs ready to die in their turn. Far from being dissuasive, fear becomes temptation and henceforth nourishes a desire to inflict death by inflicting death on oneself. The death penalty as lex talionis, "an eye for an eye," thus turns out to be just as inefficient a vengeance as it is a useless dissuasion.

The second argument brings us back to what Victor Hugo called the "scrawny brevity of human justice"[9]: the judiciary lottery, its fallibility. In the name of which institution do men and women allow themselves the right to pronounce and apply a mortal condemnation?

The third argument is expressed in murmurs because it is addressed to the victims and those close to them. Some of them feel that even if putting criminals to death doesn't avenge their crimes or dissuade those who would follow in their footsteps, at least it gets rid of their author. The death penalty as elimination would consequently attenuate the unbearable and appease.

But does the image of the criminal in his tomb really relieve the suffering of those who have lost a loved one, a victim of the worst of atrocities? This suffering in search of alleviation is just as inexpressible and unshareable as it is legitimate and respectable: Who would dare ignore this? No one, and above all those men and women who, outraged by the death of innocent victims, equally hope to defend and protect life in the name of its inviolability. Because they know that the notion of death as ultimate and unique recourse is a lure.

When, in effect, will we stop making the tomb our savior? Let's detach ourselves from the *jouissance* brought about by the vengeful act. Victor Hugo's elevated words already alerted us to this religion of death as salvation: "Do not open a tomb in the middle of us with your own hands," he writes in Guernsey. "You who know so little and can't do anything about it, you are always face to face with the infinite and the unknown! The infinite and the unknown: this is the tomb." I understand: Don't hope to find "the unknown or the infinite"[10] in the sacrifice of the condemned. And I add: there is no other unknown, no other infinity than those of human passions—of which we never stop deepening our experience and establishing our knowledge [*connaissance*].

By abolishing the death penalty, we're not screaming victory over death as Paul de Tarse would have it, calling for belief in the Resurrection. We invite a better knowledge [*connaître*] and accompaniment of the passions and among these the most terrible: the death drive.

Psychoanalysis discovers that *Homo sapiens* is both *Homo religiosus* and *Homo economicus* and is a *Homo eroticus* inhabited not only by a life drive but also by a death drive. The death drive that Freud—as if he had a premonition about the Shoah—explored at the end of his life, and that contemporary research continues to elucidate today.

The human being is a fundamentally binary being: digesting the good and expelling the bad, oscillating between inside and outside, pleasure and reality, the forbidden and transgression, his ego and the other, body and mind/spirit. Language itself is binary (made up of consonants and vowels, and other dual forms that so delighted structuralism). The child thus attains to the difference between *good* and *evil* from the very moment he learns his mother tongue; the universe of meaning invites a distinction between *good* and *evil* before refining its nuances, perceiving its polyphonies, its excesses, its transgressions, and before creating works of art.

Our desires are revealed as more or less compatible with the desires of others. They draw us toward the other, up to the point of love, but a love carrying an aggressiveness within: *je t'aime, moi non plus*, hatred and culpability: such is the alchemy of words [*le verbe*]. It is precisely on these convergent and divergent libidinal interests, underpinned by our conceptions of *good* and *evil*, that the most elevated values are constructed and enter into concurrence or conflict. Desires and values dictate religions and philosophies, as well as the ideologies living off them, killing each other or attempting to explain and understand themselves.

Often, so-called "values" capture destructiveness, which then takes the form of a fascination with evil, an evil to be sought in the other: henceforth, all that remains is to track down the scapegoat in order to exterminate him with no remorse, for the benefit of the sovereign good, my own good, my religion. Such is the logic of a fundamentalism that wages a merciless war in the name of an absolute ideal erected against the other. Whether individual or collective, this fundamentalism is nourished by a total, blind faith that tolerates no questioning whatsoever. As I argued previously, condemning a fundamentalist to death doesn't eliminate fundamentalism; to the contrary, it makes its agent a martyr and exalts his logic—a logic with economic and social roots but also a psychosexual nervous system running through the very structure of his passion, remaining untouchable unless it's deactivated from the inside.

Here, however, it is only a question of the superficial layers of radical evil. A pure death drive equally exists, dissociated from all desire (one might say: uncomplicated by desire). This death drive sweeps aside the distinctions between good and evil, between ego and other, and abolishes the meaning and dignity of self and other. The destructiveness I just pointed out cedes here to its own undoing. These extreme states of the quasi-total detachment of the death drive touch the limits of *Homo sapiens* as a speaking being capable of values (beginning with *good* and *evil*). The person who has fallen prey to this detachment expresses himself in a language that is no longer anything but simple mechanics, an instrument of destruction with neither code nor communication: without any why, without remorse, neither expiation nor redemption.

Such liminal states [*états limites*] find refuge not only in hospitals or on the analyst's couch. They do not only plague serial killers, nor do they only brutally explode within the chaos of adolescence destined to indifference and insensitivity in the face of the foreigner [*étranger*] to be suppressed. The death drive's liminal states also unfurl in sociopolitical crises and catastrophes. Abject, these states can lead all the way to the cold, planned extermination of other human beings; this was the case with the Shoah and other genocides.

I hear your question and share your indignation: So, abolitionists want to spare those criminals' lives?

If I've taken my reflections all the way to the point of dehumanization, it is only to demonstrate better that the humanism vindicated by partisans of an abolition of the death penalty is a wager against horror. Even if an understanding of the human passions renders us neither all-powerful nor capable of annihilating this genocidal pathology when an entire society suffers from it, this knowledge does allow us to approach these liminal states and accompany them within a clinical context. But after Ezekiel, Paul de Tarse, and Maimonides, after Beccaria, Voltaire, Hugo, Jaurès, Camus, Badinter, and so many others, it seems that a better understanding of the spectre of human passions is the only way to uncover and confront the many faces of this radical evil. When compassion and forgiveness abdicate because they no longer have any hold on evil, it nevertheless does become possible to sound the depths of evil. How?

> By relaying the emotional horror produced by a more precise diagnosis of the consequences of radical evil. Vigilance, objective analysis, treatment, and education do nothing to efface criminals' guilt, but they do mobilize us from the very first symptoms of evil;
> by replacing the death penalty with rigorous criminal penalties that prevent recidivism;
> and, finally, by organizing a support system for convicted criminals and political prisoners [*criminels politiques*] in order to lead them as far as possible toward possibilities for restructuring and to attempt to elucidate the triggers of destructiveness and the detachment that generated the crime.

Hannah Arendt, philosopher and political journalist, denounced the Nazi horror as an unprecedented radical evil—by arguing, however, that it's not *evil*, but rather good, that's radical. Because *good* isn't the symmetrical opposite of evil; it resides in the infinite capacities of human thought to find causalities and the means to combat unhappiness [*le mal-être:* "evil-being"] and the *malignity of evil*.

Permit me to finish on a more personal note. As a child in my native country of Bulgaria, I heard my parents evoke the executions carried out by the previous Parliament's Communist regime but also by the Stalinist trials and purges. I was already learning French when my father, a man of faith, explained to me that, even if revolutionary terror had been inevitable, language, like French culture, also contained enlightenment. I was already in France when he was hospitalized for a minor operation and killed in a Bulgarian hospital, several months before the fall of the Berlin Wall in 1989—at the time they were experimenting on the elderly. Although the death penalty was abolished in 1988 in Bulgaria, today 52 percent of those questioned in this country still say they support its application.

It's not a question of saving society, which perpetuates itself only by walling itself off from the infinite complexity of the passions. Rather, it's a question of putting our knowledge of these passions in the service of the human in order better to protect ourselves from ourselves. The new humanism should be up to the task of defending the inviolability of human life and applying it to everyone, without exception, as well as to other extreme situations in the life experience: eugenics, euthanasia, and so forth. I am far from idealizing human beings, nor do I deny the evil of which they're capable. They can always, however, be cared for, and by abolishing the death penalty—which is a crime, let's remember—we're combating both death and crime. In this context, the abolition of the death penalty is a rational revolt, the only one that counts against the death drive and, definitively, against death: abolitionism is the secularized version of the Resurrection.

You know, of course, that the Italians illuminate the Coliseum, a bloody memorial to the innumerable gladiators and Christian martyrs put to death, every time a country abolishes the death penalty or declares a moratorium on executions.

I propose that every night when a country renounces the death penalty, its name be displayed on giant screens installed at the Place de la Concorde (formerly Place de la Révolution) and the Hôtel de Ville (formerly Place de Grève) for just this purpose, in memory of Madame Roland, Madame du Barry, Charlotte Corday, the *tricoteuses* (knitting women), the guillotine, Fouquier-Tinville, André Chenier, and others. Would this supplementary expense exacerbate the state of our economy? Optimists predict that most of the world will have abolished the death penalty by 2050. It's up to us to do what it takes to make the majority support this abolition.

Translated by Lisa Walsh

Rethinking Power and Responsibility

Punishment, Desert, and Equality:
A Levinasian Analysis

Benjamin S. Yost

The last forty years have witnessed a spectacular increase in the number of incarcerated Americans. In 1970 the U.S. penal population stood at 330,000; it now stands at over 2.4 million. This is a 700 percent increase, measured against a population increase of 150 percent. Our current level of incarceration is far out of line with almost every other country in the world. The United States imprisons 743 out of every 100,000 citizens, while Germany imprisons 85 per 100,000. The United States' closest competitor is Russia (607 per 100,000), followed by Cuba (487) and Ukraine (360).[1] This dubious achievement is made possible by the popularity of "getting tough on crime" by means of three-strikes laws and mandatory minimum sentencing schemes. And tough these schemes are, though their draconian punishments are often wildly disproportionate to the corresponding offences. Consider the not unusual punishment meted out to Leo Andrade. Andrade, a father of two, stole five children's videotapes worth $85 from a California Kmart and was caught by a security guard as he was leaving the store.[2] Two weeks later, he stole four more children's videotapes worth $69 from a different Kmart and was again caught by a security guard. Andrade was arrested for both thefts. Andrade had been a heroin addict since leaving the Army twenty years earlier and was in and out of jail, but his most serious offense was burgling three houses when no one was home. Both Kmart thefts were charged as "petty theft with a prior," which is punishable by a maximum of three years and eight months in prison. This may seem like a harsh sentence, but unfortunately for Andrade, his burglaries counted as a "serious or violent" felony for the purpose of California's three-strikes law. Just as unfortunately, in California petty theft with a prior is a "wobbler" offense, which can be charged as a misdemeanor or as a felony. The prosecutor chose to charge Andrade with two felonies. A jury convicted Andrade on both counts, and in accordance with the three-strikes schedule, he was sentenced to two consecutive terms of twenty-five years to life, a sentence in excess of those imposed on rapists and many murderers. Andrade appealed his case to the Supreme Court, which declined to vacate his sentence, holding that a fifty-years-to-life sentence was not cruel and unusual punishment for a $150 theft.[3]

Another important factor in U.S. incarceration rates is the War on Drugs, which has supplied more than half of the increase.[4] Drug offenders now make up a quarter of the penal population and half of the federal prison population.[5] A quick bit of math shows that there were more people incarcerated for drug offenses in 2013 than there were people incarcerated for *all crimes combined* in 1970. The consequences for African Americans have been particularly devastating. The number of prison admissions for African Americans is twenty-six times higher than it was at the beginning of the War on Drugs.[6] More importantly, African Americans are disproportionately incarcerated for drug offenses, making up roughly half of those incarcerated for drug offenses at the state level and close to half of those at the federal level.[7] This disparity exists even though whites and African Americans use and sell drugs at the same rate. If there is any significant difference indicated in the relevant research, it is that whites are more likely to deal drugs than people of color.[8]

Even this quick sketch of the unequal treatment of white and black offenders suggests that our penal system is unjust, and sentencing reform is urgently needed. But while these normative claims have obvious intuitive appeal, they run up against what I call the "noncomparativist challenge." Some philosophers, using a "noncomparative" conception of justice, argue that the justice of a type of punishment is *independent* of the fairness of its distribution, and that the aforementioned facts do not, by themselves, impugn the justice of contemporary practices of punishment. If you do the crime, you deserve the time, and so unequal punishment does not unjustly burden those groups who are disproportionately punished. The noncomparativist challenge garners support from the priority of noncomparative justice over comparative justice in most thinking about penal justice, including contemporary Fourteenth Amendment jurisprudence. In what follows, I will offer philosophical support for sentencing reform by defending the claim that the disproportionate application of punishment to disadvantaged social groups is unjust. After describing the noncomparativist challenge in more detail, I will argue that Levinasian conceptions of desert and responsibility enable a theory of penal justice according to which comparative considerations have priority over noncomparative ones. In so doing, I will show that the noncomparativist challenge can be met.

In the second section of the chapter, I will discuss a slightly different type of injustice. At the time of this writing, no one responsible for the financial crisis of 2008 has been convicted of a crime, even though the ensuing events lowered Americans' household wealth by $19.2 trillion,[9] sapped retirement accounts of $3 trillion, put 12 million people out of work, and increased the number of Americans needing food stamps by 13 million.[10] (The S.E.C. has made one attempt at a conviction, charging a junior ex-Citigroup executive named Brian Stoker with fraud. Stoker was acquitted by a federal jury, who suggested in an unusual note to the judge that they were frustrated that they were not sitting in judgment of the senior executives responsible for the crisis.[11]) This should be no great surprise: white-collar crime is far more costly to society than all the FBI Index crimes combined, yet white-collar criminals are almost never arrested or charged, and when they are, they are treated far more leniently than poor offenders.[12] If we compare the good fortunes of financial executives to the tragedies that befall people like Andrade, who are routinely subject to lengthy prison sentences for minor property crimes, we are confronted with an injustice that looks similar to the one discussed previously: the wealthy are underpunished, and the poor are overpunished.

These grim reminders of the plutocratic nature of American society and its effect on punishment set the stage for the actual point I want to make. When we assess the moral blameworthiness of the well-off compared to the disadvantaged, it can seem *more* blameworthy for the well-off to commit crimes (excluding violent crimes) than the disadvantaged, even when the harms caused by their wrongdoing is of similar magnitude. Put more prosaically, part of many people's anger at the instigators of the financial crisis stems from the fact that the malefactors are inordinately well-off. In some ill-defined way, this makes their actions seem worse. Yet it is very hard to specify what, exactly, is worse about them, and as a result, one might suspect that these judgments of blameworthiness are products of *ressentiment.* But as I will argue, again on Levinasian grounds, these inchoate intuitions are correct, and the advantaged *are* more blameworthy for committing crimes that are equal in severity to crimes committed by the disadvantaged. (This claim is not aimed solely at the 1 percent, though I will refrain from defining what it means to be "advantaged.")

The Noncomparativist Challenge

To start, I want to explain the distinction between noncomparative and comparative justice. Very broadly, treating someone in accordance with comparative justice requires us to think about how we are treating other people; not surprisingly, comparative justice involves comparison. In contemporary political philosophy, comparative justice is at home in discussions of distributive justice, and it stands for a specific normative principle: like cases should be treated alike, and different cases should be treated differently. This principle regulates the distribution of benefits and burdens in two ways. On one hand, it tells us that we must make comparisons when we are gauging whether to give someone her due. On the other, it tells us that we must make comparisons when we are determining what is due to her. The first version of the like cases principle requires us to give everyone the same percentage of what they are due. (Ideally, we would give everyone everything they are due, but since this is impossible, we should give everyone the same percentage of what they are due.) The second requires us to look at relevant comparisons when determining what someone is due. An example of the latter application is grading: the like cases principle states that we ought to give shabby papers worse grades than excellent ones. In the second case especially, comparative justice stands in stark contrast with noncomparative justice. Noncomparative justice requires us to treat people in accordance with what they are due, the assessments of which are independent of comparative considerations.[13] In other words, noncomparative justice requires us to treat people in accordance with what they *deserve*. For example, imagine that you fail a student for plagiarizing, and he complains that his grade is unjust because his friend's equally egregious plagiarism went undetected. If you are unmoved by his plea, you are assessing him in terms of noncomparative justice.

There are unintuitive and intuitive aspects of noncomparative justice. Many find it extremely unjust that African Americans are far more frequently jailed for drug offenses than whites. Many also find it unjust that those who commit white-collar financial crimes are treated much more leniently than petty thieves. Yet if we *just* look at the individual offender, then so long as he is guilty, and the punishment proportionate, punishment does seem "deserved" in some sense, even in contexts where punishments have a racially disparate impact. Much seems to depend on our perspective: as one philosopher of punishment puts it, "justice and injustice seem alternately to flit in and out of focus like the pictures in an optical illusion, depending on whether we consider comparative or noncomparative factors."[14]

But while both perspectives have intuitions on their side, the noncomparative perspective is more deeply rooted in contemporary penal thought and practice. Noncomparative justice is tied to penal justice—at least the retributivist variant I'll be discussing in this chapter—by means of the concept of desert. Both noncomparative justice and penal justice state that we ought to treat people in ways that accord with what they deserve. (By contrast, most philosophers deny that desert plays a role in distributive justice.[15]) The concept of desert plays two crucial roles in penal justice. First, it is often thought that someone is liable to be punished only insofar as she is a morally responsible being and her actions can be imputed to her; that is, she is liable to be punished only if she is capable of deserving punishment. Desert, then, is a necessary condition of morally permissible punishments. Second, and more importantly, desert is often cited as one of the reasons for punishing lawbreakers.[16] Desert, along with the illegality of the lawbreaker's act, are thought to form a set of jointly sufficient conditions of punishment. As such, desert, along with criminal conduct, constitutes a conclusive reason to punish, even in situations where other lawbreakers who have committed similar crimes are not so punished.

A point of clarification: for my purposes, desert is important because it helps answer the question of why a state should punish particular offenders, *not* because it helps answer the question of why a state should employ punishment as opposed to some other method of dealing with crime. Some philosophers have assigned the latter function to the concept of desert, and have justified the practice of punishment in retributivist terms, arguing that the *purpose* of legal punishment is to give people what they deserve. However, others believe that it is incoherent (or illiberal) to justify the practice of punishment in this way. These philosophers think that the practice of punishment should be justified in consequentialist terms, though they allow that the punishment of individual offenders is best justified in a retributivist fashion. I take no stand on this debate, as I am mainly concerned with the justification of the punishment of individuals, and on this point almost everyone is in agreement.

The noncomparativist challenge should now be clear. If desert is a jointly sufficient condition of legitimate punishment, this licenses the conclusion that someone who commits a crime, and is subsequently punished for it, is treated justly *even though* someone else who commits the same crime is not punished. It licenses the conclusion that someone who commits a crime, and is subsequently punished for it, is treated justly *even though* someone else who commits the same crime is not charged with the crime, is charged with the crime but never convicted, or is convicted but punished less severely.[17] On the noncomparativist view, the fact that a legal institution overpunishes some people of color relative to whites (or the poor relative to the rich) does not imply that a person of color or a person of minimal means fails to *deserve* that punishment. And since desert functions as part of the jointly sufficient conditions of punishment, justice requires the punishment of the offender in question. Now, for the noncomparativist, there *is* a problem with unequal punishment, though it has no relation to those who are punished. The problem is that the wrongdoers who go unpunished do *not* get what they deserve.[18] But on this construal of the problem, overpunishment is not unjust.

At this point, I would note that the dispute between comparativists and noncomparativists is not a mere academic quibble. Noncomparativists have friends in high places. The Supreme Court holds that comparative considerations have no bearing on the constitutionality of an individual offender's punishment. In the landmark case *McCleskey v. Kemp*, the Court was presented with a study that concludes, on the basis of a rigorous analysis of over two thousand murder cases in Georgia, that the race of murder victims significantly influences sentencing decisions. The Baldus study shows that when victims are white, murderers are eleven times more likely to receive a death sentence than when victims are black.[19] The *McCleskey* dissent argues that such bias clearly violates African Americans' right to equal protection under the law, but this argument does not carry the day. While the majority disagrees neither with the Baldus study's methods nor with its conclusion that the victim's race is one of the most important factors determining a murderer's sentence, they deny that this is reason to give McCleskey relief under the Fourteenth Amendment. The Court believes that unless a petitioner can show evidence of *intentional* racism in his or her case, his desert is not in question, and there is no constitutional complaint. In short, the Court holds that penal justice prioritizes noncomparative over comparative justice.[20]

If the noncomparativist challenge is to be defeated, the conceptual privilege accorded to noncomparative justice must be revoked. In the following pages, I will argue that a Levinasian account of penal justice shows comparative justice to have priority, thus defeating the noncomparativist challenge.

Justice and Equality

To begin, we need to get a handle on Levinas's multifaceted conception of justice. "Justice" has different meanings in different periods of his philosophical development, many having little to do with how justice is ordinarily conceived.[21] *Otherwise than Being* is his first major text containing a conception of justice that makes room for some of the term's ordinary meanings. In its broadest sense, which applies to both moral and political realms, justice refers to an ideal in which everyone possesses equal moral standing.[22] In a more specific sense, justice names a characteristic of societies in which equal rights are asserted, defended, and respected,[23] and it is here that Levinas's conception of justice overlaps with more traditional ones. To my mind, one of the most important developments of Levinas's work in the 1980s is to move beyond the extremely thin description of justice contained in *Otherwise than Being* to gesture toward what one might call a Levinasian theory of legal and political justice.

To understand this latter conception of justice, it is helpful to understand Levinas's critique of mainstream liberal justice. According to the latter, "justice" names the virtue belonging to institutions that respect, enable, and protect freedom and equality. In the liberal conception of justice—and I am painting with a very broad brush here—individual autonomy and fair treatment are basic values that legitimate political and legal institutions strive to exemplify. Liberal societies are ones in which legal and political institutions enable people to pursue their private conception of the good and run their lives effectively and efficiently. In addition, liberal societies arrange matters so that the burdens and benefits of social cooperation are distributed fairly, and no one gets the fruits of social cooperation without taking on social burdens proportional to their benefits, or vice versa.

Levinas often casts a critical eye on this conception of justice, as we see in passages where justice is described as "bookkeeping," "a balance of accounts in an order where responsibilities correspond exactly to liberties taken."[24] More fundamentally, Levinas rejects its metaphysical underpinnings, exemplified by Kant's claim that freedom is the essence of humanity, and his axiological claim that autonomy is the fundamental ethical and juridical value. In Levinas's view, liberal justice, with its emphasis on freedom and autonomy, is geared toward honoring an implicitly libertarian *conatus essendi*; it delineates a sphere that surrounds each individual self, protecting their ability to reach their vision of the good life and minimizing all non-self-initiated claims on their time, money, and labor—in short, enhancing individuals' ability to persevere in their chosen way of being. For Levinas, of course, this way of thinking renders us incapable of understanding our fundamental ethical responsibilities.

But at the same time, Levinas states that "institutions and juridical proceedings are necessary," even ethically necessary.[25] In fact, Levinas explicitly endorses liberalism, claiming that it is the specific features of liberal justice that distinguish praiseworthy legal and political regimes from totalitarian or fascist ones.[26] He says that states *ought* to fairly apportion rights and responsibilities, to strive for equality in benefits and burdens.[27] At first glance, these claims might seem to be in tension with his critique, but they are not. They reflect a clear-eyed recognition of the ways in which liberal justice—or at least a Levinasian version of liberal justice where justice is conceived as subservient to ethics—furthers the aims of ethics. Again, Levinas's considered view is that liberal justice, properly understood, is ethically necessary. To see why this is the case, we need to take one more step back.

Levinas conceptualizes ethics on the basis of a fundamental normative relationship between the self and the other. For Levinas, responsibility for the other is the source of all normativity, be it political, legal, or ethical; it is in "responsibility for the other . . . ," he writes, "[that] the adjectives unconditional, undeclinable, [and] absolute take on meaning."[28] He contends there would be no normative orientation in a world without it. Levinas follows Kant in thinking that the very possibility of normativity depends on the existence of an unconditional moral authority. But Levinas puts responsibility where Kant—and the liberal tradition more generally—would put freedom: to be a moral agent is to be responsible. For Levinas, it is the other, not pure practical reason, that is the unconditional authority. The other's needs, not my freedom, constitute the fundamental normative fact that orients ethics. Likewise, moral requirements derive from the commands of the other, not from rational principles constitutive of free will.

Levinas's analysis of responsibility for the other is notoriously difficult to understand. Roughly speaking, my responsibility for the other is the fact that I am literally responsible for everything that happens to the other, responsible in the sense that I am answerable to the other for everything that happens to her. Being responsible for others is also about attending to the needs of the other without deliberating about what we "owe" to her. As a result, our responsibilities for others cannot be determined by, or limited by, the responsibilities others bear for us. Moral duties are not cut from the cloth of reciprocity. This may seem outrageous, but Levinas's argument, which I will not be able to defend here, is that only by conceiving of responsibility in this way does it make sense to posit the existence of unconditionally binding moral duties. In his view, theories that privilege freedom put conditions on our duties to others that make a mockery of the notion of unconditional obligation.

To see how justice serves the aims of ethics so construed, we need to consider a problem that arises in virtue of the fact that there is more than one other in the world: the self is responsible for all others. Implicit in this responsibility for everyone is a deep normative tension, namely, every other's claim is *equally* valid. In rushing to someone's assistance, I turn my back on another who makes an equally valid claim on me. And what if I tried not to turn my back on anyone? I would be paralyzed, overcome by the impossibility of taking any specific course of action. I would be like Buridan's ass, which, confronted with equally attractive bales of hay, starves to death for want of an ability to decide between them.

Since our responsibility compels us to act, we must do something, but to do anything we must have some criteria for determining which responsibilities to act on. For Levinas, these criteria are provided by the fundamental principles of morality and by the basic principles of legal and political justice. So justice is *ethically* necessary because the requisite criteria for action are provided by principles of justice, or more specifically, by the catalogue of rights and duties generated by principles of justice. Furthermore, equality demands that I apply these criteria as impersonally as possible, so as not to favor those familiar to me. This necessity generates a need for *institutions* to make authoritative decisions in this arena. More specifically, institutions are needed to make impersonal judgments regarding the content of our more or less indeterminate rights (e.g., the right to life) and also to make decisions when our rights claims come into conflict (your right to life versus my right to self-defense). We also need institutions to determine procedures for the acquisition of rights (acquiring property, making contracts, passing laws, etc.). Finally, we need institutions to *enforce* our rights and duties, and to impose sanctions when they are violated. (Although Levinas says virtually nothing about punishment, I think this last point indicates how he would justify the practice of punishment. On his view, punishment is legitimate insofar as it serves justice by enforcing compliance with our duties.[29]) These needs make it ethically necessary to institute legal institutions. As Levinas puts it, "Institutions are necessary to carry out decisions. . . . Justice and the just State constitute the forum enabling the existence of charity within the human multiplicity."[30] In our society, legal institutions just are the institutions in question. So while Levinas and liberal theorists agree on the necessity of legal institutions and, at a general level, would explain that necessity in similar ways, for Levinas the *purpose* of law is not primarily to protect our rights—though it must do that as well—but to equitably distribute responsibilities. Put differently, for Levinas law is a response not to the threat of Hobbesian violence or free-riding but to overwhelming responsibility.[31]

As a consequence of these considerations, legal justice must be understood as essentially comparative. The necessity of equal treatment flows from the purpose of law, which provides normative direction to every aspect of legal practice. Since the purpose of law is to equitably distribute responsibilities, each branch of the legal system is normatively governed by the principle of equality. In other words, equality is an *essential* feature of legal justice. And since legal justice is comparative all the way down, penal justice, as a type of legal justice, must also be comparative.

To better understand the novelty of Levinas's approach, it will help to draw a contrast with more traditional explanations of equality. Take, for example, a family of theories of equality that I will call "liberal" theories of equality. We can trace the importance of equal treatment in these theories to their conception of the purpose of law and their justification of legal coercion. On a liberal view (again, painting with a very broad brush), a legal institution is justified in exerting power over citizens insofar as it protects and enhances their freedom or autonomy. Here equal treatment is important because citizens have equal moral standing qua autonomous beings or rational agents, and equal treatment respects our equal standing. But this explanation of the importance of equality licenses the use of noncomparative practical judgments and establishes the permissibility of unequally applied punishments. If deliberations about who is to be punished and how much they are to be punished are guided (and constrained) by the value of autonomy, our decisions will privilege noncomparative justice, for the simple reason that autonomous beings can be said to *deserve* punishment. They deserve to be punished because they have chosen to break the law and to commit wrongful acts. Since respecting people's autonomy involves treating them as autonomous beings, respecting autonomy involves holding them morally and legally accountable for their wrongdoing, *regardless* of how others are treated.[32] Furthermore, nothing in the concept of autonomy precludes punishing members of an overpunished group for their wrongdoing; autonomy is violated only if there is no good reason for the punishment. So insofar as fundamental norms of liberal justice are shaped by the value of autonomy, legal justice is not comparative all the way down, and noncomparative justice is not excluded from the ambit of penal justice.

We can now more clearly see what makes Levinasian justice distinctive and what enables it to repel the noncomparativist challenge. On Levinas's account, the justification of legal coercion, and the corresponding justification of punishment, is developed on the basis of a conception of the purpose of law that excludes a noncomparative conception of legal justice. The values central to this conception generate side constraints on the means states may use to control crime. Most importantly for our purposes, they prohibit unequal punishment. While liberal values also place side constraints on punishment, like the prohibition against dehumanizing punishments, the principle "no punishment without a crime," and so on, liberal values do not generate the prohibition in question.

It is important to note that establishing the priority of comparative justice does not mean that the Levinasian account must forgo the concept of desert altogether. Desert can still function as a necessary condition of legitimate punishment: we can still say that the state may punish only those who *deserve* to be punished. This makes room for the traditional requirement to assess a wrongdoer's state of mind and ensure that he is culpable for his actions. Furthermore, as I discuss later on, desert can still play a role in sentencing determinations. Desert, in its connection with blameworthiness, can help us determine how much to punish a lawbreaker by helping us pick out which crimes are the most severe and merit the most severe punishment. What desert *cannot* do is function as a sufficient condition of legitimate punishment.

Demonstrating the injustice of unequally applied punishment is an important step to reform, but it leaves a critical question unanswered. How should we remedy the injustices we find? As I mentioned earlier, the United States disproportionately punishes African American drug offenders; the ratio of drug convictions to drug offenses is higher for African Americans than it is for whites. Justice requires us to remedy this situation and pursue equality. But equality could be pursued in one of three ways. We could punish more white drug offenders, we could punish fewer African American drug offenders, or we could decriminalize drug possession and distribution. Of the first two options, the second is more attractive, at least if we accept the validity of the moral principle "first do no harm." Since unequal punishment is illegitimate, the state actively harms the African American drug offenders it punishes. The state does not harm those it fails to punish. The "do no harm" principle would therefore direct sentencing authorities to reduce convictions of African Americans.

As for the final option, a good case can be made for decriminalizing possession and distribution of recreational drugs on both consequentialist and retributivist grounds. But to make this case, we need the sort of substantive moral argument that cannot be found in Levinas, and so Levinas will not help us settle this issue. (Obviously decriminalization would be a much more controversial way of solving the problem of unequal punishment of violent crimes such as first-degree murder.)

Unfortunately, things are not so simple with respect to crimes that involve severe moral wrongdoing. Imagine a world in which minority group M is overpunished for the crime of kidnapping. Would we want to refrain from punishing kidnappers who belong to group M? I am not sure that in this instance the "first do no harm" principle would carry the day; it may be preferable to focus efforts on ratcheting up punishment of nonminority offenders.[33] But for the purposes of this chapter, we need not settle this question.

Levinasian Desert

In this part of the chapter, I want to consider the consequences of Levinas's conception of justice for our understanding of what wrongdoers deserve, or what they are due. It is a commonplace of retributivist theories of punishment that a lawbreaker's punishment ought to be proportionate to the moral gravity of her offense. On the standard account, the moral gravity of an offense is a function of two variables: the culpability of the offender and the severity of her offence. Culpability refers to someone's responsibility for their act. For someone to be culpable at all, they must be reasonably mature and of sound mind. Once this threshold is passed, culpability admits of degrees. Someone who intentionally harms someone else is more blameworthy than someone who foreseeably but unintentionally harms his victim. The severity of an offense is typically based on the amount of harm caused by the wrongful act. To take an easy example, premeditated murder is one of the gravest offenses, because it intentionally causes an immense amount of harm. But in many cases, determining the precise amount of moral blameworthiness attached to an act of wrongdoing is a difficult task.

Legal institutions use various shortcuts to simplify assessments of desert. Culpability (*mens rea*) is differentiated into intentional, knowing, reckless, and negligent wrongdoing. (*Mens rea* need not be demonstrated for strict liability offenses.) The severity of the criminal act (*actus reus*), along with the elements of the act, are statutorily defined. While the Eighth Amendment gives sentencing bodies fairly wide latitude in determining punishment, most jurisdictions try to honor the principle that a lawbreaker's punishment should fit her crime. The basic idea of fittingness, or proportionality, is that crimes and punishments are ranked in severity (where severity includes the severity of the underlying offense, culpability, and sometimes criminal history), and punishments are attached to the crimes to which they are equal in severity. For example, if we ranked punishments and crimes on a scale of 1 to 10, a crime of severity 8 would merit punishment of severity 8.[34] Legal institutions that punish a crime of 8 with a punishment of 8 punish properly, and those that punish the same crime with a more or less severe punishment punish improperly. Since first-degree murder intentionally causes grievous harm, proportionality tells us that first-degree murderers will deserve some of our most severe punishments.[35] (For the purposes of this discussion, I want to focus on crimes that are *mala in se* rather than *mala prohibita*, i.e., wrong in themselves rather than wrong by legal fiat, as the latter involve complications that distract from the task at hand.[36]) In the United States, these considerations are distilled into federal and state sentencing guidelines.

On a *Levinasian* theory of desert or blameworthiness, we must add one more variable, which I will call "capacity," to the calculus. For the purposes of this chapter, capacity can be thought of as material resources and social capital, though this characterization is not exhaustive. In Levinas's view, or so I will argue, when we assess someone's blameworthiness for a particular wrongdoing, we must take into account her social and economic status. This addition captures the idea, presented earlier, that some crimes are more blameworthy when committed by a well-off offender than a disadvantaged one.

The scaffolding of this conception of blameworthiness begins with Levinas's claim that the other's need functions as a sufficient condition of my duty to meet that need. While the fact that I live in a world surrounded by many needy others absolves me from the requirements of the singular ethical relation (i.e., my "infinite responsibility"), the other's need does not cease to impose obligations. Now, if we convert this point about need into a determinate moral principle, it would look something like Peter Singer's famous claim that the better-off must donate their wealth until they reach the point of marginal utility. And this principle might seem so demanding as to be implausible. But I do not think that Levinas is arguing for such a specific principle, though I cannot defend this interpretation here. (If there is a general principle to be extracted, it is that those of us who are decently provisioned are blameworthy for not sacrificing *any* of our comfort.) Rather, Levinas wants to show that a common moral intuition—I ought to assist someone in need, because they are in need—gets morality exactly right. If we privilege this intuition, as Levinas suggests we do, moral deliberation will *start* from the fact that other people's needs make a prima facie claim on us and only then ask whether there are reasons for believing that these needs fail to generate conclusive duties. Need is a sufficient condition of moral obligation, and so these needs impose duties, unless there are excusing conditions. By contrast, the standard mode of deliberation places the burden on the person with needs, demanding an argument showing that we really ought to give her what she needs.

To be sure, in Levinas's view considerations of justice *do* allow me to weigh my needs against the other's. This means that if I am in a situation of equal need, our needs cancel each other out, and I might not be obliged to renounce my right to the resources I possess. But these excusing conditions are limited; my only excuse is my own need. Since the well-off have no such needs, they possess no justification for failing to attend to the needs of others. For the well-off, the duty to assist others is almost always conclusive.

To my mind, the view just described is implied by the theory of responsibility developed in *Otherwise than Being*, though it is not made explicit. Levinas does, however, endorse something like the position I am attributing to him in one of his Talmudic readings, where he writes: "The problem of a hungry world can be resolved only if the food of the owners and those who are provided for ceases to appear to them as inalienable property, but is recognized as a gift they have received for which thanks must be given and to which others have a right. Scarcity is a social and moral problem and not exclusively an economic one. . . . A community must follow the individuals who take the initiative of renouncing their rights so that the hungry can eat."[37] There are a number of points to be noted here. First, this passage clearly expresses the idea that a good society must privilege the needs of the seriously disadvantaged over the rights of the advantaged. This indicates that a good society is an *egalitarian* one: social policies governing distributions of resources will favor the less well-off. Moving from the political to the moral themes of the passage, we see that it is the "owners" and "those who are provided for" who are first and foremost responsible for the feeding of the hungry and that the claims for assistance made in the name of those with less capacity primarily target those with abundant capacity. This responsibility is incurred simply by means of being able to ameliorate the suffering. It has nothing to do with whether one has done anything to *cause* the suffering; as Levinas puts it, "To leave men without food is a fault that no circumstance attenuates; the distinction between voluntary and involuntary does not apply here."[38] Finally, desert does not lessen or attenuate these responsibilities. Those who are well-provided for do not deserve what they have, even if they have worked hard for it. Instead, they must recognize that their possessions are a "gift," presumably in the Rawlsian sense that the fundamental conditions of individual flourishing are distributed according to luck rather than desert.

But these points apply more broadly. Levinas is not simply talking about our responsibility to give food to those who are starving; he is talking about responsibility for the others' needs as such. So the well-off are more responsible than the disadvantaged for not meeting any of the needs of others: as Spider-Man's Uncle Ben intones, "With great power comes great responsibility."[39] And a well-off person is, *ceteris paribus*, more blameworthy than a disadvantaged person for not meeting the needs of others. The conclusion to draw from this is that for some types of actions and omissions, *blameworthiness is a function of capacity*. For our purposes, the act and omission types in question all have to do with the distribution of resources. Although I will not make this preliminary typology any more definite, one clarification is in order. The act and omission types in question do *not* include violent crimes. Nothing in Levinas suggests that the disadvantaged have fewer responsibilities with regard to respecting the other's physical and emotional integrity.

To see what difference Levinas's account makes, consider a competing theory of morality. For Kant, autonomy is the basic moral value. All moral duties are, in this sense, derived from the requirement that we respect the autonomy of ourselves and others. This theory of morality does *not* place higher demands on the well-off, because everyone, advantaged and disadvantaged alike, is equally capable of respecting themselves and others. (Kantian morality does require us to advance the happiness of others, but this is an indirect duty, and an easy one to discharge.[40]) So for Kant, blameworthiness is a function of culpability and harm, where harm is conceptualized in terms of infringements on autonomy.

But for Levinas, blameworthiness is not merely a function of culpability and harm; it is also a function of capacity. So when we deliberate about how we ought to treat others, we must take note of our capacities. And when we make moral assessments of other people, we must take their capacities into consideration, along with the harm done and their level of culpability.

There are two practical consequences of this view that need to be distinguished. First, the inclusion of capacity means that some act or omission types typically thought to be morally blameless will be considered blameworthy. It lengthens the list of moral offences. As I have already suggested, the inclusion of capacity would ground the claim that the wealthy are to be blamed for not helping those in need. Second, this inclusion modifies *existing* calculations of blameworthiness; it makes certain previously defined wrongful acts more blameworthy when committed by someone who is well-off.

The first consequence involves a special complication for a theory of punishment. Even if the well-off are *morally* blameworthy for not helping those in need, it is still an open question whether they should be *legally* blameworthy for failing to do so. And it is an open question whether any of the moral offenses on the newly lengthened list should be criminalized. So anyone who wants to defend the criminalization of such conduct would need to offer a separate argument defending their view. States do not criminalize all immoral conduct, nor do any philosophers of punishment or legal theorists think that criminalizing every moral offence is anywhere near a good idea. Furthermore, identifying the immoral conduct to be criminalized is an extremely difficult philosophical task. On the one hand, criminalizing immorality often curtails liberty; the more a state criminalizes immorality, the less freedom its citizens maintain to pursue their own conceptions of the good. On the other hand, morality is, in many cases, a matter of serious disagreement. And the dominant "positive morality" of a society is often deeply unjust and immoral.

I feel the force of these difficulties, but I will set them aside. This is partly because I am not sure how to address them. But mainly it is because the second consequence mentioned earlier is sufficient to support the argument I want to make, and it does not introduce such problems. Legal institutions can give effect to the Levinasian modification of blameworthiness by means of legal practices already in existence. In many jurisdictions, a sentencing body is allowed to consider aggravating and mitigating factors. If aggravating factors are demonstrated at trial, a sentencing body can impose a more severe punishment on the defendant; common aggravating factors include prior felony convictions, use of a deadly weapon, and excessive cruelty. The point of statutory aggravators is to enable criminal law to achieve proportionality in the following kind of case: offender is guilty of committing a criminal act A, which is an instance of criminal act-type T; the blameworthiness of T is codified in the jurisdiction's sentencing scheme, but A is clearly more blameworthy than T. To make the punishment better fit the crime associated with A, statutory aggravators direct the sentencing body to impose a more severe punishment than is usually imposed for T.[41] (Mitigating factors are used in the opposite way.) Employing this model, the law could incorporate aggravators that capture variations in defendants' capacities. While there are some difficulties in specifying the type and level of capacity that would constitute the aggravator, they would be no more difficult to overcome than the ones inherent in identifying "especially cruel or heinous" circumstances, to take an infamous example.

To see how this works, consider a pair of malefactors. One, a wealthy CEO, cheats on his taxes. The other, an Army veteran living in a homeless shelter, steals some DVDs from Kmart. Let's stipulate that the harm involved in both cases is the same, and that both men were of sound mind. On the standard way of calculating desert and blameworthiness, both offenders would be equally morally blameworthy. But if we use the Levinasian way of calculating blameworthiness, we will include consideration of capacity, and the CEO turns out to be more blameworthy. As a result, there exist good reasons to sentence the CEO more severely than the veteran, and we need not worry that the intuitions motivating the present argument are products of *ressentiment*, or that they lack philosophical support.[42]

The conclusions reached previously might surprise those who possess prior acquaintance with Levinas. Levinas is often considered to be *the* proponent of ethical asymmetry, the champion of a relentless responsibility that singles us out and submits us to duty on top of duty, leaving no room for excuses. And while my analysis does not *excuse* the least well-off, it does show that they are less blameworthy for their wrongdoing. But I do not think that this result is in tension with Levinas's fundamental philosophical commitments. It is true that Levinas argues that the normativity, or binding force, of morality derives from the asymmetrical relationship of the one-for-the-other. However, as I have argued here, if we pay attention to Levinas's theory of justice, we find that his radical theory of responsibility grounds a liberal concern for equality as a legal and political principle. I have also shown why this admittedly cumbersome Levinasian baggage should appeal to those interested in punishment reform. The normative reach of the traditional liberal principle of equality, insofar as it is grounded in freedom and autonomy, does not extend so far as to properly regulate the institution of punishment. Only on Levinas's account is equality in punishment necessary.

Prisons and Palliative Politics

Ami Harbin

This chapter examines a common occurrence in North America: prisoners dying of illness in prison. With prison populations in the United States and Canada growing, and with rising numbers of older prisoners, prisons have needed to consider how to address the needs of those facing terminal illness and death in prison. In recent years, the number of prisons that have instituted formal hospice care has grown substantially, in many cases with prisoners providing end-of-life care to their peers. These hospice programs have garnered substantial attention, in documentaries,[1] photographic collections,[2] and in many writings from prisoners, activists, and bioethicists.[3] In this chapter, I aim to critically reflect on prison hospice programs by considering the relational experiences of those facing death in prison (both incarcerated people who are dying and those volunteering to care for them) and argue that the programs are significant and needed for reasons other than those articulated in previously discussed accounts.[4] Hospice programs make life and death in prison more livable.

Hospice care in prisons is needed and important for many reasons, including the following three that I focus on here: (1) it helps ensure material needs are met for prisoners who are very ill and at the end of their life;

(2) it allows for needed relationships among people living and working in prisons; and (3) it helps recognize the significance and importance of prisoners' lives, against the background of systems that otherwise make prisoners' illnesses and deaths seem insignificant. While prisons purport to treat inmates equally and enforce rules evenly, meeting the "basic needs" of all prisoners, what needs should be considered basic is, of course, contentious. Beyond food, shelter, and some degree of medical attention, depriving prisoners of relationships with others both inside and outside of prison and clearly communicating the insignificance of prisoners' lives and deaths are and should be seen as failures to meet prisoners' basic needs. As I will argue, responding to the moral question of what kind of end-of-life care should be provided to people dying in prison requires resisting reductions of "basic needs" to the bare minimum needed for temporary physical survival, understanding the broader context of who is most likely to live and die in prison, and focusing on what value their health and lives are seen to have.

In arguing for the significance of prison hospice programs, I aim to contribute to two distinct lines of conversation. In bioethics, those who have addressed prison hospice programs (surveyed in the next section) have not yet discussed the second and third aforementioned consequences of prison hospice (i.e., that it allows for needed relationships and helps recognize the significance and importance of prisoners' lives), which I take to be central functions of end-of-life care in prison. At the same time, in mainstream representations of prison hospice programs, critical awareness of prison demographics and harms is troublingly absent, so that accounts of the importance of hospice programs have a tendency to be reduced to simplistic narratives of how prisoners are given opportunities to redeem themselves in end-of-life contexts. My goal is to intervene in both of these contexts by providing a richer account of the significance of hospice programs in harm reduction.

Angela Davis describes life in prison (and outside of prison for those with records of incarceration) as a kind of "civil death":

> When we consider the disproportionate number of people of color among those who are arrested and imprisoned, and the ideological role that imprisonment plays in our lives, I want to suggest that the prison population in this country provides visible evidence of who is not allowed to participate in this democracy, that is to say, who does not have the same rights, who does not enjoy the same liberties, who cannot reach the same level of education and access, who cannot be a part of the body politic, and who is therefore subject to a form

of civil death . . . Prisons catch the chaos that is intensified by de-industrialization. People are left without livable futures.[5]

In addition to failing to provide survivable physical conditions particularly for the ill, old, or dying, prisons deprive prisoners of contact and relationships with other people and persistently communicate to prisoners that their lives and deaths are insignificant and unrecognized. In this sense, I will argue, prisons harm prisoners by making their lives and deaths *unlivable*. Building on Davis's understanding of "livable futures," I draw on Judith Butler's account of livability, where in order for a person's life to be livable, the person must be recognized in relationships with others as significant and worthy. The question I think must be examined most closely here is: *what can make life and death in prison livable?* My claim is that the relationships developed in prison hospice programs go some way—imperfectly but perceptibly—toward resisting this civil death for prisoners and toward making life and death in prison more livable for those prisoners dying, those grieving, and those who know they will be in prison when they die.[6]

I do not mean to suggest that addressing these aspects of prison life would be sufficient for addressing all the harms that exist so long as a prison system exists. For some prison theorists and activists, prison reforms can be seen as unimportant or even counterproductive, for the way they make slight improvements to a devastating prison system rather than focusing on a more thorough reworking of criminal justice frameworks. Hospice programs are by no means a perfect or final solution to the needs of ill, old, and dying prisoners. They are easily co-opted by prison administrations as evidence of their generosity or the efficacy of prison rehabilitation programs, while, in fact, prisons can profit from the cost-saving measures of prisoners working as unpaid hospice volunteers. Even so, I argue that hospice programs are and will be needed so long as there are people dying in prison, and they are needed for more reasons than those writing about them have so far articulated.

In order to argue this, I draw on the insights of a feminist and relational bioethics. Feminist bioethicists are acutely aware of how systems of oppression constrain marginalized groups' possibilities for health and well-being (especially for women, non-cisgendered groups, queers, racialized groups, lower-class groups, elderly, groups with disabilities, and others), and they think at the group level about oppression's harms.[7] Given that prisons are currently populated mostly by members of the most vulnerable social groups (especially on levels of class, race, and ethnicity), and that group-based oppression can be exacerbated by prison, the health and well-being of those in prison is and should be of concern to feminist bio-ethicists. Some health care practices and systems are especially harmful for oppressed groups; other health care practices reduce harm for members of oppressed groups; and still other practices work to more broadly trans-form oppressive institutions and systems. In all kinds of institutions (in-cluding prisons), feminist bioethicists should ask how marginalized groups are harmed, could be less harmed, and could be better supported in health and well-being. Feminist bioethicists bring an awareness of how dynam-ics of power and disempowerment can play out through health care sys-tems and interaction within those systems. Relational bioethics employs a relational lens to understand how all individuals are constituted by their relationships, only have autonomy in a relational sense, and can be harmed in part by constraints on their relationships. Here, I bring feminist and relational bioethics together to properly situate hospice care in prisons as an example of health care practice that works to reduce harm for members of oppressed groups.

In the next section, I will briefly characterize the circumstances of those dying from illness in prison: the particular vulnerabilities of imprisoned populations, what distinguishes deaths from "natural/unnatural causes" in prisons, the overall "graying" of prison populations, and the introduction of formal hospice care in prisons in the United States and Canada. I bring together first-person accounts and other research on the experiences of aging, being ill, and dying in prison, with and without formal hospice care, and the experiences of those working in hospice, caring for other prisoners at end of life. In the third section, I consider these accounts, emphasizing Butler's analysis of livability, asking the question: what makes life, death, and grief in prison livable? I conclude by arguing that adequately consider-ing the complexity of prison hospice programs requires attending not just to how, where, and with whom prisoners are dying but also to who is most likely to be imprisoned, how their relationships are likely to be constrained, and how their lives and deaths are most likely to be perceived (both inside and outside prisons). Formal and informal hospice programs are important not only for the way prisoners provide basic care to each other within them but for the way they also allow for recognizing and mourning those who die in prison, as significant, remembered, and grievable.

Natural Causes: Illness and Incarceration

Journalists have recently reported on multiple factors contributing to a rise in the number of prisoners dying in prison. In February 2012 Sadhbh

Walshe reported in *The Guardian* that "according to bureau of justice statistics, around 4,000 inmates died in prison and jails (both public and private) in 2009; and over half of those deaths were illness-related. A comprehensive nationwide survey on the health and healthcare of US prisoners carried out by Harvard Medical School researchers found that over 40% of US inmates were suffering from a chronic medical condition, a far higher rate than other Americans of similar age. Of these sick inmates, over 20% in state prisons, 68% in jails, and 13.9% in federal prisons had not seen a doctor or nurse since incarceration."[8]

Ill people get imprisoned and imprisoned people get ill.[9] Like people on the outside, prisoners have and can develop health conditions that require preventive care, acute care, long-term care, and eventually end-of-life care. Imprisoned populations can be more susceptible than others to particular illnesses and health conditions, in part because prison work environments, housing conditions, nutritional standards, and access to consistent, quality health care can make some illnesses more readily contracted, developed, undertreated, and hard to recover from. Where drug use and sex practices are not openly addressed, and where there is no access to material protections, rates of HIV/AIDS and other contractible diseases can be high. So some illnesses can be made increasingly available by prison environments. Furthermore, the same populations that are overrepresented in prisons (e.g., African Americans, Latino/as, First Nations people, queers, transgender people, and people living in poverty) can be more likely to lack access to adequate preventive and acute health care, food and water, security, holistic health care, housing, and social supports. So there can be a correlation between people likely to be in prison and people likely to be ill.[10]

At the same time, as people in prison are especially vulnerable to some chronic conditions, the number of aging prisoners is also rising in the United States (i.e., the prison population is said to be "graying"), as is the number of people serving life sentences who die within prisons.[11] As Linder and colleagues summarize the state of prisons concerned about the health of ill and aging prisoners who are increasingly facing sentences that mean they will die in prison: "The number of inmate deaths per year, the percentage of deaths from natural causes excluding acquired immune deficiency syndrome (AIDS), and the average prisoner age on entry into prison all show long-term increases. . . . The health concerns of older adults, including coping with chronic, degenerative, or terminal illnesses, are also a source of growing concern for departments of corrections and public safety nationwide."[12] In sum, prison administrators have on their hands a large number of people in need of care for chronic and terminal illnesses, and they are required to meet some standards of humane health care while at the same time controlling costs.

Those in prison are at the mercy of their institutions for medical care. In some cases, inmates will be treated within prison hospitals or infirmaries, either at their current institution or by being transported to another centralized prison hospital facility. In other cases, patients can be sent to outside hospitals for testing and treatments not available on-site. If an inmate receives attention and a diagnosis of a terminal illness, end-of-life care options may then be available. In some cases, medical parole/compassionate release is an option, but it is not widely granted, and in the few cases where it is, it is often delayed until the very final days of life.[13] Prisoners for whom medical parole is not granted will die in prison. For many long-term or permanently incarcerated people with terminal illnesses, death in prison is inevitable.

In some institutions, no formal hospice care is provided. In 1998 a *Special Issues in Corrections* report stated that twelve of fifty-three correctional jurisdictions (forty-seven state departments of corrections, plus select other jurisdictions including Correctional Service Canada) had formal hospice programs in operation in one or more sites, and eight more had programs in development. The number of prisons with formal hospice care available has grown substantially since 1998, but it is still not universally available. Those prison administrations that are in favor of supporting organized hospice care for inmates face the question of how to establish such programs at minimum cost, without compromising the mandates to ensure public security and punitive measures. Bioethicists have noted that in some ways, hospice care in prison is similar to hospice care on the outside: "Hospice for inmates is comprised of the same core services as hospice in the free community: an interdisciplinary team with physician-supervised care, routine nursing and social work intervention, spiritual and bereavement care, volunteers and allied professionals. The focus is on patient comfort and the relief of suffering. To qualify, patients must have a life-limiting condition and a prognosis of 6 months or less to live."[14]

The bioethical questions involved in how to organize hospice care in prison include those regarding palliative care on the outside: what medical professionals are best suited to different tasks, how can physical spaces be made most comfortable for patients, how can pain relief be ensured, how can the family and individual be prepared for processes of dying, and how can patients, family members, and medical professionals be supported in grieving? In other ways, however, as Linder et al. summarize, prison hospice programs face a number of unique considerations: among others, how or whether to integrate hospice with general medicine patients, how to work with restrictions on opioids and other medications, how to deal with patients who are admitted into hospice and later released with improved prognoses, and how hospice will affect or intersect with compassionate release programs where they exist.[15] Patients in prison hospice care who are judged competent are in some cases given options for advance directives, to opt for "do not resuscitate" (DNR) orders or to refuse or withdraw nutrition, hydration, and ventilation at advanced stages of terminal illness. Even where this is possible, however, not all patients in prison hospice feel able to trust that prisons and hospice staff will respect their wishes at end of life or have their best interests in mind.[16] The role of family in end-of-life decision making for people in prison is also complicated by imprisonment. Families, partners, children, and friends of prisoners are often not informed or informed too late about the situations of their loved ones, sometimes geographically far from the prisons where they are being kept, and in almost all cases not able to have the relationships with their loved ones they otherwise would at end of life. As Linder and Meyers explain: "'Family' may also mean other inmates. This adds a layer of complexity to an ill inmate's decision to self-identify as having special health needs. Institutional policies may neither recognize nor support inclusion of other inmates as 'family.'"[17]

Experiences of facing death in prison can include long-term illness; partial, infrequent, or insufficient medical care; isolation; and boredom. James Ridgeway's 2012 article "The Other Death Sentence" reports extensively on the experiences of men aging and living with illness in prisons without formal hospice care: "In recent months, I have been corresponding with several older men in Massachusetts state prisons, and have visited one of them in person. . . . Their letters tell of lives filled with daily indignities—trying to heave an aging body into the top bunk, struggling to move fast enough to get a food tray filled or get a book at the library, fighting off younger troublemakers. But worst of all is the pervasive nothingness and isolation."[18] Ridgeway reports that struggling with mobility or other health issues means prisoners often cannot access available opportunities for socializing: "The activities available—which are few, since lawmakers wiped out most rehabilitative programming during the 1980s and 1990s—are accessible only to inmates who can walk long prison hallways or climb stairs. For some old-timers, a cell is their entire world; doing time simply means awaiting death."[19]

Where able, prisoners have in many cases developed informal end-of-life care for one another. Such was the case for eighty-two-year-old Massachusetts prisoner William "Lefty" Gilday, who suffered from Parkinson's disease and other conditions. A number of other prisoners formed what Ridgeway describes as an "ad hoc hospice team," bringing Gilday food, helping him to the toilet, and taking him outside.[20] Ridgeway reports that no hospice programs are available in Massachusetts prisons.[21] At Iowa State Penitentiary in Fort Madison, hospice volunteer Bertrum Berkett explains the situation before hospice care was introduced on-site:

> I'll just speak on what I do know and that's the "real effect" the hospice unit named "Sail to Serenity" by its convict volunteers has had on both the young and old. . . . Until 2005, convicts would simply die in the cell or the infirmary in a cold lonely room, hurting physically and mentally from the pains of the disease [that] ravaged their bodies, minds and souls. They would see a nurse when and if she had the time. But after she shut the door, they'd return to their lonely world of thoughts, doubts, despair and uncertainties. Most would die alone; with only the sounds of nature to give whatever comfort or compassion one can receive from such an unfair fate.[22]

Suffering at end of life can be exacerbated for those living with HIV in prison.[23] Benjamin Fleury-Steiner's research focuses in particular on forty-three HIV-positive individuals who died in a segregated HIV-positive unit at Limestone Prison in Harvest, Alabama, between 1999 and 2003.[24] Fleury-Steiner quotes Tamara Serwer, a lawyer working to bring attention to the lack of treatment for HIV-positive prisoners at Fulton County Jail in Georgia: "A good number of guys—I mean we saw so many deaths in that early part of the lawsuit—were actually cared for by each other, changing their sheets or helping one of the terminal guys. I mean, the nurses didn't want to touch them."[25]

Beyond the fact that basic care for prisoners at end of life is already scarce, and adding to that the phobic responses of prison staff around prisoners with HIV, this comment points also to the constraints on relationship (i.e., prisons are places where staff are not encouraged to see themselves as in relationship with, or as having responsibilities to, those living in prison) and the failure to recognize the significance of the life and health of those in prison.

Much of the attention to formal prison hospice programs focuses on not only the experiences of those dying but on how in order to staff hospices, prisons rely on the unpaid labor of prisoners who volunteer to provide end-of-life care to their peers.[26] Prisoners who would like to volunteer in hospice programs are often required to submit applications, pass rigorous screening processes for abuse in criminal records and their time in prison, be interviewed and questioned about their intentions, and be evaluated by prison medical and hospice staff, competing for a limited number of unpaid positions. Those who succeed are then trained by prison and medical staff, and sometimes by veteran hospice volunteers. The documentary *Serving Life* (2011) observes the workings of hospice at Louisiana State Penitentiary, known as Angola.[27] *Serving Life* profiles the two-week training period of a number of hospice volunteers. Hospice volunteers are taught to always wear gloves and how to change sheets, dress bedsores, and move patients for their comfort. In very large prisons like Angola, hospice workers and patients are sometimes meeting one another for the first time in hospice. Angola does not disclose to the hospice volunteers what crimes the men they care for have been convicted of committing. Berkett describes the first patient of hospice care at Fort Madison, Herbie Schnee, also one of the original hospice workers:

> We cared for Herbie. We were with him 24 hours a day and for the first time in Iowa State Penitentiary history a convict died, pain free, with convict volunteers all around him, holding his hands, praying and caring for his last earthly needs. . . . After his death, we cleaned the body and prepared him to be picked up by the funeral home, we even washed every drop of ink from his fingers after he was fingerprinted for the final time. We also placed his body on the gurney and zipped up the body bag. . . . Now we have 2 hospice rooms up and ready, we also have 6 ADL [Attention for Daily Living] rooms ready to care for convicts who cannot care for themselves and who are not terminal but need daily assistance to maintain a positive manner of living.[28]

Volunteers hold the hands of men who are very near death, cut their hair, shave their necks, or hang out in their rooms, talking or playing cards. When a patient seems to be very near death, the hospice volunteers are called in to provide twenty-four-hour vigil in four-hour shifts, so no one will die alone.[29]

Caskets and Quilts: Conditions of Prison Life

From the perspective of harm reduction, it seems clear that it is better for a prison to have a hospice program than not to have any form of hospice or end-of-life care. The existence of any degree of more comfortable rooms and beds, access to pain relief, and the aim of providing volunteers to sit with and talk with people as they are dying is better than for incarcerated people to die in cells in pain and alone. At the same time, hospice programs in prisons must be understood as motivated by the need to deal with the huge number of aging and dying prisoners, in ways that will be cost-effective within often overpopulated buildings and facilities, while meeting standards of mandatory health care for incarcerated people. Fleury-Steiner writes of Limestone, "Indeed, it is a clear demonstration of cost cutting in the extreme that despite the obvious awesome responsibilities and specialized training that hospice work entails, such work had become transformed inside the HCU into 'just another opportunity to volunteer.'"[30] Prisoners are marginalized in Iris Marion Young's sense of marginalization as "systematic exclusion from meaningful participation in social life."[31] Hospice programs do not prevent more people from entering or facing long sentences in prison. These programs are still largely under the control and subject to the decisions of prison administrations, with prisoners being allowed to play only some roles as unpaid workers in such programs, even in cases where prisoners were the ones lobbying for hospice care in the first place. Given all this, the nonideal circumstance of hospice care in prisons must be carefully considered, especially when it is done so by academics like me, without direct experience with such programs. Theorists need to be taking the lead from those who live in prisons, or who have more direct connections to prison life, if we are to account for realities that might otherwise go overlooked—like the highly variable experiences and commitments of guards and other paid prison workers, or the long-standing informal work of prisoners that may be eclipsed by a focus on the good will and originality of prisons now committed to the development of formal hospice.

Importantly, the administrative decisions within prisons can have serious and sometimes unintended consequences for everyday life. For example, the way prison hospices allocate time and space can facilitate relationships that prisons otherwise work to constrain. As has already been noted, some of the punitive tactics of prisons involve the restriction of relationships: those in prison are prevented from having regular contact with loved ones, friends, communities, and co-workers on the outside, and other potential relationships are never allowed to begin (e.g., with teachers one might have encountered if one had continued in school or college, with children one might have raised). Beyond this, relationships on the inside are also constrained: prisoners are allowed to develop limited relationships with prison staff and professionals who occasionally work in prisons (e.g., professors, chaplains, medical professionals) but only within certain parameters and always with the knowledge that they may end without notice (e.g., if a prisoner is transferred or suddenly placed in a higher-security unit). And relationships among inmates are severely constrained, often from stated concerns about safety and security, where what counts as a safety or security concern is decided by prison staff and management rather than by those living in prisons.

Yet against this background, unpaid hospice workers and patients in hospice have recently become expected to develop, and in fact are tasked with building, particular relationships, and those relationships are recognized as legitimate by prison administrators within specific constraints. This means that some people in prison are allowed to access hospice wards and spend time with one another in ways they otherwise would not be. In the broader context of relationships between prisoners being severely constrained and seen as inherent threats by high security prisons, and with multiple levels of solitary confinement widely employed, any facilitation of relationships among prisoners is an exception.[32] At the same time, kinship among prisoners can still go unrecognized and prisoners can be denied the right to officially identify one another as partners or family. As Berkett notes, "They say that you are not family, but when you spend 24 hours a day, seven days a week with each other, you become more than family."[33]

Judith Butler has in numerous accounts defended a vision of "livability," where livability means more than mere survivability. For a situation to be livable in Butler's sense, it must be a context where an individual can survive, maintain a sense of one's own value, and be recognized by oneself and others as a person with dignity. Communities made vulnerable by the realities of joblessness, shifts in production, and dwindling access to material resources are left without options for livable futures, which increases the likelihood that they will face futures in prison. Although Butler's focus is not limited to people in prison or currently vulnerable to incarceration, she makes a related point about livability in *Undoing Gender*: "What makes for a livable world is no idle question. . . . It becomes a question for ethics, I think, not only when we ask the personal question, what makes my own life bearable, but when we ask, from a position of power, and from the point of view of distributive justice, what makes, or ought to make, the lives of others bearable? Somewhere in the answer we find ourselves committed to a certain view of what life is, and what it should be, but also of what constitutes the human."[34]

What does it mean to make dying and grieving livable in prison? What is it to be granted a livable death? Part of what hospices in prisons do is give prisoners the promise that, for as long as current administration and funding holds, hospice care will be available for themselves, their friends, and their loved ones in prison when they die. Although a tenuous promise, it seems better to have that than to know that prison administrations lack the will to develop hospice or that they are actively resisting prisoners' campaigns for such hospice care, as Ridgeway reports has been the case with the Massachusetts Department of Corrections.[35] Historically at Angola, prisoners were buried in cardboard boxes. Now, prisoners have been allowed to build wooden caskets and hospice volunteers prepare bodies for burial. In *Serving Life*, volunteer Steven Garner is shown sewing memorial quilts, sometimes to give to people who are dying, sometimes to drape over their caskets during memorial services. One is inscribed "No More Chains Holding Me." Patient Kevin Hollingsworth arrives in hospice awaiting a biopsy before he receives his official diagnosis of cancer and is given two weeks to two months to live. As he is dying, Hollingsworth is able to request that Garner, his one-time dorm mate, be there with him. Garner is shown sewing a quilt to be presented to Kevin, saying: "I can't wait to get this done so I can rest." The livability of dying and grieving depends partly on material things that make possible respecting, dignifying, acknowledging, and remembering those who are dying and those who have died.

For dying and grieving to be livable in prison means that individuals need space to experience and share death and grief in relationships with others. Recognition of the life of someone means recognizing details of who they were. In *Serving Life*, volunteer Shaheed says of one patient: "I used to play softball with him. He was a good third baseman." Recognizing the life of someone also means taking their own accounts of their lives seriously. The recognition by others of the significance and importance of one's own life is part of what makes it possible for individuals to die with some form of comfort. Of course, as we have seen, public and relational recognition of the death of friends and kin in prison—in other words, the making of time and space to acknowledge and grieve the lives of other prisoners—existed long before formal hospice care and has not depended on prison support. Ridgeway reports of Lefty Gilday, whose friends had provided informal end-of-life care for him: "When Lefty died last September, his friends were denied permission to hold a memorial service in the prison chapel, so they ended up holding it in a classroom. The service culminated in some 80 men sailing paper planes into the air as a tribute. 'We loved the old man,' Joe Labriola wrote me in a letter."[36] In grieving Gilday, his friends recognize that this is not just another death of a prisoner, that Lefty had a place in the world, in the lives of those around him, and has left relations in grief. In other words, they recognize that the person who died had been alive, even as he had survived the "civil death" of imprisonment.

Theorists and activists who consider the position of hospice programs within broader criticisms of prison systems as a whole emphasize the need for strategies other than improved hospice care for prisoners. Some recommend more use of existing medical parole/"compassionate release" programs in the case of terminally ill or elderly prisoners, sentence diversion for ill or elderly prisoners, and in some cases specifically *no prison hospices*.[37] I would push back on particularly the last of these recommendations: in cases where prison hospice exists, we can see significant ways in which life inside is made more livable, through the relationships that can come to exist among prisoners and prison workers in palliative care. Prison hospice care, wherever it happens (with or without institutional support) can be most significant for the relationships it facilitates among people currently in prison.

In *Serving Life*, we see volunteer Boston Rodgers being briefed on end-of-life decisions made available to prisoners, including the possibility of DNR orders and the ending of life-sustaining measures. At first, Rodgers says he would want all possible supports to extend his life. Later, after some time working in hospice, he says he has changed his mind; he would not want extreme measures taken. He does not talk more about his reflections or how he has come to think differently, so it cannot be surmised what he was thinking. But the case raises one issue about what might make death in prison more livable: the sense that the reality and significance of one's life will not end when one cannot live anymore; the sense that it is not only up to me to insist my life gets recognized. Knowing that others will remember and memorialize one's life can make one's life and death more livable. Practices of memorializing others' lives can make grieving them and preparing to die ourselves more livable. Members of marginalized groups outside of prison might experience a sense of their own social insignificance so persistently in social worlds—a feeling they get from school, health care, economic, or other systems that their particular lives, and the lives of others like them, does not matter, is not a priority, and would not be missed—that they internalize a sense of their fungibility, insignificance, and unimportance. Prison environments can exacerbate this diminished sense of one's own significance. For some in prison, a felt sense of one's own irrelevance may manifest as depression, nihilism, withdrawal, violence, or suicide. Others may respond to this sense of irrelevance with an explicit struggle to stay alive and fight for recognition as having lived a significant life. Against backgrounds of racism and classism that actively portray some individuals as expendable, the struggle to stay alive may even become imperative or burdensome. Hospice workers have the potential to challenge an individual's felt sense of expendability if the person dying comes to know that they have not died without recognition of their particularity, which makes it possible to go through the dying process with some willingness to allow oneself to die, and to allow others to care for you, which makes it possible to have some relief from the fight to stay alive, to not die, to be recognized as alive. Insofar as the existence of hospice in prison makes these relationships more possible, they can make death and grief in prison more livable. Butler describes the power of grief when she writes: "I am not sure I know when mourning is successful, or when one has fully mourned another human being. . . . It may seem that one is undergoing something temporary, but it could be that in this experience something about who we are is revealed, something that delineates the ties we have to others, that shows us that those ties constitute a self, compose who we are, and that when we lose them, we lose our composure in some fundamental sense."[38]

The insistence of prisoners to recognize the death of others in prison by lobbying for hospice provisions, caring for them informally and formally, and holding memorials for them is partly expressive of what Butler describes: a recognition that those who died were crucial parts of our lives and of the social world, were and are important parts of who we are, and are grievable—even as many would try to exclude and forget them.

Life Expectancies: From Palliative Ethics to Palliative Politics

The moment where hospice care in prisons gets attention in mainstream press is a relatively rare moment for prisoners' lives to show up to those of us not in prison, those who do not have direct connections to prison, or those who would deny that they are in any form of relationship with prisoners. What representations of prison hospices communicate will be constrained by both deliberate and unintentional misreadings, and by prisoners having limited or nonexistent opportunities for revising and critiquing what nonprisoners quote, print, or exhibit about them. As such, we on the outside should be extremely cautious about interpreting representations of prison hospice. As Warden Burl Cain does in *Serving Life*, one might emphasize individualistic accounts of the benefits of hospice—showcasing individual prisoners who receive good care in hospice, individual hospice volunteers as having transformational or redemptive experiences, or individual prison workers/wardens who have the good will to treat prisoners more humanely. It is imperative that individualistic stories of redemption and generosity be understood critically and brought into conversation with realities of how more and more people are imprisoned, facing very long sentences, making it likely that they will die in prison (in hospice, or out of it). When observing such representations, the questions we should ask are: Who is doing the work of providing basic care to dying prisoners? How are prison hospices addressing harms created by an expanding prison system? How are hospices allowing for needed relationships that are otherwise constrained? How are hospices helping us recognize the significance of individuals whose lives and deaths are otherwise made unimportant?

Individualistic approaches to bioethics that focus on patient autonomy, informed consent, and one-on-one interactions between a physician and patient are not able to fully consider the complex situation of prisoners in need of end-of-life care. Feminist and relational approaches recognize and resituate dying prisoners in their relationships, social groups, and broader systems of power. Prisoners reach end-of-life in prison after, in many cases, facing the likelihood of poorer health and shortened life expectancy throughout their lives. Prison hospice care, as a complex kind of cooperative, community-based health care in a very complicated context, does more than meet the health needs of individual prisoners. Though it is by no means insignificant for each terminally ill prisoner who is fed and assisted with cleaning himself or herself, it is important for the way it responds to the needs of all those facing death in prison to be in relationships and be recognized as relevant by others. It attempts to prefigure a system of meeting individuals' material needs, prioritizing relationships among individuals, and esteeming, remembering, and missing individuals after their lives come to an end—even when those individuals have been convicted of crime.

Expanding critical bioethics from palliative ethics to palliative politics, in and outside the prison, requires that theorists understand who is most likely to suffer ill health and lack of quality health care, and how their lives might be bettered. As a field that attends to the multiple ways in which suffering can and should be reduced, even if the suffering of facing death always to some extent remains, palliative ethics is fundamentally addressing the nonideal.[39] It requires that bioethicists consider the important questions of end-of-life experiences of patients, loved ones, and health care providers (including those who are unpaid and/or incarcerated) in the broader social context of some people having less access to good health care and palliative options than others and some people's lives being seen as more livable and grievable than others. Beyond the ways hospice can help palliate the pain and suffering that can accompany illness, old age, and death, I have been interested here in the ways hospice programs can go some distance toward palliating the suffering of civil death, in Davis's sense.

Prisoners' work in hospices demonstrates the resistance of those imprisoned to crushing harms and the importance of advocates working to expand possibilities for relationships and expressions of experience as a mode of harm reduction while prisons exist. Politics, Butler says, is concerned with the question of how to create a world where those who fail to fit in normative social structures can live "not only without the threat of violence from the outside, but without the pervasive sense of their own unreality. . . . [T]here is a normative aspiration here, it has to do with the ability to live and breathe and move and would no doubt belong somewhere in what is called a philosophy of freedom. The thought of a possible life is only an indulgence for those who already know themselves to be possible."[40]

Much of the power of those working in hospice programs might consist, in Butler's terms, in challenging the pervasive sense of prisoners' unreality. Palliative ethics for prisons needs to move beyond notions of the rights of the dying to comfort (e.g., palliative sedation) and final wishes (e.g., about where to die) to account for all the dimensions of oppression that harm prisoners up until their death. Attention to ways that health care and other systems might better relieve suffering at the level of oppression, marginalization, and civil death is the task of palliative politics.

Sovereignty, Community, and the Incarceration of Immigrants

Matt S. Whitt

Readers of this volume probably know that the United States incarcerates more people per capita than any other nation on record. Approximately 2.2 million people are confined in U.S. jails and prisons, and another 4.8 million are under correctional supervision in the form of probation or parole.[1] It is perhaps less well known that noncitizens make up the fastest-growing segment of this population.[2] Since the mid-1990s, and especially since 2001, the United States has increasingly used its massive network of jails and prisons to confine noncitizens, many of whom have not been convicted of a criminal violation and never will be. These noncitizen detainees are often targeted by racial and class profiling, and many are effectively denied legal counsel, bail, and visitation as they languish in facilities designed to punish felony offenders. The growing number of noncitizens in this situation is not due to increasing rates of undocumented immigration but to legislation stipulating mandatory detention for suspected immigration violators, newly created categories of violation, increased patrolling, and lengthened detention periods.[3] In other words, noncitizens make up the fastest-growing sector of U.S. jail and prison populations because the

United States increasingly uses its vast carceral apparatus as a means of border control.

This recent "criminalization of immigration" has been denounced by defenders of civil liberties, advocates for immigration reform, anti-incarceration activists, and governmental officials. In this chapter, I lend my voice to this chorus by interrogating the productive functions that the criminalization of immigration plays in the United States. By "productive," I do not mean that I will focus on what is "good" or "worthwhile" about criminalizing immigration. Rather, I mean to identify the activities and capabilities that are produced—enabled and occasioned—by this development. Specifically, I seek to understand what criminalizing immigrants *does for* the state that criminalizes them. This task is intended as a necessary component of transformative criticism.[4]

On its face, the productive function of criminalizing immigration seems straightforward. By treating undocumented immigration as crime, the state builds a case for expanding its coercive apparatus, increasing surveillance, and intensifying its government of individuals and groups.[5] This preliminary analysis is compelling so far as it goes, but it says little about the productive function of criminalizing *immigration* in particular. We must still ask: What ends are served by criminalizing *specifically* immigration and immigrants?

I answer this question by focusing on the state's prerogative to not merely govern a political community but also *constitute* that community by deciding on questions of membership. By criminalizing immigration, the state channels the rhetorical, moral, and legal idiom of criminality in order to (re)shape the political community in ways that it otherwise could not. Specifically, the state employs the punitive force of the prison apparatus to differentiate between the members and nonmembers of the community— "us" and "them." Because this force falls mainly upon noncitizens who cannot access the criminal justice protections reserved for (some) citizens, and because immigration enforcement technically falls within the sphere of civil rather than criminal law, the state can treat its coercive (re)constitution of the political community as a merely administrative affair.

The prerogative to differentiate members from nonmembers, and thereby constitute a political community, is the most fundamental aspect of state sovereignty. This prerogative has long been linked to territorial boundaries, which provide a framework for the insider/outsider dichotomies enforced by sovereign authority. However, in a globalizing era, territorial boundaries cannot consistently play this role, leading some commentators to perceive a "waning" of state sovereignty.[6] I am not convinced. Indeed, the criminalization of immigration represents one way that state sovereignty adapts to globalization by developing new ways to perform the acts of inclusion, exclusion, and differentiation with which it constitutes political communities. By criminalizing immigrants, the United States reconstitutes itself through violently coercive acts in an era when globalization threatens the sovereign prerogative to do just that. Today, the United States defines itself as a community by not only expelling but also *punishing* those it seeks to exclude.

The chapter proceeds as follows. In the first section, I briefly outline the concept of state sovereignty to establish that sovereign authority constitutes political communities by opposing them to whatever and whomever they exclude. In the second section, I examine in detail two main institutions of sovereignty—borders and prisons—to show that they do not merely secure or police political communities but actively constitute them. In the third section, I turn directly to the criminalization of immigration, which I analyze as a convergence of border and prison apparatuses. By punishing undocumented immigration as a crime, I argue, the United States performs acts of inclusion, exclusion, and differentiation that neither borders nor prisons can accomplish alone. In so doing, the state reasserts its sovereign prerogative to not merely govern but also constitute the political community—even as traditional frameworks of sovereignty become obsolete. In the fourth section, I conclude by suggesting that critics of the criminalization of immigration must also challenge the norm of sovereignty itself.

The Enduring Ideal of Sovereignty

Sovereignty is the ideal of political authority claimed by modern states. It is characterized by internal supremacy (the sovereign is the ultimate authority over all actors within its jurisdiction) and external independence (no actor outside a sovereign's jurisdiction may intercede in its authority). This classic and still-dominant ideal of sovereignty implies a firm distinction between the interior and exterior of a sovereign's jurisdiction. For this reason, sovereignty is often theorized as supreme, independent, and *bounded* political authority.[7] The boundaries of sovereignty are the boundaries of the political community over which sovereign authority is exercised.

Unlike other forms of political authority, sovereignty claims to control these boundaries itself. At bottom, the supremacy and independence characteristic of sovereignty are its license to regulate the borders of its own jurisdiction and to decide upon questions of membership. By differentiating insiders from outsiders, members from nonmembers, or citizens from noncitizens, sovereign authority does not simply rule over a particular community. More fundamentally, sovereignty *constitutes* that community.[8] By performing acts of inclusion, exclusion, and differentiation, sovereign authority founds and refounds the political community as a particular, coherent "us" in contradistinction to "them"—the individuals and groups it designates as outsiders.

Sovereignty produces this "us"/"them" dichotomy as a matter of opposition rather than simply difference. The community constituted by sovereign authority is founded *against* its outside; its coherence and particularity are secured by its opposition to whatever it is not. This oppositional logic is illustrated by the charged dichotomies that characterize classic theories of sovereignty: civilization/barbarism, body politic/state of nature, friend/enemy, and *bios politikos*/bare life.[9] In practice, these dichotomies incite and condone violence against the individuals and groups—such as indigenous populations—that sovereign authority designates as the community's "others."

Although sovereignty has been the dominant norm of the modern state system, much has been made about its purported eclipse in an era of globalization.[10] Because sovereignty has long been linked to the territorial boundaries of the modern state, globalization's reterritorialization of political life would appear to threaten the future of sovereign authority. However, this view presumes that sovereignty is essentially territorial. Elsewhere, I have argued that it is not; territoriality is a prevalent strategy used to achieve and exercise sovereign authority, but it is not a necessary element of sovereignty.[11] Once sovereignty is analytically distinguished from territoriality, we can see that globalization does not necessarily and directly undermine sovereign authority.

In fact, once sovereignty is correctly understood as the supreme and independent authority to constitute a political community through oppositional acts of inclusion, exclusion, and differentiation, we can acknowledge that sovereignty is alive and well, but changing, in the contemporary moment. As traditional configurations of territory, authority, and community change, sovereignty persists by adopting new, potentially nonterritorial ways to constitute political communities. As I will argue, the criminalization of immigration represents one of these new ways. In the United States at least, sovereignty thrives in an era of globalization by turning one of the state's most violent tools—the prison apparatus—toward the task of civic (re)constitution. In order to make this argument, I now examine the ways that borders and prisons individually serve sovereign authority, before examining their convergence in the criminalization of immigration.

Borders and Prisons as Institutions of Sovereignty

At first glance, it would seem that borders and prisons perform different functions upon different populations: borders look outward from the community to regulate the flow of nonmembers, while prisons look inward to enforce laws governing members. This "Janus-faced" dichotomy is characteristic of classic accounts of state sovereignty, which typically presume a clearly established distinction between inside and outside.[12] However, I will complicate this perspective by showing that the operations of borders and prisons do not map onto any such simple dichotomy. Rather than conforming to a presupposed difference between inside and outside, these institutions actually *create* such differences by designating individuals as members, nonmembers, and partial or submembers. In so doing, borders and prisons actively constitute the community, defining the sphere of members *against* individuals deemed "unfit" for full membership. This is their function as institutions of sovereignty.

BORDERS

If we assume that national borders are meant to secure a community by separating it from outsiders, then we must admit that borders routinely fail at their intended purpose. Even where they feature fences, walls, and guards, borders do not fully separate one community from another, keep out unauthorized entrants, or consistently distinguish between foreign and domestic spheres. This is because borders are spaces of convergence as well as separation, and they incite movement and contact rather than simply prohibiting them. But if they do not effectively separate and secure political communities, then, what do they do? As a primary vehicle of sovereignty, the border apparatus (meaning borders themselves, together with the policies, institutions, and people that enforce them) actively constitutes and reconstitutes the political community. It does so in at least four ways.

First, national borders constitute a political community by inciting and channeling movement in ways that differentiate members from nonmembers. Official checkpoints force authorized crossers to travel through designated corridors, regardless of their destination. Unauthorized crossers must also route their travel through particular channels, in this case unregulated zones where they are more likely to cross without proper documentation. These zones are themselves mobile, as patrolling in urban areas shifts unauthorized crossings to mountains, deserts, and rivers.[13] Not confined to territorial boundaries between states, the border apparatus also channels movement *within* and *beyond* the community. This is most visible in the practice of deportation, which has increased more than threefold since the mid-1990s.[14] Deportees are often apprehended far within the interior of the United States, transferred to detention centers, and then expelled far beyond the boundaries of the political community to receiving areas inside other states. This suggests that instead of obstructing movement or keeping individuals "on their own side," the border apparatus creates circuits of transfer and dislocation that *re*mobilize certain individuals, pushing them through channels that extend deeply within, and far beyond, the community's territorial limits.[15] The border apparatus mobilizes members and nonmembers differently and uses this difference to structure the limits and interior of the political community.

Second, the border apparatus actively shapes the political community by filtering potential entrants according to particular criteria. Historically, U.S. immigration policy has expressed explicit preference for immigrants of particular races, classes, and ethnicities. This filtering continues today, although usually it is informal and implicit. Visa regulations favor Europeans, men, and professionals; border patrols and traffic stops disproportionately target Latino/as and working-class immigrants; and procedures for identifying deportable persons at airports focus on male noncitizens from Muslim and Arab countries.[16] Through such preferential and discriminatory treatment, the border apparatus filters entrants according to the community's vision of itself, its needs, and its desires.[17] By selecting potential members according to this vision, the border apparatus does not merely secure or separate the political community; it actively (re)constitutes the community according to its collective values.

Third, the border apparatus disciplines migrants into behaviors, dispositions, and modes of social participation that are deemed "appropriate" for noncitizens.[18] This happens explicitly when border agents question potential crossers and when naturalization procedures train would-be citizens into the knowledge and norms required by the state. However, the border apparatus also disciplines undocumented entrants. In his excellent analysis of the Mexico–U.S. border, Nevzat Soguk argues that border enforcement does not eliminate undocumented entry to the United States so much as it forces undocumented entrants to acclimate to the vulnerability, frustration, clandestinity, and lack of official recognition that characterize unsanctioned crossing. In this way, the very experience of entering the United States without authorization prepares successful entrants for an economy that demands hard work, ingenuity, and personal sacrifice in exchange for little reward, recognition, or protection.[19] Recent attempts at border hardening, together with economic uncertainty, have only intensified this disciplinary function so that more is demanded of undocumented entrants while even less is implicitly promised. Rather than effectively separating the community from its outsiders, reinforced borders more harshly select and prepare different outsiders for different roles within the community, thereby directly shaping the community's internal constitution.

Fourth, precisely because it does not separate the political community from "unwanted" and "unfit" persons and populations, the border apparatus creates and regulates subordinate statuses within the community. Most dramatically, legally sanctioned visitors are distinguished from undocumented noncitizens—so-called "illegal aliens"—who are designated a precarious position and subordinate status within the community. As Mai M. Ngai writes, "Marginalized by their position in the lower strata of the workforce and even more so by their exclusion from the polity, illegal aliens might be understood as a caste, unambiguously situated *outside* the boundaries of formal membership and social legitimacy," even while they reside *within* the geographic limits of the community.[20] This caste of internal outsiders is not simply tolerated by the border apparatus but actively *created* by it. The porosity of the border enables undocumented entry while immigration policy deems it illegal, thereby turning undocumented crossers into aliens and criminalizing not only the act of crossing but also the status of alien itself.[21] In many cases, this status corresponds to the constant threat of deportation, exploitable employment, and lack of access to important public goods. The border apparatus thus functions as a machine for producing so-called "criminal aliens" and assigning them to precarious or subordinate roles within the community. In this way, the border apparatus further refines the heterogeneous and hierarchical constitution of the community.

Taken together, these four functions reveal that national borders do not simply separate the political community from "outsiders" or regulate the entry of nonmembers. More fundamentally, the border apparatus performs acts of differentiation that create the very distinction between inside and outside and constitute the community in opposition to what it excludes—even if what is excluded remains within the territorial limits of the community. This constitution-through-opposition is the hallmark of sovereign authority.

PRISONS

Like national borders, prisons are key sites where sovereign authority constitutes political communities through acts of inclusion, exclusion, and differentiation. Here, too, a vast apparatus (including not only prisons but also other institutions of the criminal justice system) is arrayed to differentiate a civic "us" from a purportedly uncivil or semicivil "them"—those persons deemed "unfit" for society.[22] However, whereas the border apparatus typically differentiates citizens from *non*citizens, the prison apparatus usually creates distinctions within the community of citizens itself. [23] In this way, the prison apparatus creates a caste of "internal outsiders" and, in contradistinction to this caste, constitutes the community of purportedly full and free citizens.

　This constitutive function may be obscured by a prevalent way of viewing the U.S. incarceration system. Since the abandonment of rehabilitation aims in the 1970s, U.S. crime-control policy has focused on incarceration itself—lockup, plain and simple—to house purportedly dangerous populations and manage risk. As David Garland puts it, "The prison is used today as a kind of reservation, a quarantine zone in which purportedly dangerous individuals are segregated in the name of public safety."[24] This accurately summarizes contemporary penal strategy, but that strategy itself presupposes an objective and evident distinction between "dangerous individuals" and the "public." In fact, the prison apparatus *creates* this distinction by designating some individuals as criminals, former criminals, or latent criminals and subjecting them to punitive confinement, intensified governance, and preventative surveillance.[25] At the same time, the apparatus designates other individuals as noncriminals, presuming them to be innocent and allowing them to retain typical access to rights, benefits, and social participation.[26] Importantly, those who are most criminalized are not necessarily dangerous, while perpetrators of some dangerous crimes— such as domestic abuse, sexual assault, and police brutality—make up a disproportionately small segment of the criminalized population. The quarantine metaphor only goes so far, then, because there are not two distinct populations that can be simply segregated from each other. Rather, the populations are produced by the prison apparatus itself, which constitutes the community through a series of oppositions mirroring those performed by the border apparatus.

First, like the border apparatus, the carceral apparatus incites move-ment. Prisons do not only immobilize individuals, locking them in "quar-antine zones" segregated from the rest of society.[27] Rather, prisons also *re*mobilize individuals by compelling them to move *through* society in ways that continually displace them from homes, families, employers, and social networks. This movement often crosses state boundaries—especially in the federal system, where prisoners can be "extradited" from state to state. Moreover, as economically stagnant counties compete for prison con-struction, the carceral apparatus is extended farther away from the dense population areas that many prisoners call home. The result is a widespread displacement of urban (largely African American and Latino/a) offenders to detention facilities situated in rural (largely white) areas.[28] This forced migration is reversed when ex-offenders return to their home cities and towns. High recidivism rates mean that the circuit of movement is often repeated, as more than 40 percent of former inmates are rearrested and moved back to jail or prison.[29]

One does not have to be incarcerated to have his or her movement re-mapped by the prison apparatus. Outside of prisons and jails, criminal-ized individuals are prohibited from travelling to particular locations, in-cluding former homes—especially those in social housing projects—and other areas specified by restraining orders, parole restrictions, and court jurisdictions. At the same time, they may be required to travel to specific locations for drug testing, parole meetings, and counseling. In these ways, the carceral apparatus moves convicted offenders through society rather than out of it. As it does, it dislocates criminalized individuals from their former lives, places, and networks while pushing them through circuits of surveillance, confinement, and discipline that differentiate them from other community members.

Second, the prison apparatus differentiates criminalized individuals by filtering their access to the rights, public benefits, and modes of political participation that other members enjoy. Individuals targeted by the appa-ratus—and especially those confined in prison—are routinely denied free movement, association, employment, and education, as well as enjoyment of property and other bases of autonomy and social recognition. Beyond prison, a felony record legitimates employment and housing discrimina-tion, and it often bars ex-offenders from welfare benefits, food stamps, and public housing assistance.[30] Additionally, almost all states in the United States prohibit felony offenders from voting while they are incarcerated, and in most states, probation and parole also disqualify ex-offenders from voting and jury duty. In some cases, felony disenfranchisement is permanent.[31] Such restrictions "send the unequivocal message that 'they' are no longer part of 'us,'" by denying offenders and ex-offenders the basic modes of social recognition and political agency that give a person "standing" in the political community.[32]

Third, the prison apparatus disciplines individuals into particular behaviors, dispositions, and roles within the community. Through arrests, courtroom proceedings, sentencing, incarceration, release hearings, parole, and probation, the behavior of offenders and ex-offenders is declared deviant and in need of normalization.[33] Formally and informally, the voice of authority echoes throughout the prison apparatus, telling individuals where to go, how to comport themselves, what to wear, what to read and not read, whom to associate with and whom to avoid, what to strive for, how to live, and what to believe.[34] Aside from explicit imperatives and prohibitions, more subtle disciplining is effected by prison work and literacy programs, which orient inmates toward the low-wage and low-skill roles that the community expects them to fill. Even when released, this disciplining can be especially pronounced when the restrictions of parole and probation clash with the license afforded to other members of the community.[35] This disciplining is not inexorable, but it reinscribes the regimes of surveillance, vulnerability, economic insecurity, and lack of support that, for many prisoners, characterize life prior to, during, and after incarceration. Through this disciplinary function, the prison apparatus differentiates its targets from other members of the community, thereby internally (re)structuring that community.

Fourth, and most importantly, the prison apparatus stratifies the political community by subordinating some individuals to the role of subcitizen. By criminalizing some persons and groups and presuming others innocent, the prison apparatus creates and assigns statuses such as deviant, felon, exoffender, parolee, and recidivist. These statuses deeply shape the modes of social interaction and participation available to the persons assigned them. Felony status has the most obvious impact; as Michelle Alexander writes, "Once a person is labeled a felon, he or she is ushered into a parallel universe in which discrimination, stigma, and exclusion are perfectly legal, and privileges of citizenship . . . are off-limits."[36] However, the prison apparatus also interpolates its targets in other ways, for instance by profiling certain individuals—such as African American residents of public housing projects—as *likely* offenders or *latent* criminals who require "proactive" policing.[37] Similarly, incarcerated prisoners may be designated as especially high risk, a status used to justify solitary confinement and other degrading, depersonalizing forms of treatment.[38] By creating and assigning these statuses inside and outside prison walls, the prison apparatus acts as "a unique mechanism of state-sponsored stratification" that divides the political community into hierarchies of membership, security, and agency.[39] Within these hierarchies, criminalized individuals are reduced to subcitizenship, or what is sometimes called "social death," insofar as they formally remain members of the community, but are substantively stripped of citizenship benefits and social recognition.[40]

In sum, the prison apparatus does not merely segregate "dangerous individuals" from the "public." Rather, it criminalizes some individuals and differentiates them from other members of society by dislocating them, filtering their access to the bases of social recognition and political agency, disciplining them, and relegating them to subcitizenship. In so doing, the prison apparatus actively creates the populations that it is said to merely separate.

This means that the prison apparatus constitutes the *entire* political community. By creating a caste of internal outsiders and opposing that caste to the rest of society, the prison apparatus also reshapes, recomposes, and resignifies the population of full citizens who are *not* criminalized and are presumed innocent. As with national borders, the carceral institutions that designate some individuals as second-class members also implicitly designate others as first-class members. Thus, the carceral apparatus helps create and confirm the hegemonic social position against which subcitizenship is defined. In an era when approximately 6.9 million individuals are locked up, on parole, or on probation, to be a full citizen of the United States is, in part, to *not be* reduced to subcitizenship by its hypertrophied penal system. By criminalizing some individuals and apparently passing over others, the prison apparatus actually interpellates us all, building sovereignty's opposition of "us versus them" into the core of the community it constitutes.

Crucially, the prison apparatus constitutes the political community as a *particular kind* of community, namely a white supremacist and classist one. In the United States, the prison apparatus disproportionately criminalizes lower-class people of color, designating them as the community's internal outsiders. This dynamic is especially manifest with regard to offenses— such as drug use and drug dealing—that are most often committed by whites but for which people of color are most often imprisoned.[41] Overall, African American males are six times more likely to be incarcerated than white males, and African American females are two and a half times more likely to be incarcerated than white females.[42] As Michelle Alexander notes, "The United States imprisons a larger percentage of its black population than South Africa did at the height of apartheid."[43] Sociologist Loïc Wacquant confirms the racial targeting of mass incarceration but also emphasizes class and place, arguing that "the expansion and intensification of the activities of the police, courts, and prison . . . has lead to the *hyper*incarceration of one particular category, *lower-class African American men trapped in the crumbling ghetto*."[44] The prison apparatus overwhelmingly positions people of color, and especially lower-class African American men, as the internal outsiders in opposition to whom sovereign authority constitutes the community of full and purportedly free citizens.[45]

Activists and scholars have argued that racialized mass incarceration continues the work of infamous institutions of racial and class-based social control, including slavery, the convict lease system, and Jim Crow laws.[46] Echoing their arguments, I want to emphasize that these historical institutions were not merely mechanisms for establishing and preserving race and class dominance; they were also mechanisms of social and political constitution. They *created* and recreated, rather than simply defended, a political community structured by intersecting white supremacist and classist hierarchies. Today, mass incarceration continues this creative project.[47] Through acts of coercive and disruptive differentiation, the U.S. prison apparatus actively constitutes a political community structured by racial and class opposition, even as the community proclaims those oppositions obsolete.

Constitution through Crime

In the previous section, I analyzed borders and prisons as institutions of sovereignty—that is, as institutions through which state authority constitutes the political community in opposition to those whom it designates as nonmembers, partial members, or submembers. In this section, I turn to the convergence of these institutions in the criminalization of immigration. To adequately understand this convergence, I argue, we need to view the criminalization of immigration as a mode of constitution rather than a mode of securing or governing a community. By treating undocumented immigration *as if* it were a crime, the United States frees itself to employ its hypertrophied carceral apparatus as tool for coercively (re)constructing the *demos*—the "We the people"—of American democracy. In an era where globalization challenges the boundaries and coherence of political communities everywhere, the United States' choice to criminalize immigration represents an adaptation—but also the persistence—of sovereignty's prerogative to constitute the community over which it rules.

In the United States, the current wave of criminalizing immigrants can be traced back to the mid-1980s. Although immigration violations are classified and prosecuted as civil law rather than criminal law, three decades of legislation have vastly expanded the use of surveillance and detention to not only remove undocumented migrants but also *punish* them in ways typically reserved for suspected criminal law violators. Most notably, the Illegal Immigration Reform and Immigrant Responsibility Act of 1996 (IIRIRA) authorized detention for undocumented border crossers and residents whose visas have expired.[48] Moreover, IIRIRA created new categories of aggravated felonies, minor offenses that would not usually result in jail time for citizens but require mandatory detention, without bail, for noncitizen suspects.[49] At the same time, a steady stream of legislation has eroded the public benefits available to noncitizens, regardless of whether they have been convicted of a crime, mirroring laws that filter out felony offenders.[50] Finally, legislatures in Arizona, Alabama, and other states have recently attempted to make undocumented immigration itself into a criminal law offense, along with certain forms of aiding and doing business with undocumented residents. This legislation has not been fully successful, but it nonetheless demonstrates a self-consciously punitive turn in U.S. attitudes and policy concerning undocumented migration. Today, "lawmakers see immigrants as criminals and criminals as subcitizens."[51] By treating undocumented immigration as a threat to the social compact, the law seemingly justifies the use of punishments previously reserved for criminal offenders.

Importantly, U.S. immigration law has incorporated the idioms, techniques, and procedures of criminal law in only a "*selective, asymmetrical*" way, by adopting models of *enforcement*, but not models of *adjudication*, from the criminal justice system.[52] As a result, "the nominally civil immigration system has increasingly assumed the punitive features of the criminal law system, but without the procedural protections that generally apply in criminal proceedings."[53] Suspected immigration violators are now punished like criminal law violators, but they are denied rights that are (supposed to be) afforded to citizen violators of criminal law, and they are barred from avenues of contest that are built into the criminal justice system.

These developments have significantly increased the number of noncitizens kept behind bars as they await trial or deportation. U.S. Immigration and Customs Enforcement (ICE) houses many detainees in its own detention centers, which mirror the prisons used to house felony offenders: "There is considerable resemblance between the policies governing prisons and immigration detention regimes. . . . According to its adopted standards—and despite the fact that detention facilities do not hold prisoners serving criminal sentences—ICE conceived and currently operates its detention centers along the model of the criminal prison."[54] However, ICE apprehends far more undocumented individuals than it can detain in its own facilities, so it subcontracts with county jails and state prisons to house the overflow. These facilities are administered by a variety of public and private actors, and ICE retains little control over the treatment of noncitizen detainees. Once inserted into prisons and jails, noncitizens are "subject to the same kinds of punitive detention as criminal defendants," even though they have not been convicted of a criminal offense.[55] In a few respects, their detention can be extra harsh, because immigrant detainees cannot avail themselves of the protections afforded by the criminal justice system.[56] Moreover, the mixed use of specialized detention centers, jails, and prisons requires ICE to frequently transfer noncitizens between facilities, disrupting contact with families, support networks, and legal counsel.[57] In short, thanks to the recent development of punitive immigration policies, new categories of immigration offense, and mandatory detention laws, suspected immigration violators are now penalized in many of the same ways, and often by the same people and in the same facilities, as suspected criminal violators.

What are we to make of this convergence of border and prison apparatuses? One possible response is to decry immigrant detention as "unjustifiably punitive" given the "noncriminal" status of those detained for immigration violations.[58] But this response uncritically accepts "criminal" and "noncriminal" as opposed statuses that individuals incur through their own actions. Thus, it fails to recognize that the prison apparatus actively produces and assigns criminal and noncriminal statuses to members of different populations at different times, based on different criteria. The United States has long overcriminalized lower-class African American males for acts that other segments of the population perform just as often, if not more.[59] Now it is criminalizing undocumented noncitizens in much the same way. It is a mistake to appeal to their noncriminal status, then, because precisely what is at issue is the *creation* and *deployment* of that status by the state.

To better understand the criminalization of immigration, we should ask what it *does for* the United States. What productive function does it perform? One compelling but limited answer argues that the criminalization of immigration enables the state to expand its power in an era when such expansion is challenged domestically by cries for smaller government and internationally by the forces of globalization. By targeting noncitizens with convergent border and prison apparatuses, the state intensifies its ability to monitor, discipline, and govern *all* members of the political community, even as it extends these operations beyond the community's limits. Because the state treats undocumented immigration as a crime, it can legitimate its increased power in the name of preserving order.[60]

This analysis presents the criminalization of immigration as an instance of what Jonathan Simon calls "governing through crime."[61] According to Simon's broadly Foucaultian analysis, crime itself, the fear of crime, and the punishment of crime all comprise the main occasions or contexts through which the U.S. government now exercises power over the political community and its individual members. Studies by Teresa Miller, Mary Bosworth, and Jennifer Chacón extend this idea to immigration control, arguing that the state now relies upon punitive techniques to more intensely govern not only citizens but also noncitizens who might otherwise be outside the reach of state authority.[62]

This governing-through-crime analysis is valuable because it acknowledges the criminalization of immigration as productive, in the sense that it *produces* new opportunities and contexts with which the state performs and expands its activities. However, the analysis does not clarify what the criminalization of *specifically immigrants* does for the state. By criminalizing any group (citizen activists, for example), the state might expand its power to govern while using the idiom of law and order to justify that expansion. But the criminalization of undocumented immigrants in particular allows the state to do something more.

Extending the work of the previous sections, I propose that by criminalizing immigrants and immigration, the state augments its sovereign authority to not merely govern but also *constitute* the political community it governs. Through the convergence of crime and immigration-control techniques, the state asserts and attempts to legitimate its authority to compose, preserve, and alter the community qua community by sorting individuals into members, nonmembers, and partial or submembers. Whereas the governing-through-crime analysis suggests that there are two distinct and preexisting populations that may be the objects of government (citizens and noncitizen immigrants), in reality the state creates those two populations, opposing them to each other and thereby defining the community of citizens. This is not merely government through crime but *constitution through crime*.

By augmenting one of its weaker functions—policing the boundaries of the political community—with one of its most hypertrophied functions—

incarcerating members of that community—the state can perform acts of civic inclusion, exclusion, and differentiation with increased force, reach, visibility, and violence. At the same time, the idiom of crime control works to legitimate this violence. By treating undocumented immigrants as criminals (i.e. violators of the social compact), the state implicitly justifies the use of punitive coercion for the purpose of constituting the political community. In this way, the United States defines who it is, as a community of purportedly law-abiding and free citizens, by criminalizing and seizing the freedom of those it defines itself against.

It matters that the targets of this coercion are undocumented immigrants, because their status enables the state to adopt the techniques of criminal law enforcement without also adopting the criminal law protections that are ostensibly guaranteed to citizens. The state is less burdened by the Constitution when it targets noncitizens with its coercive apparatuses.[63] At the same time, because immigration enforcement still technically falls within civil law, rather than criminal law, the punitive incarceration of noncitizens is treated by the state as a merely administrative matter. In short, by criminalizing specifically immigrants and immigration, the state frees itself to intensify the acts with which sovereign authority constitutes the political community in opposition to those it deems "unfit" for membership.

This perversely moralistic mode of boundary drawing resignifies the statuses of member and nonmember in order to reproduce the United States' traditional self-conception as an exceptional political association.[64] First, by criminalizing undocumented immigration, the United States resignifies political membership as a highly covetable status that nonmembers risk incarceration to merely approximate. In opposition to criminalized immigrants who "forfeit" freedom for a chance to participate in the community, the community is constituted as a unique and choice-worthy space of civic freedom.[65] Second, membership is resignified as a moral status, insofar as the criminalization of immigration casts undocumented immigrants as moral compromisers who pursue membership, or its approximation, through punishable—and therefore morally "wrong"—means. This reflects back on full citizens who are presented merely by contrast as having attained their status by the "right" means, implying their moral superiority vis-a-vis "criminal aliens"—even when many have "earned" their citizenship merely by being born in a particular time and place. Thus, the community is constituted as a morally virtuous association in opposition to morally suspicious outsiders.[66] Finally, membership is also resignified as the necessary condition for social stability, recognition, and belonging.

The convergence of the border and prison apparatuses renders the lives of undocumented immigrants precarious, because the state constantly threatens to apprehend them, shuffle them through a series of carceral facilities, seize their assets, sever their means of support, and essentially "disappear" them from their families and communities. Because even documented immigrants can be reduced to undocumented status, full citizenship is signified as the only plausible guarantee against this precariousness.[67] Thus, the community itself is constituted as a space of security and stability in which citizens' access to public and private goods appears consistent, at least when compared to the precarious fates of noncitizen residents.

Put bluntly, in a time of wounded national pride, internal political division, moral blunder on the world stage, and emigrating wealth, criminalizing undocumented immigrants allows the United States to constitute itself as a political community in accordance with the image of exceptional virtue and prosperity that it has always imagined for itself. To be a full member of this community is to be a free and equal citizen—that is, to not be subject to the coercion, subordination, and precariousness that the border and prison apparatuses individually and jointly inflict on those they designate as noncitizens and subcitizens. In short, what criminalized immigration *does* for the United States is sharpen the oppositions through which sovereign authority constitutes the community while working to legitimate that constitution through the idioms of criminality and order.

This development has obvious significance in a historical moment when the traditional markers of sovereignty are becoming less and less relevant. In recent years, it has become commonplace—although not uncontroversial—to declare sovereignty's traditional dividing lines of territory and nation obsolete in the face of contemporary globalization. This apparent obsolescence is sometimes taken as a sign that state sovereignty itself is "waning."[68]

The analysis here suggests otherwise. Through the criminalization of immigration, the government of the United States asserts its claim to specifically sovereign authority—the authority not to merely rule a community but to compose, define, and sustain or alter it by deciding upon questions of membership. Rather than relying on coherent and relatively static boundaries of territory or nation, sovereign authority criminalizes certain individuals, assigns them subcitizen or noncitizen status, and constitutes the political community of U.S. citizens *against them*. Thus, the state's violently punitive techniques become the everyday means by which the community defines itself. The civic "we" of the United States—the community of members deemed "fitting" for full citizenship—is constituted through criminalization, confinement, and coercion. *We* define who we are by locking *them* up.

Rethinking Community, Challenging Sovereignty

The phrase "We the People of the United States" does not name a settled collective identity. Rather, the phrase is a mode of self-interpellation, and the community to which it refers changes with the moment of utterance. As the community changes, so, too, do the mechanisms by which sovereign authority constitutes it. I have argued that the criminalization of immigration should be understood as one of these mechanisms—one specially adapted for contemporary conditions. If correct, this analysis raises a number of rich and urgent philosophical questions.

First, there are pressing philosophical issues concerning the use of coercive violence to police the boundaries of community.[69] In an excellent essay on incarceration and race, economist Glenn C. Loury identifies these issues as moments where descriptive social science must give way to normative theory. He writes, "Deciding how citizens of varied social rank within a common polity ought to relate to one another is a more fundamental consideration than deciding which crime-control policy is most efficient. The question of relationship, of solidarity, *of who belongs to the body politic and who deserves exclusion*—these are philosophical concerns of the highest order."[70] Loury is correct that philosophical work is needed here. However, he misses the higher-stakes philosophical questions, because he does not acknowledge the ways that exclusion actively constitutes the body politic. At issue is not simply the matter of who belongs to the body politic and who deserves exclusion but the very character and identity of a polity that defines itself through coercive and violent exclusion. What sort of community constitutes itself not merely by excluding nonmembers but also by *punishing* them? What kinds of social relations are produced or foreclosed by making punitive violence central to the constitution of the community? In short, *who are we*, if the "we" of political community—the demos of U.S. democracy—defines itself by locking "them" in prison?

Second, there are deep philosophical questions concerning the freedom enjoyed by even the full citizens of a community constituted by denying freedom to others. Democracy is idealized as the form of political association in which members relate to one another as free and equal citizens; the association makes political freedom and equality possible. But what happens when the community "of the free" defines itself as such by violating the freedom of nonmembers and partial members? In this case, the freedom of full citizens is conditioned—simultaneously made possible but also limited—by the unfreedom of others. Does this not also undermine or contaminate even their freedom? I do not see how the freedom of some can flourish when it is purchased with the unfreedom of others.

Undoubtedly, prison is a mechanism of violent coercion. It strips individuals of their freedom, severs families and communities, exploits bodies for commercial gain, and imposes upon individuals terrifyingly concrete versions of the very tyranny that canonical liberal philosophy rails against in the abstract. If the prison apparatus has any legitimate role to play in contemporary U.S. society, it is not as a tool for constituting the democratic body politic. However, in order to challenge the present situation, it is not enough to challenge the particular institutions through which sovereignty performs its violent acts of oppositional constitution. Confronting the "prison-industrial complex" is unquestionably important work, but critical thinkers—and especially philosophers—need also to challenge the social and political ideals that call for, and purportedly legitimate, the present state of affairs.

I have argued that borders and prisons are institutions of sovereignty and that the criminalization of immigration is a new, adapted manifestation of that aging political ideal. A radical challenge to the convergence of prison and border apparatuses should therefore include a challenge to sovereignty itself. Throughout its history, the ideal of sovereignty has implicitly legitimated violence against what the political community seeks to exclude—so-called nature, barbarians, aliens, enemies, and bare life. In the contemporary United States, this violent negation focuses especially, but not only, on the individuals confined, remobilized, disciplined, exploited, and reduced to subcitizenship or social death by the converging institutions of the border and prison apparatuses. To challenge this situation, we need to overcome the political ideal that calls for it. Sovereignty itself deserves thoroughgoing critique—not because it has been made obsolete by globalization, but because even in a globalizing world, sovereignty still demands the sharp oppositions between "us" and "them" that borders and prisons impose through state sponsored violence.

Without the Right to Exist:
Mass Incarceration and National Security

Andrea Smith

> Arabs and Muslims have been socially constructed as Black,
> racially profiled, and treated in a discriminatory fashion as
> that status has historically implied. The specific stereotype
> of "terrorist" has enhanced their sense of "otherness" and
> permanent de-Americanization, whether they are citizens or
> not. Their personal, political, and legal plight was bleak before
> September 11, but has become much worse since then . . .
> CRT [Critical Race Theory] can offer some solutions.
>
> —ADRIEN WING

> Mass imprisonment in the US can only ever serve as a referent
> for some other phenomenon. As such, it is presented as *the*
> prototypical experience of disappearance, but one that is
> necessarily abstracted (and thus taken for granted, as what
> goes without saying) in order to make concrete all other
> forms of disappearance against which we must mobilize.
>
> —SORA HAN

The never-ending war on terror has prompted many scholars to argue that
Arab and Muslim peoples are now positioned as Black peoples within the
growing security state. Consequently, many critical race scholars, such as
Adrien Wing, have argued that it is important to go beyond the "black-
white" binary to examine how other peoples of color are treated "like
Black people."[1] Other scholars have argued that this call to go "beyond a
black-white binary" erases the specificity of anti-Blackness as well as the
complicity of other people of color in anti-Blackness.[2] I have argued elsewhere that this move tends to presuppose that white supremacy operates
under a singular logic.[3] This move toward equating anti-Black racism with
the forms of racism faced by other peoples disappears the specificity of
anti-Blackness. This disappearance then effectuates the logic of anti-Black

racism whereby Black peoples are equated as property by making Black struggle the property of other social justice struggles who in turn owe no obligation to Black struggle.

This anti-Blackness is the unspoken foundation of even progressive proposals to address the issues faced by those held as "enemy combatants." The assumed preferred method by which the U.S. government should treat suspects in the war on terror is to subject them to the U.S. criminal justice system.[4] Instead of terrorists or enemy combatants, suspects can be designated as "criminals." What gets normalized in these proposals, as Sora Han argues, is the mass incarceration of Black peoples within the criminal justice system so that the criminal justice system can be rendered as the benign alternative to indefinite detention. Instead of [extraordinary] mass detention, we should have [ordinary] mass incarceration.

Thus, on one hand, scholars will argue that Arab peoples are now being treated like Black peoples. But then on the other hand, the actual mass incarceration of Black peoples disappears from concern in order to present the criminal justice system as the alternative approach to the mass detention of terrorist suspects. Black peoples are sacrificed in this proposed solution for addressing the competing concerns of national security and civil liberties.

Thus, a critical approach toward national security must question not only who is deemed "terrorist" but also who is deemed "criminal." As Native studies scholar Luana Ross notes, the genocide of Native peoples has never been a crime in the United States.[5] Similarly, the prison industrial complex, an institution that oppresses and brutalizes communities of color, is not considered a criminal enterprise; it is considered the solution to crime.[6] As Ruth Wilson Gilmore notes, the United States is structured under the "state-sanctioned and/or extralegal production and exploitation of group-differentiated vulnerability to premature death" for people of color.[7]

In this chapter, I will argue that the elision of mass incarceration within even progressive responses to the war on terror rests on the uncritical assumption that the nation-state has an unquestioned right to assist. As a result, the equating of "national security" with the well-being of the government rather than the governed erases from concern the perpetual premature deaths that enable this security. Rather than presume that the only form of governance that exists is a biopolitical state in which some must be sacrificed so that the "nation" can live, we can build new forms of security by building movements that would create new nonbiopolitical forms of governance that ensure the well-being of all peoples.

The National Security/Civil Liberties Trade-off

> With other scholars, we argue that there is a tradeoff between
> security and liberty. The basic idea of the tradeoff is not original
> with us; indeed, it is one of the oldest theories of emergency
> powers. Our contribution is to analyze the comparative statics
> of institutional performance, of both government and courts, in
> striking the security-liberty balance during both emergencies
> and normal times. We pursue the tradeoff thesis to its ultimate
> conclusions without flinching at its implications, particularly its
> implications for judicial review of government action in times of
> emergency. The tradeoff thesis can be stated in simple terms. Both
> security and liberty are valuable goods that contribute to individual
> well-being or welfare. Neither good can simply be maximized
> without regard to the other. The problem from the social point
> of view is to optimize: to choose the joint level of liberty and
> security that maximizes the aggregate welfare of the population.

ERIC POSNER AND ADRIAN VERMEULE, *Terror in the Balance*

> Terrorism presents a special challenge to a democratic society:
> how to prevent and punish ideologically motivated violence
> without infringing on political freedoms and civil liberties.

DAVID COLE AND JAMES X. DEMPSEY, *Terror and the Constitution*

Legal scholars across the political spectrum have debated on what should
be the proper relationship between national security and civil liberties.[8]
More conservative scholars such as Eric Posner and Adrian Vermeule have
argued that civil liberties must be sacrificed to protect U.S. national security against terrorist threats.[9] More liberal scholars such as David Cole
and James X. Dempsey, also just cited, argue that the war on terror has
sacrificed too much in terms of civil liberties without actually strengthen-
ing national security. Despite the significant differences in these positions,
however, both conservative and liberal legal scholars agree on the framing of the issue; there is a trade-off between national security and civil
liberties. They may disagree on where the trade-off should occur, but they
agree that the two goods that must be balanced are national security and
civil liberties. Consequently, I argue that the national security and civil
libertarian sides of the debate are more similar than different. While civil
libertarians advocate passionately for polices that would no longer target

politically marginalized peoples in the interest of national security, they do not question the framework of national security itself. Yet, it is the framework of national security that is itself the white supremacist foundation that enables the racial targeting of certain peoples in the name of security. This framework rests on logics of biopower in which some populations must be perpetually subjected to premature death in order to secure the life of the nation-state.

Mass incarceration is the necessary foundation for this framework. Just as mass numbers of "criminals" are to be incarcerated in order to save "us" from crime, so, too, should mass numbers of "terrorists" be detained in order to save "us" from terrorism. The underlying assumption is that state violence in the forms of the interlocking systems of the prison and military industrial complexes are necessary to save "us" from criminal and terrorist violence. This mechanism only occurs when racialized bodies can be expelled from the category of "us" and the well-being of the nation-state— which is ultimately really what is being protected by these mechanisms— becomes equated with the well-being of the peoples residing within the nation-state.

It is important to stress, however, that detention is not "like" mass incarceration. As numerous scholars have noted, Black struggle often becomes the empty signifier to explain other struggles. The conditions of anti-Black racism are presumed to be a given that can then explain the racism faced by other groups, such as Arab and Muslim peoples. Rather, it is important to examine how these distinct forms of racism are not equivalent but are distinct and yet interrelated. Thus, it is not that the war on terror is equivalent to mass incarceration. Rather, the war on terror rests on the normalization and hence disappearance of anti-Blackness and mass incarceration. In turn, this normalization is enabled through a settler colonial logic that presumes the givenness of the nation-state. This logic cannot be dismantled without dismantling the presumption that any nation-state has an inherent right to exist or that the well-being of the nation-state should be equated with the well-being of the peoples living within the confines of that nation-state. Through an engagement with critical race/indigenous theory, this chapter will explore alternative possibilities for reframing the national security/civil liberties debate.

Critical Race Theory and National Security

What might it mean to expand who occupies the category
of our disappeared, from those killed in the World

Trade Center, to consider also those noncitizens in detention?
Our government has taken them, and we do not know
where they are. Are those in detention our disappeared?
If not, why not? I raise this to provoke a rethinking of
what bodies are centered in our consideration and what
bodies disappear. Who is the "us" in the U.S.?

LETI VOLPP, "The Citizen and the Terrorist"

The CRT [Critical Race Theory] approach does not
mandate a finding of deliberate malfeasance on the part of
government actors. The approach, however, does require
close scrutiny in situations where ostensibly neutral
governmental decisions result in the socially disenfranchised
bearing the greatest burden of those decisions. The
post–September 11 government flight from civil
liberties has certainly involved such a situation.

MARIO L. BARNES AND F. GREG BOWMAN,
"Entering Unprecedented Terrain"

Leti Volpp as well as Mario Barnes and F. Greg Bowman implicitly interrogate the biopolitics of the national security debate.[10] Ostensibly, civil
liberties in the abstract must be sacrificed to ensure the well-being of the
nation-state. However, as critical race theorists have noted, this "sacrifice"
is not shouldered by all peoples equally. Certain populations—racial/re-
ligious "others"—are repeatedly sacrificed supposedly for the well-being
of all.

As Foucault articulated in his concept of biopower, nation-states depend
on the continual expulsion of racialized others. In *History of Sexuality* as
well as in a lecture series published as *Society Must Be Defended*, Foucault
asks the question: why in this period of so-called liberal democracy are
so many wars of genocide committed, and yet these wars are *not* seen as
contradictions to democracy? While we often articulate racism as an aber-
ration to democracy or as a result of scapegoating in times of social crisis,
Foucault argues that racism is in endemic and permanent relation to the
modern state. Society simultaneously polices collective bodies and man-
ages them as populations. In the service of life, others are allowed to die.
"One might say that the ancient right to take life or let live was replaced by
a power to foster life or disallow it to the point of death . . . One had the
right to kill those who represent a kind of biological danger to others."[11]

Consequently, entire populations get marked as expendable because they are viewed as threats to the colonial world order. "Wars are no longer waged in the name of a sovereign who must be defended; they are waged on behalf of the existence of everyone; entire populations are mobilized for the purpose of wholesale slaughter in the name of life necessity; massacres have become vital. It is as managers of life and survival, of bodies and the race, that so many regimes have been able to wage so many wars, causing so many men to be killed."[12] Racism is the necessary precondition that marks certain people for death in a society based on normalization. This death, however, does not even appear to be death—it is simply the necessary precondition to ensure the life of the nation-state. Genocide becomes rational in the modern state because the modern state, to ensure the health of its social body, is entitled to destroy those that represent permanent threats. Genocide then does not become an ethical contradiction for democracy. When the United States kills thousands of people in the war on terror, those deaths disappear because they are necessary sacrifices in to ensure the well-being of "Americans."

As Dylan Rodriguez argues, this normalization of terror is accomplished through the logics of mass incarceration. That is, the effect of mass incarceration is not just to imprison mass numbers of people but also to legitimize brutality and punishment as appropriate technologies of the state. "To situate the prison's strategies and technologies of violence and human subjection as a normal and 'everyday' regime of punishment . . . is to suggest that . . . brutality, torture, and excess should be understood as an essential element of American statecraft, not its corruption or deviation."[13]

This biopolitical logic is evident in rationales articulated by legal scholars who defend the sacrifice in civil liberties as necessary to secure national security. Eric Posner and Adrian Vermeule, for instance, argue that racial minorities must sacrifice their rights for the well-being of the nation:

> The racial profiling policy affects this balance in a special way: the reduction in liberty is suffered only by the minority group, while the benefits from enhanced security are enjoyed by all. The fact that the benefits and burdens are not equally shared, of course, hardly distinguishes this law from any other. In the case of ordinary regulatory laws, the numerical minority is outvoted, but the regulations are accepted because, in some rough sense, the benefits to the majority outweigh the losses to the minority, and the minority that loses in this case may participate in different majorities that win in other settings. The mere fact that a particular policy reduces the liberty of one group in order to

enhance the security of another group does not show that it is the result of a democratic failure.[14]

By arguing that racial profiling benefits "all," Posner and Vermeule are essentially arguing that people of color are not included within "the nation." The death of people of color, rather, is necessary to protect white America. Posner and Vermeule are also admitting, essentially, that this racism is not a democratic failure—rather, it is endemic to American democracy itself, which was fundamentally constituted through the enslavement of African Americans and the genocide of Native Americans. Their rationalization of this explicit support for racist policies is that those who constitute affected "minority" groups will change as different minority groups are targeted at different times. However, the interventions of critical race theory demonstrate that certain bodies are perpetually the ones targeted by these policies. These racialized bodies never end up sharing in the "benefits of the majority." As the quotes from Volpp and Barnes demonstrate, it is people of color who are perpetually sacrificed in the interest of national security. They are never effectively included in the nation. Furthermore, as Jared Sexton argues, this analysis by Posner and Vermeule disappears the fact that some "minority" groups do not actually change their position within the racial state.[15] Black peoples are permanently profiled through a perpetual strategy of containment. This disappearance, however, is necessary to effect the Posner/Vermeule justification for racial profiling. That is, racial profiling is acceptable because it is temporary and always shifts from group to group. An acknowledgment that some groups, Black peoples, remain permanently profiled would demonstrate that Posner and Vermeule are advocating a white supremacist state that is founded on the collateral expulsion of racialized others.

Derrick Bell's work in particular has pointed to the fact that some peoples are definitionally constituted as outside the body politic. He argues that racism is permanent within U.S. society. Rather than seek representation *within* the law, Bell calls on Black peoples to "acknowledge the permanence of our subordinate status."[16] He disavows any possibility of "transcendent change."[17] To the contrary, he argues that "it is time we concede that a commitment to racial equality merely perpetuates our disempowerment."[18] The alternative he leaves behind is resistance for its own sake—living "to harass white folks"[19] or short-term pragmatic strategies that focus less on eliminating racism and more on simply ensuring that we do not "worsen conditions for those we are trying to help."[20] In his famous story, "Space Traders," aliens come to planet Earth promising to solve the world's problems if world leaders will simply give up Black people to the aliens. This story narratively illustrates how thin white liberal commitments to social justice are. First, the white people do give up Black people to the aliens without much thought. But what more dramatically illustrates this point is that the reader knows, almost without a doubt, that if this were to happen in real life, Black people certainly would be given up.

Interestingly, Posner and Vermeule implicitly make the same argument. In arguing against allowing for judicial review of executive and legislative policies during national crises, Posner and Vermeule contend that there is no reason to think judges will be any more protective of racial minorities than anyone else. Essentially adopting a Foucauldian framework, they argue that racial minorities are not particularly targeted because of national crises. Rather, they are targeted irrespective of national crises because of the racism within U.S. polity itself. "Minorities undoubtedly are scapegoated during emergencies, but they are during normal times as well, albeit in less visible ways; it is not clear that emergencies change anything other than the rhetoric or rationalizations surrounding the majority's actions."[21] They do not, however, question the inherent goodness of U.S. polity, given that it is admittedly structured on the basis of white supremacy.

Bell argued that the law could be used strategically for short-term gains most effectively when one did not presume that the law was in and of itself just.[22] For instance, in the "Racial Preference Licensing Act," Bell suggests that rather than criminalize racial discrimination, the government should allow discrimination, but tax it. Taxes accrued from this discrimination would then go into an "equality" fund that would support the educational and economic interests of African Americans. Bell denies that the Constitution could "work toward just ends." Rather, it suggests that Bell thought it might be possible to engage in legal reform in the midst of these contradictions if one foregoes the fantasy that the law is morally benevolent or even neutral. In doing so, more possibilities for strategic engagement emerge.

Even Bell's analysis, while not necessarily reflecting any faith in the possible goodness of the law, still relies on the presumptiveness of the permanency of the United States and its current legal regime. Consequently, it is not a surprise that critical race scholars who are informed by Bell's analyses did not follow his analysis to its logical conclusion. Under the racial realism framework, one is forced to either adopt a project of racial progress that contradicts the initial analysis of the United States being inherently racist or forego the possibility of eradicating white supremacy. The reason for these two equally problematic options is that this analysis presumes the permanency of the United States. Because racial theorists often lack an analysis of settler colonialism, they do not imagine other forms of governance that are not founded on the racial state. When we do not presume the givenness of settler states, then it is not as difficult to recognize the racial nature of nation-states while simultaneously maintaining a nonpessimistic approach to ending white supremacy. We can work toward "transcendent change" without presuming it will happen within the confines of the U.S. state. For instance, whereas Matsuda advocates for "reparations" for indigenous peoples in Hawai'i, for instance, indigenous scholars advocate for decolonization and the creation of new forms of governance not structured as nation-states. They do not believe that it is possible to support Matsuda's call for "a radical constitutionalism that is true to the radical roots of this country" because these so-called radical roots are founded on the genocide of indigenous peoples.[23] The fact that the United States itself could not exist without the past and continuing genocide of indigenous peoples in particular does not strike liberal legal reformists as a contradiction. Ironically, then, the same U.S. government that codified slavery, segregation, anti-immigrant racism, and the genocide of indigenous peoples now becomes the body that will protect people of color from racism.

As I have discussed elsewhere, Derrick Bell suggests an alternative framework for engaging in short-term legal strategies. And, as I have argued, our short-term legal strategies are more likely to be effective if we adopt them based on their strategic effects rather than on the attempt to make the law conform to some notion of "radical constitutionalism."[24] However, it is not necessary to resign ourselves only to short-term strategies. And indeed, it is not possible to further a project against mass incarceration and for prison abolition without simultaneously advancing the project of abolishing the nation-state. In the end, the prison industrial complex is simply an arm of a nation-state form of governance that rules through logics of violence, domination, and control. A world without prisons requires a world with different governance structures.

Critical Indigenous Theory and Unsettling the State

> The state cannot be defeated militarily because it has too much
> physical force at its disposal. To this kind of power we must
> defer. But the authority of the state is something we *can* contest.
> The legal and bureaucratic structures that manage the state's
> power are vulnerable because they rely on people's cooperation
> in order to function. This kind of power we must defy. And

> state legitimacy is the most imperceptible yet crucial form of
> power. It lies on the psychological and social conditioning of
> people to create an acceptance of the state and the forms of
> power it normalizes . . . The first and most important objective
> of movements against state power must be to deny the state's
> legitimacy in theoretical and concrete ways. In the long term,
> legitimacy is the most important form of power the state possesses.
>
> TAIAIAKE ALFRED

> If all of America is based on the fundamental denial
> of freedoms (including the right to life) to Indigenous
> Peoples, then any attempt toward justice must consider the
> elimination of the U.S. government as a political entity.
>
> WAZIYATAWIN

Recently, critical indigenous theory has intervened in the presumptions that have structured critical race theory.[25] Critical indigenous theorists such as Taiaiake Alfred, Waziyatawin, Glen Coulthard, Scott Morgensen, Jodi Byrd, Robert Nichols, Chris Finley, and many others have argued that the nation-state is not only inherently white supremacist but also settler colonialist. As such, they do not presume the permanency of settler states such as Canada and the United States. They feel less bound by the contradictions articulated by Mari Matsuda of striving for legal reform even as one critiques the racial state, because they think it is possible to build new governance systems that are not racial states. That is, their work does not simply question the legitimacy of settler states but the presumption that governance can only occur through nation-states. As I have argued elsewhere, Native peoples have advocated for nations founded on indigenous principles of inclusivity, radical relationality, and egalitarianism. The nations are not based on land commodification in which one group of people can own and control discrete territory but are based upon care and responsibility for land in which we can all share.[26] They resist carcerality because they challenge the western epistemological framework from which carcerality emerges. That is, as Denise Da Silva has argued, the western subject constitutes itself as over and against other selves. It defines itself as self-determining because it compares itself to racialized others it deems not self-determining. Thus, not surprisingly, the nations that emerge from this sense of self are bounded and exclusivist. Indigenous scholars and activists, by contrast, argue that selves are constituted through their radical relationality to all other selves as well as to creation in general. Consequently, the nations that emerge from this sense of self are inclusive and interconnected to other nations.

Taiaiake Alfred argues that indigenous nationhood entails distinguishing between peoples and the government that claims to represent them. He notes that the colonial governance system is premised on the ability to exercise power through the state by means of coercion and domination. Traditional forms of indigenous governance, by contrast, are based on different understandings of power:

> The Native concept of governance is based on . . . the "primacy of conscience." There is no central or coercive authority and decision-making is collective. Leaders rely on their persuasive abilities to achieve a consensus that respects the autonomy of individuals, each of whom is free to dissent from and remain unaffected by the collective decision. . . .
>
> A crucial feature of the indigenous concept of governance is its respect for individual autonomy. This respect precludes the notion of "sovereignty"—the idea that there can be a permanent transference of power or authority from the individual to an abstraction of the collective called "government." . . . In the indigenous tradition, there is no coercion, only the compelling force of conscience based on those inherited and collectively refined principles that structure the society.[27]

Alfred suggests an alternative approach to understanding "national security." Instead of national security focusing on maintaining the current government system, it could focus on ensuring that the relationships between peoples and all of creation within that nation are healthy. If the current government structure is creating unhealthy relationships between peoples (especially through white supremacy, settler colonialism, heteropatriarchy, and other forms of oppression), then national security would require that we dismantle that government system and create a new system that would promote healthier relationships. Of course, such ideas are easily dismissed because indigenous peoples are always positioned in an anterior relationship to modernity and hence their "primitive" values are not seen as having relevance for today's complex problems.[28] But, as indigenous scholars have also noted, one of the legacies of settler colonialism is that colonialism also structures our imagination. Colonialism continues to exist because it naturalizes itself. It creates the appearance that there cannot be an outside to this current oppressive system. However, indigenous and queer of color theorists in particular are calling for a decolonization of our imagination—to begin to imagine an outside to the system.[29]

This critique of settler colonialism has emerged in critical race theory. Dean Spade intersects Derrick Bell's critique of the racial state with indigenous critiques of the settler state to question the critical race theory's aspirational approach to the law. Spade argues that our very aspiration to be represented in the law forecloses the possibility of alternative political formations that could challenge the capitalist hierarchies that can never be addressed through the law. Furthermore, the quest for representation does not question the manner in which the law defines the subjects who can be recognized by the law. For instance, as Elizabeth Povinelli has argued, for indigenous peoples to have their "rights" recognized under the law, they must position themselves as "authentically indigenous" in order to seek recognition.[30] Thus, the only indigenous person that can be recognized under the law is colonial fantasy that does not actually exist. Thus, suggests Spade, rather than seek recognition through gender and racial legal classificatory schemes that are themselves white supremacist and heteropatriarchal, we should challenge these regimes as themselves the problem:

> The anti-discrimination . . . strategy relies on the belief that if we change what the law says about a particular group to make it say "good things" . . . and not "bad things" . . . then those people's lives will improve. This approach to law reform relies on an individual rights framework that emphasizes harms caused to individuals by other individuals who kill or fire them because they are members of the group. It seeks remedies that punish individuals who do those harmful things motivated by bias. This analysis misunderstands how power functions and can lead to approaches to law reform that actually expand the reach of violent and harmful systems. In order to properly understand power . . . we need to shift our focus from the individual rights framing of discrimination and "hate violence" and think more broadly about how . . . categories are enforced on all people in ways that have particularly dangerous outcomes.[31]

Similarly, Denise Da Silva has argued against what she terms critical race theory's "racial exclusion thesis," that the problem with the system is that it excludes people of color. Rather, the system itself is structured on the logics of white supremacy. People of color, she argues, cannot seek inclusion without seeking their obliteration.[32] Rey Chow has similarly argued that the problem with this exclusion thesis is that the idea that the social order is bad because it excludes me also implies that the social order is good if it includes me. But the system does not operate simply through exclusion but selective inclusion.[33] If a person from a marginalized group is ostensibly included in the system, the assumption of that person is that the system must be fair, and hence that person feels entitled to take part in excluding any other peoples from that group who were not chosen to be selectively included.

These strands within critical race and indigenous theory point to the possibility of justice beyond the current political/legal regime. While the current regime exists, short-term legal strategies are needed. But the end goal is not simply a kinder, gentler settler state founded on genocide and slavery, just as the goal is not kinder and gentler prisons. The end goal is the creation of a world without prisons effected through new forms of governance that are liberatory for all peoples.

National Security without the Inviolable Right to Exist

[Richard] Posner is best known as one of the founding fathers
of the law and economics movement, so it is hardly surprising that
his judgments are powerfully informed by an economist's
fetish for cost-benefit analysis. (One might almost say determined,
except that, as we will see, the valuation of costs and benefits in
this area is almost entirely indeterminate.) In the end,
constitutional interpretation for Posner is little more
than an all-things-considered balancing act—and when
the potential costs of a catastrophic terrorist attack are
placed on the scale, the concerns of constitutional rights
and civil liberties are almost inevitably outweighed.

DAVID COLE

Civil libertarian David Cole critiques Richard Posner's cost/benefit approach to balancing national security concerns against civil liberties in public policy.[34] However, as discussed earlier, Cole and other civil libertarians also ultimately adopt a balancing test approach as well—they just weigh civil liberty concerns more strongly than do more conservative scholars.[35] But what Cole's analysis points to is the fact that if we accept that the issues should be framed in terms of national security versus individual rights, ultimately national security will always win. Thus, John Yoo's justification of torture follows from this framework. Ultimately, he argues that whatever the problems around the legality of torture may be, it is justified in the interest of national self-defense:

As we have made clear in other opinions involving the war against al Qaeda, the Nation's right to self-defense has been triggered by the events of September 11. If a government defendant were to harm an enemy combatant during an interrogation in a manner that might arguably violate a criminal prohibition, he would be doing so in order to prevent further attacks on the United States by the al Qaeda terrorist network. In that case, we believe that he could argue that the executive branch's constitutional authority to protect the nation from attack justified his actions. This national and international version of the right to self-defense could supplement and bolster the government defendant's individual right.[36]

Similarly, Posner and Vermeule argue that courts should apply a less exacting standard than strict scrutiny for policies that are racially discriminatory in times of national emergency.[37] Under this rationale, individual rights (at least the individual rights of racialized subjects) will always seem less important than national security. As Sora Han argues, the debates around whether courts should still apply strict scrutiny tests for discrimination cases during times of national emergency are largely irrelevant because courts will always find that national security interests meet strict scrutiny, as seen in *Korematsu*. "Is national defense ever anything other than compelling, necessary, urgent?"[38] Self-defense will trump any other concern. In addition, this analysis does not allow us to focus on how the sacrifice in rights is consistently forced on entire racialized populations. Further, this framing does not let us question whether those who are attempting a hostile takeover of the U.S. government may, in fact, be better suited to govern than those in the current system. This framework also presumes that those perpetually sacrificed populations in the interest of national security have no right to a new governance system that does not sacrifice them.

The United States as National Emergency

American Indians are fully aware of terrorist attacks. We also remember our ancestors who perished at Wounded Knee and Sand Creek. We remember those who perished during the "Trail of Tears" and the Potawatomi "Trail of Death." All of these tragedies occurred on American soil.

NATIVE NEWS NETWORK

The United States is not at war; the United States *is* war.

SORA HAN

Bruce Ackerman proposes the development of an "emergency constitution" as a way to address temporary national emergencies.[39] Because the U.S. constitution is relatively silent on how to address national emergencies, it is tempting for the executive to act extra-constitutionally, thus undermining in the long run the authority of the Constitution. At the same time, when the United States is under attack, panic strikes because the governing authority of the United States is in question. To address both concerns, Ackerman proposes that an emergency constitution be developed that suspends normal constitutional rights for a short period until the emergency is contained. This emergency constitution would be temporary, and it would exist under review from Congress:

> Call it the reassurance function: When a terrorist attack places the state's effective sovereignty in doubt, government must act visibly and decisively to demonstrate to its terrorized citizens that the breach was only temporary, and that it is taking aggressive action to contain the crisis and to deal with the prospect of its recurrence. Most importantly, my proposal for an emergency constitution authorizes the government to detain suspects without the criminal law's usual protections of probable cause or even reasonable suspicion. Government may well assert other powers in carrying out the reassurance function, but in developing my argument, I shall be focusing on the grant of extraordinary powers of detention as the paradigm. . . . My aim is to design a constitutional framework for a temporary state of emergency that enables government to discharge the reassurance function without doing long-term damage to individual rights.[40]

As the statement from the Native News Network suggests, who decides when there is a national emergency and for whom? Why is 9/11 seen as a national emergency because of mass deaths that occurred but the massacres at Wounded Knee and Sand Creek are not? Why is slavery and the afterlife of slavery not viewed as a national emergency? Why are the actions of Black revolutionary groups considered terrorist activities (i.e., the placement of Black Liberation Army leader Assata Shakur on the FBI Most Wanted Terrorist List) while the actions of white supremacist groups are not? Why is the mass incarceration of Black peoples not considered a "national emergency?"

Richard Posner makes an interesting distinction in his argument for why speech by those who aim to overthrow the United States government should be criminalized. He contends that the Brandenburg test, which allows for the constitutional criminalization of speech when (1) there is a substantial likelihood of imminent illegal activity and (2) the speech is directed to causing imminent illegality, is insufficient. It does not criminalize enough speech that can be threatening to U.S. national security. He contends that the Brandenburg test applies in a case of white supremacist hate speech but not "terrorist" speech: "It is a disservice to judges to treat their general statements, which necessarily reach beyond the facts of the particular cases in which they are made, as if they were statutes. Clarence Brandenburg was not Osama bin Laden; he was merely a Grand Dragon of the Ohio Ku Klux Klan."[41] Although Black deaths caused by the KKK far outweigh the number of deaths caused by Osama bin Laden, white supremacist violence is not a significant threat to national security. Clearly, according to Posner, Black deaths do not threaten the well-being of the "nation."

As Mary Dudziak argues, this attempt to delineate special "war times" and "national emergencies" by which constitutional rights can be abrogated tend to presume there is a sharp distinction between war and peace time:

> Much attention has been paid in recent years to wartime as a state
> of exception, but not to wartime as a form of time. For philosopher
> Giorgio Agamben, a state of exception "is a suspension of the juridical
> order itself," marking law's boundaries. Viewing war as an exception to
> normal life, however, leads us to ignore the longstanding persistence
> of war. If wartime is actually normal time . . . rather than a state of ex-
> ception, then law during war can be seen as the form of law we in fact
> practice, rather than a suspension of an idealized understanding
> of law.[42]

As Dudziak and Sora Han note, the United States is perpetually at war; contra Ackerman, the Constitution is already an "emergency constitution." Public officials already routinely act extra-legally. The United States is already a state of exception. This fact is particularly clear given that George Bush's declaration of war against terror admits to being a war without end. "Our enemy is a radical network of terrorists, and every government that supports them. Our war on terror begins with al Qaeda, but it does not end there. It will not end until every terrorist group of global reach has been found, stopped and defeated."[43] This war on terror exists concurrently with the wars against indigenous peoples, Black peoples, and other people of color since its founding. The question then arises: what would a national security approach look like that centered white supremacy and settler colonialism as national emergencies?

Conclusion

A critical race/indigenous theory on national security policy changes the
question before us. The question is not "how can we ensure national security and protect civil liberties?" The question is "what forms of governance
can we build that do not rest on the continual deaths of racialized others?"
If we do not presume that the current U.S. government should or will
always continue to exist, then movements that are engaged for the productive purpose of building new systems of governance that are not structured
on anti-Blackness and indigenous genocide would be seen as movements
that promote "national security."

Prison Abolition and a Culture of Sexual Difference

Sarah Tyson

Violence against women is a public issue because of feminist movements. This huge cultural shift is certainly worthy of celebration. Making sexual assault, domestic violence, and family violence public issues is not, of course, the primary goal of feminists—ending them is. But it would be counterproductive impatience to fault feminists for not having yet eradicated these widespread problems—entangled as they are with the main structures of social life, including family, law, rights, and gender. So it makes sense that we should applaud feminism's outing of violence against women, even as we work to eliminate it more fully. There is, however, a recalcitrant and troubling problem in much feminist antiviolence work that presents a formidable obstacle to reaching its ultimate goal: many feminists working to eradicate violence have come to rely on prisons and the apparatus of the carceral state more broadly.

In this chapter, I recount briefly how feminist antiviolence work has become complicit with mass incarceration. Then, I make the case that support of mass incarceration is at odds with the feminist goal of ending violence against women. I suggest that, for help in thinking beyond prisons, we look to grassroots organizations already working within communities to find noncarceral responses to violence; my analysis focuses particularly on Communities Against Rape and Abuse (CARA) based in Seattle.[1] Finally, I turn to the work of Luce Irigaray to argue that organizations like CARA are not just anticipating life after prisons but creating the conditions necessary for life without prisons. The primary aim of this chapter is to further develop theoretical resources for feminist prison abolitionist work as part of the struggle to end violence against women.

Feminists and the Carceral State

Marie Gottschalk has shown that the founders of many of the early rape crisis centers viewed the state and hierarchical professions as part of the larger problem of patriarchy that allowed and facilitated a culture of violence against women. Gottschalk notes that the founders of the first rape crisis centers "self-consciously maintained a distance from law enforcement agencies, hospitals, and conventional social services and assumed a militant stance toward professionals in such organizations. . . . A number of feminists involved early on in the anti-rape movement looked askance at the punitive arm of the state."[2] However, in the quest to legitimize the importance of the issue of violence against women, as well as to garner state and federal funding, "women's groups entered into some unsavory coalitions and compromises that bolstered the law-and-order agenda and reduced their own capacity to serve as ideological bulwarks against the rising tide of conservatism."[3]

We can see this larger historical trend in the history and prehistory of CARA. Its earlier incarnation, Seattle Rape Relief (SRR), one of the first rape crisis centers in the country, closed in 1999.[4] Although there are many reasons for SRR's closing, including monetary ones, Alisa Bierria and CARA write that the center "was impacted by the professionalization of a once-grassroots antiviolence movement, and SRR's volunteers identified this shift in the organization's political identity as the main reason for its demise."[5] CARA, organized by volunteers in the aftermath of SRR's closing, eventually received a large portion of the city government funding that had previously been allocated to SRR, the result of which has been an organizational struggle within CARA. The struggle has been to maintain two public images, one they describe as "more palatable to local politicians" and another, more radical image they describe as "authentic" for their constituents.[6] As the dual life of the organization becomes increasingly untenable, Bierria and CARA anticipate a complete move away from government funding.

The story of SRR's closure and the founding of CARA illustrate the complexities of creating radical responses to sexual assault within current structures. It may be tempting to suggest that CARA abandon state funding but doing so would severely limit their outreach and accessibility. CARA maintains a critical view of the state and especially its punitive function, even as they recognize the need for state funding. For instance, CARA writes, "We've found that, when organizations both inside and outside the non-profit structure have fewer financial resources, what gets cut first is resources for accessibility—for people with disabilities, for children, for parents, for people whose first language is not English, for poor people, and for all of us who need support to participate in movement building."[7] Thus, part of my interest in this chapter is to make urgent the question: Is there a state that could not just tolerate CARA's radical critique of violence but could be born from it? Beginning to elaborate an answer to that question is part of my reason for turning to Irigaray.

Further, feminist alliance with and reliance on the punitive arm of the state has not been limited to the coalitions and compromises of the political realm. Chloë Taylor has shown how much feminist theory also relies on prisons as a solution. Taylor notes, "While it is . . . not uncommon for feminists to observe that law enforcement is not the ultimate solution to sex crimes, and to focus on social reeducation and prevention instead, it *is* uncommon for feminists to say anything about what should happen to sex offenders other than to call for stiffer penalties or object to light ones."[8] In other words, in both theory and practice, many feminists have supported the creation of what Loïc Wacquant calls a "genuine prison society."[9] Hence, part of my reason for turning to CARA is to question that support in Irigaray's work and in feminist theoretical work more broadly.

Prisons Are Violence against Women

Is this reliance on prisons a problem for feminism? After all, if locking up sex offenders keeps women safe, then we may have no reason to resurrect early feminist suspicions about the state. To think about this question, let's begin by considering what happens in prison. Don Sabo explains, "In the muscled, violent, and tattooed world of prison rape, woman is symbolically ever-present. The prison phrase 'make a woman out of you' means that you will be raped. Rape-based relationships between [male] prisoners are often described as relations between 'men' and 'women' and in effect conceptualized as 'master' and 'slave.'"[10] Prisons reproduce rape culture, even when women are not present.

Prince Imari A. Obadele also criticizes prisons for their role in perpetuating a culture of violence against women. He writes about the phenomenon of men masturbating when they are in sight of a female guard, a practice known as "killing." Obadele calls those who engage in killing "proxy-rapists"[11] and explains: "Understand that [I] don't give a damn what happens to a prison guard. It wouldn't bother me one bit if these same killers were using guns and knives and other instruments of death on these same guards. But they are not. And the culture of killing does not bode well for the safety of little girls and wimmin."[12] In other words, Obadele is concerned about the practice of "killing" not because it disrespects guards, who he sees as part of the problem, but because the practice is a form of misogyny training that extends beyond the prison walls. Obadele further underlines the connection between what happens in prisons and what happens on the outside: "These same killers, the majority of them, are going to the streets one of these days and they will be peeping at your mothers, daughters, sisters, and wives from behind the walls and around the corners, or swinging like [T]arzan snatching up [J]ane."[13]

Don Sabo, Terry Kupers, and Willie London document how prisons cultivate and reinforce "destructive forms of masculinity."[14] That reinforcement is not incidental to prison systems but integral to it. Prison guards, for instance—a group that by no means escapes the violent consequences of mass incarceration—use sexual violence as a means of controlling the inmate population.[15] Sabo, Kupers, and London write, "Guards tolerate some sexual domination among prisoners because it serves to divide them into perpetrators and victims, thus diminishing the likelihood of united resistance."[16] Stephen "Donny" Donaldson observes, "Guards are also involved in setting up some rapes and sexual encounters in exchange for payoffs or for such diverse purposes as the destruction of the leadership potential of an articulate prisoner."[17] Sexual assault in prison serves multiple interests and, like all sexual assault, it is not only a crime of interpersonal violence but also a means of social control.

Another way to consider how prisons are not keeping women safe is to consider women's experience of incarceration, noting that it is poor women and women of color who are disproportionately imprisoned. Since 1981, women have been the fastest-growing prison population.[18] While violence is widely recognized to be endemic in men's prisons and jails, evidence is amassing that violence is a prominent feature of women's institutions as well. A 2002 study found that 27 percent of inmates in one female facility had been sexually assaulted in prison.[19] Another study in 2006, which received funding through the Prison Rape Elimination Act (PREA), found a victimization rate of 21 percent within a state prison system.[20] The 2007 report from the Bureau of Justice Statistics undertaken to fulfill PREA statistic-gathering requirements reported lower rates of incidence than these earlier studies but still found rates of sexual assault as high as 10 percent in women's facilities.[21] Thus, if we are concerned with violence against women, prison must be a site of our concern.

Further, as the introduction to the INCITE! anthology observes, "for all women prisoners, the state acts as a punitive perpetrator of violence, subjecting women to invasive body searches, emotional and physical isolation, and physical and verbal abuse."[22] Women do not have to be sexually assaulted in prison to experience violence there. In April 2012 the Michigan Department of Corrections (DOC) finally stopped conducting routine vaginal inspections for every woman who met with a visitor. These searches were conducted even when the woman had been under supervision at all times with no suspicion of her hiding anything.[23] The ACLU, which was involved in petitioning the Michigan DOC to stop the searches, received letters from more than sixty inmates who were adversely affected by the searches, including women who avoided meetings with family members in order to avoid the searches that would follow them.[24]

Feminists seeking to end violence against women must also consider the relationship between life on the inside and life on the outside for many women. In "Women in Prison: How We Are," Assata Shakur illuminates the parallels between women's imprisonment at Rikers Island and their lives on the outside. She writes of life in prison: "The fights are the same except they're less dangerous. The police are the same. The poverty is the same. The alienation is the same. The racism is the same. The sexism is the same. The drugs are the same and the system is the same."[25] Shakur's point is not to deny the devastation created by imprisonment; rather, she is underscoring that prisons are *another* institution of dominance and inequality in the lives of the women who do time in them.

Another way we can see prisons as a problem for feminism is the fact that women of color are more likely to be sent to prison for the same types of crimes that typically result in probation for white women.[26] African American women are incarcerated at four times the rate of white women.[27] That is what has led INCITE! to ask: "What would it take *to end violence against women of color?* What would this movement look like? What if we do not presume that this movement would share any of the features we take for granted in the current domestic violence movement? . . . When we shift the center to women of color, the importance of addressing state violence becomes evident. This perspective benefits not only women of color, but all peoples, because it is becoming increasingly clear that the criminal justice system is not effectively ending violence for anyone."[28] Recognizing that prisons are complicit in violence against women is part of the work of making feminism a movement to end oppression for all.

But imagine that PREA does its work and rape is eliminated from prisons. Let's go further and imagine that men's facilities no longer train men in destructive masculinity. Prisons would still be involved in perpetuating violence against women for the ineliminable fact that prisons remove people from community relations, including removing male partners from women's lives. As Ruth Gilmore observes, "Looking around the block at all the homes, research shows that increased use of policing and state intervention in everyday problems hasten the demise of the informal customary relationships that social calm depends on (Clear et al. 2001). People stop looking out for each other and stop talking about anything that matters in terms of neighborly well-being."[29] Incarceration does not just wreak havoc on the families of those incarcerated; entire neighborhoods and communities are also affected. Again, Gilmore explains, "The 'tipping point' when things start to get really bad is not very deep. Only two or three need to be removed from N to produce greater *instability* in a community of people who, when employed, make, move, or care for things."[30] Prisons make communities more, not less, vulnerable to violence.

This destruction of community does not end with the prison sentence, either. Once people are released from prison, they face onerous fees associated with parole, no access to public housing, trouble finding work or being considered for it because they must disclose their history of incarceration, ineligibility for food stamps if the conviction was drug-related, as well as lifelong disenfranchisement in many states.[31] The ability of people facing these obstacles to support a family or meaningfully contribute to their community is severely limited. Indeed, as Michelle Alexander argues, the illegal economy becomes the only rational solution for many people once they are released from prison.[32]

My analysis and arguments in this section have shown the short sightedness of attempting to redress interpersonal violence with state violence. It is clear that feminists have ample reason not to support the policies and practices of mass incarceration. How, then, do we really make women safer?

What if Not Prisons?

In their introduction to the volume, the editors of *Color of Violence: The
INCITE! Anthology* write: "The challenge women of color face in combating personal *and* state violence is to develop strategies for ending violence
that *do* assure safety for survivors of sexual/domestic violence and *do not*
strengthen our oppressive criminal justice apparatus."[33] As I mentioned
earlier, part of the reason that the editors frame the challenge as one faced
by women of color is because it is largely these women who have critiqued
feminist complicity with the carceral state and who have been marginalized for this antiviolence activism. The activist writings of these women
of color provide a cache of resources that can help us radically reimagine
mainstream feminist responses to violence.

The example I highlight, CARA, does not offer a formula for addressing violence. Rather, CARA offers "the bones for each community-based
process [and works] with survivors and their communities to identify their
own unique goals, values, and actions that add flesh to their distinct safety/
accountability models."[34] They specify that their mission is "to better understand the nature of sexual violence and rape culture, nurture community values that are inconsistent with rape and abuse, and develop community-based strategies for safety, support, and accountability."[35] Central
to the accountability processes that CARA helps communities develop is
the refusal to treat survivors as irreparably "damaged"[36] and aggressors as
irredeemably monstrous.[37]

Guiding CARA's accountability work are ten principles, two of which I
will focus on here. The first is the mandate to "recognize the humanity of
everyone involved."[38] In relying on mass incarceration, however unthink-
ingly, theorists fail to apply this principle. CARA differentiates between
rage and anger on the one hand (which they value as appropriate responses
to violence) and dehumanization on the other. CARA avoids dehumanization of aggressors for the following reason: "alienation and dehumanization of the offending person increases a community's vulnerability to being
targeted for disproportional criminal justice oppression through height-
ening the 'monster-ness' of another community member."[39] By refusing
to contribute to the images of criminality that overwhelmingly implicate
minority communities, CARA acknowledges the multiple ways in which
violence happens in a community and incorporates that awareness into
their response to violence.

CARA's conception of criminality is deeply social. We can see the relational aspect in their observation: "If we separate ourselves from the of-

fenders by stigmatizing them then we fail to see how we contributed to conditions that allow violence to happen."[40] Implicit in the principle of recognizing the humanity of everyone involved is an analysis of how the community was involved in creating the conditions for violence to occur in the first place. Within the framework that CARA employs, that analysis does not relieve the aggressor of responsibility but rather contextualizes the violence in order to demystify it. One case study presented by CARA reports an accountability process that was started in response to the rape of one member of a punk music community by another member.[41] Through their work with CARA, the community became involved in a sustained discussion of its values and cultural forms rather than continuing to demonize the person who committed the rape or to blame the survivor—the two predominate responses within the community when the rape was made public.

Another of CARA's principles is: "identify a simultaneous plan for safety and support for the survivor as well as others in the community."[42]In their critiques of alternatives to prisons such as Restorative Justice programs, feminists have rightly criticized programs that left survivors unprotected from aggressors. (In these cases, women were either pressured to drop charges or to accept mediation in order to protect the community from state violence.)[43] In response to this concern, CARA emphasizes a multidimensional concept of safety that includes not just the physical but also the emotional, economic, political, and social well-being of the people involved. CARA emphasizes a community response to violence that undercuts the temptation to see safety as a zero-sum game. The survivor's safety must be thought of in a relational web. A solution that exposes the community as a whole or any member in it to more violence violates this principle.

As indicated in my brief exploration of their principles, CARA has done a great deal of self-theorization. Thus, my turn now to Irigaray may seem unnecessary. Further, Irigaray's argument for sexuate rights may seem like an unlikely contribution to prison abolition, as her proposals aim at overcoming the constitutive exclusion of women from culture. In other words, Irigaray's articulation of sexuate rights, which she describes as rights for women,[44] are clearly a resource for thinking about violence against women, but how can she help us to address the broader understanding of violence developed in CARA's critique of the prison system?

A large part of the reason I want to analyze Irigaray's work in relation to CARA's is because these theorists of violence can help us to see understand why the feminist goal of ending violence against women must also include abolishing prisons. My hope and contention is that Irigaray can help us appreciate the radical nature of the work CARA is doing and theorizing, not just at the level of institutions and practices but also at the level of subjectivity. At the same time, I argue that CARA's self-theorization can help us to improve Irigaray's theory by showing that the revolutionary change she theorizes cannot maintain a reliance on prisons. Thus, by creating a discussion between CARA and Irigaray, I seek to contribute to feminist antiviolence theory and activism that is also, because it must be, in support of prison abolition, not in some distant future but right now.

Transforming Communities

Tina Chanter writes, "For Irigaray it is not only necessary to become '*politicized*' (TS: 165; CS: 159), it is also necessary to recast the political so that it does not merely reinscribe patriarchal forms of domination, or, as she puts it, 'from a feminine locus nothing can be articulated without a questioning of the symbolic itself' (TS: 162; CS: 157). Irigaray is skeptical of feminism if it is understood simply as a process of politicization that does not also question the models and ideals that govern politics."[45] Through their community accountability work, I argue that CARA is not only putting into question the models and ideals that govern politics; they are putting into practice new ideals and models that could guide new political formations. To elaborate how I think CARA is doing this, I will build on Irigaray's efforts to think a nonsacrificial political order.

Central to Irigaray's work on recasting the political is overcoming a singular model of subjectivity and bringing about a culture of sexual difference. Particularly in her early work, Irigaray exposes the dominance of masculine subjectivity and its dependence on the sacrifice of feminine subjectivity. That critical work shows how a culture of sexual difference has been made impossible.

One way to understand Irigaray's critique is to return to the quotation from Sabo: "In the muscled, violent, and tattooed world of prison rape, woman is symbolically ever-present. The prison phrase 'make a woman out of you' means that you will be raped. Rape-based relationships between prisoners are often described as relations between 'men' and 'women' and in effect conceptualized as 'master' and 'slave.'"[46] It might appear that an acknowledgment of sexual difference is implicit in the threat to "make a woman out of you," but Irigaray's point is that this apparent acknowledgment of difference actually works as a support for a phallocratic order, an order based on the dominance of masculine subjectivity. The symbolic presence of women in men's prisons does not amount to a recognition of sexual difference. Rather, the symbolic presence of women as those who are raped vividly illustrates the sacrifice of feminine subjectivity to the consolidation of masculine subjectivity.

Irigaray's work has shown that this sacrifice operates at many levels—philosophical and political, economic and linguistic. As Chanter writes, "The problems women face in their attempt to change the process of othering that has defined them through the eyes of men extend to fundamental assumptions about what it means to be a subject, assumptions that are embedded in the function of language and institutionalized in socio-political norms."[47] Irigaray is clear that mere reversal of this process of othering would not instantiate the change that she seeks—a culture of sexual difference.[48] Rather, Irigaray argues that we must transform subjectivity so that it no longer relies on the sacrifice of feminine subjectivity, which requires a revolution in language, religion, civil life, family structures, and legal orders.

Anne Caldwell well describes how the logic of sacrifice operates: "Irigaray argues that Western social orders sacrifice materiality and difference, reducing them to a static ground or constitutive outside on or against which concepts and subjectivity emerge."[49] The social order achieves its coherence and stability, to the extent that is does, through this sacrifice. Caldwell, working through Irigaray, shows in detail how such a logic of sacrifice works within liberal democracy, psychoanalysis, and deconstruction. Importantly, Caldwell also notes that much feminist theory has accepted the necessity of this logic.[50] Irigaray, by contrast, critiques that sacrifice of materiality and difference, as well as its presumed necessity. CARA is also involved in such a critique in their unwillingness to sacrifice either the survivor or the aggressor in an attempt to ensure community safety. Thus, I agree with Caldwell that "Irigaray's critique of sacrifice in particular makes her recent work worth examining,"[51] especially for developing noncarceral responses to violence and in conversation with CARA.[52]

Throughout her work, Irigaray links the sacrifice of feminine subjectivity, the sexual indifference of culture, to the lack of appropriate responses to violence against women.[53] For instance, in "The Question of the Other" Irigaray writes, "But it's not a good thing, either for women or for relations between the sexes, that women as the injured party be put in the position of simply being accusers. If there were civil rights for women, the whole of society would be the injured party in the case of rape or all the other forms of violence inflicted on women; society, then, would be the plaintiff or co-plaintiff against the harm caused to one of its members."[54] A lack of civil rights specific to women results in women only being able to take up the role of accusers. From CARA's accountability work, we can already see why relegating the survivors of violence to the role of accuser is problematic. The role of the accuser reduces the survivor to "a symbol of an idea instead of an actual person."[55] In Irigaray's terms, such reduction sacrifices the survivor to the order of the judicial process.

Irigaray links the end of such sacrifice to a change in the discourse of rights and the organization of the state: "Our need first and foremost is for a right to human dignity for everyone. That means we need laws that valorize difference. Not all subjects are the same, nor equal, and it wouldn't be right for them to be so. That's particularly true for the sexes. Therefore, it's important to understand and modify the instruments of society and culture that regulate subjective and objective rights. Social justice, and especially sexual justice, cannot be achieved without changing the laws of language and the conceptions of truths and values structuring the social order."[56] Could Irigaray's proposals for civil rights for women help build the sort of revolutionary system that CARA calls for? I would like to complicate any approach to this question by suggesting that Irigaray's proposals are not as straightforward as they might initially appear. While these rights can and have been read as literal proposals for rights to be enshrined in the state, I wish to highlight the critical reflection they provoke about the current order. I am taking up the possibility proposed by Penelope Deutscher when she writes: "What if we think of Irigaray's declaration of sexuate rights as a declaration of a radical political perspective? . . . Perhaps what is being performed is not the founding of sexuate rights but the founding of a critical perspective."[57] Thus, rather than suggesting that Irigaray supplies the vision for the revolution CARA is working to build, I suggest that it is Irigaray's critical perspective that is most useful for supporting CARA's work.

What I propose is that we read Irigaray's conception of sexuate rights not as an attempt to found a determinate identity for women but rather as a critique of the constitutive exclusion of sexual difference from liberal democracy. The importance of this critique is not just relevant to women's exclusion but also to culture more broadly. As Irigaray writes, "What has to be defined as women's rights is what the male people, the between-men culture, has appropriated as possessions, including in this respect not only women's and children's bodies, but also natural space, living space, the economy of signs and images, social and religious representations."[58] In other words, through her work on the constitutive sacrifice of women, Irigaray helps us to understand why the institutions to which victims of sexual assault turn are likely to oppress or ignore their appeals.

To understand Irigaray's proposals for sexuate rights as an ally in gaining critical perspective on mass incarceration, let's look at the second right she enumerates. In *je, tu, nous*, Irigaray writes:

> The right to *human identity*, that is . . . the legal encodification of
> *virginity* (or physical and moral integrity) as a component of female
> identity that is not reducible to money, and not cash-convertible by
> the family, the State, or religious bodies in any way . . . The rights
> would enable us to get away from simple penal sanctions and to enjoy
> civil legality as far as women's rights are concerned. I'm thinking of
> rape and incest cases, for example, or cases against forced prostitution,
> pornography, etc., which are always enacted with a view to punishing
> the guilty rather than in accordance with civil society's guarantee of
> positive rights appropriate to women. . . . If there were civil rights for
> women, the whole of society would be the injured party in the case
> of rape or all the other forms of violence inflicted on women; society,
> then, would be the plaintiff or co-plaintiff against the harm caused to
> one of its members.[59]

In order to discuss this right's relevance to the work of organizations like CARA, I must first suggest an amendment. Not only would the whole of society be the injured party, but it would also be the injuring party.[60] That is, not only is harm inflicted *on* one society's members, but it is also inflicted *by* one of its members.[61] Such recognition does not require a claim that society would be equally harmed and harming or that plaintiff and defendant would be the same; both options fall into the traps of equality and sameness that Irigaray identifies as foundational to a culture that excludes sexual difference.

Rather, as CARA underscores: "A consciousness of rape culture prepares us for the need to organize beyond the accountability of an individual aggressor. We also realize we must organize for accountability and transformation of institutions that perpetuate rape culture such as the military, prisons and the media."[62] In other words, we must acknowledge the role of larger social structures, including norms, in perpetuating violence. CARA writes, "The community we are working to build is not one where a person is forever stigmatized as a 'monster' no matter what she does to transform, but a community where a person has the opportunity to provide restoration for the damage she has done."[63] Giving the role of accuser to the survivor relegates the aggressor to the role of criminal and even monster. CARA asks for much more from aggressors. Although accountability plans are tailored to each situation, they uniformly ask aggressors to engage in transformative work, which may involve direct support by the aggressor's community. Public shaming may be a step in an accountability plan, but accountability extends beyond that.[64] CARA gives examples of terms of accountability such as: "You can attend our church, but you must check in with a specific group of people every week so that they can determine your progress in your reform."[65] CARA's attention to the aggressor forces us to consider what it would mean to see the whole of society as not just the injured party (as Irigaray would have it) but also as the injuring party.

To create cultures that do not rely on sacrifice, Irigaray suggests that we take the limitation of our subjectivity upon ourselves rather than projecting it onto an other, work that she calls, reworking Hegel, the labor of the negative.[66] Caldwell explains the ethics born of this labor: "An ethics of the negative works to undermine the traditional subject's transfer of its disavowed materiality onto others . . . Such an ethics facilitates a nonantagonistic intersubjectivity by acknowledging our own partiality and limits, rather than shifting them to others."[67] The labor of the negative requires our acknowledgment that we are not self-sufficient and that we never can be. The importance (and difficulty) of this point for rethinking responses to violence is that it asks us, even in the face of our injury by the other, to take the labor of the negative upon ourselves. In other words, we cannot eliminate our interdependence, even when we have been harmed by the other. As CARA's work shows us, not relying on prisons means we also cannot rely on a reduction of the other to a monster, a criminal, or even a defendant (though Irigaray's language of plaintiff risks engaging this powerful binary). We must continue to acknowledge our interdependence.

Refusing to reduce the other to such functions allows, as Irigaray argues, for communication between us. In writing of a "citizenship appropriate to the necessities of our age," Irigaray writes: "Education for civil life becomes an education in being, rather than in having: being oneself, being with others, male and female, being in and with nature, being a moment of History, etc. The development of certain values is indispensable for this new form of citizenship: values of communication, not only in the sense of the transmission of information but as communication-between. Relations between individuals are thus prioritized, with respect for things and possessions following as a consequence."[68] Irigaray calls for the cultivation of citizens who can communicate and not just transmit information. The challenge CARA presents and takes up is the creation of this communication—in the face of an aggressor's refusal of the labor of the negative and in the creation of a community that invites the aggressor into this labor. CARA's work asks us to consider what it would look like to refuse to sacrifice members of our community even when a member has refused the labor of the negative.

In developing accountability strategies, it is important to keep in mind that it is not just the carceral system that has failed to invite aggressors into such work. Many communities and organizations that have sought alternatives to incarceration have also resisted such work. As Critical Resistance and INCITE observe: "The various alternatives to incarceration that have been developed by anti-prison activists have generally failed to provide sufficient mechanisms for safety and accountability for survivors of sexual and domestic violence. These alternatives often rely on a romanticized notion of communities, which have yet to demonstrate their commitment and ability to keep women and children safe or seriously address the sexism and homophobia that is deeply embedded within them."[69] Irigaray gives us one way to understand that failing as more than just an irony of activist work. Because we live in cultures in which the labor of the negative is projected onto an other, a critique of one its components is necessary, but not sufficient, to achieving a different social order.

In other words, we should expect to find the sexual indifference that Irigaray critiques even in radical politics, unless we engage in the work of bringing about a culture of sexual difference. As Critical Resistance and INCITE! write: "Because activists who seek to reverse the tide of mass incarceration and criminalization of poor communities and communities of color have not always centered gender and sexuality in their analysis and organizing, we have not always responded adequately to the needs of survivors of domestic and sexual violence."[70]

But there is an apparent mismatch between CARA's activism and Irigaray's proposals that deserves attention. CARA presents their accountability work by alternating personal pronouns to indicate that both men and women can be survivors and aggressors. As they succinctly point out, "This reflects the realities of our work."[71] Further, earlier I spoke of the widespread phenomenon of rape in men's prisons. Irigaray, on the other hand, speaks of women only as the survivors and for the needs of women to have civil rights. Is Irigaray operating with an outdated or even regressive notion of sexual violence?

My answer to this question requires a yes and a no. Insofar as Irigaray implies or explicitly states[72] that women are the only victims of rape, incest, and other forms of sexual abuse and harassment, she is clearly not recognizing the vulnerability to violence of men, boys, transgender individuals, and those who do not conform to gender norms.[73] But if we return, once again, to Sabo's description of prison rape as a gendering practice, I think we can see compelling reason to consider how sexual violence is involved in the discursive creation of men and women, as well as to the creation of that binary. I am thinking here of Sharon Marcus's argument that rape feminizes women[74] and Christine Helliwell's argument that rape is a practice that "masculinizes men as well."[75] Helliwell points to prisons as a site in which we can see this effect of rape; she writes, "This masculinizing character of rape is very clear in, for instance, [Peggy Reeves] Sanday's ethnography of fraternity gang rape in North American universities (1990b) and, in particular, in material on rape among male prison inmates. In the eyes of these rapists the act of rape marks them as 'real men' and marks their victims as not men, as feminine."[76]

Thus, Irigaray's proposals for civil rights for women could be read as a critique of discursive practices that render women vulnerable to sexual assault and define women as those who are vulnerable to sexual assault, while concomitantly rendering men as those who commit sexual assault and define men as those who commit sexual assault. That is, Irigaray's demand for bodily integrity for women can help us to see the extent of social and cultural transformation that would be necessary to guarantee such safety, as well as the extent to which vulnerability to assault defines what it means to be a woman in many cultures. Thus, Irigaray offers a powerful critical tool by proposing bodily integrity for women to illuminate the production of women as vulnerable, even as she sometimes fails to acknowledge that women are not the only people vulnerable to violence.

The existence of cultures without rape gives us crucial evidence that sexual assault need not be the only way that gender is constituted and reaffirmed.[77] Irigaray's proposals for sexuate rights can show us how far we are from achieving cultures free from such assault. But so can a glance at crime statistics. The importance of Irigaray's proposals for sexuate rights is their provocation to think about the formation of gendered subjectivities and what might be required to end sexual assault in our own community, given how gendering currently happens. CARA has already begun such work.

By working to redress violence without creating accusers, monsters, criminals, plaintiffs, and defendants, CARA creates new possibilities for subjectivity and community. Irigaray's work shows that such work requires a critique of current structures, including the structure of subjectivity, and a process of transformation toward new structures that we cannot fully determine, now or in the future. Rather, we must acknowledge that no model of subjectivity can be the universal model of subjectivity, which requires that we take the labor of the negative on ourselves and create communities that foster such labor.

Isolation and Resistance

Statement on Solitary Confinement

Abu Ali Abdur'Rahman

In June 2012 Illinois Senator Dick Durbin chaired a hearing on solitary confinement in the federal prison system. Survivors of solitary confinement, legal representatives of presently confined persons, and officials from U.S. prisons testified to the Senate Judiciary Committee's Subcommittee on the Constitution, Civil Rights and Human Rights. Abdur'Rahman sent this testimony to the Committee.

I am Abu Ali Abdur'Rahman, formerly known as James L. Jones. I am an American citizen and though I am a student of Islam, I am not of the non-spiritual un-Islamic renegade sects. That you needed to know, so that you will not assume and despise me. My voice needs to be heard. I appreciate this moment and thank you for your attention.

Presently, I am confined at Riverbend Maximum Security Institution. I am housed in Unit 2, the Death Row Unit. I've been on Death Row since July of 1987. It has been a journey and a struggle. I've managed to make it to this point in time. I have been blessed! My dream, to speak with you, has come to be. Praise be to the GOD of us all.

Isolation. Solitary confinement began with me a long time ago. I was born in the year of 1950. At the age of eight, my father (who is now deceased), a military man, 503rd military police, 82nd airborne, confined me to a clothing closet for a long period of time as a disciplinary measure. In this closet, I laid hog-tied with a thin piece of leather tied to the end of my penis, the other end tied to the clothing hook above. The psychological effect it had on me was not to be determined until later on in life. I ask the question: is this a productive form of discipline? I am the end result.

Because no one cared or [wanted] to get involved, I fell prey to unforeseen traps during my delusional attempts to find a space without the elements of pain. In 1970 my defects led me to a reformatory in Petersburg, Virginia. There, I experienced sexual harassment. Reporting my concerns to the proper officials served me no good. Each time I sought help, I was put in solitary confinement for protection, so said the officials. I was being punished for not wanting to be a jailhouse punk. Being confined in such a way for seeking help took a toll on me. I became much more bitter, and I hated certain male figures who I thought were dictators and bullies.

Because this form of isolation was so torturous, in every instance I made myself believe I could withstand the pressure. Each time, I asked to go back into population. Each time, because the officials were not properly trained, and because they didn't care, I was put back into population.

It happened. In February 1972 two Black males sexually assaulted me. I've been told now that that incident caused me to disassociate. With the encouragement of others, I had to prove myself to be a man. In April 1972 rumors led me to believe that I was going to be attacked again. I didn't want to go back to isolation. The officials knew about the incident and yet they didn't care.

I decided to confront the situation, and one thing led to another, until, impulsively, I thought I was defending myself. I stabbed one of the individuals who, rumors told me, was going to make me his boy. I was trapped and isolated in my head. Where was I to go? And who was I to turn to?

From then until 1980, I lived in isolation, solitary confinement—from one dark space to another. The irony of this is that everything that I am now saying is already in the records. No one stepped forth to help me. And even though there are existing documents directing people in positions of power to help me, the records reflect that I was ignored and dismissed.

I tell you these things now because you said you wanted to know what is taking place here in this country's penal system. I have no ulterior motives. With certain information, perhaps future policies can help people who are experiencing similar defects of the mind.

We come from abusive and destitute environments. Our lives were built on anger, fear, hatred, and lack of love. You have to have insurance or the right amount of money before you receive the proper help. Without the proper help, there will be failures, low esteem, and no sense of direction. It's the poor Whites, the Chicanos, the Native Americans, and the African Americans who bear the brunt of this. The penal system is full of mentally disturbed people. Because of their disabilities, they are being considered misfits, rejects, and undesirables, isolated from public view and sentenced under the criminal code. The present policies criminalize mental illness.

In the year 2000, my legal team was able to find people who undertook the task to help me understand how to recover. Every day is a challenge. I get up every morning at 5:00 to prepare myself for the occurrences of that day. The fact that my legal team was able to uncover my full record has helped the process toward healing. Though I still have nightmares, they are[n't as frequent]. I am able to write you this testimony because of the people who have finally come into my life. People who actually care about my welfare.

My testimony is not meant to debate whether people who are supposed to be a danger to others should be scrutinized, for I know too well the problems that people can sometimes present. My concern is the method. If the intent is to transform behavior, then agitating an emotionally disturbed person is counterproductive. I think correctional officials should hold degrees in developmental psychology and sociopsychology. The goal of the law and the field of correcting disordered, defective behavior should be interdisciplinary. That being said, restorative and transformative justice will both contribute significantly to the purpose of initiating contrition and that desired result—habilitation.

Thank you for allowing me this opportunity. I hope that what I have said made sense.

The Violence of the Supermax: Toward a Phenomenological Aesthetics of Prison Space

Adrian Switzer

The Problem of Supermax Violence

As Peter Scharff Smith explains in his study "The Effects of Solitary Confinement on Prison Inmates," a "primary rationale for supermax prisons has been to lower the level of violence in prison systems."[1] The supermax prison is characterized, Smith continues, by "solitary confinement twenty-three hours a day in a barren environment, under constant high-tech surveillance."[2] More generally, maximum-security incarceration, which first came to prominence in the United States in the late 1970s and early 1980s, involves the isolation of prisoners in separate cells, limitation of access to communal areas and activities, and the regular and systematic use of solitary confinement. The logic of the supermax is that by dividing the prison population into discrete units and limiting the time and space of group interactions, less prisoner-on-prisoner violence will occur: fewer occasions for prisoner interactions leads to fewer altercations.

Further articulating the anti- or counterviolent logic of the supermax, Lorna Rhodes reports on the following from a conversation she had with a guard in an "intensive management unit" in a prison in Washington.

According to the guard, the "control unit" is a vast improvement over the conditions in the prison in the 1970s and early 1980s; because of the "control unit," the prison overall "[has] gotten less violent." Rhodes interjects at this point: "Control units . . . are a product of the rationalized management" of prisoners; by design, they are "tightly organized, brightly lit, and maximally visible in every corner." The origin of this new form of "control unit" imprisonment in which prisoners are isolated from one another and confined to blank, featureless cells for long uninterrupted periods of time is historically identified with the federal prison in Marion, Illinois, in 1983. Rhodes writes, "There a week of violence led to a prolonged emergency lockdown, a 'large-scale experiment in solitary confinement' that continues to this day. As the number of people being incarcerated rose dramatically in the 1980s and 1990s, prison systems all over the country began using isolation to 'tighten up' on their inmates." Though labor intensive in requiring guards to escort each prisoner from one area to another, deliver meals, and search cells, "[prison] administrators . . . argue that it is worth the price to keep the 'worst' prisoners locked down where they can do no harm."[3]

Yet, as Smith points out, citing the research of Castellano, the desired effects of supermax confinement have not been realized over the past forty years. In Smith's terms, the "effectiveness" of supermax prisons in curbing prison violence remains, at best, "speculative."[4] Violence persists within maximum-security prisons—prisoner-on-prisoner violence, as well as the excessive punishments of prisoners by guards. Despite the anecdotal evidence to the contrary offered by the guard Rhodes interviewed in the Washington state penitentiary system, prisons with "control units" are not sites free of violence. Here, we find one of the central paradoxes of the contemporary prison system: Why have changes made to prisons in order to decrease the incidents of violence not brought about the intended results?

We might answer this question by appealing to the types of persons who are incarcerated in the supermax (e.g., violent criminals, persons with long criminal records, drug addicts, persons with mental or developmental disabilities, etc). In this regard, recall the aforementioned administrative view of confined prisoners as cited by Rhodes: it is the "worst" prisoners who require "loc[k] down." From these assumptions about the population in maximum-security facilities, and in the "control units" within these prisons, the persistence of the problem of violence in supermax prisons is a matter, simply, of the violent persons confined therein. Regardless of security precautions, and no matter how structured and ordered the prison becomes, the violent character of prisoners overrides these safety measures.

Misconceptions about the current prison population aside, what the aforementioned line of reasoning fails to explain is not just the *persistence* of violence in the supermax prison but its *aggravation*. Again, citing Castellano, Smith shows that occurrences of violence are higher and more frequent in maximum-security prisons than in other incarceral settings.[5] In the argument sketched in the previous paragraph, according to which violence in prisons is caused by the violent characters of prisoners, the further assumption would have to be made that persons now imprisoned in supermax facilities are in some sense more violent than persons who were imprisoned prior to the introduction of this form of prison. If the supermax itself is to be counted out as a nonfactor in explaining prison violence, then *all* empirical trends would have to be explained in terms of the prisoners alone.

Statistics on prison populations in the United States in the past thirty-five years do not support this line of reasoning. With the rapid increase in prison populations since the late 1970s, persons incarcerated for violent crimes are per-capita a *smaller* proportion of the overall prison population than before the mid-1970s. Citing the research of Hindelang and Gilliard and Beck, Irwin et al. calculate the percentage of violent offenders held in the prison system at 57 percent in 1978 and 47 percent in 1997.[6] Continuing, Irwin et al. argue that "[m]ost of the growth in America's prisons since 1978 is accounted for by nonviolent offenders."[7]

Similarly, Ruddell notes that the "steepest and steadiest increase in incarceration rates began in 1980" and continued for the next five years "without any change in the crime rate." Accounting for this increase in the prison population by citing the increase during the same time in violent crimes is statistically untenable: "it is difficult to explain the totality of increases in the use of imprisonment based only on changes in the number of violent crimes. While violent crime doubled [between the late 1970s and early 1990s], the use of incarceration quadrupled."[8] Moreover, citing the work of Rennison and Rand, by 2002, which Ruddell terms "the height of the imprisonment boom," "rates of violent crime reached their lowest point since the 1950s."[9]

The sociological evidence, then, presents us with three incongruous aspects. First, the record shows a decrease over the past forty years in the relative percentage of prisoners who are incarcerated for committing violent crimes. Second, there has been a near-exponential increase over the same time period in the number of supermax facilities in the United States. Third, over the same time period, there has been an increase in violence in prisons. The focus of this chapter is on the last of these three aspects of the contemporary prison-(post-)industrial complex. While focused on violence in the supermax prison, the aim of the present chapter is to offer an explanation of this phenomenon without appealing to the unfounded equation of violent prisoners and violent prisons.

A further assumption on which this last identification rests is that it is the most violent criminals who are incarcerated under supermax conditions. That is, it is assumed that only the "worst" criminal offenders are housed in maximum-security facilities with arbitrarily imposed and extended periods of solitary confinement, as well as severely restricted access to interpersonal interactions in public communal spaces. Here, too, the sociological evidence contradicts the "anti- or counterviolence" argument for maximum-security incarceration. Citing legal filings in the case of *Wilkinson vs. Austin*, Smith calculates that there are at least fifty-five supermax prisons in the United States; citing Rhodes, Smith estimates that the number might be even higher.[10]

With the rapid increase in the number of incarcerated persons in the United States since the early 1980s—the so-called "prison boom" of the past three decades—and with an increased use of the supermax model for redesigning and building new facilities, a larger and larger proportion of the prison population is housed in high-security facilities. This is one of the overlooked senses of the contemporary prison as an "industrial complex," namely, the mass reproduction and regularized design and construction of prison facilities. Though, today, the prison system in the United States is fully postindustrial, for the previous thirty-five years prisons followed in their design, construction, and function the trend set by broader socioeconomic forces in commodity production.[11] During the same time period, the supermax became the design model for the mass-industrial production of prisons—hence, the "industrialized" character of the prison despite the postindustrial character of prison life and operations.

The effects that the mass-production of prisons had on design and layout are predictable: interior spaces were stripped of defining marks and features; prison exteriors became monolithic and box-like; a "placelessness" permeates the supermax inside and out, regardless of their geographical location. Earlier, we read Rhodes's comment on the "brightly lit" and featureless spaces of the supermax control units. If Bentham via Foucault offered a design ideal of centralized disciplinary power in the Early Modern prison,[12] the contemporary prison design of the supermax is more akin to a planned corporate park or "campus," or a subdivision of prefabricated homes: repetitive; homogeneous; built on a principle of maximized "usability."[13] Later on, I will return to the design of the supermax—to the spaces of mass-reproduced and absolutely "functionalized" confinement facilities. Specifically, my interest is in the designed and built space of the supermax as a determining factor in its violent character.

Leaving aside, for the moment, this link between the highly regularized space of supermax prisons and the basic "mode," in a phenomenological sense, of such a space, let us conclude our brief review of the sociological record on prison violence. As noted previously, the modern history of prison redesign and construction in the United States has followed the example of the supermax. Prior to a very recent and partial reversal of this trend, the number of maximum-security prisons in the United States had steadily increased since the 1980s. Concurrent with the increase in the number of maximum-security prisons was a decrease in the number of persons incarcerated for violent crimes. The prison-population trends over the last thirty-five-year period show a rapid rise in nonviolent criminal incarcerations. Thus, the sociological evidence undermines the legislative arguments for the need for supermax facilities to house an ever-growing number of violent criminals who need to be "locked down." Per-capita, nonviolent offenders make up a greater proportion of the United States prison population than ever before.

From these different sociological trends, the question of increased violence within supermax prisons remains open. The wont is to answer, simply, by appealing to the violent character of prisoners founders on the fact that today's prison population is comprised of fewer and fewer violent offenders. In turn, the claim that the supermax is unique in the contemporary prison landscape in housing only the most violent criminals is contradicted by the industrial mass-production of supermax facilities. Persons incarcerated for nonviolent crimes are now confined under supermax conditions. The reason for this, in part, is because of overcrowding as the new construction of prisons lags behind the growth of the prison population. Another reason for the same trend is from the punishments imposed on persons for "illegal" acts committed while imprisoned—though many such intraprison "crimes" are nonviolent acts. In this way, a drug dealer with an original sentence of a few months can find herself isolated for a long period of time in a "control unit" for an altercation with another prisoner in a low-security facility. In all these respects, trends would predict a *decrease* rather than an *increase* in prison violence. However, even this counterprediction is made on the assumption that the cause of prison violence is the violent character of incarcerated persons, and it is this equation that I would like to resist in order to take a different approach to the problem of violence in the supermax prison.

Generally, my argument is nonempirical and nonsociological. I begin with a brief review of the sociological record in order to sketch in outline a live problem in the contemporary supermax prison: *Why has a facility that was instituted to decrease incidents of violence been marked, instead, by increases in violence?* Further, why has an increasingly nonviolent prison population within supermax facilities been subject to higher rates of violence? If the solution to this problem does not lie with the population in the supermax, and if a psychological account that identifies violent acts with violent persons does not accord with the research findings, then the problem begs for an alternative approach.

A Transcendental Phenomenology of Space

My aim is to sketch a nonsociological and nonpsychological account of the violence of the supermax prison. What I outline is a potential answer to the question of supermax violence that, though nonempirical, still accords with the sociological evidence considered previously. My approach is philosophical; specifically, it is phenomenological. We are led from the outset by indications of there being *something* to the supermax environment itself that contributes to prison violence. By setting aside an experiential and psychological approach to the problem of supermax violence (and this is why I adopt a phenomenological approach), we allow the form of maximum-security incarceration to be counted as a factor in addressing this problem.

Further, my phenomenological account of the violence of the supermax prison is transcendental in Husserl's sense, which is to say it locates such violence at a basic and constitutive level of the prison environment. For Husserl, the transcendental constituents of a horizon of consciousness, of an intersubjective horizon of consciousnesses, and, most generally, of the world as the most general object-correlate of transcendental subjectivity determine the experienceable characteristics of that horizon and world. The supermax prison, here, is treated as a horizon of consciousness, or as a world of intersubjective consciousness, in Husserl's sense. In these terms, the claim of this chapter is that violence is a basic and objective constituent of the world of the supermax.

By such phenomenological means, we revert from the level of the psychological causes of prison violence to the Husserlian level of the transcendental. As Husserl writes in the Encyclopedia Britannica essay "Phenomenological Psychology and Transcendental Phenomenology" (1927)—making a point that he repeated throughout his career—"[a] phenomenological pure psychology is absolutely necessary as the foundation for the building up of an . . . empirical psychology." In turn, a phenomenologically pure psychology must itself be grounded in phenomenology as a transcendental science.[14] Accordingly, in offering a phenomenological account of the violence of the supermax prison, we turn from the level of prisoner psychology, whether phenomenologically pure or empirical, and consider such violence at a transcendental and constitutive level.

A number of considerations recommend a transcendental phenomenological approach to the question of violence in the supermax prison. First, as noted previously, there are a number of incongruities in the sociological record on prison violence, incongruities that tend to persist even upon further empirical study. Further, almost all studies in this area share the assumption that the violence *of* the supermax is a matter of the violence of the persons *in* the supermax—abandoning this premise leads us to the level of the nonpsychological and nonempirical. Finally, the turn to a transcendental account of the violence of the supermax is motivated by the facility it gives us to consider the prison itself as a determining factor in the violence that occurs within the space of the prison (i.e., in brief, the aim is to explain the violence *of* the supermax as a phenomenologically identifiable state of affairs that differs from violence *in* the supermax).

In terms borrowed from Husserl's *Ideas I* (1913), our interpretive attention shifts from the noetic to noematic features of intentional consciousness. With the idea of a noema, Husserl introduces into phenomenology an element that has "objective relation" in itself; further, it is a noematic objectivity that has its own sense and significance.[15] As Husserl continues in *Ideas I*, the basic determinant of a noema considered in itself is the spatiality of all objects.[16] While Husserl is interested in the objective significance of noematic space (i.e., the way in which it contributes to and is a factor in the fulfilled meaning syntheses of intentional consciousness), my interest, instead, is in space's basic modality, that is, its quality, or, what Heidegger, developing Husserl's phenomenology, would call its fundamental "*Stimmung* [mode; or, mood]."[17]

As a philosophy of the subjective and objective constituents of cognition and possible experience, phenomenology overcame the long-standing epistemological "problem" of the objective validity of subjective thought: objective significance is shown by Husserl to be always already a feature of transcendental subjectivity.[18] Because of its two-term analytic framework, phenomenology also enables philosophy to consider each of these poles in relative isolation from each other. By adopting a phenomenological approach, one is able to conduct separate analyses of the subjective and objective determinants of intentional consciousness against the backdrop of their mutual worldliness. Further, the transcendental character of phenomenology enables us to consider each determinant at a basically constitutive level.

In focusing on the objective and spatial character of the supermax prison—in reversing Husserl's usual procedure from noesis to noema—I am not thereby ignoring the subjectivity of the *experience* of that space. After all, the violence of the supermax is experienced by persons in body and mind; though constitutive of that subjective experience, the objective space of the supermax is not itself violated. Rather, I accent the object-correlate of the noematic pole of intentional consciousness in order to reveal its transcendental quality and basic modality. In this regard, I am following Husserl's recognition from the persistence of the object, or what he terms the "determinable x" of the noema, of a distinct transcendental determinacy to objects, which underlies their noetic predicative determination by consciousness.[19] Accordingly, space is treatable as a transcendental determinant in its own right. Most basically, space is an insuperable "other" to noetic determination.

Consider in this regard Husserl's familiar phenomenological account of the perceptual experience of an object. As embodied and situated consciousnesses, we are only ever immediately present to one side or one dimension of a perceived object. The other sides, hidden to immediate perception, are in a sense given in the ordered character of intentional consciousness. The actually unavailable sides of the presently perceived object are given as what Husserl calls "adumbrations." In the mode of projection or anticipation, we "walk around" the object and fill out its missing sides through our specific conscious intentions toward those for-now unavailable sides.[20]

From this phenomenological account of the structure, orientation, and makeup of an object of perception, we might still ask: what status does the spatiality of the object have? In *Thing and Space: Lectures 1907*, Husserl answers that this spatiality, the alterity and other-sidedness of all objects of perception, is an "inauthentic perception" (i.e., the "apperceptive surplus" atop the "pure perceptual tenor" of what is immediately—and authentically—perceived of the object).[21] The philosophical problem that Husserl faces with this answer is that the perceptually intuited proximate side of an object is thereby treated as similar-in-kind to the other sides of the object as intimated in this perception. But this undermines what is unique and particular to actual perception: Husserl's answer risks converting perception into a form of signification. The alternate answer is no more satisfying. On this alternative, Husserl would have to extend perceptibility to the unperceived other sides of the object, thereby obscuring the difference between actual and possible acts of perceptual consciousness.

Without answering these issues, or, more precisely, without tracing through his corpus, Husserl's various efforts to answer these questions suffice it to note that space as a condition of the object-correlate of noema has a problematic status for phenomenology. One way to understand space in a Husserlian phenomenological context is as the condition of the irreducible otherness—and unavailable "other-sidedness"—of all transcendent objective reality. Space, after all, is not immanent to transcendental consciousness; or, to the extent that it is, it is available only analogically with the temporal succession of internal time-consciousness.[22] Thus, the need for a further condition for the determination of other-sidedness of perceivable objects is supplied by space as a nonimmanent element of transcendental consciousness. In more technical terms, while the spatiotemporal form of all possible experience is a feature of transcendental subjectivity, space as the *actualizing* condition of objective other-sidedness has a distinctly transcendent character. Though Husserl obscures this difference earlier in using the terminology of "authentic" and "inauthentic" perception, as if the other side of objects is a mere difference-in-degree of perception, his recognition of objects as *actually* other-sided intimates a perceptual difference-in-kind.[23]

The relevance of these theoretical considerations for our present interest in the violence of the supermax prison is that they show space to have a foreign and "other" character from a phenomenological perspective.[24] The alterity of space as a transcendental condition of *actual* objectivity suggests further that it might have its own determinations and modalities. In these terms, what I am interested in is space's transcendental modality of non-subjective alterity and inexperienceability. Rather than solving the Husserlian problem of the spatial character of the object as thing, we can allow this problem to signal a significant fact about space, namely its otherness relative to the immanent transcendental character of consciousness. Space is thereby engaged transcendentally and phenomenologically without framing our analysis in terms of the immanent noetic aspects of consciousness. Space becomes, in its own right, the object of a non–subject-oriented transcendental phenomenology: an objective phenomenology whereby the basic structures and modalities of space can be revealed in themselves. Despite this refinement of our phenomenological approach, still there are limits to a phenomenology of space that requires a supplementary aesthetics of the same. Later on, I return to these limits in conclusion and suggest a few elements of such a supplementary aesthetics.

By whatever means the basic modality of space is revealed, whether phenomenologically or aesthetically, its significance for the space of the supermax—the physical, architectural, and designed interior space of maximum-security prisons—is that this modality determines, transcendentally, the experiential horizon of the world of the prison. Further, because the transcendental character of space in itself is "other" and actually unavailable to human experience, the space of the prison is determined as hostile and foreign to the prisoners. This is because the space of the supermax approximates the bare alterity of space as a transcendental determinant and radical "other" to meaningful conscious experience. The violence of the supermax, then, is rooted in the space of the prison because of the latter's nondeterminate featureless character. The plain homogeneous spaces of supermax design approximate the basic character of space itself, revealing its inaccessible character and building a nonsubjective otherness into the lived environment of incarcerated persons.

Though I have followed Husserl, to this point, in arguing from the empirical and experiential level of the supermax to its underlying transcendental character, phenomenology's interest in the basic character of space extends well beyond Husserl. In fact, other phenomenological resources help us articulate the basic modality of space: what Husserl leaves in the mode of "otherness" and alterity, Bachelard defines more fully as the "hostility" and "inhospitability" of empty space.

In reflecting on space in itself, and before poetically transforming it through memory and creative imaginings—akin to what Husserl calls the "retentions" and "protensions" of intentional consciousness—Bachelard notes its basic "hostil[ity]." The promise of a subsequent "habitab[ility]" of space is a further determination affected through experience, whether lived experience or artistic creativity.[25] Featureless bare space is not the space of the geometer, which the phenomenological tradition rejects for an idea of space integrated into conscious and embodied experience, or, in the case of Bachelard, the space of home life, both real and imagined. The "hostil[ity]" of space "in itself" that Bachelard notes is not a matter of its Cartesian coordinates or its describability in mathematical terms. In short, basic space is nonconceptualizable; equally, the modality of bare space is nonconceptual. Rather, indeterminate space registers phenomenologically at a preexperiential level: its hostility is nondiscursive and immediate; it is constitutive; such "hostility," for Bachelard, is "the space of hatred and [of] combat."[26]

In its generically homogenized design and featureless layout, the space of the supermax prison approximates the character of space with which

Bachelard begins his phenomenological reflections. As do all spaces, so, too, does the featureless blank space of the supermax invite experiential determination and particularization. Yet, because of the great regularity of the spaces within the supermax facility—the regularly spaced cells, the modular cell design, the flat fluorescent lighting, and so forth—the possibility of experiential determination is always frustrated. Aesthetic changes that a prisoner makes to his/her cell are counteracted by the otherness and insignificance of the wider prison space within which he/she lives. Similarly, and to appease the worry that I am considering the space of the supermax in too idealized a form, the gradual deterioration and disrepair of maximum security facilities also does little to offset their basic design character: a dilapidated minimalism and functionalism remains at root minimalist and functionalist. Indeed, phenomenology as a transcendental philosophy enables us to engage objective reality at this basic, nonempirical level without treating such objectivity as ideal.

What emerges within the space of the supermax, then, is space in what Bachelard identifies as its bare hostility and uninhabitability: it is a blank environment that overwhelms the subjectivity of the prisoner. As Anthony Vidler writes in reference to Ioan Davies's work *Writers in Prison* (1990), "The space in prison is of a different order, being, in Bachelard's sense, both familiar and hostile." What Davies means by this, Vidler continues, is that the space of prisons is "voiceless [and] sightless"; it is a "mechanized physical structure" that reproduces in an uncanny and inaccessible fashion space as something familiar and potentially experienceable. However, in its regularity and homogeneity, the space of the prison leaves such familiarity always out of reach and unrealizable.[27] The context of Vidler's comments is an essay on the violence of space (i.e., the un- or underconsidered manner in which the spaces we inhabit have a constitutively harmful character all their own)—a violence that comes to the fore in sanitized spaces stripped of all defining features.[28]

Consider, in this regard, the following description of the confinement units at a maximum-security prison in Northern California: "[The] cells [are] approximately five feet wide by eight feet long. The cells are without fresh air or daylight, both ventilation and lighting being poor. The lights in some cells are controlled by the guards."[29] Similarly, a *New Yorker* article on solitary confinement in contemporary supermax prisons describes a cell at the maximum-security prison at Walpole, Massachusetts: "[the cell is] thirteen-by-eight-foot" painted all in "off-white." Several concrete structures are present in the cell as furniture: a "smal[l] slab" that protrudes from the wall as a desk; a "cylindrical concrete block" on the floor is a chair. Finally, and unlike most solitary confinement units, the Walpole cell has a seven-inch "ribbon-like window" cut into the concrete.[30] The slight light variability introduced into the space by the thin opening differs from the more common light design of prison cells: an overhead bank of white fluorescents that are controlled externally by a guard; when lit, the unit is washed with unshadowed light; whatever defining features of the space are effectively erased by the light. In writing about the solitary confinement units at Elmira Correctional Facility, William Blake describes it as a "timeless" place of "austere sameness."[31] Though I am concerned with the whole space of the supermax prison, these descriptions—both firsthand and secondhand accounts—of the confinement units provide a clear image of the brutal plainness and unadorned homogeneity of maximum-security facilities. The "regularization" of the supermax, which was undertaken to diminish aggression and check intrapopulation divisions and hierarchies, leads to the protrusion of the space of the prison. In the language of Blake, quoted previously, the "austere sameness" of the space emerges prominently and deleteriously into the everyday consciousness of the prisoners.

Phenomenology anticipates just such a spatial "presence." One of the key insights shared by Husserl, Heidegger, and Merleau-Ponty is the lived character of space. What in the history of philosophy and science had tended to be construed as self-subsistently given and defined by regular geometrical proportions is in phenomenology the space of intersubjective intentional consciousness (Husserl), concernful being-in-the-world (Heidegger), or desire-oriented embodiment (Merleau-Ponty). In all three phenomenologies of space, subjective mobility is further constitutive of lived space. For example, as Husserl writes in *Ideas II* (1952), "In all perception and perceptual exhibition . . . the body is involved as freely moved sense organ," a mobility which is in part constitutive of "the spatial world."[32] Yet, with the interruption of everyday lived experience and corporeal motion that ensues upon incarceration, the spatial-objective correlates of intentional subjectivity emerge from their habitual background: space "presents" itself in its bare otherness.

At an experiential level, what the supermax prison does to space, as basically oriented and ordered through embodied mobile experience, is to rearrange it and disorder it. The concerns that direct us in the world and give meaningful direction to our actions—and thus the concerns that structure the space of the world within which we live—are disrupted by incarceration. This is not to say that prisoners do not have end-oriented concerns and desires that enable them to arrange and order the spaces of their world. Rather, it is that the given concerns of communal life—

from which we draw our own cares to constitute the space of our personal lives—are absent within the supermax prison. As Drew Leder writes in phenomenological terms about the space of the prison, "We might . . . refer to this space as *disoriented*. The spatiality of home and neighborhood is oriented by vectors of meaning, possibility, and preference. Far less so is the spatiality of prisons."[33]

Prisoners adopt different strategies and responses to the breakdown of the familiar lived spatiality of "outside" life. In conversation with prisoners at the Maryland State Penitentiary, Leder notes that some leave the space of their cells untouched and generic; others, in an effort to claim the space as their own, paint and decorate their cells: "Michael Green: . . . I got a friend that every cell he moves in he paints to the max. I refuse to paint one of these cells or lay it out like it was home . . . Charles Baxter: . . . I call my cell my palace . . . I got my Oriental rugs laid down. I don't care where I'm at; I'm going to make it heaven while I'm there."[34] It is not insignificant that prisoners respond aesthetically to the protrusion of bare space into their everyday lives. What practices of rearranging the objects in their cells, pasting up magazine cutouts, or displaying their own art suggests is that prisoners are affected by the bareness of the prison space at a non- or preconceptual level. The aesthetic responses of prisoners to the bareness of their cells suggests that there is an indeterminacy to what it is about that space that calls for a response; accordingly, prisoners react in the simplest aesthetic manner, by adding color and altering the light.

For now, let us set aside these aesthetic responses of prisoners to the "disoriented" and "disorienting" space of the supermax prison. In conclusion, as already noted, I will consider an aesthetic supplement to the present phenomenological account of prison space. Instead, I would like to underline the point that the experience-based ordering of space with which we are all familiar in an everyday setting is disrupted upon incarceration. With such interruption, space itself protrudes for the prisoner who now finds him/herself confined to a maximum-security facility. What the prisoner must do is shape, give meaning to, and inhabit the unfamiliar spaces of the prison; he/she must endow his/her environs with sense and value through his/her desires and purposes. Because of the generic design and structure of the interiors of the supermax, these efforts are checked by a space that persists as indeterminate and other. The "work" of constituting a world in such an aesthetic environment is physically and psychically taxing; and here, on an experiential level, we note a manifestation of the hostility of the space of the prison.

If meaningful space must be opened and maintained through the projected cares and concerns of each prisoner, as various phenomenologists argue, then the trespass of another prisoner into that defined space, and the intersection of differently ordered spaces of meaning and value, could lead a prisoner to react in anger from the sense that his/her very world—the very spatiotemporal fabric of his/her life—is being violated. However, all of this is true for prisons in general, and not just for supermax facilities. On this traditional phenomenological account of the embodied or care-ordered nature of space, there is nothing spatially unique about the maximum-security prison: all prisons would "look" and be experienced the same. Moreover, because of the extreme isolation exercised on prisoners in supermax prisons, the spaces of separate prisoners' worlds do not regularly overlap. If the work of constituting a spatiotemporal world is threatened in a "control unit" environment, it is threatened by something other than other prisoners. So, the problem of the violence unique to the supermax is not fully explained in traditional phenomenological terms of disoriented lived space. For this reason, and within the context of a phenomenology of prison violence, we are again returned to considerations of what *does* define these spaces uniquely, namely their generic design and absolute homogeneity. Once more, we are compelled to shift our phenomenological gaze from the subjective constituents of the supermax as a lived world to its objective built-character. In short, because of the insufficiencies of a phenomenology of disoriented lived experience in explaining the violence of the supermax, we are returned to a transcendental level.

What recommends a transcendental analysis of the problem of violence in maximum-security prisons, and, in particular, a phenomenology of the space of those facilities as constitutive of such violence, is its anticipation at a transcendental level of the protrusion of space into an unfamiliar environment and un- or underdetermined setting. As strained as the analogy might be, what incarceration affects is a kind of phenomenological *epochē*—a suspending or bracketing of the natural everyday attitude in which time and space are experienced as the nonintrusive and seamless context of our thought and action. We inherit a lifeworld already overlain and intersected with meaning and value; we are "thrown," in Heidegger's terms, into already-determined horizons of sensible action. It is this inheritance that is lost, or, at least, that might only, at best, be carried over into and partially recreated within the generically homogenized cells and hallways and confinement units of the supermax. In these terms, what I have suggested throughout is the character of space that is revealed through the incarceral *epochē* of everyday embodied comportment in the collective life-world "outside" the prison. My interest is with space, not as it is "in itself" in the sense of a substantially given phenomenon, nor as a mathematizable phenomenon. My interest is in space in its transcendental character (i.e., bare space defined in its own basic modality).

Still, for all of its analytic potential, phenomenology ultimately is insufficient to the task of defining this basic modality. My tone, throughout, has been tentative and suggestive; repeatedly, I have referred to the current project as a "sketch" or an "answer in outline." My reason for doing so follows, in part, from this last point: phenomenology remains too general in its analysis of the transcendental character of space to capture the specificity of the space of the supermax. What Bachelard names outright as the "hostility" of bare space, and what Husserl intimates in the language of the "alterity" and actual "otherness" of space, is all still too abstract to account for the particular modality of violence in specific supermax environments. Though it is beyond the scope of this chapter to complete this project, in conclusion I offer an aesthetic "supplement" to a phenomenology of space—a turn to aesthetics anticipated in Heidegger and Merleau-Ponty's respective phenomenologies of art.

What the prisoner undergoes upon incarceration, and what figures the insufficiency of a strictly phenomenological account of the prison space, is an absolute rupture in the time and space of experience. What the prisoner enters into is a wholly different experiential setting. As Alyson Brown shows in "'Doing Time': The Extended Present of the Long-Term Prisoner," the general temporal structure of "normal" experience is not merely disordered upon and during incarceration; it is altered absolutely. Further, the time and space of experience is altered for the prisoner in so profound a way as to persist even upon release from prison.[35] From Brown's findings, space and time are *not* (somewhat) stable structures that carry over from the "outside" into the "inside" world; experientially, the two worlds are significantly different and actually incomparable *even at the spatiotemporal level*. Here, in more technical terms, is my reason for avoiding an existential analytic of the space of the supermax and adopting a transcendental approach: at an experiential level, the spatiotemporality of long-term imprisonment is unlike other worldly horizons.

In light of the radical break in experience that occurs with imprisonment, the question is whether a transcendental phenomenology can rid itself of every vestige of "normal" experience and consider the objective constituents of a world without appeal to a suspended everyday empiricism. In so doing, can phenomenology show the transcendental character of space in itself and specify its "otherness" *specifically* as violent or hostile? Merleau-Ponty, who in the phenomenological tradition comes closest to analyzing space directly without connecting it to time, still tends to frame space existentially. In *Phenomenology of Perception* (1945), Merleau-Ponty even identifies space and experience: "[S]pace is existential; [and] we might just as well say that existence is spatial."[36] Despite such "experientialization," elsewhere Merleau-Ponty offers spatial analyses that draw closer to space itself without appeal to an experiential frame.

Continuing in the same passage in *Phenomenology of Perception*, Merleau-Ponty criticizes Kant for reducing space to a sensible intuition — or, to the form of sensibility — because it makes of it something "spatialized" rather than as something "spatializing."[37] With the latter concept, Merleau-Ponty tries to capture a primary sense of space, one that precedes ontologically the discursive constitution of the experienceable world. Subsequently, Merleau-Ponty describes "spatializing" space in the following terms: "When, for example, the world of clear and articulated objects finds itself abolished, our perceiving self cut off from its world imagines a spatiality without things . . . [Such a spatiality] is not an object in front of me, it envelops me, it penetrates through all of my senses, it suffocates my memories, it almost erases my personal identity."[38] As Mikel Dufrenne characterizes space as Merleau-Ponty here presents it, "[It has] the aspect of otherness, as what is always outside . . . and as an elsewhere opposed to the here which we are."[39] The question is whether such a description of transcendental space implicitly appeals to the experiential frame of all phenomenological analyses. Though the body is something more for Merleau-Ponty than an experiential datum, and it is through the body that we "commun[e] with the [spatializing] world" before all thought,[40] to describe the prediscursive character of space Merleau-Ponty still must appeal to experiential and discursive forms: in a sentence elided from the aforementioned excerpt, Merleau-Ponty figures bare space as "like the night" in blanking out all horizons of perception and suffocating the self in darkness.

What my analysis of the space of the supermax reveals, then, is a limit of a phenomenological approach to the analysis of space. In enabling us to consider space at a transcendental level, phenomenology has allowed us to set aside the psychological and experiential assumptions of a sociology of prison violence. Yet, because phenomenology remains dependent upon an experiential context to translate its transcendental findings, it disables us from *specifying* the basic constitution of space without reverting to an empirical level — the very level at which the violence of the supermax presents contradictory aspects. In short, since we are concerned with the transcendental modality of space "in itself," we seem, still, to require the context of everyday experience for the articulation of that modality, and it is just this "everydayness" that Brown tells us disappears upon incarceration. To describe bare space as "inhospitable," "hostile," or "violent" is implicitly to translate the transcendental mode of space into a determinate discursive form; such discursivity at least adjoins, if it does not completely coincide with, natural everyday experience.

It is for this reason that I point forward, in conclusion, to the possibility of an aesthetic supplement to a phenomenology of space in its basic modality. Where a transcendental phenomenology fails to articulate the basic character of space without appealing surreptitiously to the subjective framework of experience, works of art might succeed. A turn to art is also motivated by the aforementioned response of prisoners to supermax confinement: many have their cells repainted; they decorate the walls with pictures and drawings, and so forth. What these practices suggest is a potential in art to overcome the prominent "presence" of hostile space in the supermax prison. In conclusion, then, let us consider briefly Heidegger's and Merleau-Ponty's aesthetic reflections as specifying additions to the aforementioned transcendental phenomenology of the space of the supermax.

A Phenomenological Aesthetics of Bare Space

At various points in his *œuvre*, Heidegger presents a phenomenology of space. In *Being and Time* (1927), space is described in terms of the care-structured orientation of *Dasein* as being-in-the-world; elsewhere, Heidegger offers an aesthetic phenomenology of space. In this latter context, consider Heidegger's claim in the essay "The Origin of the Work of Art" (1935) that the work of art is a "setting up" in the sense of an establishing and opening of a "world."[41] Included in what it means for an artwork to open a world, Heidegger, too, describes it as a basically "spatializing" operation.[42]

Given my interest in the constitutive hostility of bare space, the pertinent feature of "world-opening" art is its relation to what Heidegger calls the "earth." While from an intraworldly perspective the "earthliness" of artworks can be construed as the opaque limits that frame every horizon of meaningful activity, we can also take "earth" to name the basic materiality or substantial spatiality of a world. Indeed, at one point in the essay Heidegger makes explicit the link between the thingly materiality of artworks and the partial concealment of a world by the earth: "Th[e] setting forth of the earth is achieved by the work as it sets itself back into the earth," which is like, Heidegger continues, how the "sculptor uses stone" to craft his works.[43]

What Heidegger is pointing to in the paired notions of "thingly" art-works and "earth-bound" worlds is their basic givenness or "facticity." In terms of aestheticized space, we might translate Heidegger's insight into the fundamental "objectivity" of space; an objectivity that Jeff Malpas describes, phenomenologically, as being present "at a level immediately below the level at which our attention is primarily directed"—one that is accessed, if at all, by works like Cézanne's late paintings of Mont Saint-Victoire.[44]

According to Heidegger, the open world of concern-oriented time and space—of experience, in general—stands in contrast to the subsistent spatiality of the "earth" over against which it is set. World and earth, Heidegger continues, strive against each other: "In setting up a world and setting forth the earth, the work [of art] is an instigating of this striving [. . .] s[uch] that the strife remains a strife."[45] In the language of the "strife" between the space (and time) of experience and space in its basic facticity and objectivity, we should hear the "otherness" of space as constitutively uninhabitable or inhospitable. Art, and more particularly a phenomenological aesthetics, is able to reveal the antagonistic character of bare space without translating it into an experiential context. In Heidegger's terms, the "strife" of world and earth is constituted *between* the two modes of space; as such, it is not reducible to the experienceable domain of the world alone.

Consider in this same phenomenological aesthetic context Merleau-Ponty's late philosophical reflections on the invisible and on the "irrecusable" and "enigmatic" character of the invisible. Such invisibility is comparable, I would maintain, to the "otherness" in which bare space subsists apart from experience.[46] In order to specify the mode of this spatial otherness, Merleau-Ponty has cause, like Heidegger, to refer to the domain of art. In "Eye and Mind," an essay written at the same time as the *Visible and Invisible*, Merleau-Ponty argues that Cézanne's color palette enables him to depict an "unstable" and chaotic spatiality.[47] Questions of the viability of this as an interpretation of Cézanne's work aside, what Merleau-Ponty finds depicted in the paintings is the instability and chaos of "invisible" space (i.e., space as undetermined by experience).

Similarly, in the early essay "Cézanne's Doubt" (1945), Merleau-Ponty describes the "nature" that Cézanne tried to paint as a "chaos" and Cézanne's self-destructive project as a matter of rendering in art the primitive "matter" of space prior to its "form[ation]" into perceivable phenomena.[48] What I have been referring to—following Bachelard—as the "hostility" of bare space is discernible in Merleau-Ponty's reflections on Cézanne's madness. While setting himself the unachievable painterly task of spatializing the canvas in order to recreate on it the depth of natural space, Cézanne's struggles are perhaps better read at a more basic level, namely that he put and held himself in relation to space in its most primitive formlessness. Subjectively, these are maddening circumstances; objectively, this is space at its most unavailable and inexperienceable. To go beyond impressionism, which Merleau-Ponty announces as Cézanne's artistic goal, the last safe vestige of organized sensory perception had to be abandoned: primitive space, or what Cézanne called simply "nature," had to be engaged directly. In making himself one with nature, or, in allowing nature to create through him, Cézanne embodies the otherness of space in himself: an embodiment that looks, subjectively, like madness.

Arguably, the work-character of artworks would have to be eradicated if a phenomenological aesthetics were to reveal in full the hostility of space in itself: the organizing structure of the artwork *as object* imports space-as-experienced into the otherwise bare spatiality of the aesthetic context. To complete a phenomenological aesthetic of bare space, then, we would need to turn from Heidegger's and Merleau-Ponty's traditional preferences for sculpture and painting to art forms that are nonobjective, such as the post-War minimalist gallery preparations of Donald Judd, Robert Morris, Dan Flavin, or Sol Lewitt. Developing such a nonwork aesthetics of minimal space is beyond the scope of this chapter.

Even with an incomplete phenomenological aesthetics of bare space, still the most relevant feature of that space for considerations of the violence of the supermax has been revealed. Space, in itself, stands in "rift"-like opposition to the space of experienceable world; space in its "natural" form, in Cézanne's sense, is chaotic, unstable—and, it leads to madness. If, as I have argued, the space of the supermax approximates space in this bare form because of its homogeneity and featurelessness, then what these last aesthetic reflections show is that such space is not merely other and non-subjective but specifically characterizable as inexperienceably hostile. In being designed and built into the very form of the supermax, a basic mode of hostility thus pervades the spaces of the prison, and it is a hostility that modally constitutes the violence of these facilities.

All of which is no argument of strict causation or immediate determination. To claim, as I have, that the bareness of the space of the supermax is constitutive of its violence is not to reduce prison violence to the structural aspects of the space within which it occurs. A "transcendental determinant" in the phenomenological sense is not a cause but a constitutive element: the space of the supermax does not cause its violence; the space constitutes—it structures in a formal manner—the prison environment as violent. The physical, psychological, and emotional violations faced each day by a person held in maximum-security facilities express and manifest the formally constitutive hostility of the space.

If my phenomenological analysis of bare space and my brief aesthetic exemplification of the same have revealed an overlooked aspect of the supermax, the question remains of what might be done to address prison violence at such a basic level. Repeatedly, previously, I noted the efforts of prisoners to alter the aesthetics of their world by hanging photos, magazine cutouts, self-made drawings, and so forth. While this response shows the significance of the aesthetics of the space of the supermax and the importance of responding in the same register to that space, the problem is that such strategies address existentially what I have argued is a transcendental feature of the prison.

A solution to the problem of the violence of the space of the supermax must occur instead at the level at which the problem is rooted, namely, the structural design and build of these facilities. The difficulty is that the design of the supermax, as noted previously, is part of a larger conception of the contemporary prison as an industrial—and now postindustrial—complex. Changes to the space of the prison that were something other than cosmetic would have to coincide with broader landscape changes (i.e., how built-space, in general, is designed and realized; how sameness and plainness are adopted as design rules in the name of utility and functionality; how postindustrial spaces are reclaimed or built over rather than being left in—and as—ruin, etc).[49] Such broadening of a reform agenda is again in keeping with my phenomenological approach. After all, though we have attended to the object-aspect of transcendental phenomenology, that aspect is always fit within a broader horizon and world. The thought of remedying the problem of supermax violence simply by making the spaces of the prison more hospitable to life and experience is to overlook this key phenomenological insight into the worldliness of all phenomena, whether subject- or object-centered.

Prison and the Subject of Resistance:
A Levinasian Inquiry

Shokoufeh Sakhi

Death, imprisonment, and physical and psychological torture are among the responses of state power to its others. These others are categorized and identified according to the self-definition of the state but also in relation to what they represent or signify. Regardless of the state and the nature of its prisoners, as Foucault shows in his *Discipline and Punish*, prisons not only exact retribution but also act as subjugating institutions with the intention of reconstructing subjects. In this sense, prisons function as totalizing systems.[1] Important variants notwithstanding, these prisons (like their states), turn out to have much in common. For what they share, what makes them "totalizing" is their continuously renewed effort to engineer not just the complete eradication of all opposition but the complete elimination of all distinction between human subjects and imposing systems, replacing all that is not themselves with themselves. Of course, both this intention and its implementation indicate the primordiality of human resistance. Within this context, prisons, and more pronouncedly politically motivated prisons, become the concentrated sites of the struggle between resistance and capitulation.

To emphasize the psychologically sophisticated and systematically complete nature of the totalizing procedures of this intention, I call them *the paideia of totalizing systems.* It is a "paideia" in the sense that, through the application of an ensemble of strategic manipulation of the subject's sense of being, it intends an ontological transformation, reducing the subject as such to a "for-the-system" being. Contrary to the common sense dictum that everyone breaks down under pain and fear of death, the persistence and intensity of totalizing practices, within prison systems for instance, are evidence of the possibility and actuality of resistance.[2] Yet, to investigate the human potentiality for resistance one needs to begin with the basic questions. Why, under the paideia of the totalizing system, do we so often come to lose our ethical bearings, our social identities, such that we capitulate in this way? Yet again, why is it that we also so often resist when resistance seems so impossible, and how might we more effectively resist?

In what follows, I shall argue that to conceive effective opposition to this paideia, we must look to the fundamental *meaning* of resistance itself, specifically, its *ethical* meaning. This meaning may tend, generally, in one of two directions: (1) withdrawal into a state I shall call the "survival-ego," a condition in which one's life is "rationalized" through the subordination, finally, of everything to concern for survival, a reduction to a slippery slope to complicit capitulation, or (2) expansion toward solidarity with other beings, and, ultimately, I shall argue, beyond being itself—to what Emmanuel Levinas refers to as the "otherwise-than-being,"[3] where a responsibility more ancient than the formation of being itself may be interrogated. It is from the latter that I extrapolate the germ of a resistance beyond the resistance of being itself, what I refer to as *effective resistance*, that is, a resistance that neither succumbs nor emulates the tendency to totalizing, to saming all to itself.

While the interrogation of the ethical meaning of resistance may be informed by any number of theoretical approaches, the meaning itself is, of course, lived. The sites of the meanings of resistance are to be found in the engaged suffering of people confronted, invaded, coerced in the context of contingent institutions and their personnel. The treatment of political prisoners and their responses offers a privileged site for examining the systematic instrumentalities of this intention.

Political Prison and the Survival-Ego

To state the bare bones in advance: the objective of prison systems for political prisoners is the production of the survival-ego by applying techniques of physical torture, environmental manipulation, and indoctrination—central components of the paideia[4] of totalizing systems—with, at its most insidious, the systematically related goals of getting the prisoner to reduce herself to an object of survival and, on that foundation, breaking her down until she identifies with and participates in the system's meanings and intentions. This is a process of attempting to isolate her from others, physically, ethically, and, ultimately, existentially (i.e., to reduce her to self-referentiality), removing what autonomous social existence she brought with her. The final phase consists of testing the efficacy of the process and solidifying the results through engaging the agency of her newly internalized identity on behalf of the system itself against her own former ego, her family, her fellow prisoners, and her culture generally.

The process of attempting to install this regression begins with the application of physical torture, an approach to be sure with many functions beyond the goals of finding out what of immediate use the prisoner knows. These include creating a willingness to be used for propaganda purposes, producing an example, and furthering political control through public confessions and other such exercises in humiliation designed for public consumption. Though this process, euphemistically called "conversion," can be divided analytically into reciprocally reinforcing aspects of the paideia, they form a constellation under the rubric of *varieties of torture*, which may be treated together and which, for reasons of space, will be the approach here.

The fundamental intention of the initial phases of this paideia is not limited to the experience of pain and suffering as such, nor even solely the fear they engender. Fear of pain and suffering, yes, but whatever else these may be, they are essentially means to achieving the great anxiety of constant insecurity and the longing for comfort that this fear brings with it. Regardless of ideological venue, it aims at, and often succeeds in, breaking the will. A Chinese prisoner recalls: "I was really accepting things in order to make myself more comfortable—because I was in great fear. . . . In this situation your will power completely disappears. . . . You accept because there is a compulsion all the time—that if you don't go on their road, there is no escape. . . . [Y]ou become passive."[5] An Iranian political prisoner writes of her experience of being blindfolded as the moment she lost her humanness: "I became a donkey. They tied my eyes and I became a donkey, an ass." She continues later: "With my eyes closed the whole world went dark. . . . Fear and anxiety about the future, torture and death became dominant."[6]

The basic achievement, reduction to the survival-ego, is accomplished if and when the prisoner identifies herself exclusively as a survivor at all costs.

And this torture-induced focus is the slippery slope at the end of which is the totalizing systems' desired total capitulation, because, reduced to the survival-ego, the prisoner's agency is virtually theirs. Nothing of the prisoner remains inaccessible; reality itself is the system's reality.

By means of isolation, surveillance, and the concomitant unpredictability and insecurity that together they provoke, this *reality* is then used to support and extend the torture-induced anxiety and render it constant.[7] It is crucial here to induce the sense of incessant imminent threat, the insecurity of the unpredictable, as illustrated, for example, in many prison memoirs of the political prisoners under the Islamic Republic of Iran.[8] The experience just after the pain of the chord hitting the bottom of the feet is one of expectation: when is the next one coming? Torturers, of course, develop a sense of timing that emphasizes unpredictability and thus maximizes the anticipatory fear and anxiety in the intervals. The benefits of such intervals are highlighted in the CIA's interrogation manual: "There is an interval—which may be extremely brief—of suspended animation, a kind of psychological shock or paralysis. It is caused by a traumatic or subtraumatic experience which explodes, as it were, the world that is familiar to the subject as well as his image of himself within that world."[9] One *lives* in this anticipatory interval. Here, the tendency all too frequently is to turn the fear against oneself, to fear oneself, if not for the aggression one may feel against the domination of the all-too-powerful system, then for the eruption of one's old personality (and, under the conditions of the constantly observed survival-ego, it *is* experienced as a previous and very dangerous personality). Thus is solidified the survival-ego, a state of constant anxiety that an imminent annihilation will surprise the next second. Insofar as the system has been successful, a state is achieved in which a little hope can often complete the conversion. Thus, according to Kubark, when the prisoner experiences the "loss of autonomy,"[10] it is time to institute and administer the paternal relation: "Now the interrogator becomes fatherly. Whether the excuse is that others have already confessed ("all the other boys are doing it"), that the interrogatee had a chance to redeem himself ("you're really a good boy at heart"), or that he can't help himself ("they made you do it"), the effective rationalization, the one the source will jump at, is likely to be elementary. It is an adult's version of the excuses of childhood."[11]

Whether the totalizing system be Iranian, Chinese, American, or otherwise, the process of regression and identification with the interrogator as a father figure[12] initiates variations on the same form: restriction of access

to any but the given ideology, intense and repetitive indoctrination, forced
self-negation through "frank" public disclosure, "authentic" repentance of
one's "crimes," and then, as a reward, social "recognition" as a successful
convert. Thus is accomplished the identification with the new ontology of
the survival-ego.

The integration of the "true convert" into the totalizing system is, of
course, insidious. For example, in "revolutionary" Iran, as in China, the
prisoner began in unofficial settings to "help" other prisoners "confess."
The process moved on, flowing organically from the informing-and-
denouncing "education," to informing on the slightest appearance of "in-
correct" behavior or attitude on the part of other prisoners, other "true
converts," even guards, and, of course, on themselves in the form of increasingly subtle "confessions." Then, one could become, to use one of
Robert J. Lifton's phrases for the Chinese convert, a "prisoner-official," a
convert so advanced along the road of "reform" as to act as an interrogator (i.e., a *samed*[13] subject), an object of the system and her own survival, a
for-the-system subjectivity. Eventually, the "prisoner-official" finds herself
torturing confessions from newcomers, going out as a guide and informer
with the guards on search and arrest missions against members of her former political group and other political groups, against the most distant
members of her extended family, and against husband, wife, mother, father,
and children. From witnessing executions, she would move on to participating in the killing.[14]

What, then, in the face of such systematic paideia, could constitute an
effective resistance? Both experience and analysis suggest that the attempt
to use the modern techniques (merely glimpsed here) to replace the content of the resistant identity with that of a totalizing system, be it Islamic,
Maoist, or modern Western, has met and continues to meet with mixed
success and more than occasional failure. However, experience and analysis also point in another direction, toward sources of meaning both beyond
and within the self, sources capable of continuously resisting reduction of
one's self to the survival-ego or subjectivity-unto-the-system, sources, in
short, of effective resistance.

Remembering, referring to my prison notes, and discussing with other
former Iranian political prisoners, I find that many had an intuitive sense
of something of the sort. Caring for humanity and life itself as such, and
sensing/hoping/believing such caring would remain outside the power
game, fortified the resolve not to participate in the slippery slope of the
rational strategic action of survivalism: one must *begin* with the knowledge
that in playing the game that ends in betrayal of that *meaning*, in becoming

a convert, the instrument of surrendering oneself and others to the system, one is already dead.

Interrogating the Meaning of Resistance

If the totalizing system attempts to supplant the "otherness" of the prisoner with the identity it prescribes, and if it has access to our being and its solidarities, it is finally our otherness that must be preserved. But the slippery slope is indeed slippery. All too often, attempts to theorize resistance, in their well-intended efforts to explain it, finally become complicit in the reduction of the other to the same. If, somehow, in the process of actual resistance, people find, in so many instances, sources within themselves that access a responsibility to and care for humanity, a space of otherness, it may be this very otherness itself that lies behind the often-recognized sense that humanity itself is the ultimate resistance to totalizing systems. It is to give what Max Horkheimer called this "banal"[15] sense of humanity an articulated meaning that we turn to Levinas. But, in so doing, it is crucial to avoid reducing Levinas's interrogation of ethical alterity to a generalized statement on the praxis of resistance, to preaching a new strategy, rather than interrogating a meaning of resistance that may lie in the depths behind several of its guises. Such strategies, falling into ends/means rationality or dialectical transformation with the totalizing system as its other, are merely defensive. And, while defenses are a necessary part of the process, they are (when abstracted from care-for-the-other) ultimately susceptible to reduction to the being of the person who is imprisoned within the "reality" of the system and thus to the slippery slope. So the last thing we need is another model of resistance, another method of suffering by which, through its employment, one could learn to suffer successfully without capitulation and become a "hero" of resistance somehow more morally attuned than the survival-ego. A fundamental and disqualifying limitation of the heroic identity is that it is, as ego-identity, an extension rather than a transcendence of the self-enclosure of the survival-ego. Constrained within its self-referentiality, it tries with all its might to cleave to its determination against the will of the torturer, like trying to hold one's breath until it is over; it is still quite vulnerable to the paideia of the totalizing system that remains its "other." Moreover, it is doubly susceptible in its tendency to stand (until it falls) in some morally superior relation to the "lesser" political prisoners who fail in their efforts to resist, explaining that failure is due to an absence of adequate quantities of will, faith, loyalty, and so on. To pretend to explain or even understand—let alone to assume a competence to judge—the intricate complexities of the soul of an individual prisoner is to remain trapped in the enclosure of one's being. It is not only to fail to respect the otherness of the other but also to participate in the very hubris of the totalizing system. It is, in short, completely to miss the point.

It is to locate a site of potentially *effective* resistance against, among other things, such strategies of being that we turn to Levinas. What we hope to encounter, in short, is another "reality," another level of meaning unencumbered by strategies of being of whatever ilk. This is a reality that, while occluded within the hegemonic survivalist "realism," has nonetheless been accessed by many in the darkness of their suffering as such denizens of totalizing systems, as political prisoners.

Levinas strips away the deep occlusions of this experience, disclosing its sources at a level of humanity phenomenologically more ancient than culture, consciousness, or even the formation of the "I" as a subject. Here, he interrogates an inherent responsibility to and care for the other that relates in fraternity all who have ever lived, live now, or will ever live, which relates them in a common humanity-of-the-being-for-the-other that is immanent to everyone. One indication that this relation is not an illusion of slave morality, the ultimate defense of the soul's "retreat to the inner citadel,"[16] is to consider what a potent obstacle the resistance of humanity must be, if totalizing systems go to such lengths in their attempts to overcome it . . . and so often fail.[17]

It is, then, with the recognition of the mystery of alterity as the ultimate horizon, an otherness that resists both explanation and coercion, that a human meaning of resistance may be approached; this potentially effective resistance, I argue, is ultimately the resistance of otherness itself, a praxis of resistance beyond resistance, humanity itself as resistance. With this approach, then, the following interrogation adumbrates a phenomenology of resistance, beginning with a brief interrogation of the limits to approaches to resistance based on the power of the individual will.

The Will of the "Pure I"; the Passivity of the "Naked I"

Levinas puts his finger on limits to the power of individual will that turn out to be pertinent to elucidating resistance at the level of being when, in *Totality and Infinity*, he presents the will as combining a contradiction. On the one hand, it claims sovereignty against all external attacks, having a power beyond any possible quantifiable adversary: "Not for eternity will I waver."[18] On the other hand, there is contained here an insurmountable proneness to error, an untrustworthiness, an unreliability, "to the point that voluntary being lends itself to techniques of seduction, propaganda, and torture."[19] As he says, the will can make it seem as though the difference between cowardice and courage consists in nothing more than the mechanical differences between quantities of energy put into resistance and quantities put into overcoming it (which, were it true, would mean that individual resistance in the context of the committed totalizing system might indeed be futile). He continues,

> When the will triumphs over its passions, it manifests itself not only as the strongest passion, but as above all passion, determining itself by itself, inviolable. But when it has succumbed, it reveals itself to be exposed to influences, to be a force of nature, absolutely tractable, resolving itself purely and simply into its components. In its self-consciousness it is violated. Its "freedom of thought" is extinguished; the pressure of forces initially adverse ends up appearing as a penchant. In a sort of inversion it loses even the consciousness of the bent of its penchants. The will remains on this moving limit between inviolability and degeneration.[20]

This I of the will is an I folded in on itself, a folding that puts the subject in the grip of being and the violence that this folding does to me. This "folding in" to self-referentiality, placing the I in solitude, is its degeneration, its reification as an object.[21] But, fortunately, no matter how much history of being and how much hypostasizing theory, the I never wholly resides in itself.

Suffering and Patience

In the isolation and other tortures of the totalizing system, one is thrown back, inevitably, upon her will and its defenses, where, sooner or later, she reaches the limits of heroism. Recuperating and marshaling all forces of her will to block the invasion, the attempt to conquer her inner life, she closes her eyes, turns inward, away from the face of the other. She tries to fold in on herself, building a fortress of solitude; she tries to become an impermeable thing, resisting all incursions. Against the violation that the system imposes upon both her psychological and physical being in order to reach and eliminate the otherness inside and the others through her, she closes her eyes behind the blindfold, turns inward to her familiar world, and musters everything available to deny its breaching. In this dynamic of invasion and denial, courage itself thus becomes a tool of the system, finally isolating a pure-I, that is, one restricted within the meagerness of its own ego. This isolated ego *is* the entrance to the slippery slope to becoming the inverted will, the samed, the system's reified thing.

This inverted will, an "inversion" in which "'freedom of thought' is extinguished" and "the pressure of forces initially adverse ends up appearing as a penchant" in the case of the convert—the *samed* prisoner—is not, however, inevitable. For, while the inversion threatens the will "in its dignity as *origin* and identity," "it *only* threatens, is indefinitely postponed, is consciousness."[22] Here in consciousness, as Levinas interrogates it, our relation to time, the nonidentity of the "instant,"[23] is the site of resistance at the limits of the will: "Consciousness is resistance to violence, because it leaves the time necessary to forestall it. Human freedom resides in the future, always still minimally the future, of its non-freedom, in consciousness—the prevision of the violence imminent in the time that still remains."[24]

Suffering thus remains ambiguous. The I is turned into a thing, but simultaneously there remains a distance from the reification, "an abdication minimally distant from abdication."[25] This is because one retains consciousness, even if it is only consciousness of oneself as an object of torture. And, of course, the torturer cannot do without this consciousness, for awareness of the suffering is the fundamental requirement of the exercise: the I must witness its suffering. This minimal distance that consciousness provides is the locus of the potentiality of what Levinas calls "patience": "This situation where the consciousness deprived of all freedom of movement maintains a minimal distance from the present, this ultimate passivity which nonetheless desperately turns into action and into hope, is *patience*—the passivity of undergoing, and yet mastery itself."[26] Here, in this consciousness, says Levinas, the will achieves a "mastery" in a new sense, not a willful mastery over, but one beyond the reach of the fear of death: "[t]he egoism of the will stands on the verge of an existence that no longer accents itself."[27]

It is in this existence that no longer accents itself that the opening for resistance beyond the enclosure of being and its will is to be found. In patience, "the violence the will endures comes from the other as a tyranny."[28] Violence can only come about in ". . . a world where I can die *as a result of someone* and *for someone.*"[29] Thus, suffering in patience changes the *meaning of death*, distancing it from the isolation of my will and my enclosure within the poignancy, the desolation, of its being *my* death. "In other words," writes Levinas, "in patience the will breaks through the crust of its egoism and as it were displaces its center of gravity outside of itself, to will as Desire and Goodness limited by nothing."[30]

What is potentially accessed in the dark night of the soul of the prisoner of the totalizing system, both inside and outside of prison, is a suffering beyond the suffering of the individual being, a suffering in and for the other. What is received is exposure to responsibility and, so I claim, care for-the-other that is prior to, more ancient than, being itself, a responsibility of the "naked I" that, potentially accessible to everyone, Levinas helps us articulate. Again, only the barest indications of these notions can be presented in what follows.

The Passivity of the Naked I as Resistance

The freedom of the subject of torture exists by virtue of the necessary distance between the subject-as-object and the consciousness of what is being done to that object—putting the subject minimally distant from the present and thus the immediacy of the pain and suffering. This freedom may render resistance on the level of being possible, but even when successful, this possibility says nothing about the fundamental question: "Why resist?" And without an unshakable response to that question, the minimal distance provided by consciousness, though sometimes enough to prevail, is a poor defense indeed. In the long run, the retention of the subject against the tyranny of the totalizing prison system cannot adequately rely on defenses of any kind but rather depends upon the meaning of resistance itself.[31]

But what is the site of meaning here if it is not this consciousness of one's pain, of one's self-knowledge, or knowledge of one's precarious life? Levinas responds, "[I]t is a "consciousness" that, rather than signifying a self-knowledge, is effacement or discretion of presence."[32] It is a "bad conscience" in which one has to "respond for one's right to be, . . . in the fear for another." This bad conscience "is a shaking and an inversion by which, as *myself*, I pierce beneath the identity of the being and may henceforth speak of *my* shaking, of *my* conatus, of *my* persistence in being, of *my* being put in question, just as I speak of my being put into the world; an entry into the concern-for-the-death-of-the-other-man—an awakening of a 'first person' within the being. This is problematicity at its origin in the guise of my awaking to responsibility for the other, in the guise of a sobering up from my own existing."[33] The I's right to be comes into question as its being is threatened. Blindfolded, in a solitary cell, on the torture bed, in the interrogation room, one is always already in the presence of the other. Prison, with all its techniques and procedures, provides one with ample motives for assuaging one's self with the "good conscience" of holding on to one's being. But "is not my existing, in its quietude and good conscience of its *conatus*, equivalent to letting the other man die"?[34] In the dark night of the soul, retention of one's subjectivity against a system that would reduce it, the refusal to become an object for the self and the system, points toward the very meaning of one's subjectivity and, hence, its resistance.

It is in the bad conscience of the for-the-other in its "passivity" that one may locate an imminent "resistance beyond resistance," a naked resistance of the for-the-other itself. Here, I find a sense of the resistance potentially experienced in the dark night of the soul of the prisoner, a resistance that remains beyond the reach of the totalizing system with its access to being. With the interrogation of this passivity, in its distinction from passivity on the level of being, one may locate an ethical "self" in contradistinction to the self as it appears on the level of being.[35]

This passivity *must* remain beyond the world of action, beyond even the material being that is the site of action: "The prereflective I in the passivity of the *self*: it is only by the self, or by the I-in-question, that this passivity is conceived. This is the passivity more passive than any passivity, more passive than that which, in the world, remains the counterpart of an action of some sort and which, even as materiality, already offers a resistance: the famous passive resistance."[36] Levinas means to distinguish the sense of passivity, chosen or imposed, within the order of being from that of the naked I as a "passivity more passive than any passivity." The passivity of being is already no longer the naked passivity of the prereflective I, the "I" of the bad conscience; it is already resistance of the ego-being of the pure I, the I confined to its will, already defensive and/or aggressive, calculating and negotiating, already a strategy of being—and thus as indifference on the level of being already complicit in the order of being of the totalizing system:

> They called me to participate in a public religious ceremony. I had
> never participated in these programs before, but, at this moment, I
> was in a state of indifference. I felt the heaviness of this indifference
> on my being; this scared me. I feared for my future. What would they
> want from me? How far could I retreat; where could I stop and tighten
> my belt again? In those days, I was thinking that I could hold out, was
> holding out, preserving my strength for bigger battles. Was this only
> a justification for my growing indifference, for allowing myself to
> be led?[37]

I would argue, however, that the passivity of the naked I is always already a resistance, a resistance more passive than passive resistance on the level of being, a resistance beyond resistance that may perhaps even be recognized as the ultimate source of all ethical resistances. In its very being-for-the-other, it is always already a resistance to the saming intentions of the totalizing system. Here, then, beyond the "disengagement within engagement" of the "patience" available to consciousness on the level of being, is—to reverse Levinas's emphasis—a potential *engagement within disengagement*, the engagement of the fraternal humanity immanent to the naked I, and thus, however occluded, to the I of being. This resistance is the resistance of the being-for-the-other, which, in the disengaged passivity itself, stands beyond the machinations of the totalizing system. It is the ethical praxis as a fundamental engagement.

Thus, the praxis of engagement within disengagement is to be distinguished both from any consciously empowered resistance on the level of being and from the withdrawal of the psyche from pain and suffering under the stress, fear, and anxiety of torture. One's passivity here is not a withdrawal from one's being as may happen, for example, in traumatic experiences such as rape or other torture of one's being. The engagement in disengagement is not a withdrawal into the no-place of traumatic shock, not simply the flooding of the ego by anxiety, but rather is as precisely opposed to this withdrawal as it is opposed to submission in the service of happiness or the contradictory responsibilities of the order of being. Here, in engaged disengagement, the meaning of life itself is transformed. From avoidance of suffering, it becomes acceptance of suffering as intrinsic to life, and it becomes *responsibility-in-suffering*. Here, then, both happiness and suffering are aspects of being, but one is not reduced to the seeking of happiness as the avoidance of pain and suffering as the survival-ego is reduced. Withdrawal into traumatic shock, into the nowhere of an ego-less being, draws one, when the ego returns, toward the survival-ego: traumatic shock is . . . traumatic; one tends to fear the experience, tends to compulsive avoidance of its repetition. In short, one is impelled toward the capitulation and compromise of the survival-ego. The engagement of disengagement is one's connection with others rather than a disconnection from everything—a solidarity rather than a retreat into solitude: the openness to which, by its very existence within the context of the totalizing system, *is* engagement.

What can be said, then, about commitment to resistance confronted with the contradictory responsibilities on the level of being? What is the appropriate response to those who, from love and responsibility, council capitulation (feigned or real): that sometimes one is faced with a choice between contradictory responsibilities and should choose the greater, the responsibility to "God," the "nation," "the people," "humanity"? No![38] What the totalizing system wants is beyond my being, is my sociality, ultimately my naked I, my for-the-other self itself; it wants to convert it to a survival-ego and from there to a for-the-system self. It is the meaning in the passivity of resistance beyond resistance in its absoluteness that remains external to, other than, such systems' instrumental strategies of causality. If I, accepting my solitude, my identity as a pure I, an in-itself and for-itself, oppose my responsibilities on the level of being to the system—Levinas is quite right here—I contaminate my resistance as a naked I with the motivations and countermotivations of the conflicting responsibilities we necessarily encounter in the world of being. Again, no. My ethical responsibility is not a choice to be weighed in a cost-benefit analysis of consequences of whatever stamp. It is rather an acceptance of an opening unto responsibility for the other immanent from the beginning—that is why it cannot be reduced to just another option of "conversion" produced in the dark night of the soul; it is not a conversion but an opening. Thus, in full recognition of the horrible consequences of my continuing resistance, I *must*, beyond all excuses and explanations, in the defenseless passive patience of my denuded self, abandon my being, along with all its responsibilities, to this original naked responsibility. My apology for this resistance must be without apology, without the reification of any "said" that I, or Levinas, or anyone else can say.

Conclusion: Humanity as Resistance

Coming to the end of this preliminary interrogation, I want merely to explore, tentatively, a small part of its possible implications as an ethic in relation to the praxis of resistance. Here, within the limits of the few indicated notions in Levinas's work, I find not only a potential for reconsideration of our contemporary human situation in general but, within that potentiality, new appreciations of the meaning of resistance that, beyond the machinations of totalizing systems, suggest a position less vulnerable to their coercions than their contemporary power with its momentum might lead one to believe.

The shift from purposes on the level of being to meanings of the otherwise-than-being allows us to clarify the core intention of the totalizing system; it ultimately seeks to coerce and manipulate the finally insular being in order to remove its otherness, its for-the-otherness, and transform it into a for-the-system. In the face of these systems, whether those promoting non-Western or Western heteronomies, is disclosed the primacy of the impulse to *efface the face that calls us to responsibility*. Against this impulse, Levinasian interrogation, clarifying the meaning of resistance, finding the for-the-other *pre*-ontologically immanent, suggests a source of resistance (beyond resistance) that is potentially more formidable than any totalizing system: humanity as resistance and resistance as humanity.

This *meaning* is not just another moralizing cultural ethic from which to stand in judgment in the apparently vain hope of achieving a psychic economy in which guilt appears in sufficient quantities to coerce enough of us into a united humanity, a humanity with a sufficiently similar mastery of aggression, to allow if not an amorphous and all-inclusive "love" at least a capacity to "just" get along. Such moralizing, in its attempt to dominate the individual will through the application of group aggression, parallels the paideia of the totalizing system—prison institutions, camps, and societies at large—preparing the human subject for the cycles of domination and capitulation, and domination again. The intention of totalizing systems, in their frustrated narcissism, to apply aggression in order to same everything that is not otherwise annihilated, is precisely opposed to fraternity, the proximity without synthesis immanent to individuals in their relationship of responsibility to, and concern and care and love for, the other person.

The interrogation here has suggested that humanity as resistance must begin at the beginning—the first step away from absolute responsibility is the step onto the slippery slope; it must begin, prior to any reason, in the relation to the face of the other. Thus, the deontological approach, the removal of the subject as such, represents precisely the wrong direction; *humanity must refuse to absent itself from its social and political forms.*

Reflecting, then, on Levinas's ethic of absolute responsibility suggests, not without risks, a reconsideration of ethics and their relation to praxis. Of first importance here, it seems to me at the moment, is the fact that Levinas's absolute is an absolute on the level of meaning. Prior to and absolutely separated from all action (let alone praxis) is the meaning of responsibility. This absolute separation not only preserves the meaning of humanity from contamination with the ethics of consequences, the cause and effect relations, the dialectics of the practice of being human in social and political contexts (the only place they are to be found). It also preserves this ethic from contaminating the field of action as just another ideology in the name of which the ends can be said to justify the means. The absolute is absolutely separate from the strategies of being, yet without being absent from the praxis of resistance.

The ethic of the absolute responsibility for-the-other, by remaining on the level of meaning, thus remains an opening up of being to the immanent otherwise-than-being that, potentially available to everyone, may disclose humanity as resistance and, in its resistance beyond resistance, stubbornly refuse to give up its spirit to the totalizing system: in itself, it preserves human meaning. As such a preservation, however, it *speaks* to being, perhaps reminding being of its absence, the absence of the for-the-other, occluded under the shroud of solitude. Solitude, that Archimedean point of totalizing systems—whether the political prison or the prison of the isolated, privatized liberal I and its system—is precisely what responsibility denies. One is always already in relation to others, even in the solitary cell. The solitary cell, in fact, presupposes the sociality of the prisoner, targets one's being-in-relation-to-the-other. As the political prison experience underscores, submission is not just an abandonment to an isolated "nowhere" (as it appears in some versions of anxiety, fear, and death), not just a retreat into isolation. Rather, it is an opening up of access to one's for-the-otherness, an opening of a passage through which violence and death reach the other; as an Iranian prisoner says, explaining his submission in a clandestine letter from a secret prison in Tehran: "They made me lie, saying that I was a spy, that my journal was financially supported by foreign countries, name other writers, journalists and thinkers as spies, perverts. . . ."[39] This submission is incorporation as a functional and functioning part, an integer of the totalizing system.

To be sure, an ethic of resistance is not the same thing as a politics of resistance, but it is also true that they are inextricably related. Ethics of resistance is politics of resistance, too; decision in the dark night of the soul is a very political moment. Politics of resistance always occur against the background of ethics of resistance; the smallest political act is a very ethical moment. Both are always already separated and related. Thus, we find ourselves in a situation where, while both ethics and politics are always possible and always necessary, a comfortable unity within, between, or among them is not available. There is then no human situation void of tension, no place for that garrison of the survival-ego, the good conscience, in ethics or politics, let alone both.

What Levinas can perhaps help provide here is not another model or formula of resistance or of praxis but a human meaning, an accessing of a passivity beyond passivity prior to and in the process of forming political judgments and decisions. This would be a space where, as most important instances exemplify, it is impossible (and, in any case, unadvisable) to select a principle and apply it to whatever given case comes to hand. In the context of totalizing systems, the I-in-question must, then, inform being (which is, after all, where resistance must succeed or surrender) and, accepting the suffering that is inevitably concomitant with life, stubbornly resist the saming intentions of totalizing systems in the recognition, again, that it is the totalizing system that must "same," and human responsibility that must not.

In any event, to give up on humanity, to dream the dream of a planet cleansed of ourselves, is to capitulate, to succumb every bit as much as to dream the dream of a planet samed in our particular image, to make idols of the versions of ourselves that demand the death of the other, of alterity itself. In the end, these are the same thing. Thus, from the beginning one must take a stand against both. As long as there are still human beings in the world, it will be meaningful, regardless of success or failure, to offer our absolute resistance to totalizing systems everywhere, and, when it becomes necessary, to say, with Ezat Tabatabaeian: "Life is beautiful and lovely. Like everybody else I too loved life; but there comes a time when one must say farewell to it. Such a moment has come for me and I welcome it. I have no particular will to make; I would just like to say that the beauties of life are unforgettable. Those who are alive, try to make the best of your life. . . . Hello to all I have loved, I love and will love" (Ezat Tabatabaeian on the occasion of her execution).[40]

Critical Theory, Queer Resistance, and the Ends of Capture

Liat Ben-Moshe, Che Gossett, Nick Mitchell, and Eric A. Stanley

One of the most notable accomplishments of queer studies has been in showing how various regimes of normativity are interconnected and mutually constitutive—how reproductive futurity and heteronormativity are articulated in relation to racialization, (dis)ability, and other socially structuring and institutionally enforced axes of difference—in such a way that much work done under the rubric of queer studies today takes for granted that queerness can be defined as against (and as other to) normativity writ large. Perhaps as a consequence of such success, the relationship between queerness and antinormativity can become vaguely tautological—what is queer is antinormative; what is antinormative is queer—and so elastic that useful distinctions between how different normativities get enforced in practice can begin to fade. Conversely, what is now being called critical prison studies, as a field, has had relatively little to say about trans/queer people, or how queer theory and/or politics might differently mitigate its optics. Here then, we have gathered to think about the uses and limits of both queer theory and abolitionist analysis in our work toward collective liberation.

QUESTION: To what extent or in what ways is this formulation of queerness-as-antinormativity useful for thinking about the politics of gender and sexuality that shape the prison industrial complex (PIC)? Are there ways in which thinking about the specificity of queer and trans existence in and resistance to the PIC that reverberate back to challenge or complicate these assumptions about what queerness is and what work it can be used to do?

ERIC A. STANLEY: I think there is, and must be, an antagonism between *queer* as an optic, a way to read and to act against normative and normalizing power, and *queer* as a sexual and/or gendered identity. The radical potentiality of queer is in this antagonism becoming a feedback loop, where its own work is constantly under self-erasure and revision. To this end, however, I believe that a queer analysis can and must extend beyond those who identify as such.

There is also the critique that queer theory, as a field and/or methodology, can normalize antinormativity, against its own aims. Or an argument that in its reach to be infinitely antinormative it produces, by way of excess, new normativities. I think, however, this would be a misreading inasmuch as queer, under my definition, like all deconstructive projects, continues to evade those forms of legibility. Queer, then, becomes a placeholder for a horizon and a way to speak toward that which remains beyond representation but also threats representation itself.

The emerging analyses and practices of prison abolition are working in a similar way. Here, abolition is not a specific political platform; however, there are a number of demands we might do make under its banner. This is one of the common misconceptions of prison abolition—that those of us who organize toward it already know, and must already know, in advance, the best ways to address the various forms of violence and harm the PIC purports to attend to. The affective common sense of carceral life that we all inhabit works in part by naturalizing its own necessity and by not allowing us to imagine beyond its domain. Abolition, like queer theory and perhaps deconstruction, too, makes us not know in advance. As analytics, they are about expanding space in an ever more psychically and physically contracted world.

However, it is also important that we continue to argue for the importance of understanding how trans and queer people, specifically trans women of color, are uniquely targeted by the PIC. For far too long, and this continues, the "prisoner," at least in much U.S.-based prison scholarship and activism, remains a straight, nondisabled, nontrans male. There are, of course, the important feminist interventions of the 1980s and 1990s that have begun to highlight women in prison. However, much of this work, for various reasons, has had little to say about trans and or queer people. This is not a call to add trans/queer people to obligatory lists but for all of us working against prisons, to act in solidarity with trans/queer imprisoned people and to use trans/queer theory when thinking about incarcerating logics at large.

CHE GOSSETT: In thinking about queer and/or trans abolitionist imaginaries, gender self-determination, and critical theory, I'm drawn toward queer, trans, intersectional, and AIDS activist of color genealogies and the revolutionary trans and queer liberationist political coordinates they crystallized. Struggling from within and against racial capitalism, the antiqueer and antitrans violence of criminalization and left movement exile,[1] organized abandonment via the state, political repression and surveillance,[2] carceral containment and the slow violence of neoliberal sociopolitical and economic rationality that threatens to exhaust radical organizing potentiality, and queer left and trans revolutionary political formations have historically pushed against and beyond the policed and policing boundaries of assimilationist political paradigms and sought to materialize alternate pathways and landscapes of radical queer and/or trans futurity.

In contrast to the antifuturity institutionalized via domestic warfare, mass incarceration, deportation, and so forth, on the one hand, and nonfuturity evidenced by the well-resourced forward momentum of "LGBT" neoliberal "diverse/multicultural" nonprofitization in the name of "progress" and "feminism" from which sex workers, homeless people, street youth, trans women of color, those living with HIV/AIDS, and (dis)abled are evacuated on the other, radical queer and trans liberationist, AIDS activists of color have imagined queerly utopian alternatives. Ortez Alderson, black queer liberationist and antiwar and AIDS activist, and many others have fought to bring into being radical queer erotic lifeworlds that were also resolutely determined in constant struggle against forces and forms of antiqueer, antitrans, and antiblack violence.[3]

Not only do these political formations continue to provide queer left, revolutionary trans, and AIDS activist inspiration for current organizing against the criminalization of HIV/AIDS and sex work, for example, they are also articulations of yearnings for freedom that shape abolitionist political imaginaries and inform queer and/or trans critical theories of abolition.

Gender self-determination, in the face of policing, was dramatized and actualized in the uprisings against police violence by trans people of color (from Compton's to Dewey's to Stonewall). Gender self-determination is abolitionist in its antipolicing ethos and is ultimately an abolitionist political project. The prison industrial complex is a site of antiblack penal slavery in which gender is violently regulated and trans identities/embodiment are treated as invalid and nonexistent within the bio (and necro) political logic of penology/penality.[4] Part of the radical potentiality of queer and/or trans PIC abolitionist critical theory lies in the horizontal/participatory design and overlapping nature of much of the work that situates and grounds it, as well as scholarship and political theory that centers trans resistance and resilience in the face of forced disappearance. Conditions faced by incarcerated trans and gender-nonconforming people have historically been overlooked in (anti) prison studies and discourse, as Eric points out. Many studies are non-trans-centric and frequently tautologically link medically/coercively binary assigned sex ("male/female") to binary gender ("man/woman"), which results in both the invisibilization of intersex and reinforces the hegemony of binary gender. In the *Captive Genders*[5] anthology edited by Eric Stanley and Nat Smith, however, we find incarcerated and nonincarcerated queer and/or trans voices articulating—albeit through distinct and even dissonant optics—critiques of the PIC harmoniously unified in an abolitionist calling for the end(s) of capture.

It speaks volumes about neoliberal multicultural carceral culture (and nonprofit rhetoric) that the PIC is portrayed and positions its assemblage-like self-/state-constituted being as necessary and, especially, culturally competent. "LGBT" people—especially low income and of color—can now be, or already are, incorporated into the culturally competent and politically relevant PIC—complete with trans-specific and queer-specific cages (initiated in Los Angeles, for example, by two gay police officers honored at Pride).[6] Queer and/or trans prison abolitionist critical theory reinvigorates queer and/or trans abolitionist imaginaries and collective energies so often at risk of dissolution into exclusively nonprofit brand forms of organizing that are compatible with, rather than dynamically and principally opposed to, prevailing neoliberal carceral multicultural culture.

Finally, in thinking about the ways in which queerness has been outlawed, as Eric points out, I wonder if we might repose the question around queerness as antinormativity and the PIC. Rather than exclusively asking what queerness might contribute to PIC abolition, which figures queerness as an addendum PIC abolition rather than immanent within it, perhaps we might consider how abolition is already eroticopolitically queer. In the face of policing, closets, and cages—abolition is a queer desire.

NICK MITCHELL: I think the antinormative reflex that has habituated so much queer studies scholarship over the last decade or so has a lot to offer those of us who are thinking about how to both theorize and historicize the modern carceral state in the service of prison abolition. Habituating ourselves in attending to the violent consolidation of regimes of gender and sexual normativity in particular might enable us to better understand how the structures of everyday life that sustain the carceral state get reproduced. Here, I'm thinking, for example, of Roderick A. Ferguson's genealogy (in *Aberrations in Black*) of the postslavery *production* of the black family in the United States through the punitive regulation and policing of black sexuality. Abolitionist thought and praxis often takes for granted that the abolition of slavery was incomplete, and that that incompleteness is marked by the ways in which the political and economic functions of slavery—along with their terroristic regime of subjection—found a new life in various forms of criminalization. These include the formal and informal institutionalization of white supremacy through the Black Codes and the convict lease system. What Ferguson gets us to understand is, first, that in this postabolition-but-not-quite-postslavery moment, heteronormativity is actively conscripted to do the work of white supremacy, and, second, that the mode of power that disciplines nonheteronomative black American populations gets consolidated, at the turn of the twentieth century, through the social sciences in general and through the disciplinary apparatus of sociology in particular.

I would be in favor of abolitionist theory and praxis attending to this double movement whereby the white supremacist freight of heteronormativity is implemented both at the level of social structure and in the institutions of knowledge. Whether we call the nonheteronormative "queer," it is through such a queer optic, as Eric puts it, that we can trace the complicity—at times, even the symbiosis—between disciplinary knowledge and the carceral state. At the turn of the twentieth century, W. E. B. Du Bois was already writing, in *The Souls of Black Folk*, of how sociologists "gleefully count [the Negro's] bastards and his prostitutes" and connecting it to how white supremacy insinuates itself as "purity against crime."[7] So we are already, at this point, in the presence of a discourse whose criminalizing gaze is trained upon black sex workers and black children. And it's also through such a queer analytic that we can come to regard the heteronormativity that underwrites the institution of the family as a problem rather than a solution. Criminological literature often celebrates the heteronormative family as a solution to recidivism. Yet for many queer and trans prisoners, "family" does not necessarily hold the promise of refuge and is often a space in which relations of violence are repeated and even intensified.

Regarding the use of the concept of antinormativity, the question for me has to do with whether, and how, antinormativity can found a politics that lives beyond oppositionality. Perhaps it also has to do with the fact that oppositionality, that is, the taking of a stand against the norm, may not exhaust all the political possibilities that become available to us when we are asking about how not only to oppose directly but also to *inhabit* normativity in a way that is corrosive to it. Without fetishizing the political as such, I do think that the experimental, practical, and concrete ethos that is at work in the practice of the aspiration toward prison abolition is worth learning from. We don't know what abolition will look like, but we do want to try working in these directions to establish abolitionist organizational forms, we do want to try and forge these kinds of connections. It's a well-established point, in the work of Critical Resistance, that the principle of collective self-determination in the context of communities that live under the death-making forces that combine conditions of impoverishment with the apparatuses of surveillance and policing is one that's corrosive to the PIC. Whether that principle is, in fact, true is a question that has to be worked out on the ground, a question that is worked out in praxis. Thinking about that, I am always wondering: What is the practical context that would put pressure on the use value of the concept of antinormativity? It's a question that I don't yet know how to answer but one that I think needs continuously to be posed if the concept is to continue to live a useful life. And I continue to take seriously Cathy Cohen's challenge to queer politics back in 1997 as a reminder that the "anti" in antinormativity does not guarantee "an encompassing challenge to systems of domination and oppression."[8]

LIAT BEN-MOSHE: Current scholarship on imprisonment (take, for example, *The New Jim Crow*[9]) doesn't take up antinormatively as its

main scope, as Eric mentions. What drew me to focus on resistance
to incarceration as an activist/scholar is what I thought was the core
question of sociology—where are the people, what are they doing, how
are their lives connected to structures of oppressions and privilege?
As disability studies was my guiding framework of analysis, it became
quite clear that those considered abnormal, deficient, deviant, crazy,
malformed, and maladjusted are the main populations interpolated and
disappeared by a variety of spaces and processes of containment and
confinement. In that sense, I think that we have to bear in mind the
composition of who is incarcerated, and included in it are also those
not yet segregated but considered the most vulnerable to the threat
of confinement: what I have been calling, following Harriet McBryde
Johnson[10] and Robert McRuer,[11] "the incarceration yet to come." As
Che mentions (later on in our conversation), many of those currently
incarcerated in prisons are aging there, because of mandatory minimums
and three-strikes laws, among other factors that have made life
without parole much more prevalent over the last decade. In addition,
a disproportionate number of those imprisoned report having mental
health issues or crises, and, as we can imagine, the prison environment
itself is quite disabling (in terms of environmental hazards, aging in such
toxic spaces, sharing of needles and the spread of hepatitis and HIV, and
the compromised and diminished capacities that happen from living in
a prison for prolonged periods of time). In short, carceral forces both
target particular populations as disposable and amenable to incarceration
(and as profitable through the PIC and nursing home industry), and
they also construct and reproduce members of these populations as
nonnormative subjects while doing so.

I think that this antinormative stance, enabled by a queer and disability
studies/disability justice position, can be, and should be, the starting
point of any abolitionary discussion and action, and it has been the stance
adopted by some of the activists behind successful closure campaigns of
carceral spaces. Let me explain what I mean here.

A question raised often in the context of abolition of carceral spaces,
such as prisons, psychiatric hospitals, and residential institutions for those
with intellectual and other disabilities, is what to do with those deemed
as having the most challenging behaviors. In prison abolition circuits,
this discussion is known as "what to do with the dangerous few," and in
the developmental and psychiatric disabilities realm it is the question of
"what to do with the most significantly/profoundly disabled."

Robert McRuer suggests that crip theory, which combines disability and queer studies, will "draw attention to critically queer, severely disabled possibilities in order to bring to the fore the crip actors who . . . will exacerbate in more productive ways, the crisis of authority that currently besets heterosexual/ able-bodied norms."[12] By "severely disabled," McRuer is not merely referring to the level of impairment a person is presumed to have but also to a queer position. By reclaiming severe as "fierce" or defiant, McRuer reverses able-bodied standards that view severe disabilities as the mark of those who will never be integrated (the adage of "everyone should be included, except for . . ."). From their marginal state, "severe disabilities" and queer subjects are positioned to reenter the margins and point to the inadequacies of straight and nondisabled assumptions.

Translated to praxis, some prison abolitionists and activists in the fields of developmental disabilities and antipsychiatry indeed begin their critique and suggestions for alternative social arrangements from the positionality of "severe" cases. A lesson learned from successful closures of residential facilities for those with intellectual and psychiatric disabilities was that people who are labeled as those with the most significant needs should move to community placements early on in the process of closure and throughout the process. If left to the end, such people would most likely be placed in segregated settings. For example, in the early 1970s Jerome Miller, commissioner of the Massachusetts Department of Youth Services at the time, closed the state's major juvenile offender facilities and placed youths in community programs or homes instead. Those deemed as the most violent and dangerous youth were the first to be decarcerated.[13] Another example is the work of prominent prison abolitionist Fay Honey Knopp. After working to draft the abolitionist manual *Instead of Prisons*, Knopp sought to work with what the public perceives as the "toughest" cases, and she devoted the rest of her life to working with sex offenders and sexual abusers.[14] The thought behind this commitment was that if she could demonstrate the ineffectiveness of prisons for this segment of the imprisoned population, then there will be no doubt that prisons are also an ineffective response to lesser criminalizable acts like theft or drug use. I think these examples illustrate the ways we should center nonnormativity in general in our discussions, as the question suggests, and begin our conversations from the position of those who are perceived as the most "severe" and defiant in imagining more just futures.

QUESTION: Citing gays in the military, gay marriage, and gender responsive prisons, many have argued that our contemporary moment is one of neoliberal "inclusion." How are these politics and others working to expand rather than reduce the scope and practices of incarceration? For example, both prison reform and mainstream LGBT politics make constant demands in the name of the U.S. Constitution, which in turn legitimates it. Beyond a simple legal strategy, there seems to be a fetishistic attachment to the law. What drives this physical and affective attachment, and how might it obscure the ways we might imagine new forms of governance beyond and against the state?

ERIC: I find it terrifying how thoroughly legalized our social movements and, in turn, our political imaginations have become. "The Constitution" or an action's constitutionality is now the baseline for everything from work against solitary confinement and capital punishment to arguments for gay marriage. While I understand that it is the only material way to make a claim before the court for many of these issues, the reliance on this strategy seems to also be dictating much discussion beyond its more strategic deployment. My primary concern here is not the actual argument but for the affective afterlives that such practices produce and the possibilities they foreclose.

For us to believe in, or to make arguments on the basis of, an action's constitutionality beyond the court legitimates settler colonialism and chattel slavery. Abolition reminds us that the law is not the arbitrator of justice and is perhaps its primary inhibitor; this is a point that Jacques Derrida also makes in "Force of Law."[15] I wonder then, what are the deep psychical attachments people have to the law? It seems in part a symptom of the cultures of scarcity that have been politically produced. Or maybe people cling to the law, even with its violence, because they are afraid that things could get even worse?

NICK: First of all, I want to register my appreciation for the form of the question, precisely because I think it allows us to get away from the question of whether this or that legal reform is good or bad and to move toward asking about the law itself as an object not only of critique but of love, attachment, seduction—how else could it so thoroughly capture the dominant imaginary? Gina Dent always opens up her "Women and the Law" course by talking about the force that is our dominant culture's "love of the law," a love that is so prevalent that it is made to feel like legal reform is the natural, if not the only, way of pursuing justice on a large scale. So we think about our love of the law not only to form a critical relation to our own habits of thinking and feeling about the law but also to imagine the law and the state as entities—as *subjects*, really— that both solicit such feelings and attachments, and also institutionalize and naturalize the forms that they take. So before dismissing that form of attachment, I think it may be worth attending to it in order to learn something about it. If, as Lauren Berlant suggests, affects are the way that the present presents itself, turning to the form of dominant attachments to the law might tell us something about the *historicity* and the *contingency* of the present.[16]

The question becomes, then, why have these calls for neoliberal inclusion gained the kind of momentum that they have in the present moment? The mainstream LGBT movement has been brilliant in forging strategic partnerships with the military and PICs that confer legitimacy onto and often enhance institutions that historically and contemporarily continue to perpetuate imperialist, antiqueer, and racist violence. As Priya Kandaswamy puts it in a brilliant essay, "The language of marriage has effectively been used to undermine welfare rights and to depoliticize economic inequality altogether."[17] By enhancing prison sentences through "hate crimes" legislation, the state is able simultaneously to position itself as *against* hate and *for* love, even as it supports neoliberal policies that corrode the very material conditions that make loving relationships sustainable. We need to consider the most recent explosion both of gay marriage and of *anti*gay marriage legislation against the background of the subprime mortgage and state budgetary crises. Because it's here, I think, that we have an example of the state actively soliciting confidence not only in its capacity to recognize love but also in *its status as an object of love* in a moment when it, and its citizens, appears most bankrupt.

The distinction Eric makes between law and justice is such a crucial one, precisely because it is the distinction that the legalistic imagination wants to obliterate—not only by training us to see law and justice as synonymous and thereby positing legal reform as the ultimate horizon of sociopolitical transformation but also by violently circumscribing the scope, depth, and shape of transformation to which we might aspire.

LIAT: I want to continue on this thread that Nick and Eric provided, about the seduction of the legal system and its incompatibility with notions of justice and extend it to the ways in which those imprisoned have attachments to the law even when it has wronged them. The fact that those imprisoned use the law to find ways to fight their own oppression and subjugation by the same system should, of course, not be surprising, and I am not trying to critique individual acts but rather to discuss the lure of the legal system in fixing what is a *social* injustice. Mumia Abu-Jamal, writing about jailhouse lawyers,[18] observes that it is the people who try to fight the system using its own tools (i.e., the legal route) that end up the most wounded at the end of the process. In his own words, they literally go crazy, as something snaps when they realize that the system does not follow its own rules for everyone. Many of them believe that once they find the right case law or loophole and can cite it to a judge, they will be vindicated. But that rarely happens, and when it does not, the same jailhouse lawyers lose all hope in the system. So ironically, it is the inmates who are rebellious and have no faith in the system from the get-go who have a better chance of accepting their incarceration, not as just but as a fact of life in an inherently unjust social structure.

And of course, this attachment to the law needs to be analyzed precisely, because even seemingly progressive or liberatory laws and regulations are based on assumptions that cut against any efforts for justice and equality. To give some literal examples, like the clause in the Thirteenth Amendment, court cases dealing with the institutional release of people with disabilities, prison release, and early release construct clear boundaries of who is worthy or unworthy of rights and freedom. The contention by mental health groups like NAMI (National Alliance of Mental Illness) that jails are becoming the biggest mental health facilities in the United States is cited often in antiprison circles but does very little in the way of abolition. What such calls do is to emphasize that so-called "mentally ill" people should not be in jail because they need treatment, not incarceration. However, that further legitimates the boundaries of freedom. If "they" don't "deserve" to be incarcerated, that means that others, in fact, should be incarcerated.

This is, of course, the neoliberal/multicultural inclusion impetus that Eric discusses and the question poses. Wendy Brown further insists that rights must not be confused with equality and that they "are more likely to become sites of the production of identity as injury than vehicles of emancipation."[19] For instance, Brown suggests that if a woman's rights are violated, it is then up to the state to uphold those rights as they have been written into law. Protection is then institutionalized, creating a female dependence on state power. There is no discussion of transcending the existing patterns of male dominance within the masculinist state because women have been granted equality under the law. The liberal philosophy of writing rights into law thus entrenches and subjugates women into the existing systems of traditional subordination, allowing no real way out of the cycle of dependency, protection, and regulation. The state is being sought as a source of remedies to catastrophes of its own creation. In the same vein, one can also discuss the legislation, and later on implementation and enforcement, of hate crime laws to be used as punishment against those who perpetrate homophobic-based violence against LGBTQA folks. What such legislation does is to increase the net of the carceral state, while we know it disproportionately affects LGBTQA people much more. Additionally, such forms of activism (which are not based on intersectional holistic abolitionist approaches to harm reduction) also obscure the ways in which the state itself is an agent of violence against LGBTQ people via its use of incarceration, for instance in the CeCe McDonald case.[20] The organization Justice Now, for example, looks at incarceration as a form of violence against women and thus changes the terms of the debate in relation to suggested responses to domestic violence and other forms of violence targeting women. The same analysis can be used in the case of LGBTQ hate crime legislation. The queer antinormative stance suggested earlier could be used as a corrective to discourses of rights and inclusion, as well as to open up ways of discussing their allure and seduction, as is further elaborated in the writing of Dean Spade, for example.[21]

QUESTION: Without assuming a codified distinction between theory and action, what is the place of "theory" or the academy in a movement against an apparatus that determines life and death in the present? Or, given the current landscape of social and physical death that is the PIC, how might theory be pressed to free people both intellectually and materially?

LIAT: I want to reply by connecting this important question to the first question about the connection between queerness, as antinormativity, and the politics of penal/prison/carceral abolition. For me, prison abolition and anticarceral and antisegregationist mindsets are both theoretical and practical frameworks. I perceive them as a utopian stance, as suggested by Munoz[22] and others. It helps us imagine a different world and opens up possibilities for conversations, actions, and potentialities that could move us into the future we want to have. In a recent conversation with Noam Chomsky, Angela Y. Davis reminded us that the future is always connected to the present and past, and that twenty years ago the present we have now (in terms of violence, rate of incarceration, oppression, racism, etc.) was unimaginable as the future. In the same vein (but from the opposite stance), she pushed us to imagine the most radical future possible, further than our lifetime and further than our present. It's this radical imagining that I see as the role of "theory," the constant link between now and then. So in essence, I think of theorizing abolition as engaging in "the politics of the future."

To complicate things further, though, I also think that the latest conversations in queer theory about the figure of the child and notions of the future (see Edelman,[23] Munoz, etc.) could be both aided and complicated by a prison abolitionist stance. What does it mean to think about the future if (for some) there is no future? Ruthie Gilmore defines racism as "the state-sanctioned or extralegal production and exploitation of group differentiated vulnerability to premature death."[24] This definition connects racism to discussions of no future or, in Lauren Berlant's parlance, slow death, as related to the politics of incarceration. Slow death, according to Berlant, refers to "the physical wearing out of a population and the deterioration of people in that population that is very nearly a defining condition of their experience and historical existence."[25] Thus, Berlant moves us from a discussion of control to a discussion of management, or from thinking about epidemics to rethinking the endemic, using Foucault's classification. As Berlant reminds us, "In this shift Foucault dissolves the attention to scenes of control over individual life and death under sovereign regimes and refocuses on the dispersed *management of the biological threat* posed by certain populations to the reproduction of the normatively framed general good life of a society. Slow death occupies the temporalities of the endemic."[26]

I think that this "management of threat" is where we are at right now in terms of the politics of incarceration and decarceration, especially if we take an intersectional analysis that looks at processes of state preparation of (certain) populations for both premature death and slow death, via mechanisms of segregation and disappearance, taking into account the matrices of race/gender/ability/class. In their call for prison abolitionists to think about carceral (as opposed to prison or penal) abolition, Piche and Larsen[27] write about the increased use of preventative detention in Canada and state that "governing through security is about shaping the present in response to the imagined harms of the future."[28] So it is again the future that haunts both abolition and incarceration. More specifically, the politics of risk management seem to be at the core of contemporary practices of imprisonment and segregation, in relation to preemptive detention (based on racial and gender profiling) and of being labeled "at risk" of doing something or having something done to oneself (which often leads to psychiatric hospitalization and treatment, being a "potential threat to oneself or others"). In essence, it is not about "crimes" or "illness" but about the possibility of being a future threat (which is discussed further by Deleuze[29] and Puar[30]).

ERIC: Picking up on what Liat just began with, specifically the figure of the child, we also see the reliance on this figure for both proprison expansion (saving the children from dangerous predators) and in antiprison work (critiquing the school to prison pipeline). This is a point that activist/scholar Erica Meiners is really helping us pay attention to. This kind of analysis, which pushes our organizing beyond even the limits of what we might know, is, I think, the promise of trans/queer theory. At its best, it can help us anticipate responses and prefigure a politics that also makes demands that go beyond response or reaction.

Thinking about our current moment, it seems the biopolitical shift toward the management and production of populations that Foucault began to sketch at the end of *History of Sexuality Vol. 1* is still useful. However, I wonder if perhaps we are in a different or perhaps another epoch, along side the biopolitical? I suggest this because I'm not sure the state, at least the United States, is working primarily though ideology of *security*. Certainly, the rampant Islamophobia post 9/11 (and before) in the United States would be good evidence of this; however, I am unsure if it is as orderly as Foucault might have it. There are definitely moments of the "internal enemy" discourse that have material effects, but I think the reality that ideology has given way to a new form of power is an even more horrifying reality. This is to suggest that the formations of domination (not that he would have used that word) that Foucault points us toward are far more complex than he was able to anticipate, and perhaps even contradictory. Returning to the question of the academy, I think it's important to point toward its limits in relation to abolitionist politics. The academy is, after all, a highly classed, raced, ableist, and gender normative space (even in its gender nonnormativity). There is a conservatizing logic I always see at work, where once people are given tenure-track jobs they often become part of the same systems that their "research" is built on critiquing. For me, this is different from saying "activists" are outside the academy or an argument like that. This attachment to normative power is always at work in the nonprofit activist world as well. The question for me, then, is not who the real activists are but how might we use our analytic vocabularies, and even our direct action skills, to press upon the academy, as we might any hierarchical institution, so that another university might be? This might even mean leaving this university in the ruins it is in and building something else.[31]

Of course we know that the academy is not the only, nor even the primary, place where what gets called "theory" lives. For example, we know that prisoners themselves produce the most powerful theorizing about the PIC. I think the challenge for us all is how we might, under the duress of capitalism, be in these institutions and not of them.

CHE: In considering questions about the temporal and the political—specifically forms of futurity that we are all going to be able to inhabit—recent empirical prison studies, most saliently perhaps one called *The Graying of Prisons*, show that the fastest-growing segment of the prison population are people over fifty years of age (deemed elderly in the United States).[32] This dismal reality is yet more proof of the astonishing and imperiling reach of what Foucault called the carceral continuum that stretches not only throughout space in its construction of sites of confinement, detention, and incarceration but also throughout time. When people die in prison, their bodies are often placed in unmarked graves on the prison grounds if they don't have legally related family. In *Precarious Life*, philosopher Judith Butler examines what makes certain lives grievable (i.e., human) and others expendable/disposable in relation to Israeli militarized state warfare against Palestinian people struggling for self-determination (i.e., existence). Carceral violence is also an instrument of Israeli apartheid and Palestinian political repression as well as mass detention of African migrants, labeled "infiltrators" under antiblack racist and xenophobic Israeli laws.[33]

Turning this optic inward and examining the U.S. context, there is a domestic frame of war and an ideological front to the carceral that we need to dismantle along with the material dimensions of the PIC, and this is where queer and/or trans critical theory of abolition is instrumental. The figure of the criminal so central to neoliberal carceral culture is one that the public is urged to turn away from in disgust, fear, and hatred—fear, disgust, and loathing of blackness, of the poor, of gender-nonconformitivity, (dis)ability, and queerness. Yet queer and/or trans abolitionist critical theory provides us with a counterdiscourse, in the case of texts like *Queer (In)Justice* by Joey L. Mogul, Andrea J. Ritchie, and Kay Whitlock, and Dean Spade's *Normal Life*—which might be thought of as both offering a queer and/or trans abolitionist discursive frame and working within an emergent queer and/or trans abolitionist discursive field—where the ableist, antiqueer, and antitrans dimensions of the figure(s) of the criminal are demystified. Most importantly perhaps, along with the demystification of the figure(s) of the criminal, is the collective queer and/trans organizing for the support of human beings who are *criminalized*, as seen in the work of organizations like the Hearts on a Wire Collective in Philadelphia, Pennsylvania; the Sylvia Rivera Law Project in New York City; the Transgender, Gender Variant and Intersex Justice Project in San Francisco; and the Bent Bars Collective in London. Such queer and/or trans abolitionist political formations work for social transformation, support incarcerated queer and/or trans people, and call for forms of accountability that do not rely on the forms of violence, abjection, dehumanization, and inhumanity so fetishized and lionized within neoliberal carceral culture and instrumentalized in prisons throughout the allegedly "post-racial"—though actually antiblack—neoliberal capitalist carceral United States.

QUESTION: How are certain identities pitted against each other, by activists, scholars, and the state, in the struggle for liberation from the PIC? For instance, the practice of compassionate release, exemption from the death penalty, and even the language of "innocent" versus "guilty" all, in different ways, produce deserving and undeserving prisoners.

ERIC: The pitting of differently oppressed groups against each other, or what we sometimes call lateral violence, is perhaps the primary methodology the state uses in maintaining its power. We know that the raw force of the state, while brutal and relentless, cannot alone contain the desires and needs of all the people who suffer under its domain. We are seeing this in the current immigration debates in the United States as many mainstream "immigrants' rights" groups are arguing that *their* immigrants are law-abiding, tax-paying, Harvard-attending, otherwise model citizens. While one might understand the need for such rhetoric to be used strategically in specific cases, its proliferation has produced the categories of "good" versus "bad" immigrants; this is something that Yasmin Nair has written about at length.[34]

This bifurcation is also evident in the claims that the PIC is horrid only because it sometimes, or oftentimes, captures "innocent" people. While this is true, this argument renaturalizes the necessity and justifies the use of prison for those who are "truly guilty." Prison abolitionist groups like Critical Resistance remind us that "abolition is for the guilty," or that the real fight for abolition must be done not based on the position of the people in its grips but on the grounds that the prison is itself a space of violence that reproduces destruction.

Further, what has recently become known as trans theory is useful for thinking about this innocent/guilty binary. Trans theory continues to press on us to see the ways the gender binary and the powers that binary upholds are central to the ordering of modernity. In other words, this kind of trans theory is pushing itself beyond its proper objects of trans and gender nonconforming people. To this end, using trans theory for thinking about the question of innocence, we can see how building a politics based on innocence has effects beyond itself. That is to say that we must work these binaries not to the point that we finally have some clarity but as an endless process that knows that, even at the moment of deconstruction, new formations appear.

LIAT: I can think of various examples in which these processes are at play (of pitting identities or struggles against each other and revealing both the potential and danger of some forms of coalitional politics). Some of the most obvious have to do with the tension between abolition and reform, of course, in which calls for reform in some areas lead to the net expansion of the carceral regime as a whole. In my work, I have seen this happen with the ways that carceral spaces tend to linger and reproduce themselves. For instance, from the early 1960s (in the field of mental health) and 1970s (in the field of intellectual and developmental disabilities) many pushed for the closure of psychiatric hospitals and large state institutions that warehoused people with a variety of impairments. In most states in the United States, this push led both to the decarceration of these populations and to the closure of many of these edifices. However, it may not be very surprising to learn that many of these vacated institutions later reopened as prisons, as Foucault stressed the way the continuity of confinement operates across settings.

Another example is the use, by the state but also by progressive activists and abolitionists, of exceptions in the struggle for liberation. For instance, in the case of abolition of the death penalty, many fought for the creation, and later on enforcement, of exception to the death penalty in the hopes to chip away at the carceral beast (what is referred to as "abolition by attrition"). The problem with these exceptions is that they tend to reify specific populations as vulnerable and "special" and therefore in need for such exceptions. This happens with the strategy of compassionate release as well, which aims at decarceration of those with terminal illnesses and certain medical conditions. In both cases, in order to successfully decarcerate or ward off execution it has to be legally demonstrated that the person is defined as "mentally retarded" (in the case of the death penalty), that they have a debilitating condition that will make them a burden on the state, or that they are dying. In making the case, though, one has to rely on ableist assumptions and rhetoric in order to achieve such exceptions for specific individuals. Once decapacitation has been proven, that only serves to prove symbolically and legally that people with disabilities are indeed a burden on the state and/or that they are not responsible for their actions, which creates a slippery slope in terms of identity, activism, legality, and ethics in relation to other decisions for people with (specific) disabilities (e.g., the right to bear and raise children, the right to vote, to have a bank account, etc. are all contentious issues for people with intellectual disabilities). Simultaneously, what such activism does it to demonstrate that *some* people don't belong in prison or should not be on death row. But of course this call ends up bypassing the question: Who does belong in prison? Whose lives are worth fighting for?

QUESTION: How might AIDS and abolitionist critical theory cooperatively and productively challenge HIV criminalization and the forced disappearance of politics and peoples that the PIC aims to maintain? And how might disability justice help to bring these communities and analytics together?

ERIC: Before I can attempt to answer this, I think it's important to note the disappearance of both AIDS activism and what we might call "HIV/AIDS theory." This powerfully signals the extent to which the ablism of the assimilationist gay agenda in the United States is working to expel, quite literally, bodies that do not fit into the narrative of American progress. People often argue that even if the gay marriage movement, for example, is not helping most of us, it is not hurting either. But I am reminded of how the annual benefit for the AIDS Emergency Fund was recently split with half the proceeds now going toward Marriage Equality California.

That said, there is much amazing organizing going on that already understands work on HIV/AIDS as the coming together of disability justice and queer theory/politics. I am thinking about AIDS Action Now! in Toronto and the current iterations of ACT UP, which unlike those before are placing issues of HIV criminalization, HIV inmate segregation, and "condoms as evidence" all at the center of their organizing work. I think disability justice, prison abolition, and trans/queer politics are useful in thinking about how we might organize, in our contemporary moment, against this HIV criminalization in ways that do not work to simply argue that "All People With AIDS are Innocent" as ACT UP famously did in the 1990s. While the sentiment of the poster and slogan are both necessary and true, our moment calls on us to argue not only that people with AIDS are innocent but that innocence/guilt or freedom/ unfreedom as binary oppositions need to be undone. This is precisely where an abolitionist analysis can push us beyond claims made in the name of normativity.

CHE: Building on Eric's observation about the recent resurgence in AIDS activism, current AIDS activist work is clearly prioritizing issues faced by people of color, sex workers, queer and/or trans people, namely, HIV and sex work criminalization. Linking the War on Drugs to the escalation of the HIV epidemic, this speaks the ways in which PIC abolition is central to HIV/AIDS prevention and treatment. Collectives and organizations—from ACT UP chapters in San Francisco, New York City, and Philadelphia, to Queerocracy, to the SERO Project—are drawing much-needed attention to HIV criminalization and the War on Drugs as penal enterprises that disproportionately target homeless, sex workers, queer/trans, and/or people of color. This summer, I was a part of the inspirational and moving "We Can End AIDS" march at the International AIDS conference in Washington, D.C. The march was led and comprised primarily of poor people of color, sex workers, queer, and/or trans people. Yet, despite the much-celebrated "lifting of the HIV travel ban," sex workers and drug users from abroad were denied entry into the United States under "moral turpitude" regulations and so a parallel conference took place in India. It was a powerful merge into an AIDS activist collective social body (representing both those who were present and those who have passed away), which, like the Occupy movement, formed a multitude with an assemblage of political aims—decriminalizing HIV, sex work, lifting the needle exchange ban, etc.—united in the intention that radical change is in motion.

Yet, I also wonder: how might decriminalization campaigns be in sync with abolitionist end(s) to capture? How might AIDS activism for HIV decriminalization, sex work decriminalization, and an end to the War on Drugs incorporate an abolitionist politic(s) that moves beyond moral and political economizing in relation to the PIC? How must the push for decriminalization move away from the rhetoric of innocence (we are not criminals, don't treat us like criminals) that shifts the burden of carceral containment instead of continuing to dismantle it? One of the strengths and singularities of abolitionist political theory writ large is that it argues that every measure of carceral confinement is unacceptable in its inhumanity and dehumanization. It is not only "mass" incarceration as excess that is unjust but rather *any and all forms* of confinement constitute modes of destructive relationality that must be abolished in its entirety. Campaigns to decriminalize HIV and sex work are crucial. It's powerful to witness the resurgence of activism about prisons and criminalization as an AIDS issue, especially in a political environment focused so much on neoliberal ways of talking about AIDS as an individual problem or stigmatizing character flaw (bad/shameful behaviors, etc) rather than a political issue. Yet, how can we organize and theorize in such a way that we win the immediate campaigns for decriminalization without sacrificing abolitionist political horizons? Abolition forces us to continually question and rework our political paradigms and thought styles, with the recognition that prisons and cages work in the service of heteropatriarchy, white supremacy, antiblackness, and other synchronized oppressions.

AIDS theory and cultural critique have grappled with critical questions of survival, resiliency, outrage, and activism under the duress and anguish of loss and mourning. These questions have been engaged across academic disciplines, from sociology and anthropology of AIDS to cinema studies and art history. Marlon Riggs and Essex Hemphill both engaged those topics while also addressing questions about blackness and the politics of authenticity: the meanings and violence of racial representation. Riggs and Hemphill spanned artistic disciplines and infused artistic forms. Riggs and Hemphill used film (*Black is, Black Ain't* and *Brother to Brother*) as well as liberatory poetics (*Conditions*) as optics through which they posed a fundamental existential and theoretical challenge to white supremacist sociosymbolic order. Black queer love was indeed a "revolutionary act," especially within the context of the Reagan antiblack, antiqueer epoch of AIDS, the political contours of which Cathy Cohen has dynamically mapped out in *Boundaries of Blackness: AIDS and the Breakdown of Black Politics.* Black self love in and as black queer love remains a "revolutionary act" in the face of white settler colonial bio and necropolitics of heteropatriarchy, gender binary normalization, and medically assigned sex naturalization, which aim to police the boundaries of blackness through the regulation of sexuality, (inter)sex, and gender(s). In terms of a wider scope of decoloniality and AIDS activism, anthropologist Adriana Garriga-Lopez has critically analyzed the sociology and anthropology of AIDS in relation to genealogies of Puerto Rican AIDS activism in her *New Proposals* journal article "Boricuas ACTing UP in New York and San Juan: Diasporic Puerto Rican HIV/AIDS Activism and Anthropology."[35] Extending the legacy of ANC member and AIDS activist Simon Nkoli, South African AIDS and sex work activist groups like SWEAT and Treatment Action Campaign have been doing mass mobilization against sex worker criminalization.[36] There is an enduring need for more theoretical work at the intersection of AIDS (activist) theory and prison abolitionist critique, considering the ways in which carceral logic and rhetoric—risk, phobia, threat—and ableist logic and rhetoric (which has roots in a eugenic hierarchy of "the human") continues to frame so much of the discourse of HIV/AIDS, in both public health/epidemiology and the doctors office ("high risk behavior" etc.).

NICK: The transnational struggles against HIV/AIDS, from the 1980s to the contemporary moment, provide one powerful way of grasping the historicity of the queer collective thought that provided the conditions of possibility for a queer studies. The point of tracing that legacy should not be to mine activist roots for the academic legitimacy they might be converted into but rather to think about the multifarious forms of struggle that make collective and collectivizing knowledge possible, by offering them a sense of urgency that cannot be found when collectivities are not on the move. This is by no means the only intellectual, organizational, or political legacy that makes our field possible, of course, but it remains a crucial site to be able to think and move with, a site that can place pressure onto the theoretical and political claims we might make and a site that can move us toward geopolitical connections, analyses, and solidarities that we might not see as necessary to our political organizing.

ACT UP, from the start, has taught us to recognize epidemics as social phenomena and to recognize the state's response to HIV/AIDS as one of generating surplus life and populations, populations that can be dispensed with, populations whose death can be seen as the effect of their mismanagement of their own lives (whether through drug use or sexuality) and not of state machinations. Unsurprisingly, such ideologies go hand in hand with the procedures of criminalization, and they have the effect of renovating older and more obsolete forms of racism, racialization, and antiqueerness. At the same time, I think it's important for activists who are trying to challenge the PIC to turn to anti-HIV struggles in places like South Africa, which have challenged the state not only to imagine but also to *plan* for public health outcomes that might under different conditions have appeared impossible. It is a serious and complicated victory that South Africa's National Strategic Plan is working toward the outcome of no new HIV infections by 2032, while at the same time fighting AIDS-related stigma and discrimination, and supporting the rights of people with AIDS.[37] How might we plan concretely and think transnationally, for instance, to completely end prison expansion in the same period?

QUESTION: How does paying attention to the expansion of neoliberal practices such as the "freeing of markets" and the "confining of borders and bodies" in this historical moment aid us in broadening what we mean by confinement to include other sites of incarceration? And how might centering abolition and antiprison perspectives change our analysis of everyday life for those free and unfree, inside and outside carceral spaces?

CHE GOSSETT: Neoliberal multicultural carceral culture hails us and beckons us to abandon hope and to become desensitized to the violence that is happening to people in prison and to the prison as violence. As anyone with a loved one who is/has been locked up affectively knows, you suffer agonizing loss. We are instructed not to care about the sexual violence that happens to hundreds of thousands of incarcerated people each year, *especially to queer and/or trans and gender-nonconforming people*—as has been documented in the studies informing the Prison Rape Elimination Act—even though this sexual violence for many incarcerated survivors is a routinized and legalized constant, as Angela Davis points out in *Are Prisons Obsolete?* Davis talks about incarcerated people being abused and humiliated in ritual acts of sexual violence like the "strip search," which is common practice in prisons, often both before and after one is visited by family and friends. Not only is the incarcerated subject made to suffer but in the penological/criminological rhetoric "associates" are made to feel vicarious trauma/shame as well, as anyone who's ever visited someone in jail or prison has affectively experienced.

As a visitor, you are made to feel only a degree of what the prison is functionally designed to do—violate and destroy one's sense of meaning, self, and bodily integrity—although this happens every time you visit, so its accumulated intensity over time. There's the waiting—you wait because time is not yours to control, you are on prison time.[38] You remove your belt, shoes, any metal objects, go through the metal detectors, and the metallic electronic doors close behind you, sealing you into the world of the prison, a world set apart from the nominally free world, although for so many of us—as black, poor, queer, and/or trans people—those boundaries are porous and unstable. You are often denied touch; you must communicate through bulletproof glass, with a phone, across these barriers and controls that constitute the deadening reality of carceral space and time.

Futurity is haunted by the violence of carceral time and space to come. Carceral space to come is both virtual as in biometric criminological surveillance and real/material as in cages and white bare concrete walls and panopticons and "Secure Housing Units." It is against this antifuture that guarantees both the continuance of captured life and the "premature death" that Orlando Patterson wrote of in *Slavery and Social Death* and generates alternate forms of sociality, freedom dreams, and collective liberation to which abolitionist critical theory and action aspire. Here, the historical and ideological differences between liberal constitutional promises of "emancipation" and black abolitionist imaginings of freedom have continued relevance and resonance. Queer and/or trans abolitionist critical theories deconstruct "freedom"—as the violence of neoliberal modes of governmentality and quasi-democratic representative state power (concretized in what philosopher Antonio Negri theorizes as "constituted power," which delimits and contains revolutionary change).[39] Queer and/or trans abolitionist critical theory works against the grain of the "repressive tolerance" of the PIC, through which, as Marcuse cautioned: "Tolerance is extended to policies, conditions, and modes of behavior which should not be tolerated because they are impeding, if not destroying, the chances of creating an existence without fear and misery."[40]

ERIC: I also see how this expanded understanding of the carceral is allowing for important connections to be made in solidarity work against pinkwashing. Pinkwashing, in this context, is primarily a media campaign produced by the Israeli government through which they promote Zionism by arguing that Israel is the only "gay friendly"

country in the region. A transnational network of queer Palestinians and
non-Palestinians have built an analysis that understands the practices
of apartheid used by the Israeli government to be a formulation
of capture, not unlike that traditionally used in prisons, which not
only responds to the practices of pinkwashing but also deepens our
analysis of settler colonialism in Palestine and elsewhere. To this end,
antipinkwashing activists are critiquing not only the PIC but also the
forms of isolation, segregation, and destruction mandated by Zionism
crystallizing in the continued practices of Israeli occupation of '48
Palestine.[41]

LIAT: It seems to me that queer and disability theory and justice
aids us in understanding non- and antinormatitvity in relation to the
capture, containment, and incarceration of a variety of nonconforming
body/minds. This focus should lead us to an expansion of what gets
constituted as the carceral to include analysis/activism around detention
centers, psychiatric wards, group homes, nursing homes, and residential
placements (for people with disabilities, populations that are perceived
being "at risk," aboriginals/native peoples, especially in Canada, etc.).
Neoliberalism, ubercapitalism, racism, and every other oppressive and
alluring force certainly doesn't care where people disappear into and
neither should we, in our analysis of and struggles against incarceration.
This point is demonstrated by the "sequence occupance" described earlier
or the continuity of confinement, by which many psychiatric hospitals,
TB hospitals, and asylums closed down (as a result of a variety of forces
including budgetary cuts but also changes in discourse and the direct
advocacy of those most affected by these spaces), but a few years later,
prisons opened on the same ground and often in the same building as
these so called "historical" carceral spaces. Another intersection is the
increasing prevalence of the use of psychopharmaceuticals in all these
residential placements. And their continuations beyond the walls of
particular institutions into compliance with drug treatment orders, as
discussed by Erick Fabris[42] as "chemical incarceration," which Fabris does
not use metaphorically but quite literally to explain the restraint of people
and the making of docility through means that go into one's body and
psyche without the need for physical cages.

I want to stress here, though, that I don't think that prisons are "just
like" psychiatric hospitals, for example, or vice versa. It is certainly the
case that many self-advocates (a descriptor for people with labels of
intellectual disabilities who are involved in organizing) describe their

time in residential facilities as "being imprisoned," but it is also the case that they are often seen as "innocent" or "eternally child-like." Perhaps they are the eternal children but not the ones thought of in discussions of futurity, as many of them (especially those who lived in residential facilities up until the 1970s) were castrated and/or forced to take birth control or abort children once pregnant, so their own reproductive power had been denied to them (and, of course, what is a prison sentence without visitation rights if not the complete denial of reproductive rights?). So in essence, we do not have the same image or reasoning for incarcerating people with intellectual disabilities as we do with people with some other Othering conditions, such as men of color, sex workers, or people who are perceived to be mad or crazy (as in almost any case of stop and frisk or "driving while black," or even the recent mass shootings in Sandy Hook Elementary in which the shooter was immediately proclaimed to be "mentally ill" and later as "aggressive autistic"). So what is important to keep in mind is not that all these cases and forms of containment and carceration are the same but that they operate on the logic of disappearance, which is related to the logic of neoliberalism more broadly. It is perhaps the core of the discourse of "safety," "danger," and precariousness that is demarcated on the bodies (and minds) of some but not others.

NICK: So much of what we are talking about is related to the ways in which prison continues to operate at and as a border, to cite the well-known dialogue between Angela Y. Davis and Gina Dent.[43] Today, with the Obama administration's massive efforts to increase the deportations of brown people—now up to approximately 400,000 per year—the border function of carcerality and the carceral function of the border is even more pronounced. The alibi for these enhanced efforts is, of course, in President Obama's words, the claim that his administration is not targeting undocumented peoples in general but undocumented people who commit violent crimes in particular—he promises that deportation efforts will center on undocumented people who are "criminals, gang bangers, people who are hurting the community" rather than "students" and "folks who are here just because they're trying to feed their families."[44] So here again, we see the line being drawn between "good" and "bad," "innocent" and "criminal" undocumented folks, even as the statistics show that far fewer a percentage of the people being deported have any sort of criminal record.

QUESTION: If liberation is the goal of trans/queer prison abolition, what work is making this materialize now? Or, where might we look to see the edges of capture, if not yet their ends?

ERIC: As desperate as it often feels, and perhaps is, in our struggle against the PIC, I also see the ways an abolitionist analysis continues to grow in new and unexpected ways. This is something I always try to emphasize when teaching, the fact that organizing against the PIC is as old as the PIC itself and that we are part of a powerful genealogy that has at times succeeded in our battles against the enormity of history. I was recently watching footage of Angela Davis being interviewed from jail, and even then, in 1972, she was calling for prison abolition. And while prison abolition is still to come, the campaign to free her was actually successful. In that instance, against the impossibility of the state apparatus, we actually won. More recently, I've been inspired by the upswell of support around the case of CeCe McDonald, a black trans woman that was sent to prison for defending herself against a 2011 racist and transphobic attack. I also look to organizations like Transgender, Gender Non-conforming, and Intersex Justice Project (TGIJP) and their work on building real leadership by and for formerly and currently incarcerated trans women of color. What these examples show us is that even if the liquidation of racialized gender nonnormativity is the intention of dominant power, the trans/queer resilience remains and even flourishes against massive destruction.

LIAT: To put a simplistic materialist claim on the table, my hope for the present and the future is that neoliberalism will implode itself, and there are signs that this is indeed beginning to be the case. With the financial downturn come measures that we could only dream of ten or even five years ago. Some of them are horrific in terms of the complete stripping of what is (barely) left of the welfare state in terms of public housing, assistance, community mental health, and health care more generally. Conversely, with austerity and budget cuts we are also witnessing the shrinkage in correctional budgets across several states and with it the closure of a number of prisons and residential institutions for people with disabilities. The question now is not so much will a certain facility close but where will they relocate the people? In other words, the fight for closure in some arenas ends but the fight against transincarceration begins and, with it, new and old and tested tactics and strategies.

One of the main challenges we face as abolitionists is perhaps not so much in the way of closing carceral spaces but in the construction of (new and old) enemies to incarcerate. Attachments to such ideas as "safety," for example, need to be examined. Sarah Ahmed[45] challenges the assumption that emotions are individual matters that come from "within" and suggests that they create the boundaries of bodies, collectives, and discourses. It is the emotional reading of fear and hatred that binds the community together and indeed constructs it as "a community." Ahmed demonstrates that these attachments work best when the "ordinary citizen" is perceived to be in crisis and under attack. In this case, it is not so much the "ordinary citizen" but normalcy itself that is seen as being under attack. The affective economy of fear creates not only a sense of shared community (community in crisis struggling to maintain its core values) but also creates what it is not (the object that is seen as threatening its existence). But while it may seem easy (even though it is hardly done enough) to apply such theorization to racist and queer/transphobic policies that encourage, support, and create police brutality, for example, we are, of course, all complicit. The practice of claiming "safe spaces" for queer or LGBTQI folks with its related symbols (e.g., stickers seen on doors of "allies" or offices across college campuses) is another form of the allure of feeling safe in particular locales (white middle-upper-class college campuses) and not others. It also means that we need to be wary of our attachment to knowledge, particularly knowing what the future holds.

Knowing the future in terms of alternatives to incarceration seems antithetical to the abolitionist mindset. Abolition can be conceptualized as a strategy beyond resistance, as it does not acknowledge the structure as it is but envisions and creates a new worldview in which oppressive structures do not exist. But it does so from the world as it is now, without waiting for all questions to be answered or alternatives to be set in place. This "refusal to wait" is further highlighted in Julia Oparah's[46] insightful article on present-day "maroon abolitionists," which brings to light the unique prison abolition perspectives of gendered, oppressed, and racialized activists who are rooted in African diasporic traditions of resistance and spirituality. Oparah refers to them as maroon abolitionists because maroon refers to the communities of runaway slaves and indigenous people who have formed in the Americas since the seventeenth century. Maroon also implies the resistance of nonblack populations such as indigenous and exiled whites. While white abolitionists were fighting against slavery because of moral, religious, and ideological convictions, "maroon abolitionists" were fighting for their communities' liberation and survival. They therefore rejected the call for gradual emancipation and called instead for an immediate end to slavery. Prison abolitionists therefore often emphasize activism that originates and takes into account those who are most affected by oppression and incarceration, as I think we should. But it is important to understand that prison abolition is not about helping prisoners, and antipsychiatry and disability justice are not about helping "people with special needs." Abolition of the segregationist mindset is about societal change that will improve the lives of all of us, inside and outside carceral spaces, the borders of which are eroding anyway.

CHE: In *Arrested Justice: Black Women, Violence, and America's Prison Nation*, Beth Richie offers a black feminist analytic through which she scrutinizes the radical loss that accompanied the rights-based gains of the antiviolence movement since the 1960s. In a chapter aptly titled "How We Won the Mainstream and Lost the Movement," Richie identifies and demystifies the underside of the Violence Against Women Act and the ways in which it was attached to the larger PIC-buoying Violent Crime Control and Law Enforcement Act signed by President Clinton in 1994.[47] The Violent Crime Control and Law Enforcement Act undid Pell Grant access for incarcerated people in federal and state institutions and dismantled hard-fought and hard-won aims for educational access, as articulated in the political manifesto authored by state captives rebelling against antiblack, antihuman conditions of penal servitude during the Attica uprising. "Modernize the inmate education system" was one of the practical proposals of the peace terms of the demands of the resistors.[48] The response of Governor Rockefeller to the Attica uprising was to eliminate the Attica rebellion, in what he confided to President Nixon was "a beautiful operation" during which forty-three people were killed.[49] In the wake of the rebellion and massacre, the push for educational access in prisons intensified and educational reform was instituted. The incarcerated activism and resistance of the Attica rebellion galvanized outside support (legislative and awareness campaigns) and changed conditions for incarcerated people across the country. Yet white supremacist, homo, and AIDS phobe Jesse Helms (also responsible for HIV travel ban legislation) introduced an amendment that would strip incarcerated people of Pell Grant access that was championed by "tough on crime" Congress.[50] The pattern of rights-based legislative reform being attached to prison and military industrial-based expansion

is historically rehearsed and contemporarily repeated, from VAWA
to the Matthew Shepard and James Byrd Jr. Hate Crimes Prevention
Act, which passed in 2009 and was attached to the National Defense
Authorization Act that allotted $130 billion for continued U.S. military
occupation in Iraq and Afghanistan.[51] As a result of these corrosive
carceral-military industrial-complex-enhancing political compromises,
what once were radical movement aims are refashioned and folded into
neoliberal carceral and military expansionist enterprises. Struggles by
incarcerated activists and their liberatory political imaginaries, seen
in the legacy of the Attica rebellion and in queer and trans liberation
organizing on the inside, are substituted for narrower political goals
and horizons. Rather than thinking about "the movement" solely from
a standpoint of the nonincarcerated, it is important to consider the ways
in which incarcerated activism also shapes the political landscape of
movement work "on the outside." It is also important to note that such
rigid dichotomies are more conceptual than material for many poor, of
color, queer, trans, sex workers, undocumented, and/or criminalized
peoples who navigate quotidian biopolitical technologies of surveillance,
punitive protocols, and police violence even when living "on the outside."
I am inspired by the work of queer and/or trans collectives such as
Hearts on a Wire in Philadelphia, Pennsylvania; Black and Pink in
Boston, Massachusetts; Bent Bars in London, United Kingdom; and
other political formations through which queer and/or trans people are
cultivating resistance and resiliency in the face of policing and penality.

NICK: I continue to turn to the efforts of Critical Resistance as an
organization that is resolutely confronting—through the work of
organizing, solidarity, and struggle in and outside the prison—the
ideological and imaginative closure that has been one of the necessary
social features attendant to the growth and consolidation of the PIC
as a solution to social problems. In my own brief work with Critical
Resistance's publication *The Abolitionist*, some of the recursive questions
have been: what kind of work is being done and what kind of work needs
to be done in order to understand the sheer capaciousness of the PIC?
Sometimes the problems cut across lines that will be familiar for most
who have been involved with left struggle—how to pursue reform work
with an agenda that is not only revolutionary in general but abolitionist
in particular? What reforms might destabilize carceral logics? Which
reforms might even throw them into crisis?

Sometimes the shape of these problems feels newer, and its newness is in some ways an effect that different left organizations have found ways to place themselves into struggle with one another, into struggle alongside one another, into struggle in order to hold open possibility for one another in ways that are profoundly productive, even promising. For instance, the January 2013 issue of *The Abolitionist*, themed on mental health struggles in and against the PIC, contains an article from members of the Sylvia Rivera Law Project that reflects, in a complex manner, on efforts by trans prisoners to obtain gender identity diagnoses in order to obtain life-sustaining health care. While acknowledging the potential for such struggles to extend the normalizing reach of the medical wing of the PIC writ large, the authors ultimately conclude that "[f]or incarcerated transgender individuals, GID [Gender Identity Disorder] becomes a powerful tool for disrupting the control of the PIC over their bodies by offering an organizing principle of their experiences and a means of affirmation."[52] It's an important reminder that even the institutions of normativity—which are also, in this case, the institutions of capture—contain the seeds of their own corrosion. An old lesson, perhaps, but one around which we are still learning to collectivize anew.

FOREWORD: LIFE AND OTHER RESPONSIBILITIES
Joy James

1. When the Secret Service attempted to intimidate antilynching crusader Ida B. Wells from publicly denouncing the mass execution of black soldiers, she dared the federal agents to arrest her and they subsequently departed. Since Wells's crusades against extrajudicial killings, campaigns have expanded against all forms of death and other penalties. The approaching fortieth anniversary of the 1976 reinstitution of the death penalty following its 1972 abolition is an occasion for reflection. The U.S. Supreme Court's 1972 ruling created a reprieve for Angela Y. Davis, as a political prisoner— Governor Ronald Reagan was seeking the death penalty against Davis based on Jonathan Jackson's taking of hostages and subsequent deaths, including that of the teenager, caused by gunfire from California prison guards. With the ruling that the death penalty was unconstitutional, Davis was released on bail and effectively worked with her defense committees to be acquitted of all charges. Jonathan's older brother, prison theorist George Jackson, author of *Soledad Brother* and *Blood in My Eye*, was killed by prison guards while Davis was imprisoned.

2. "Maroon Philosophy: An Interview with Russell 'Maroon' Shoatz," this volume.

3. Statement on Solitary Confinement, presented June 2012. Illinois Senator Dick Durbin chaired a hearing on solitary confinement in the federal prison system. "Statement on Solitary Confinement," this volume.

4. "Prison and the Subject of Resistance: A Levinasian Inquiry," this volume.

INTRODUCTION: DEATH AND OTHER PENALTIES
Geoffrey Adelsberg, Lisa Guenther, and Scott Zeman

1. Children's Defense Fund, "The Cradle to Prison Pipeline, Summary Report" (2009). http://www.childrensdefense.org/child-research-data -publications/data/cradle-prison-pipeline-report-2007-full-highres.html.

2. See, for example, David Garland, *Peculiar Institution: America's Death Penalty in an Age of Abolition* (Oxford: Oxford University Press, 2010) and Jennifer Culbert, *Dead Certainty: The Death Penalty and the Problem of Judgment* (Stanford, CA: Stanford University Press, 2008). The most important Supreme Court cases on racism and the death penalty are Furman v. Georgia, 408 U.S. 238 (1972) and McCleskey v. Kemp, 481 U.S. 279 (1987).

3. Loïc Wacquant, "Deadly Symbiosis: When Ghetto and Prison Meet and Mesh" *Punishment & Society* 3 (January 2001): 120. Michelle Alexander, *The New Jim Crow: Mass Incarceration in the Age of Colorblindness* (New York: The New Press, 2010). David Garland, *Peculiar Institution*.

4. David M. Oshinsky, *"Worse Than Slavery": Parchman Farm and the Ordeal of Jim Crow Justice* (New York: The Free Press, 1997).

5. See Matthew J. Mancini, *One Dies, Get Another: Convict Leasing in the American South, 1866–1928* (Columbia: University of South Carolina Press, 1996).

6. http://www.prisonradio.org/media/audio/memories-maroon-mumia -abu-jamal.

EXCAVATING THE SEDIMENTATIONS OF SLAVERY: THE UNFINISHED PROJECT OF AMERICAN ABOLITION
Brady Heiner

The research for this chapter was supported by a faculty research grant from California State University, Fullerton. I would also like to acknowledge the participants of the Philosophy Department Colloquium Series at CSU Fullerton and the students from my Social and Political Philosophy courses, for providing feedback on earlier versions of this work. Special thanks are due to Christopher Muller for assistance in data mining and generating Figures 3–5, to the inspiring students from my advanced directed study course on "Mass Incarceration and Prison Abolitionism": Jesus Herrera Rivera, Alejandro Fernandez, Marissa Piña, and Eric Tafolla, and to Jesus for also providing invaluable research assistance.

1. Elliot Currie, *Crime and Punishment in America* (New York: Henry Holt and Co., 1998), 21.

2. Carol S. Steiker, "Capital Punishment and Contingency," *Harvard Law Review* 125 (2012): 760–787.

3. Roy Walmsley, *World Prison Population List*, 9th ed. (London, UK: International Centre for Prison Studies, King's College, 2010): http://www .idcr.org.uk/wp-content/uploads/2010/09/WPPL-9-22.pdf.

4. I use the term *racialized* to capture the "discursive process by which particular groups have been classified as non-white; specific meanings have been attached to those groups, and those meanings have been used to support

the hierarchical distribution of power, land, and resources." See Addie C. Rolnick, "The Promise of Mancari: Indian Political Rights as Racial Remedy," *N.Y.U. Law Review* 86 (2011): 965n31; and more generally Michael Omi and Howard Winant, *Racial Formation in the United States: From the 1960s to the 1990s*, 2nd ed. (New York: Routledge, 1994).

5. E. Ann Carson and William Sabol, *Prisoners in 2011* (Washington, DC: U.S. Bureau of Justice Statistics, 2012): http://www.bjs.gov/content/pub/pdf/p11.pdf.

6. Caroline W. Harlow, *Education and Correctional Populations* (Washington, DC: U.S. Bureau of Justice Statistics, 2003); Bruce Western, *Punishment and Inequality in America* (New York: Russell Sage, 2006).

7. I write "at the time of their arrest," because many imprisoned persons throughout American history, from Malcolm X to Stanley "Tookie" Williams, pursue and actualize their education while incarcerated. This possibility has been thwarted since the Violent Crime Control and Law Enforcement Act (1994) eliminated prisoners' eligibility for Pell Grants, causing most of the over seven hundred postsecondary degree-granting programs in existence in prisons at that time to close. See Caroline W. Harlow, *Education and Correctional Populations* (Washington, DC: U.S. Bureau of Justice Statistics, 2003); and Laura Gorgol and Brian Sponsler, *Unlocking Potential: Results of a National Survey of Postsecondary Education in State Prisons* (Washington, DC: Institute for Higher Education Policy, 2011).

8. Rebecca M. McLennan, *The Crisis of Imprisonment: Protest, Politics, and the Making of the American Penal State* (New York: Cambridge University Press, 2008).

9. Joy James, *The New Abolitionists: (Neo)Slave Narratives and Contemporary Prison Writings* (New York: SUNY Press, 2005).

10. Marie Gottschalk, *The Prison and the Gallows: The Politics of Mass Incarceration in America* (New York: Cambridge University Press, 2006); Marie Gottschalk, "The Past, Present, and Future of Mass Incarceration," *Criminology and Public Policy* 10, no. 3 (2011): 483–504; Heather Ann Thompson, "Why Mass Incarceration Matters: Rethinking Crisis, Decline, and Transformation in Postwar American History," *Journal of American History* 98, no. 3 (2010): 703–758; Heather Ann Thompson, "Rethinking Working Class Struggle through the Lens of the Carceral State: Toward a Labor History of Inmates and Guards," *Labor: Studies in Working-Class History of the Americas* 8, no. 3 (2011): 15–45.

11. Angela Y. Davis, "From the Prison of Slavery to the Slavery of Prison: Frederick Douglass and the Convict Lease System," in *The Angela Y. Davis Reader*, ed. Joy James (Malden, MA: Blackwell, 1998): 74–95; "Political Prisoners, Prisons, and Black Liberation," in *The Angela Y. Davis Reader*, 39–52;

"Race and Criminalization: Black Americans and the Punishment Industry," in *The Angela Y. Davis Reader*, 61–73; "Racialized Punishment and Prison Abolition," in *The Angela Y. Davis Reader*, 96–107; "Incarcerated Women: Transformative Strategies," *Black Renaissance/Renaissance Noir* 1, no. 1 (1996): 21–34; "Masked Racism: Reflections on the Prison Industrial Complex," *ColorLines*, September 10, 1998; *Are Prisons Obsolete?* (New York: Seven Stories Press, 2003); *Abolition Democracy: Beyond Empire, Prisons, and Torture* (New York: Seven Stories Press, 2005); Brady Thomas Heiner, "'From the Prison of Slavery to the Slavery of Prison': Angela Y. Davis's *Abolition Democracy*," in *Radical Philosophy Today, Volume 5: Democracy, Racism, Prisons*, ed. Harry van der Linden (Philosophy Documentation Center, 2007): 219–227.

12. Saidiya Hartman, *Scenes of Subjection: Terror, Slavery, and Self-Making in Nineteenth-Century America* (New York: Oxford University Press, 1997); Stephen Best and Saidiya Hartman, "Fugitive Justice," *Representations* 92 (2005): 1–15.

13. Joy James, *The New Abolitionists*, Joy James (ed.), *Unfinished Liberation: Policing and Imprisonment*, a special issue of *Radical Philosophy Review* 3, no. 1 (2000).

14. Dorothy E. Roberts, "Constructing a Criminal Justice System Free of Racial Bias: An Abolitionist Framework," *Columbia Human Rights Law Review* 39 (2007): 261–285.

15. Michelle Alexander, *The New Jim Crow: Mass Incarceration in the Age of Colorblindness* (New York: The New Press, 2010).

16. Loïc Wacquant, "The New 'Peculiar Institution': On the Prison as Surrogate Ghetto," *Theoretical Criminology* 4 (2000): 377–389; "Deadly Symbiosis: When Ghetto and Prison Meet and Mesh," *Punishment & Society* 3 (2001): 95–134; "From Slavery to Mass Incarceration: Rethinking the 'Race Question' in the United States," *New Left Review* 13 (2002): 41–60.

17. Colin Dayan, "Legal Terrors," *Representations* 92 (2005): 42–80; *The Story of Cruel and Unusual* (Cambridge, MA: The MIT Press, 2007); *The Law is a White Dog: How Legal Rituals Make and Unmake Persons* (Princeton, NJ: Princeton University Press, 2011).

18. Lisa Guenther, *Solitary Confinement: Social Death and its Afterlives* (Minneapolis: Minnesota University Press, 2013).

19. Frank B. Wilderson, "The Prison Slave as Hegemony's (Silent) Scandal," *Social Justice* 30, no. 2 (2003): 18–27; Saidiya Hartman and Frank B. Wilderson, "The Position of the Unthought," *Qui Parle* 13, no. 2 (2003): 183–201; Frank B. Wilderson, *Red, White, and Black: Cinema and the Structure of U.S. Antagonisms* (Durham, NC: Duke University Press, 2010).

20. Priscilla A. Ocen, "Punishing Pregnancy: Race, Incarceration, and the Shackling of Pregnant Prisoners," *California Law Review* 100 (2012): 1239–1311.

21. Michael A. Hallett, "Race, Crime, and For-Profit Imprisonment: Social Disorganization as Market Opportunity," *Punishment & Society* 4, no. 3 (2002): 369–393; *Private Prisons in America: A Critical Race Perspective* (Chicago: University of Illinois Press, 2006).

22. For a sympathetic critique of this line of argument from a critical legal perspective, see James Forman Jr., "Racial Critiques of Mass Incarceration: Beyond the New Jim Crow," *New York University Law Review* 87 (2012): 101–146.

23. Karl Marx, *Capital*, vol. 1, trans. Ben Fowkes (New York: Penguin Classics, 1990), 163–164.

24. Edmund Husserl, *Ideas Pertaining to a Pure Phenomenology and to a Phenomenological Philosophy: First Book*, trans. F. Kersten (Boston: Kluwer, 1983), 86–87.

25. Martin Heidegger, *Ontology—The Hermeneutics of Facticity*, trans. John van Buren (Bloomington: Indiana University Press, 1999).

26. Maurice Merleau-Ponty, *Phenomenology of Perception*, trans. Donald Landes (New York: Routledge, 2012), 102.

27. The reference is to this passage in *Ideas II*: "The hand lies on the table. I experience the table as solid, cold, smooth. Moving it over the table I experience it and its determinations as a thing. At the same time, however, I can always pay attention to the hand and find on it tactile sensations, sensations of smoothness and coldness, etc. In the interior of the hand, running parallel to the experienced movement, I [also] find sensations of motion, etc. Lifting a thing I experience its weight, but, at the same time, I have sensations related to the weight located in my lived body. And thus, in general, my lived body, coming into physical contact (striking, pressing, pushing, etc.) with other material things offers not only the experience of physical events relating the lived body to things, but also [of] specific lived-bodily events of the kind that we call sensings (*Empfindnisse*). Such events are missing in 'merely' material things." Edmund Husserl, *Ideas Pertaining to a Pure Phenomenology and to a Phenomenological Philosophy: Second Book*, trans. R. Rojcewicz and A. Schuwer (Boston: Kluwer, 1989), 153.

28. Merleau-Ponty, *Phenomenology of Perception*, 147, 103.

29. Prices are those currently listed on the California Prison Industry Authority's online *Catalogue of Products and Services* (http://catalog.pia.ca.gov/store).

30. "About CalPIA," California Prison Industry Authority: http://calpia .ca.gov/About_PIA/AboutPIA.aspx (accessed January 18, 2013).

31. California Prison Industry Authority, *Report to the Legislature FY 2009–2010* (Folsom, CA: CalPIA, 2010), 11: http://www.pia.ca.gov/Public _Affairs/pdfs/CALPIA%20Report%20to%20the%20California%20

Legislature.pdf (accessed January 19, 2013); California State Auditor, *California Prison Industry Authority: It Can More Effectively Meet Its Goals of Maximizing Inmate Employment, Reducing Recidivism, and Remaining Self-Sufficient* (Sacramento, CA: Bureau of State Audits, 2011), 1: http://www.bsa.ca.gov/pdfs/reports/2010-118.pdf (accessed January 19, 2013). CalPIA revenues have declined in the wake of state realignment policies put into effect in 2011. In 2011 the U.S. Supreme Court ruled that California was violating incarcerated persons' Eighth Amendment rights against cruel and unusual punishment because of the massive overcrowding of its state prisons. The Court ordered that the state prison system reduce its incarcerated population to redress this constitutional violation. The state's realignment policy responds to the Court order by rerouting lower-level offenders to serve their sentences in county jails rather than state prison. Declining prison populations have led to declines in both CalPIA's labor supply and the demand for its products and services (much of which is consumed by incarcerated persons themselves). See James Nash, "California's Prison Factories Falter as Inmate Population Falls," *Business Week*, May 16, 2013: http://www.businessweek.com/articles/2013-05-16/californias-prison-factories-falter-as-inmate-population-falls (accessed May 20, 2013).

32. As California Penal Code 2807 and California State University Policy 224 states: "The State and its agencies (including the CSU) are required to procure any available comparable goods or services produced by the Prison Industry Authority (PIA), unless specifically waived by the PIA." California State University–Fullerton Division of Administration and Finance, *Contracts and Procurement Operations Manual* (2005), 36. The Associate Director of Contracts and Procurement at my university informed me that, while most state agencies are still required to utilize CalPIA, the CSU has been exempt from that mandate since late 2004 (personal communication).

33. California State Auditor, *Prison Industry Authority: Statutory and Cost Control Problems Adversely Affect the State* (Sacramento, CA: Bureau of State Audits, 1996), 20: http://www.bsa.ca.gov/pdfs/reports/95106.pdf (accessed January 19, 2013).

34. D. C. Carson, "Reforming the Prison Industry Authority," *California Legislative Analyst's Office* (1996), 9.

35. California Performance Review, *SO67 Procurement of Prison Industry Authority Products* (2004): http://cpr.ca.gov/cpr_report/Issues_and_Recommendations/Chapter_7_Statewide_Operations/Procurement/SO67.html (accessed January 18, 2013).

36. Prerna Anand, *Winners and Losers: Corrections and Higher Education in California* (Los Altos, CA: California Common Sense, 2012): http://www.cacs.org/ca/article/44 (accessed January 19, 2013).

37. Hansook Oh and Mona Adem, "California Budgets $1 Billion More to Prisons than Higher Education and Leaves Students Hanging," *The Daily Sundial*, September 19, 2012: http://sundial.csun.edu/2012/09/california -budgets-1-billion-more-to-prisons-than-higher-education-and-leaves -students-hanging (accessed January 19, 2013).

38. In 1998–1999, per-student spending in CSU totaled $13,502 (with 81 percent from the state and 19 percent from net tuition and fees); by 2011– 2012, total revenue had fallen to $11,971 per student (with 54 percent from the state and 46 percent from net tuition and fees). Hans Johnson, *Defunding Higher Education* (San Francisco: Public Policy Institute of California, 2012), 7–8.

39. "About CalPIA," California Prison Industry Authority: http://calpia .ca.gov/About_PIA/AboutPIA.aspx (accessed January 18, 2013); shawnna d., The Fire Inside Editorial Collective, and Edaleen Smith, "Slaving in Prison," in *Interrupted Life: Experiences of Incarcerated Women in the United States*, ed. Rickie Solinger et al. (Berkeley: University of California Press, 2010), 321–325.

40. Thomas Harris et al., *The Economic Impact of the California Prison Industry Authority on the California Economy for FY 2008/09*.

41. http://www.unicor.gov/about/faqs/faqsgeneral.cfm (accessed January 29, 2013); Ian Urbina, "Prison Labor Fuels American War Machine," in *Prison Profiteers: Who Makes Money from Mass Incarceration*, ed. Tara Herivel and Paul Wright (New York: The New Press, 2007), 109–118.

42. *Factories with Fences: 75 Years of Changing Lives* (2009): http://www .unicor.gov/information/publications/pdfs/corporate/CATMC1101_C.pdf (accessed January 29, 2013).

43. http://jointventureprogram.ca.gov/Benefits; http://jointventure program.ca.gov/Free-Venture-Program (accessed January 29, 2013).

44. shawnna d., The Fire Inside Editorial Collective, and Smith, "Slaving in Prison," 322; Prison Law Office, "Release Date Calculations and Challenging Errors in Release Date" (San Quentin, CA: Prison Law Office, revised 2012): http://www.prisonlaw.com/pdfs/ReleaseDate,Sept2012.pdf (accessed June 6, 2013).

45. Urbina, "Prison Labor Fuels American War Machine," in *Prison Profiteers*, 117.

46. shawnna d., The Fire Inside Editorial Collective, and Smith, "Slaving in Prison," 322; Urbina, "Prison Labor Fuels American War Machine," in *Prison Profiteers*, 116.

47. Steven Jackson, "Mapping the Prison Telephone Market," in *Prison Profiteers*, 235–249; Todd Shields, "Prison Phones Prove Captive Market for Private Equity," *Bloomberg News*, October 3, 2012: http://www.bloomberg

.com/news/2012-10-04/prison-phones-prove-captive-market-for-private
-equity.html (accessed February 1, 2013).

48. John E. Dannenberg, "Nationwide PLN Survey Examines Prison
Phone Contracts, Kickbacks," *Prison Legal News*, April 2011: https://www
.prisonlegalnews.org/(S(34xg4h553u305v453i4j5u45))/23083_displayArticle
.aspx (accessed February 1, 2013).

49. Drew Kukorowski, *The Price to Call Home: State-Sanctioned Monopolization of the Prison Phone Industry* (Northampton, MA: Prison Policy Initiative, 2012).

50. In 2004, 52 percent of people in state prisons and 63 percent in
federal prisons were parents of minor children. Eighty percent of incarcerated women are parents of minor children. See The Sentencing Project, *Fact
Sheet: Parents in Prison* (Washington, DC: The Sentencing Project, 2012):
http://www.sentencingproject.org/doc/publications/cc_Parents%20in%20
Prison_Factsheet_9.24sp.pdf (accessed November 27, 2012); Joanne Belknap,
The Invisible Woman: Gender, Crime, and Justice (Belmont, CA: Wadsworth
Publishing Company, 1996); Linda Evans, "Playing Global Cop: U.S. Mili-
tarism and the Prison-Industrial Complex," in *Global Lockdown: Race, Gender,
and the Prison-Industrial Complex*, ed. Julia Sudbury (New York: Routledge,
2005), 217.

51. On the financial rewards for investment bankers when prisons are
built, see Kevin Pranis, "Doing Borrowed Time: The High Cost of Back-
door Prison Finance," in *Prison Profiteers*, 36–51; and Ruth Wilson Gilmore,
Golden Gulag: Prisons, Surplus, Crisis, and Opposition in Globalizing California
(Berkeley: University of California Press, 2007), 97–102.

52. Paul Wright, "The Cultural Commodification of Prisons," in *Prison
Profiteers*, 101.

53. Ruth Gilmore's expansive study of the political economy of the
California prison system reveals that the majority (60 percent) of prison jobs,
while promised to local communities, actually go to people from elsewhere.
See, for example, *Golden Gulag*, 148–173.

54. Jonathan Franklin, "Jails Go Up, Yes, in their Backyards," *Boston Globe*,
July 31, 1994: 2.

55. Gilmore, *Golden Gulag*, 101.

56. Ibid., 111.

57. Judith Greene, "Banking on the Prison Boom," in *Prison Profiteers*,
3–26.

58. James Austin and Garry Coventry, *Emerging Issues on Privatized Prisons*
(Washington, DC: Department of Justice/Office of Justice Programs, 2001),
iii: http://www.ncjrs.gov/pdffiles1/bja/181249.pdf (accessed January 4, 2012).

59. Michael Marois, "Corrections Corporation Wins as Brown Buys California Prison Fix," *Bloomberg News*, September 9, 2013: http://www .bloomberg.com/news/2013-09-09/corrections-corp-wins-as-jerry-brown -buys-california-prison-fix.html (accessed August 25, 2014).

60. Bureau of Justice Statistics, *Prisoners in 2010* (Washington DC: United States Department of Justice, 2011), 7: http://bjs.ojp.usdoj.gov/index .cfm?ty=pbdetail&iid=2230 (accessed January 5, 2012).

61. Corrections Corporation of America, *2010 Annual Report*, 10; Amanda Petteruti and Paul Ashton, *Gaming the System: How the Political Strategies of Private Prison Companies Promote Ineffective Incarceration Policies* (Washington, DC: Justice Policy Institute, 2011).

62. Corrections Corporation of America, *About Us*: http://www.cca.com/ about (accessed January 5, 2012). Davis, *Are Prisons Obsolete?*, 86–88; *Abolition Democracy*, 38–39, 123–125.

63. Laura Sullivan, "Prison Economics Help Drive Arizona Immigra-tion Law," *National Public Radio*, October 28, 2010: http://www.npr .org/2010/10/28/130833741/prison-economics-help-drive-ariz-immigration -law (accessed January 20, 2013); "How Corporate Interests Got SB 1070 Passed, *National Public Radio*, November 9, 2010: www.npr.org/2010/ 11/09/131191523/how-corporate-interests-got-sb-1070-passed (accessed January 20, 2013).

64. For a copy of the letter, obtained by the *Huffington Post*, see: http:// big.assets.huffingtonpost.com/ccaletter.pdf.

65. *Criminal: How Lockup Quotas and "Low-Crime Taxes" Guarantee Profits for Private Prison Corporations* (Washington, DC: In the Public Interest, 2013): http://www.inthepublicinterest.org/sites/default/files/Criminal-Lockup%20 Quota-Report.pdf. For information about *In the Public Interest*, see: http:// www.inthepublicinterest.org/about-us. For a recent analysis of the way that privatization threatens democracy, see Si Kahn and Elizabeth Minnich, *The Fox in the Henhouse: How Privatization Threatens Democracy* (San Francisco: Berrett-Koehler, 2005).

66. See Andrew Dilts, *Punishment and Inclusion: Race, Membership, and the Limits of American Liberalism* (New York: Fordham University Press, 2014); Christopher Uggen, Sarah Shannon, and Jeff Manza, *State-Level Estimates of Felon Disenfranchisement in the United States, 2012* (Washington, DC: The Sentencing Project, 2012): http://sentencingproject.org/doc/publications/ fd_State_Level_Estimates_of_Felon_Disen_2010.pdf (accessed February 7, 2013); Jeff Manza and Christopher Uggen, *Locked Out: Felon Disenfranchise-ment and American Democracy* (New York: Oxford University Press, 2007); Marc Mauer, "Voting Behind Bars: An Argument for Voting by Prisoners,"

Howard Law Journal 54, no. 3 (2011): 549–566; Alec C. Ewald, "Civil Death": The Ideological Paradox of Criminal Disenfranchisement Laws in the United States," *Wisconsin Law Review* (2002): 1045–1132.

67. Christopher Muller, "How the Census Gives Wise County a Break," *The Roanoke Times*, January 30, 2005.

68. See the Prison Policy Initiative's *Prisoners of the Census* website: http://www.prisonersofthecensus.org; Brent Staples, "The Census: Phantom Constituents," *The New York Times*, February 6, 2009; Gary Hunter and Peter Wagner, "Prisons, Politics, and the Census," in *Prison Profiteers*, 80–89.

69. Georg Rusche and Otto Kirchheimer, *Punishment and Social Structure* (New Brunswick, NJ: Transaction, 2003), 5.

70. Edmund Husserl, *Crisis of European Sciences and Transcendental Phenomenology*, trans. David Carr (Evanston, IL: Northwestern University Press, 1970), 72.

71. Hortense Spillers, "Mama's Baby, Papa's Maybe: An American Grammar Book," *Diacritics* 17, no. 2 (1987): 67.

72. Jacob D. Green, "Narrative of the Life of J. D. Green," in *Slave Narratives*, ed. William L. Andrews and Henry Louis Gates Jr. (New York: The Library of America, 2000), 958.

73. Ibid., 959.

74. Ibid; emphasis added.

75. Quoted in Michael Hanchard, "Afro-Modernity: Temporality, Politics, and the African Diaspora," *Public Culture* 11, no. 1 (1999): 245–268 (quote p. 255).

76. Hartman, *Scenes of Subjection*, 41.

77. Ibid., 62, 68.

78. See Edward L. Ayers, *Vengeance and Justice: Crime and Punishment in the 19th-Century American South* (New York: Oxford University Press, 1984); David J. Rothman, *The Discovery of the Asylum: Social Order and Disorder in the New Republic* (Boston: Little Brown, 1971); and Michael Meranze, *Laboratories of Virtue: Punishment, Revolution, and Authority in Philadelphia, 1760–1835* (Chapel Hill: University of North Carolina Press, 1996). For parallel developments in England and Europe, see Michel Foucault, *Discipline and Punish: The Birth of the Prison*, trans. Alan Sheridan (New York: Random House, 1977); Michael Ignatieff, *A Just Measure of Pain: The Penitentiary and the Industrial Revolution, 1750–1850* (New York: Pantheon, 1978); and Dario Melossi and Massimo Pavarini, *The Prison and the Factory: Origins of the Penitentiary System*, trans. Glynic Cousin (London: Macmillan, 1981).

79. On the racial segregation of antebellum juvenile justice systems see, Geoff Ward, *The Black Child-Savers: Racial Democracy and Juvenile Jus-*

tice (Chicago: University of Chicago Press, 2012). On the marginal use of disciplinary codes and carceral punishments on enslaved African Americans in antebellum America, see Susa Eva O'Donovan, "Universities of Social and Political Change: Slaves in Jail in Antebellum America," in *Buried Lives: Incarcerated in Early America*, ed. Michele L. Tarter and Richard Bell (Athens: University of Georgia Press, 2012), 124–146. My thanks to Christopher Muller for bringing to my attention this latter text and the history to which it points.

80. Ayers, *Vengeance and Justice*, 61.

81. Gustave de Beaumont and Alexis de Tocqueville, *On the Penitentiary System in the United States and its Application to France*, trans. Francis Lieber (Philadelphia: Carey, Lea, and Blanchard, 1833), 15.

82. Christopher R. Adamson, "Punishment After Slavery: Southern State Penal Systems, 1865–1890," *Social Problems* 30, no. 5 (1983): 557.

83. Oshinsky, *"Worse Than Slavery,"* 6.

84. Angela Y. Davis, *Abolition Democracy*, 36–37; emphasis added. See also Angela Y. Davis, "Race and Criminalization: Black Americans and the Punishment Industry," 66–67; "Racialized Punishment and Prison Abolition," 99–100; *Are Prisons Obsolete?*, 60–83; *Abolition Democracy*, 72–74, 95–99.

85. Davis, "Racialized Punishment and Prison Abolition," 99.

86. Hartman, *Scenes of Subjection*, 116.

87. James, *The New Abolitionists*, xxviii.

88. Alex Lichtenstein also makes this point: "[I]n the New South the 'social death' entailed by the enslavement of the laborers was ostensibly rooted in their criminality, not just their race." He goes on to argue that this marked a shift from what Orlando Patterson called "intrusive slavery," in which the slave stood as an outsider, an alien, to "extrusive slavery," in which the slave was positioned as an internal exile, deprived of all claims of community because he had fallen. See James, *The New Abolitionists*, xxviii–xxix; Alex Lichtenstein, *Twice the Work of Free Labor: The Political Economy of Convict Labor in the New South* (New York: Verso, 1999), 21; and Orlando Patterson, *Slavery and Social Death: A Comparative Study* (Cambridge, MA: Harvard University Press, 1982).

89. Hartman, *Scenes of Subjection*, 115.

90. Ibid., 116.

91. Ibid., 125.

92. Ibid., 7.

93. Douglas Blackmon, *Slavery By Another Name* (New York: Random House, 2008); Mary Ellen Curtin, *Black Prisoners and Their World, Alabama, 1865–1900* (Charlottesville: University Press of Virginia, 2000); Angela Y. Davis, "From the Prison of Slavery to the Slavery of Prison"; "Political Pris-

oners, Prisons, and Black Liberation"; "Race and Criminalization"; "Racialized Punishment and Prison Abolition"; *Are Prisons Obsolete?*; Milfred Fierce, *Slavery Revisited: Blacks and the Southern Convict Lease System, 1865–1933* (New York: Africana Studies Research Center, Brooklyn College, CUNY, 1994); Brady Thomas Heiner, "'From the Prison of Slavery to the Slavery of Prison'"; Adam Jay Hirsch, *The Rise of the Penitentiary: Prisons and Punishment in Early America* (New Haven, CT: Yale University Press, 1992); Alex Lichtenstein, "Good Roads and Chain Gangs in the Progressive South: 'The Negro Convict is a Slave,'" *The Journal of Southern History* 59, no. 1 (1993): 85–110; Lichtenstein, *Twice the Work of Free Labor*; Matthew Mancini, *One Dies, Get Another: Convict Leasing in the American South, 1866–1928* (Columbia: University of South Carolina Press, 1996); David Oshinsky, *"Worse Than Slavery": Parchman Farm and the Ordeal of Jim Crow Justice* (New York: Free Press, 1996); Wacquant, "The New 'Peculiar Institution': On the Prison as Surrogate Ghetto"; Wacquant, "From Slavery to Mass Incarceration: Rethinking the 'Race Question' in the United States."

Earlier historical analyses along these lines include: Ida B. Wells-Barnett, *The Reason Why the Colored American is Not in the World's Columbian Exhibition*, reprinted in *The Selected Works of Ida B. Wells-Barnett* (1893; reprint: 1991: Oxford University Press), 67–74; W. E. B. Du Bois, "The Spawn of Slavery: The Convict Lease System of the South," *Missionary Review of the World* (October 1901): 737–745; *Black Reconstruction in America: 1860–1880* (1935, rpt. New York: The Free Press, 1998), 506, 698–700; Henry Calvin Mohler, "Convict Labor Policies," *Journal of the American Institute of Criminal Law and Criminology* 15, no. 4 (1925): 530–597; Angela Y. Davis, *Women, Race, and Class* (New York: Vintage, 1981), 89; Adamson, "Punishment After Slavery . . . ," 555–569; Christopher R. Adamson, "Toward a Marxian Penology: Captive Criminal Populations as Economic Threats and Resources," *Social Problems* 31, no. 4 (1984): 435–458; Jennifer Roback, "Southern Labor Law in the Jim Crow Era: Exploitative or Competitive?" *University of Chicago Law Review* 51 (1984): 1161–1192; Howard Rabinowitz, "Epilogue: Race Relations and Social Control," in *Race Relations in the Urban South, 1865–1890* (Urbana: University of Illinois Press, 1980); Mary Frances Berry, *Black Resistance, White Law: A History of Constitutional Racism in America* (1971; rpt. New York: 1994); Pete Daniel, *The Shadow of Slavery: Peonage in the South, 1901–1969* (1972; rpt. Urbana: University of Illinois Press, 1990).

94. See Khalil Gibran Muhammad, *The Condemnation of Blackness: Race, Crime, and the Making of Modern urban America* (Cambridge, MA: Harvard University Press, 2010) for a historical analysis of the central role of statistical discourse in forging the semiotic links between blackness and criminality, which simultaneously recodified white crime as individual failure.

95. Du Bois, "The Spawn of Slavery: The Convict Lease System of the South," 738.

96. Frantz Fanon, *Black Skin, White Masks* (1952; trans. Richard Philcox, New York: Grove, 2008), 108. I've modified Philcox's translation, which renders Fanon's *formules dissolvantes* as "corrosive stereotypes."

97. Patricia Hill Collins, *Black Feminist Thought* (New York: Routledge, 2000), 69–96.

98. I am here creatively appropriating the notions of *apperceptive transfer* and *pairing association* from Husserl's account of intersubjectivity in the *Cartesian Meditations*. However, whereas apperceptive transfer and pairing association are products of passive synthesis, ultimately rooted in the consciousness of a founding subject, my Foucault-inflected concepts of semiotic transfer and pairing aim to account for a process of sense-constitution that is social, decentered, and activated by an intentionally discontinuous series of institutional rituals and discursive and perceptual practices. See Edmund Husserl, *Cartesian Meditations*, trans. Dorion Cairns (Boston: Kluwer Academic Publishers), 110–113.

99. In *The Angela Y. Davis Reader*, 75. See also Heiner, "'From the Prison of Slavery to the Slavery of Prison.'"

100. W. E. B. Du Bois, *Black Reconstruction* (New York: The Free Press, 1998 [1935]), 699.

101. Ibid., 698.

102. See Oshinsky, *"Worse Than Slavery,"* 21; Adamson, "Punishment After Slavery," 559.

103. Quoted in Mancini, *One Dies, Get Another*, 183–184.

104. Lichtenstein, *Twice the Work of Free Labor*, 40.

105. See Oshinski, *"Worse Than Slavery,"* 20–21. The notion of the legal "improvisation" of crime stems from Karl Marx, "The Labeling of Crime," in *Crime and Punishment: Readings in Marxist Criminology*, ed. David F. Greenberg (Philadelphia: Temple university Press, 1993), 54.

106. Lichtenstein, *Twice the Work of Free Labor*, 26. Eugene Genovese and Peter Kolchin argue that the paternalistic racism of southern slavery reflected the economic and political interests of both masters and states in protecting the lives of bondspeople. "Despite the [paternalistic] efforts of the authorities and the courts," Genovese notes, "masters and overseers undoubtedly murdered more slaves than we shall ever know." See Eugene Genovese, *Roll, Jordan, Roll: The World the Slaves Made* (New York: Vintage, 1974), 37–41; Peter Kolchin, *American Slavery, 1619–1877* (New York: Hill and Wang, 1993), 111–122.

107. Cited in Mancini, *One Dies, Get Another*, 2–3. Original citation: Hastings H. Hart, "Prison Conditions in the South," *Proceedings of the National*

Prison Association (1919), 200. The postbellum racism unmitigated by paternalism was forcefully articulated by Ida B. Wells-Barnett in 1893: "In the time of slavery if a Negro was killed, the owner sustained a loss of property. Now he is not restrained by any fear of such loss." See Ida B. Wells-Barnett, *The Reason Why the Colored American is Not in the World's Columbian Exhibition*, reprinted in *The Selected Works of Ida B. Wells-Barnett* (1893; reprint: 1991: Oxford University Press), 55.

108. Lichtenstein, *Twice the Work of Free Labor*, 61.

109. *Ruffin v. Commonwealth of Virginia*, 62 Va. 790 (1871); emphasis added. It wasn't until the 1960s and 1970s that the U.S. Supreme Court recognized that prisoners retain some level of constitutional rights while imprisoned.

110. See Jacques Derrida, *Of Grammatology*, trans. Gayatri C. Spivak, corrected ed. (1967, trans.: Baltimore: Johns Hopkins University Press, 1997).

111. Hartman, *Scenes of Subjection*, 82–83.

112. Frederick Douglass, "Address to the People of the United States," delivered at a Convention of Colored Men, Louisville, Kentucky, September 24, 1883, in Phillip Foner, *The Life and Writings of Frederick Douglass, Volume 4: Reconstruction and After* (New York: International Publishers, 1950), 379; quoted in Angela Y. Davis, "From the Prison of Slavery to the Slavery of Prison," 82, and *Are Prisons Obsolete?*, 30.

113. Randall Kennedy, *Race, Crime, and the Law* (New York: Random House, 1997), 136–167.

114. Lichtenstein, *Twice the Work of Free Labor*, 60–61.

115. Jennifer Eberhardt, Phillip Atiba Goff, Valerie Purdie, and Paul Davies, "Seeing Black: Race, Crime, and Visual Processing," *Journal of Personality and Social Psychology* 87, no. 6 (2004): 876–893; Aliya Saperstein, Andrew M. Penner, and Jessica M. Kizer, "The Criminal Justice System and the Racialization of Perceptions," *The Annals of the American Academy of Political and Social Science* 651, no. 1 (2014): 104–121; Nazgol Ghandnoosh, *Race and Punishment: Racial Perceptions of Crime and Support for Punitive Policies* (Washington, DC: The Sentencing Project, 2014).

116. Lichtenstein also makes this point: "For African Americans, [the convict lease system] became a powerful symbol of injustice, linking the punishment of crime and their former status as slaves as forms of white oppression." See Du Bois, "The Spawn of Slavery: The Convict Lease System of the South," 741–742; and Lichtenstein, *Twice the Work of Free Labor*, 17–18.

117. Davis, *Abolition Democracy*, 74.

118. Friedrich Nietzsche, *On the Genealogy of Morality*, ed. Keith Answell-Pearson, trans. Carol Dieth (1887: trans. Cambridge: Cambridge University Press, 1994), 52.

119. Nietzsche, *On the Genealogy of Morality*, 53.

120. Nietzsche, *On the Genealogy of Morality*, 51–53.

121. My reading of Nietzsche's concept of genealogy here is indebted to Alison Stone, "Towards a Genealogical Feminism: A Reading of Judith Butler's Political Thought," *Contemporary Political Theory* 4, no. 1 (2005): 7–8; and Raymond Geuss, *Morality, Culture, and History: Essays on German Philosophy* (Cambridge: Cambridge University Press, 1999), 9–15.

122. Nietzsche, *On the Genealogy of Morality*, 51.

123. Stone, "Towards a Genealogical Feminism," 8.

124. Ibid.; Geuss, *Morality, Culture, and History*, 11.

125. Nietzsche, *On the Genealogy of Morality*, 51.

126. Michel Foucault, "What Calls for Punishment?" in *Foucault Live: Collected Interviews, 1961–1984*, ed. Sylvère Lotringer (New York, Semiotext[e], 1989), 427 (translation modified).

127. Nietzsche, *On the Genealogy of Morality*, 53.

128. In an interview, Angela Y. Davis indicates the historical and philosophical importance of the concept of abolitionism that guides the abolitionist movement. "I choose the word 'abolitionist' [to describe the strategy of the movement] deliberately. The 13th Amendment, when it abolished slavery, did so except for convicts. Through the prison system, the vestiges of slavery have persisted. It thus makes sense to use a word that has this historical resonance." See "Incarcerated Women: Transformative Strategies," *Black Renaissance/Renaissance Noir* 1, no. 1 (1996): 21–34, 26. See also "Race and Criminalization," 72.

129. On "ethical violence," see Judith Butler, *Giving an Account of Oneself* (New York: Fordham University Press, 2005), 41–82.

130. On participatory economics, see Michael Albert, *Parecon: Life After Capitalism* (New York: Verso, 2003).

131. On the theory and practice of community accountability, see Communities Against Rape and Abuse (CARA), "Taking Risks: Implementing Grassroots Community Accountability Strategies," in *Color of Violence: The INCITE! Anthology*, ed. INCITE! Women of Color Against Violence (Boston: South End Press, 2006), 250–266; Ana C. R. Durazo, Alisa Bierria, and Mimi Kim, eds., *Community Accountability: Emerging Movements to Transform Violence*, a special issue of *Social Justice: A Journal of Crime, Conflict & World Order* 37, no. 4 (2011–2012).

132. Herman Bianchi, *Justice as Sanctuary* (Bloomington: Indiana University Press, 1994), 164–165. René van Swaaningen, "What is Abolitionism?" in *Abolitionism: Towards a Non-Repressive Approach to Crime*, ed. Herman Bianchi and René van Swaaningen (Amsterdam: Free University Press, 1986), 13–14. See note 131.

133. Nils Christie, "Conflicts as Property," *The British Journal of Criminology* 17, no. 1 (1977): 1–15.

134. Beth Richie, *Compelled to Crime: The Gender Entrapment of Battered Black Women* (New York: Routledge, 1996). Quote from p. 5.

135. Christie, "Conflicts as Property," 7.

FROM COMMODITY FETISHISM TO PRISON FETISHISM:
SLAVERY, CONVICT-LEASING, AND THE IDEOLOGICAL
PRODUCTIONS OF INCARCERATION
James A. Manos

1. William J. Sabol, Heather Couture, and Paige M. Harrison, "Prisoners in 2006," in *U.S. Bureau of Justice Statistics Bulletin*, NCJ 219416 (December 2007).

2. Jennifer Warren, "One in 100: Behind Bars in America 2008," *Public Safety Performance Project* (Pew Center, 2008).

3. Otto Kirchheimer and Georg Rusche, *Punishment and Social Structure* (New Brunswick, NJ: Transaction Publishers, 2003); Mike Davis, "Hell Factories," *The Nation*, February 20, 1995, 229–234; Angela Davis, *Are Prisons Obsolete?* (New York: Seven Stories Press, 2002); Michael Hallett, *Private Prisons in America: A Critical Race Perspective* (Chicago: University of Illinois Press, 2006); Loïc Wacquant, *Punishing the Poor: The Neo-Liberal Government of Social Insecurity* (Durham, NC: Duke University Press, 2009); Michelle Alexander, *The New Jim Crow: Mass Incarceration in the Age of Colorblindness* (New York: The New Press, 2010).

4. Max Horkheimer, *Eclipse of Reason* (New York: Continuum Press, 2004), 87.

5. For a quick survey, see J. Thorsten Sellin, *Slavery and the Penal System* (New York: Elsevier, 1976); Matthew J. Mancini, *One Dies, Get Another: Convict Leasing in the American South, 1866–1928* (Columbia: University of South Carolina Press, 1996); David M. Oshinsky, *Worse than Slavery: Parchman Farm and the Ordeal of Jim Crow Justice* (New York: Free Press, 1996); Alex Lichtenstein, *Twice the Work of Free Labor: The Political Economy of Convict Labor in the New South* (New York: Verso, 1996); Mark Colvin, *Penitentiaries, Reformatories, and Chain Gangs: Social Theory and the History of Punishment in Nineteenth-Century America* (New York: St. Martin's Press, 1997); Loïc Wacquant, "From Slavery to Mass Incarceration: Rethinking the 'Race Question' in the US," *New Left Review* 13 (2002): 41–60; Angela Davis, *Are Prisons Obsolete?;* Douglas A. Blackmon, *Slavery by Another Name: The Re-Enslavement of Black Americans from the Civil War to World War II* (New York: Doubleday, 2008); Alexander, *The New Jim Crow*.

6. Dario Melossi makes this argument in "The Penal Question in 'Capital' [found in *Crime and Social Justice*, no. 5 (Spring-Summer 1976): 26–33]. He claims of all of Marx's works the "capitalist matrix of the penal question" is found in the first volume of *Capital*'s discussion of primitive accumulation (26).

7. For arguments claiming primitive accumulation is not an *Ur* story of capital but the logic by which it preserves itself, see Werner Bonefeld, "The Permanence of Primitive Accumulation: Commodity Fetishism and Social Constitution," *The Commoner* 2 (2001): 1–15; Mark Neocleous, "War on Waste: Law, Original Accumulation and the Violence of Capital," *Science & Society* 75 (2011): 506–528.

8. For a description of this process, see Ellen Meiksins Wood, *The Origin of Capital: A Longer View* (New York: Verso, 2002); E. P. Thompson, *Customs in Common* (Merlin Press, 2009); Peter Linebaugh, *London Hanged: Crime and Civil Society in the Eighteenth Century* (New York: Verso, 2003); Michael Perelman, *The Invention of Capitalism: Classical Political Economy and the Secret History of Primitive Accumulation* (Durham, NC: Duke University Press, 2000).

9. Karl Marx, *Capital: A Critique of Political Economy, Volume One*, trans. Ben Fowkes (New York: Vintage Books, 1977), 874.

10. Ibid.

11. Ibid.

12. Ibid.

13. Ibid., 896.

14. For more on this point, see Jeffrey Reiman and Paul Leighton, *The Rich get Richer and the Poor get Prison: Ideology, Class, and Criminal Justice* (New York: Wiley Publishing, 1979); John Irwin, *The Warehouse Prison: Disposal of the New Dangerous Class* (New York: Oxford University Press, 2004). Loïc Wacquant, *Punishing the Poor*.

15. Marx, *Capital*, 899.

16. Rusche and Kirchheimer, *Punishment and Social Structure*, 5.

17. Michel Foucault, *Discipline and Punish: The Birth of the Prison*, trans. Alan Sheridan (New York: Vintage Books, 1995), 24.

18. Rusche and Kirchheimer, *Punishment and Social Structure*, 5.

19. Ibid., 42.

20. Ibid., 24.

21. As Steve Martinot argues in *The Rule of Racialization: Class, Identity, Governance* (Philadelphia: Temple University Press, 2003), Marx's discussion of primitive accumulation leaves out the fact that it "relied on early colonialism, and the despoliation of new areas (Africa and Americas) during the six-

teenth and seventeenth centuries. The British began their industrialization in large part with shipping, and developed their shipping industry through the enormous profits made in the slave trade . . . the slave trade and plantation slavery both served to kickstart capitalism's operations" (15). See also Robin Blackburn, *The Making of New World Slavery: From the Baroque to the Modern, 1492–1800* (New York: Verso, 1997).

22. See Sellin, *Slavery and the Penal System*; Angela Davis, *Are Prisons Obsolete?*; Wacquant, "From Slavery to Mass Incarceration," 41–60; Michael Hallett, "Race, Crime, and for Profit Imprisonment: Social Disorganization as Market Opportunity," *Punishment and Society* 4 (2002): 369–393.

23. Angela Davis, "Racialized Punishment and Prison Abolition," in *The Angela Y. Davis Reader*, ed. by Joy James (New York: Routledge, 1998), 100.

24. For example, in 1833 Alabama's slave code decreed "no slave shall be admitted a witness against any person, in any matter, cause, or thing whatsoever, civil or criminal, except in criminal cases, in which the evidence of one slave shall be admitted for or against another slave." John G. Aikin, ed., "Slaves and Free Persons of Color," in *A Digest of the Laws of the State of Alabama: 1833* (Philadelphia: Alexander Towar, 1833), 391. Accessed from Alabama Department of Archives and History (Montgomery, Alabama). Retrieved online: http://www.archives.state.al.us/teacher/slavery/lesson1/doc1.html

25. Again, Section 9 of Alabama's Slave Code reads: "Riots, routs, unlawful assemblies, trespasses, and seditious speeches, by a slave or slaves, shall be punished with stripes, not exceeding thirty-nine, at the discretion of a justice of the peace; and he who will, may apprehend and carry him, her, or them, before such a justice" (Aikin, "Slaves and Free Persons of Color," 392).

26. Once more, Section 15 of Alabama's Slave Code decrees: "All runaway slaves may be lawfully apprehended by any person, and carried before the next justice of the peace, who shall either commit them to the county jail, or send them to the owner, if known, who shall pay for every slave so taken up, the sum of six dollars to the person apprehending him or her, and also all reasonable costs and charges" (Aikin, "Slaves and Free Persons of Color," 393).

27. Again, Section 5 of Alabama's 1833 Slave Code states that if a slave has left "the tenement of his master without a pass, or some letter or token" then the slave could be rounded up and carried "before a justice of the peace, to be by his order punished with stripes, or not at his discretion, not exceeding twenty stripes." Moreover, in Section 6 one finds that a slave could receive "ten lashes on his or her bare back" for each offense of trespassing on other plantations without "being sent upon lawful business" (Aikin, "Slaves and Free Persons of Color," 391).

28. Pete Daniels comments on the loose association and confusion that characterized labor in the post-war south in his essay "The Metamorphosis

of Slavery, 1865–1900" [in *Journal of American History* 66 (1979): 88–99].
Daniels writes, "Like a patchwork quilt, the new labor system in the South
was varied and complex, an unpatented blend of illiteracy, law, contracts,
and violence, confusing, if not incomprehensible, even to those closest to it"
(Daniels, "The Metamorphosis of Slavery, 1865–1900," 88).

29. One only needs to look at the "differences" between Alabama's runaway slave law in 1833 (see endnote 26) and Mississippi's runaway apprentice
law to see this. Mississippi's 1866 apprentice law states, "If any apprentice
shall leave the employment of his or her master or mistress, without his or
her consent, said master or mistress may pursue and recapture said apprentice, and bring him or her before any justice of the peace of the county,
whose duty it shall be to remand said apprentice to the service of his or her
master or mistress; and in the event of a refusal on the part of said apprentice so to return, then said justice shall commit said apprentice to the jail of
said county, on failure to give bond, to the next term of the county court."
Quintard Taylor, ed., "Mississippi Black Codes (1866)," in *African American
History: Primary Documents*, accessed at Blackpast.org: An Online Reference
Guide to African American History. Retrieved from http://www.blackpast
.org/?q=primary/1866-mississippi-black-codes.

30. Angela Davis makes this argument in "Racialized Punishment and
Prison Abolition." She writes, "In constructing prisoners as human beings
who deserved subjection to slavery, the Constitution allowed for a further,
more elusive linkage of prison and slavery, namely the criminalization of former slaves" (100). See also Khalil Gibran Muhammad, *The Condemnation of
Blackness: Race, Crime, and the Making of Modern Urban American* (Cambridge,
MA: University of Harvard Press, 2011).

31. Steven Hahn gives an excellent account of this dispossession in terms
of the transformation of general stock laws in South Carolina in the essay
"Hunting, Fishing, and Foraging: Common Rights and the Class Relations in
the Postbellum South," in *Crime and Capitalism: Readings in Marxist Criminology*, ed. David Greenberg (Philadelphia: Temple University Press, 1993),
142–168. He argues that in "the South, as in other post-emancipation societies, the fists of coercion and repression came down in efforts to restrict the
freedman's mobility, alternative employment opportunities, and access to the
means of production and subsistence, tying them to the land as a propertyless
work force" (Hahn, "Hunting, Fishing, and Foraging: Common Rights and
the Class Relations in the Postbellum South," 142).

32. Vagrancy laws were commonly employed in the post-war South to
quickly and wantonly reimprison ex-slaves. Some versions of these laws cast
quite a wide net. South Carolina's Vagrancy Law from 1865 is a great example of this and is worth reproducing in full. It states: "All persons who have

not some fixed and known place of abode, and some lawful and respectable employment; those who have not some visible and known means of a fair, honest and reputable livelihood; all common prostitutes; those who are found wandering from place to place, vending, bartering or peddling any articles or commodities, without a license from the District Judge, or other proper authority; all common gamblers; persons who lead idle or disorderly lives, or keep or frequent disorderly or disreputable houses or places; those who, not having sufficient means of support, are able to work and do not work; those who (whether or not they own lands, or are lessees or mechanics) do not provide a reasonable and proper maintenance for themselves and families; those who are engaged in representing publicly or privately, for fee or reward, without license, any tragedy, interlude, comedy, farce, play, or other similar entertainment, exhibition of the circus, sleight-of-hand, waxworks, or the like; those who, for private gain, without license, give any concert or musical entertainment, of any description; fortune-tellers; sturdy beggars; common drunkards; those who hunt game of any description or fish on the land of others, or frequent the premises, contrary to the will of the occupants, shall be deemed vagrants, and be liable to the punishment hereinafter prescribed." Section XCV. The Statute at Large of South Carolina Vol. XII containing the Acts from December 1861 to December 1866. An Act to Establish and Regulate the Domestic relations of Persons of Color and to Amend the Law in Relation to Paupers and Vagrancy, Act No. 4733. General Assembly, December 19, 1865 (Columbia SC: Republican Printing Corp., 1875), 284. South Carolina Department of Archives and History, Columbia, South Carolina. Retrieved: www.teachingushistory.org/pdfs/BlackCodes_000.pdf.

33. Angela Davis, *Are Prisons Obsolete?*, 29. See also Jessica Adams, *Wounds of Returning: Race, Memory, and Property on the Postslavery Plantation* (Chapel Hill: University of North Carolina Press, 2007).

34. As already noted, a recent report by the Pew Center on the States 2008 states that "more than one in every 100 adults is now confined in an American jail or prison" (Pew Center 2008, 3). While this fact may be striking enough on its own, when one breaks down the demographics of who is imprisoned the ratios drastically shift. One finds that while white men over the age of eighteen compose 1:106, Hispanic men over eighteen compose 1:36, and most strikingly black men over eighteen compose 1:15 (a ratio that increases to 1:9 when one looks specifically at black men between the ages of twenty and thirty-four) (Pew Center 2008, 6).

35. See Blackmon, *Slavery by Another Name*; Christopher R. Adamson, "Punishment after Slavery: Southern State Penal Systems, 1865–1890," *Social Problems* 30, no. 5 (June 1983): 555–569.

36. See Jessica Adams, *Wounds of Returning*.

37. Lichtenstein, *Twice the Work of Free Labor*, 16. See also Sellin, *Slavery and the Penal System*.

38. W. E. B. Du Bois, "The Spawn of Slavery," in *Race, Crime and Justice: A Reader*, ed. Shaun L. Gabbidon and Helen Taylor Greene (New York: Routledge, 2005), 4.

39. See Angela Davis, *Are Prisons Obsolete?*, especially chapters 2 and 5; Lichtenstein, *Twice the Work for Free Labor*, especially chapter 1.

40. Du Bois, "The Spawn of Slavery," 5.

41. Blackmon, *Slavery by Another Name*, 96.

42. Ibid.

43. Most slave codes had some clause protecting against malicious over-punishment by the master. Some of them regulated the number of lashes. Some of them, like Alabama's slave codes, gave more general prescriptions: "Any person who shall maliciously dismember or deprive a slave of life, shall suffer such punishment as would be inflicted in case the life offence had been committed on a free white person, and on the life proof, except in the case of insurrection of such slave" (Akin, "Slaves and Free Persons of Color," 391). This is lost in the transition of the slave codes to the black codes, hence the intensification of these forms of punishment at the hands of private industry.

44. As Mancini noted in *One Dies, Get Another*, the "isolation, the semi-frontier conditions of the rural south, the drive for profits, and the miserable penury of the lessees all combined to produce terrible health problems, sometimes of epidemic level. They could result in soaring death rates for some years. Mississippi recorded an 11 percent annual death rate over the entire period from 1880 to 1885—a total of 482 convicts. Fifteen of 120 convicts died in the Alabama mines in 1877; 45 of 182 died on the Cape Fear and Yadkin Valley Railroad two years later. In states where convicts were held in jails rather than being transported to their labor camps directly, mortality was higher" (66).

45. Angela Davis, "From the Prison of Slavery to the Slavery of Prison: Frederick Douglas and the Convict Lease System," in *The Angela Y. Davis Reader*, ed. Joy James (Malden, MA: Blackwell, 1998), 87.

46. Du Bois, "The Spawn of Slavery," 4.

47. Allessandro De Giorgi's excellent *Rethinking the Political Economy of Punishment: Perspectives on Post-Fordism and Penal Politics* (Burlington, VT: Ashgate Publishing, 2006) takes up the dispersal of the workforce during the rise of the post-Fordist workforce under neoliberalism. He characterizes this workforce as containing the following characteristics: "extreme flexi-bilisation," "blurring of times of work and non-work," "fragmentation and diffusion of the production process," "increasing mobility" of the workforce, and "diffusion of multi-skilled role" (xiii). The advent of the post-Fordist

workforce, De Giorgi argues, marks the end of biopolitical control and exploitation of labor power. Rather, punishment under the conditions of neoliberalism is focused on the control of the "poor, the unemployed, the immigrants: these are the new dangerous class, the 'wretched of the metropolis'" (x).

48. Lichtenstein, *Twice the Work of Free Labor*, 188.

49. For instance, in "The Permanence of Primitive Accumulation: Commodity Fetishism and Social Constitution," *The Commoner* 2 (2001), Werner Bonefeld argues, "The commodity form poses the totality of bourgeois social relations and as such a totality posits the basis of the productive practice of all individuals as alienated individuals" (5).

50. Karl Marx, "Wage Labour and Capital," in *Karl Marx and Frederick Engels Collected Works*, vol. 9, ed. Philip S. Forner et al., 50 vols. (New York: International Publishers, 1996), 198.

51. Marx, *Capital*, 300.

52. Karl Marx, *Das Kapital: Band I*, vol. 23, in *Karl Marx und Friedrich Engels Werke*, 42 vols. (Berlin: Dietz Verlag, 1962), 85.

53. In "Marx on the Penal Question," Dario Melossi argues, "After the factory had been recognized as an ideal workhouse, then prisons became ideal factories; punishment finally acquired the double characteristic of tangible representation of the dominant social ideology" (30).

54. de Giorgi, *Re-Thinking the Political Economy of Punishment*, 44.

55. See: Loïc Wacquant, "Crafting the Neoliberal State: Workfare, Prisonfare, and Social Insecurity," *Sociological Forum* 25 (2010): 197–220; Wacquant, *Punishing the Poor*.

56. Michael Hallett, "Race, Crime, and Forprofit Imprisonment: Social Disorganization as Market Opportunity," 371.

57. Ibid.

58. See: Loïc Wacquant, "Class, Race and Hyperincarceration in Revanchist America," *Daedalus* (Summer 2010): 75–90; Eduardo Mendieta, "Plantations, Ghettos, Prisons: US Racial Geographies," *Philosophy & Geography* 7 (2004): 43–59; Eduardo Mendieta, "Penalized Spaces: The Ghetto as Prison and the Prison as Ghetto," *City* 10 (2007): 384–390.

59. Wacquant, *Punishing the Poor*, 295.

MAROON PHILOSOPHY: AN INTERVIEW WITH
RUSSELL "MAROON" SHOATZ RUSSELL "MAROON"
Shoatz and Lisa Guenther

1. Eugene Genovese, "Black Maroons in War and Peace," in *From Rebellion to Revolution: Afro-American Slave Revolts in the Making of the Modern World* (Baton Rouge: Louisiana State University Press, 1979).

2. Frantz Fanon, *The Wretched of the Earth*, trans. Richard Philcox (New York: Grove Press, 1963), 128.

3. Russell "Maroon" Shoatz, *Maroon the Implacable: The Collected Writings of Russell Maroon Shoatz* (Oakland, CA: PM Press, 2013).

U.S. RACISM AND DERRIDA'S THEOLOGICO-POLITICAL SOVEREIGNTY
Geoffrey Adelsberg

1. Michael Naas, "Philosophy and the Death Penalty" (presented at the Derrida Seminar Translation Project, Caen, France, Summer 2011), http://derridaseminars.org/pdfs/2011/2011%20Presentation%20Naas.pdf.

2. Jacques Derrida, *The Death Penalty. Volume I*, trans. Peggy Kamuf (Chicago: University of Chicago Press, 2013), 22.

3. Jacques Derrida and Elisabeth Roudinesco, *For What Tomorrow: A Dialogue*, trans. Fort (Stanford, CA: Stanford University Press, 2004).

4. Ibid., 145.

5. Ibid.

6. If this analysis is right, that it is anathema for the state to give up its decision over violence reveals that the theologico-political conception has valence. It is right that any entity that we can recognizably call a state is only a state insofar as it can exercise this capacity to decide on the life and death of its citizens (thereby have at least the capacity to kill). This demonstrates that the foundational claim of theologico-political sovereignty refers to political structures as we know them. This does not prove the whole of the claims of political theology, but it does point to the valence of its fundamental premise.

7. Cesare marchese di Beccaria, *Beccaria: "On Crimes and Punishments" and Other Writings*, ed. Richard Bellamy, trans. Richard Davies (Cambridge: Cambridge University Press, 1995), 68.

8. Derrida, *For What Tomorrow*, n25.

9. Ibid., 149.

10. Angela Y. Davis, *Abolition Democracy* (New York: Seven Stories, 2005), 35.

11. Ibid., 37.

12. White women, unrecognized in the public sphere, were subject to the tremendous cruelties of the private punishments of their husbands and hence, like slaves, were largely ineligible for these more "humane" prisons.

13. Davis, *Abolition Democracy*, 37.

14. Ibid., 97.

15. Lucia Re, "Structural Discrimination and Color-Blindness in United States and European Prison Systems," *Jura Gentium: Rivista di filosofia del diritto internazionale e della politica globale* 3 (2007): http://www.juragentium.org/forum/race/en/re.htm.

16. See Jacques Derrida, "Force of Law: The 'Mystical Foundation of Authority,'" *Cardozo Law Review* 11 (1990): 920–1046.

17. My discussion here tracks, in broad outline, Judith Butler, *Frames of War: What Makes Life Grievable* (New York: Verso, 2009).

18. In contrast to the abolitionist response to Troy Davis's execution, the killing of protesters in Tahrir Square brought political action against the sovereign itself. The Troy Davis abolitionists impugned the institution of the death penalty as punishment without challenging the sovereignty of the state itself. Herein, we find a rather concrete example of the distinction between the sovereign abolition of anti-Mubarak protesters in Egypt and the phenomenal abolitionism in Georgia.

19. In Derrida's language, the mourning of the protestors in Tahrir Square exemplifies a political iteration of overdetermined, impossible mourning. He writes, "Mourning must be impossible" (159). Their deaths caused a rupture in the lives of those who mourned.

20. Derrida, *For What Tomorrow*, 159.

MAKING DEATH A PENALTY:
OR, MAKING "GOOD" DEATH A "GOOD" PENALTY
Kelly Oliver

1. "The United States ranked fifth for the highest number of executions. The U.S. takes a spot behind China, Iran, Iraq, and Saudi Arabia for the most executions in the world last year, sitting ahead of Yemen and the Sudan" (Alexis Manning, *National Geographic News*, published April 12, 2013, accessed at http://news.nationalgeographic.com/news/2013/13/130412-death-penalty-capital-punishment-culture-amnesty-international/ on January 31, 2014).

2. *Baze v. Rees* (Roberts opinion), 533 U.S. 35 (2008).

3. Ross Levitt and Deborah Feyerick, "Death Penalty States Scramble for Lethal Injection Drugs," *CNN*, November 16, 2013, http://www.cnn.com/2013/11/15/justice/states-lethal-injection-drugs/index.html.

4. "Death Row Inmate Executed Using Pentobarbital in Lethal Injection," accessed March 11, 2014, http://www.cnn.com/2010/CRIME/12/16/oklahoma.execution/.

5. "State by State Database," *Death Penalty Information Center*, accessed January 28, 2014, http://www.deathpenaltyinfo.org/state_by_state.

6. Brian Haas, "Death Penalty Stuck in Limbo in Tennessee," *The Tennessean*, April 25, 2011, http://www.timesfreepress.com/news/2011/apr/25/death-penalty-stuck-limbo-tennessee-/?news.

7. Ibid.

8. *West v. Schofield*, 380 SW 3d 105 (Court of Appeals 2012), 112.

9. *Baze v. Rees* (Ginsburg, J., dissenting), U.S. (U.S. Supreme Court 2008). For a discussion of consciousness checks in relation to phenomenology of consciousness, see Lisa Guenther, "Toward a Critical Phenomenology of Lethal Injection." *New APPS: Art, Politics, Philosophy, Science*, January 27, 2014. http://www.newappsblog.com/2014/01/toward-a-critical -phenomenology-of-lethal-injection.html. Guenther invokes Husserl's theory of consciousness to argue against the possibility of second person or external consciousness checks.

10. Erica Goode, "After a Prolonged Execution in Ohio, Questions Over 'Cruel and Unusual,'" *The New York Times*, January 17, 2014, http://www .nytimes.com/2014/01/18/us/prolonged-execution-prompts-debate-over -death-penalty-methods.html.

11. Ibid.

12. For a discussion of the death penalty and phenomenology of consciousness, see Lisa Guenther, "Toward a Critical Phenomenology of Lethal Injection."

13. For a more substantial version of this argument, see Kelly Oliver, *Technologies of Life and Death: From Cloning to Capital Punishment* (New York: Fordham University Press, 2013).

14. *Furman v. Georgia*, 408 U.S. 238 (Supreme Court 1972).

15. *Baze v. Rees*, 533 U.S. 35, 38 (2008).

16. Ibid.

17. *Baze v. Rees*, 533 U.S. 35, 119 (2008) (Ginsburg, J., dissenting).

18. Ibid., n4.

19. Alison Motluk, "Execution by Injection Far from Painless," *New Scientist*, April 14, 2005, http://www.newscientist.com/article/dn7269 -execution-by-injectionfar-from-painless.html.

20. Brian Haas, "Tennessee's Death Penalty Is Back on Track," *The Tennessean*, October 23, 2013, http://www.wbir.com/story/news/local/2013/10/ 23/tennessees-death-penalty-is-back-on-track/3168925/.

21. Ibid.

22. Ibid.

23. Austin Sarat, ed., "Killing Me Softly: Capital Punishment and the Technologies for Taking Life," in *Pain, Death, and the Law* (Ann Arbor: University of Michigan Press, 2001), 44.

24. For a discussion of the issue of pain in relation to the death penalty, see Sarat, "Killing Me Softly."

25. Jacques Derrida, *The Beast and the Sovereign. Volume II* (Chicago: University of Chicago Press, 2011).

26. Jacques Derrida, *The Death Penalty. Volume I*, trans. Peggy Kamuf (Chicago: University of Chicago Press, 2013), 42.

27. Haas, "Tennessee's Death Penalty Is Back on Track."

28. Mike Mentrek, "Failed Execution of Romell Broom Prompts Efforts to Block 2nd Attempt," *The Plain Dealer*, September 17, 2009, http://blog .cleveland.com/metro/2009/09/failed_execution_of_romell_bro.html.

29. Rommel Broom was scheduled to be executed in Ohio on September 15, 2009. After the executioners tried for over two hours to find a viable vein to administer the lethal injection, the governor issued a week reprieve, during which Broom's legal team filed another appeal.

30. Jacques Derrida discusses the tension between the concepts of *death* and *penalty* in the death penalty, a tension that is perhaps more apparent in French than in English: "What is it, this thing, the death penalty (*la peine de mort*)? Is it a penalty, a punishment (*une peine*)? . . . And what if the death penalty (*la peine de mort*) were an untenable artifact, a pseudo-concept, such that the two terms, penalty (*peine*) and death, punishment (*peine*) and capital, did not let themselves be joined, like an out of joint syntagm, and such that it would be necessary to choose between the penalty and death without one being able ever to justify their logical grammar, except by unjustifiable violence, so much so that it would be necessary to choose between the penalty and death, there where the one and the other never go together?" (quoted in Dutoit, "Jacques Derrida on Pain of Death" presented at Vanderbilt University, September 2011, from Derrida, second lecture of year two, thirteenth lecture overall, 2–3). Dutoit comments, "Derrida brings out that to put 'penalty' (punishment, pain) and 'death' together is a monstrous hybrid. Either one chooses 'penalty,' in which case one lets go of death: the convict does not get put to death; or one chooses death, which is not a punishment, a pain or a penalty, since all of those presuppose life, continued life. The 'death penalty' is impossible, an impossible concept, the existence of which and the legal theory of which, are both based on an 'unjustifiable violence,' a forcing together of law and nature as if this were possible." Thomas Dutoit, "Kant's Retreat," *The Southern Journal of Philosophy*, 50, no. 1 (2012): 107–135. For a discussion of Derrida on capital punishment, see Oliver, *Technologies of Life and Death*.

31. Immanuel Kant, *The Metaphysics of Morals* (Cambridge: Cambridge University Press, 1996), 474–475.

32. Sarat, "Killing Me Softly," 68.

33. Derrida, *The Death Penalty. Volume I*, 116; emphasis added.

DEATH PENALTY ABOLITION IN NEOLIBERAL TIMES: THE SAFE CALIFORNIA
ACT AND THE NEXUS OF SAVINGS AND SECURITY
Andrew Dilts

1. Quoted in Robert Nye, "Two Capital Punishment Debates in France: 1908 and 1981," *Historical Reflections / Réflexions Historiques* 29, no. 2 (2003): 223.

2. George Jackson, *Blood in My Eye*, reprint edition (Baltimore: Black Classic Press, 1990), 118.

3. *Gregg v. Georgia*, 428 153 (1976).

4. The final results were 48 percent in favor and 52 percent against. See http://www.sos.ca.gov/elections/sov/2012-general/06-sov-summary.pdf.

5. Tessa Stuart, "Proposition 34: Campaign to Repeal the Death Penalty Is Gaining Traction According to Poll," in *The Informer* (Los Angeles: LA Weekly, 2012).

6. While support for the death penalty in California has been roughly constant since 1978, since 2000 there was a strong shift toward LWOP as the preferable sentence for capital murder cases. Mark DiCamillo and Mervin Field, "Support for Death Penalty Still Very Strong. But Increasing Preference for Life in Prison without Parole for Those Convicted of Capital Crimes," in *The Field Poll* (San Francisco: Field Research Corporation 2011).

7. See Maura Dolan, "Former Death Penalty Supporters Now Working against It," *Los Angeles Times*, September 23, 2012. In addition, the Safer California campaign highlighted the story of Don Heller—who drafted the 1978 ballot measure reinstating the death penalty—prominently on their website; see http://www.safecalifornia.org/stories/new-voices/heller.

8. Maura Dolan, "Campaign to Abolish California's Death Penalty Begins Airing Ads," *Los Angeles Times*, October 22, 2012.

9. As with all ballot initiatives in California, the full text of the provision, independent legislative and fiscal analyses, and arguments both for and against the measure are published by the California Secretary of State and sent to all Californian households with registered voters. This publication is also available online at http://voterguide.sos.ca.gov/propositions/34/.

10. Michel Foucault, "The Anxiety of Judging," in *Foucault Live*, ed. Sylvère Lotringer (New York: Semiotext[e], 1996), 246.

11. Ibid.

12. Bernard E. Harcourt, "Dismantling/Neoliberalism," *Carceral Notebooks* 6 (2010): 22.

13. See Jessica S. Henry, "Death-in-Prison Sentences: Overutilized and Underscrutinized," in *Life without Parole: America's New Death Penalty?*, ed. Charles J. Ogletree Jr. and Austin Sarat (New York: New York University Press, 2012).

14. In particular, see Angela Davis, "Race and Criminalization: Black Americans and the Punishment Industry," in *The House That Race Built: Black Americas, U.S. Terrain*, ed. Wahneema Lubiano (New York: Pantheon, 1997); Angela Davis, "From the Prison of Slavery to the Slavery of Prison: Frederick Douglass and the Convict Lease System," in *The Angela Y. Davis Reader*, ed. Joy James (Malden, MA: Blackwell Publishing, 1998); David Garland,

Peculiar Institution: America's Death Penalty in an Age of Abolition (Cambridge, MA: Belknap Press, 2010).

15. Loïc Wacquant, "The Penalisation of Poverty and the Rise of Neo-Liberalism," *European Journal on Criminal Policy and Research* 9, no. 4 (2001); Loïc Wacquant, *Punishing the Poor: The Neoliberal Government of Social Insecurity* (Durham, NC: Duke University Press, 2009); Dean Spade, *Normal Life: Administrative Violence, Critical Trans Politics and the Limits of Law* (Cambridge, MA: South End Press, 2011); Bernard E. Harcourt, *The Illusion of Free Markets: Punishment and the Myth of Natural Order* (Cambridge, MA: Harvard University Press, 2011); Loïc Wacquant, "Three Steps to a Historical Anthropology of Actually Existing Neoliberalism," *Social Anthropology* 20, no. 1 (2012).

16. The claim that eliminating single-occupancy cells for the 725 inmates on death row in the summer of 2012 could reduce costs is somewhat ironic given that State of California is also under federal oversight to reduce unconstitutional levels of overcrowding throughout the state, as a result of the 2011 ruling in *Brown v. Plata* (2011).

17. Carrillo (currently a student at Loyola Marymount University) had not received a death sentence, a fact that opponents of Prop. 34 repeatedly emphasized in their criticisms. Carrillo did receive what is effectively a "death-in-prison" sentence of thirty years to life, plus a second life sentence.

18. *Franky Carrillo is voting YES on Prop 34*, YouTube Video, 0:30, posted by "SafeCalifornia," October 2, 2012, https://www.youtube.com/watch?v=SDlQJoiooDw.

19. "Proposition 34's Common-Sense Appeal," *Los Angeles Times*, October 24, 2012. Prop. 34 was additionally endorsed throughout the state by the *Sacramento Bee*, *La Opinón*, the *San Bernardino Sun*, and the *San Francisco Chronicle*, as well as national newspapers such as *The New York Times*.

20. "Mercury News Editorial: California Should End Barbaric, Costly Death Penalty," *San Jose Mercury News*, July 30, 2012; emphasis added.

21. *Yes on 34*, YouTube Video, 2:39, posted by "SafeCalifornia," October 23, 2012, http://youtu.be/kTXTZ3x2JjY.

22. On the developing left/right political consensus on reforming criminal justice in line with "financial" and "investment" strategies, see Keally McBride, "California Penality: The End/Price of the Neoliberal Exception," *Carceral Notebooks* 6 (2010); Christopher Berk, "Investment Talk: Comments on the Use of the Language of Investment in Prison Reform Advocacy," *Carceral Notebooks* 6 (2010).

23. See Jonathan Simon, "Janus Faced Leviathan: California's Prisons and the Universities as Two Faces of State Power," *Carceral Notebooks* 6 (2010).

24. Ashley Nellis and Ryan S. King, "No Exit: The Expanding Use of
Life Sentences in America" (Washington, DC: Sentencing Project, 2009);
Ashley Nellis, "Throwing Away the Key: The Expansion of Life without
Parole Sentences in the United States," *Federal Sentencing Reporter* 23 (2010).
On the increasing dependence by some abolitionist groups on LWOP as a
replacement, see also Rachel E. Barkow, "Life without Parole and the Hope
for Real Sentencing Reform," in *Life without Parole: America's New Death
Penalty?*, ed. Charles J. Ogletree Jr. and Austin Sarat (New York: New York
University Press, 2012); Marie Gottschalk, "No Way Out? Life Sentences
and the Politics of Penal Reform," in *Life without Parole: America's New Death
Penalty?*, ed. Charles J. Ogletree Jr. and Austin Sarat (New York: New York
University Press, 2012). Every state that currently has the death penalty also
has a LWOP option as an available sentence for capital crimes. Additionally,
many states allow LWOP for noncapital crimes, and in some cases LWOP
sentences are mandatory for specific noncapital offenses. The only categorical
restrictions on LWOP apply to juveniles. *Graham v. Florida* (560 U.S. ____
2010) restricted LWOP sentences for juveniles to capital crimes only, and
Miller v. Alabama (567 U.S. ____ 2012) bars states from having mandatory
LWOP sentences. The court, however, stopped short of categorically barring
LWOP sentences for juveniles in *Miller*. The consideration of LWOP as a
replacement for execution rests in no small part on the widespread availability
of the sentence, which spread throughout the United States in the years following the 1972 moratorium imposed by Furman.

25. See Roger Hood and Carolyn Hoyle, *The Death Penalty: A Worldwide
Perspective*, 4th ed. (Oxford: Oxford University Press, 2008), 388–389.

26. This, at least in part, helps to explain why death penalty abolitionists
in the United States have relied heavily on judicial and executive avenues,
while simultaneously working to alter public opinion. Additionally, it is
important to distinguish between legislative "abolition," on the one hand, and
judicial and executive "abolition," on the other. There have been no executions in California since 2006, when a judicial moratorium was imposed for
all executions using the standard "three-drug protocol" by the courts. In contrast, Illinois's 2011 abolition of the death penalty came after an eleven-year
moratorium issued by a controversial executive order by Governor George
Ryan, who was later convicted of corruption.

27. Contrary to the European abolitionist trend, in which most states
ended capital punishment despite popular support, death penalty abolitionists in California have to end capital punishment with a winning strategy at
the ballot box, in a popular vote. See Andrew Hammel, "Civilized Rebels:
Death-Penalty Abolition in Europe as Cause, Mark of Distinction, and

Political Strategy," in *Is the Death Penalty Dying?*, ed. Austin Sarat and Jürgen Martschukat (Cambridge: Cambridge University Press, 2011).

28. DiCamillo and Field, "Support for Death Penalty Still Very Strong. But Increasing Preference for Life in Prison without Parole for Those Convicted of Capital Crimes."

29. Henry, "Death-in-Prison Sentences: Overutilized and Underscrutinized," 68.

30. Ibid., 69. Given the incredibly low annual rate at which parole is granted, Henry argues, DIP sentences include a larger swath of inmates than just those sentenced to LWOP. In California, the difference between an indeterminate life sentence (i.e., one available for parole) and a LWOP sentence is itself questionable, given a historic 2–5 percent parole rate for lifers.

31. Quoted in Henry, "Death-in-Prison Sentences: Overutilized and Underscrutinized," 72.

32. See Sharon Dolovich, "Creating the Permanent Prisoner," in *Life without Parole: America's New Death Penalty?*, ed. Charles J. Ogletree Jr. and Austin Sarat (New York: New York University Press, 2012).

33. Emphasis added. This fact would likely be obvious to a death row warden, given that of the ninety-seven death row inmates to die in California since 1978, only fourteen have actually been executed. Fifty-seven are reported to have died of natural causes, twenty have committed suicide, and six have died from "other causes." Darrell Calhoun and Michael Martinez, "California Death Row Inmate Found Dead Hanging in His Cell" (2012/05/30 2012); available from http://www.cnn.com/2012/05/29/justice/california-death-row-suicide/index.html.

34. See, in particular, Simon Grivet's comparative history of death penalty abolition in Simon Grivet, "Executions and the Debate over Abolition in France and the United States," in *Is the Death Penalty Dying?*, ed. Austin Sarat and Jürgen Martschukat (Cambridge: Cambridge University Press, 2011).

35. Ibid. Also see Garland, *Peculiar Institution: America's Death Penalty in an Age of Abolition*, chap. 8.

36. See Thomas Dumm, "The Dead, the Human Animal, and the Executable Subject," in *Who Deserves to Die?: Constructing the Executable Subject*, ed. Austin Sarat and Karl Shoemaker (Amherst: University of Massachusetts Press, 2011).

37. Jonathan Simon, "Governing Through Crime: 2012: Hope and Change Election Too," *Governing Through Crime*, November 5, 2012, http://governingthroughcrime.blogspot.com/2012/11/2012-hope-and-change-election-too.html; Jonathan Simon, "Governing Through Crime: You Should Know: Why Death Row Inmates Oppose LWOP," *Governing Through*

Crime, September 25, 2012, http://governingthroughcrime.blogspot.com/2012/09/you-should-know-why-death-row-inmates.html.

38. Kevin Cooper, Donald Ray Young, and Correll Thomas, "Death Row Debate: Yes or No on the Safe California Act?," *San Francisco Bay View*, June 5, 2012.

39. Michel Foucault, "Pompidou's Two Deaths," in *Power*, ed. James Faubion, *The Essential Works of Michel Foucault, 1954–1984* (New York: The New Press, 2000), 419.

40. Ibid.

41. Ibid.

42. In particular, see Malcolm M. Feeley and Jonathan Simon, "The New Penology: Notes on the Emerging Strategy of Corrections and Its Implications," *Criminology* 30, no. 4 (1992); David Garland, *The Culture of Control: Crime and Social Order in Contemporary Society* (Chicago: University of Chicago Press, 2001).

43. Timothy Kaufman-Osborn, "A Critique of Contemporary Death Penalty Abolitionism," *Punishment & Society* 8, no. 3 (2006): 374.

44. See especially Angela Davis, *Are Prisons Obsolete?* (New York: Seven Stories Press, 2003); Angela Davis, "Racialized Punishment and Prison Abolition," in *A Companion to African-American Philosophy*, ed. Tommy Lott and John Pittman (Oxford: Blackwell Publishing, 2003); Angela Davis, *Abolition Democracy: Beyond Empire, Prisons, and Torture* (New York: Seven Stories Press, 2005).

45. See Dylan Rodríguez, *Forced Passages: Imprisoned Radical Intellectuals and the U.S. Prison Regime* (Minneapolis: University of Minnesota Press, 2004).

46. Michel Foucault, *Discipline and Punish: The Birth of the Prison*, trans. Alan Sheridan (New York: Vintage Books, 1995), 232.

47. In the United States, this fabrication of criminal others was deeply connected to and articulated upon discourses and institutions of racial and sexual oppression. See Joy James, *States of Confinement: Policing, Detention, and Prisons* (New York: Palgrave Macmillan, 2002); Ladelle McWhorter, *Racism and Sexual Oppression in Anglo-America: A Genealogy* (Bloomington: Indiana University Press, 2009); Davis, "Race and Criminalization"; Davis, "Frederick Douglass and the Convict Lease System"; Davis, *Are Prisons Obsolete?*; Davis, "Racialized Punishment and Prison Abolition"; Davis, *Abolition Democracy*. As each of these authors has shown, it is wrong to simply read Foucault's analysis of the birth of the prison into the "American" context without both noting its limits and producing a distinct genealogical investigation in this time and place. Nineteenth- and early-twentieth-century criminol-

ogy was intimately tied to the production of racially, sexually, and mentally "underdeveloped" others, policing the boundaries of whiteness, gender, and heterosexuality themselves. The predictable and tragic production of deeply criminal "others" was a direct outcome of the contradictory discourses of atomistic liberalism and disciplinary society, expressed through existing social and politics cleavages of difference. The delinquent, the monstrous criminal, and the dangerous individual each came to the fore as ways to productively manage inherent tensions between criminal liability attached to one's bad actions and a disciplinary regime focused on one's "bad" soul. That these figures were able to also police cleavages of difference such as whiteness, masculinity, heterosexuality, ability, and independence allowed for "American" citizenship to be shot through with criminological discourses. On this point, see especially Ladelle McWhorter, "Sex, Race, and Biopower: A Foucauldian Genealogy," *Hypatia* 19, no. 3 (2004); McWhorter, *Racism and Sexual Oppression in Anglo-America;* Khalil Gibran Muhammad, *The Condemnation of Blackness: Race, Crime, and the Making of Modern Urban America* (Cambridge, MA: Harvard University Press, 2010); Andrew Dilts, "Incurable Blackness: Criminal Disenfranchisement, Mental Disability, and the White Citizen," *Disability Studies Quarterly* 32, no. 3 (2012).

48. See Ben Golder and Peter Fitzpatrick, *Foucault's Law* (London: Routledge, 2009).

49. Michel Foucault, *The History of Sexuality Vol. 1: An Introduction*, Vintage Books ed. (New York: Vintage Books, 1990), 102.

50. Ibid., 136.

51. Ibid.

52. Ibid., 138.

53. Ibid., 137–138.

54. Michel Foucault, *Society Must Be Defended: Lectures at the Collège De France, 1975–1976*, trans. David Macey (New York: Picador, 2003), 254–256. For an especially clear reading of Foucault's account of "racism" and its relation to biopower, see McWhorter, *Racism and Sexual Oppression in Anglo-America.*

55. Foucault, *Society Must Be Defended*, 254.

56. Ibid., 255.

57. Cf. Dumm's analysis of force feeding prisoners on hunger strikes: "In this strange state of affairs, the bio-political power to allow and sustain life comes to be the bio-political power to force one to live. Mercy in the form of sustaining life therefore becomes a punishment" (166). Thomas Dumm, "From Time to Torture: The Hellish Future of the Criminal Sentence," in *States of Violence: War, Capital Punishment, and Letting Die*, ed. Austin Sarat and Jennifer Culbert (Cambridge: Cambridge University Press, 2009).

58. Michel Foucault, *Security, Territory, Population: Lectures at the Collège De France, 1977–1978*, trans. Graham Burchell (New York: Palgrave Macmillan, 2007), 6–9.

59. Ibid., 8.

60. Ibid., 9.

61. Michel Foucault, *The Birth of Biopolitics: Lectures at the Collège De France, 1978–79*, trans. Graham Burchell (New York: Palgrave Macmillan, 2008).

62. See Andrew Dilts, "Michel Foucault Meets Gary Becker: Criminality Beyond Discipline and Punish," *Carceral Notebooks* 4 (2008); Jason Read, "A Genealogy of Homo-Economicus: Neoliberalism and the Production of Subjectivity," *Foucault Studies*, no. 6 (2009); Trent Hamann, "Neoliberalism, Governmentality, and Ethics," *Foucault Studies* (2009); Andrew Dilts, "From 'Entrepreneur of the Self' to 'Care of the Self': Neo-Liberal Governmentality and Foucault's Ethics," *Foucault Studies*, no. 12 (2011).

63. Foucault, *Birth of Biopolitics*, 317.

64. See the lectures of March 14, 21, and 28 in particular. The key texts by Becker are Gary S. Becker, "Investment in Human Capital: A Theoretical Analysis," *The Journal of Political Economy* 70, no. 5, Part 2: Investment in Human Beings (1962); Gary S. Becker, "Irrational Behavior and Economic Theory," *The Journal of Political Economy* 70, no. 1 (1962); Gary S. Becker, "Rational Action and Economic Theory: A Reply to I. Kirzner," *The Journal of Political Economy* 71, no. 1 (1963); Gary S. Becker, "A Theory of the Allocation of Time," *The Economic Journal* 75, no. 299 (1965). For Schultz, see Theodore W. Schultz, "Investment in Man: An Economist's View," *The Social Service Review* 33 (1959); Theodore W. Schultz, "Investment in Human Capital," *The American Economic Review* 51 (1961); Theodore W. Schultz, "Human Capital: Policy Issues and Research Opportunities," *Human Resources* (1972). I take up the question of Foucault's relationship to these thinkers at greater length in Dilts, "From 'Entrepreneur of the Self' to 'Care of the Self': Neo-Liberal Governmentality and Foucault's Ethics."

65. See Becker, "A Theory of the Allocation of Time," 503, 516.

66. G. S. Becker, "Crime and Punishment: An Economic Approach," *The Journal of Political Economy* 76, no. 2 (1968): 176.

67. Foucault, *Birth of Biopolitics*, 253.

68. Ibid., 249–250.

69. Ibid., 258.

70. Ibid., 259.

71. Ibid., 258.

72. Isaac Ehrlich, "The Deterrent Effect of Capital Punishment: A Question of Life and Death," *The American Economic Review* 65, no. 3 (1975): 399.

73. Ibid.

74. Becker, "Crime and Punishment: An Economic Approach," 196.

75. Ibid., 198.

76. Wendy Brown, "Neo-Liberalism and the End of Liberal Democracy," *Theory & Event* 7, no. 1 (2003).

77. Pat O'Malley, "Neo-Liberalism and Risk in Criminology," in *The Critical Criminology Companion*, ed. T. Anthony and C. Cunneen (Sydney: Hawkins Press, 2008). Robert Castel, "From Dangerousness to Risk," in *The Foucault Effect: Studies in Governmentality*, ed. Graham Burchell, et al. (Chicago: University of Chicago Press, 1991); Bernard E. Harcourt, *Against Prediction: Profiling, Policing, and Punishing in an Actuarial Age* (Chicago: University of Chicago Press, 2007).

78. See, for instance, Carol Pateman, *The Sexual Contract* (Stanford, CA: Stanford University Press, 1988); Charles W. Mills, *The Racial Contract* (Ithaca, NY: Cornell University Press, 1997); Muhammad, *Condemnation of Blackness;* Robin D. G. Kelley, *Race Rebels: Culture, Politics, and the Black Working Class* (New York: Free Press, 1994); Cathy J. Cohen, "Deviance as Resistance: A New Research Agenda for the Study of Black Politics," *Du Bois Review: Social Science Research on Race* 1, no. 1 (2004).

79. Karl Marx, "On the Jewish Question," in *The Marx-Engels Reader*, ed. Robert C. Tucker (New York: Norton, 1978), 33.

80. See Wacquant, "Three Steps to a Historical Anthropology of Actually Existing Neoliberalism," 74–76; Harcourt, *The Illusion of Free Markets: Punishment and the Myth of Natural Order.*

81. Joe Soss, Richard C. Fording, and Sanford Schram, *Disciplining the Poor: Neoliberal Paternalism and the Persistent Power of Race* (Chicago: University of Chicago Press, 2011); Wacquant, *Punishing the Poor: The Neoliberal Government of Social Insecurity.*

82. Commentators have referred to the Maryland bill expressly as the "left's austerity strategy." See Kailani Koenig-Muenster, "The Left's Austerity Strategy for the Death Penalty" (03/03/2013 2013); available from http://tv.msnbc.com/2013/03/03/the-lefts-austerity-strategy-for-the-death-penalty/.

83. "End Md.'s Death Penalty," *The Baltimore Sun*, January 15, 2013.

84. John Wagner, "O'malley Calls for End of Executions, Confirming Plans for Repeal Bill," *Washington Post*, 2013/01/15/ 2013.

85. Michel Foucault, "Considerations on Marxism, Phenomenology and Power," *Foucault Studies* 14 (2012): 109. As Foucault put it in this interview from April of 1978—given two days before he lectured at the *Collège de France* on the rise of the economic reason as the "new governmentality" that has given *raison d'état* "new content"—part of what one saw (with respect to

the interplay between "problems" of childhood sexuality and the pervasive concern about specific practices) was that resistance easily became deployment of the power itself being resisted.

86. Foucault, "Against Replacement Penalties," 459.

87. Ibid., 460–461.

88. Michel Foucault, "Le Grand Enfermentent," in *Dits Et Ecrits, Tome 2: 1976–1988* (Paris: Gallimard, 2001), trans. Perry Zurn.

89. Davis, *Are Prisons Obsolete?*, 22–24.

90. For instance, see Elias Walker Vitulli, "Queering the Carceral: Intersecting Queer/Trans Studies and Critical Prison Studies," *GLQ: A Journal of Lesbian and Gay Studies* 19, no. 1 (2012); CR-10 Publications Collective, ed., *Abolition Now! 10 Years of Strategy and Struggle against the Prison Industrial Complex* (Oakland, CA: AK Press, 2008); Ryan Conrad, ed., *Prisons Will Not Protect You* (Lewiston, ME: Against Equality Publishing Collective, 2012); Eric A. Stanley and Nat Smith, eds., *Captive Genders: Trans Embodiment and the Prison Industrial Complex* (Oakland, CA: AK Press, 2011); Spade, *Normal Life: Administrative Violence, Critical Trans Politics and the Limits of Law*; Beth E. Richie, *Arrested Justice: Black Women, Violence, and America's Prison Nation* (New York: New York University Press, 2012).

91. Foucault, "Against Replacement Penalties," 461.

ON THE INVIOLABILITY OF HUMAN LIFE
Julia Kristeva

1. Victor Hugo, *Écrits sur la peine de mort* (Actes Sud, 1992), 71.

2. Robert Badinter, *Débats À l'Assemblée Nationale Sur L'abolition de La Peine de Mort En France: Intervention de M. Badinter, Garde Des Sceaux, Ministre de La Justice* (Paris: Journal officiel de la république française, 1981), http://www.peinedemort.org/document.php?choix=4738.

3. Maimonides, *The Commandments*, trans. Charles B. Chavel (Brooklyn, NY: Soncino Pr Ltd., 1984), 269–271.

4. Charles de Secondat baron de Montesquieu, *Montesquieu: The Spirit of the Laws*, ed. Anne M. Cohler, Basia Carolyn Miller, and Harold Samuel Stone (Cambridge: Cambridge University Press, 1989), 82.

5. Cesare marchese di Beccaria, *Beccaria: "On Crimes and Punishments" and Other Writings*, ed. Richard Bellamy, trans. Richard Davies (Cambridge: Cambridge University Press, 1995), 66.

6. Jean Jaurès qtd. in Badinter, *Débats À l'Assemblée Nationale Sur L'abolition de La Peine de Mort En France*.

7. Albert Camus, "Reflections on the Guillotine," in *Resistance, Rebellion, and Death*, trans. Justin O'Brien (New York: Vintage International, 1995), 132.

8. Ibid, 218.

9. Hugo, *Écrits sur la peine de mort*, 118.

10. Ibid, 121.

PUNISHMENT, DESERT, AND EQUALITY: A LEVINASIAN ANALYSIS
Benjamin S. Yost

1. "US Rates of Incarceration: A Global Perspective." Retrieved January 18, 2013, from http://www.nccdglobal.org/sites/default/files/publication_pdf/factsheet-us-incarceration.pdf.

2. Over 3,200 Americans are currently serving life terms for nonviolent offences. "A Living Death: Life without Parole for Nonviolent Offences." Retrieved January 24, 2014, from https://www.aclu.org/criminal-law-reform/living-death-life-without-parole-nonviolent-offenses-0.

3. *Lockyer v. Andrade*. U.S. 538: 63. For further discussion of *Andrade*, as well as a detailed criticism of three-strikes laws, see Erwin Chemerinsky, "Cruel and Unusual: The Story of Leandro Andrade," *Drake Law Review* 52 (2003): 1–24. California voters recently passed Proposition 36, which requires that the third strike be a "serious or violent" felony for the mandatory life sentence to be applied. However, there is a loophole: some "non-serious, non-violent drug or sex offences" can still trigger a mandatory life sentence. See "California General Election Official Voter Information Guide." Retrieved January 18, 2013, from http://vig.cdn.sos.ca.gov/2012/general/pdf/complete-vig-v2.pdf.

4. Michelle Alexander, *The New Jim Crow: Mass Incarceration in an Age of Colorblindness* (New York: The New Press, 2010), 59.

5. Douglas A. McVay, "Prisons and Drug Offenders: Federal-Specific Data." Retrieved January 18, 2013, from http://www.drugwarfacts.org/cms/Prisons_and_Drugs#Federal-Data.

6. Alexander, *The New Jim Crow*, 96.

7. Marc Mauer, "The Changing Racial Dynamics of the War on Drugs." Retrieved January 18, 2013, from http://sentencingproject.org/doc/dp_raceanddrugs.pdf. Mauer shows that the situation is just as bad for Latinos.

8. Alexander, *The New Jim Crow*, 97.

9. "The Financial Crisis Response in Charts." Retrieved January 18, 2013 from http://www.treasury.gov/resource-center/data-chart-center/Documents/20120413_FinancialCrisisResponse.pdf.

10. "The Costs of the Financial Crisis." Retrieved January 18, 2013 from http://www.bettermarkets.com/sites/default/files/CBA%20Report%20CoC%205-31.pdf.

11. Peter Lattman, "Former Citigroup Manager Cleared in Mortgage Securities Case," *The New York Times*, July 31, 2012.

12. Jeffrey Reiman and Paul Leighton, *The Rich Get Richer and the Poor Get Prison: Ideology, Class, and Criminal Justice* (Boston: Pearson Higher Education, 2010), 110–171.

13. I take this way of putting the distinction from Owen McLeod, "On the Comparative Element of Justice," in *Desert and Justice*, ed. Serena Olsaretti (Oxford: Oxford University Press, 2003), 123–144.

14. Ibid.

15. The two principles of justice found in Rawls's *A Theory of Justice* contain no reference to desert; one of Rawls's main arguments is that desert should *not* figure into distributive justice. Desert is also absent from Nozick's conception of justice in *Anarchy, State, and Utopia*. To be sure, some theorists insist that desert plays a necessary role in distributive justice; for a discussion and criticism of this position, see Arneson, "Egalitarianism and the Undeserving Poor," *Journal of Political Philosophy* 5, no. 4 (1997): 327–350. But even friends of desert could agree that distributive justice is conceptually severable from the concept of desert, while it is difficult to say that penal justice is severable in that way.

16. It is important to note that retributivism need not be associated with the proposition "evil people deserve to suffer." Retributivism also has liberal variants. On the liberal view, legal and political institutions enable us to escape the state of nature in which violence threatens our natural rights. When the rule of law prevails, cooperative arrangements are secured, and massive social benefits result. Different versions of liberalism will emphasize different aspects of this story. Kant, for example, emphasizes the former, while contemporary liberals such as Rawls tend to emphasize the latter. But either way, the purpose of law is cashed out in terms of the protection of our rights. And if law is to protect our rights, it must ensure that rights are respected. This necessity justifies the state in coercing compliance with rights claims.

17. Ernest van den Haag famously depends on this claim to argue that capital punishment is just, even when it is imposed in a racially discriminatory fashion; see "The Ultimate Punishment: A Defense," *Harvard Law Review* 99, no. 7 (1986): 1662–1669.

18. Ibid.

19. David Baldus et al., "Comparative Review of Death Sentences: An Empirical Study of the Georgia Experience," *Journal of Criminal Law and Criminology* 74 (1983): 661–753.

20. The Court is not completely immune to considerations of comparative justice. *Furman v. Georgia* deemed the death penalty unconstitutional pre-

cisely because its imposition was completely discretionary (i.e., states could provide no reason why they executed one person rather than another). Once states devised capital sentencing procedures that purported to guide juries' discretion and standardize the sentencing process, the Court found the death penalty constitutional. But requiring guided discretion does almost nothing to ensure comparative justice, and so the Court's interest in comparative justice is effectively nonexistent.

21. Elsewhere, I discuss the development of Levinas's concept of justice in detail; see Benjamin S. Yost, "Responsibility and Revision: A Levinasian Argument for the Abolition of Capital Punishment," *Continental Philosophy Review* 44 (2011): 41–64.

22. Emmanuel Levinas, *Otherwise than Being, or Beyond Essence* (The Hague: Marinus Nijhoff, 1980), 160.

23. Ibid., 160–161.

24. Ibid., 125. See also "The Rights of Man and the Rights of the Other," in *Outside the Subject* (Stanford, CA: Stanford University Press). It is important to note that Levinas never says much about law. He devotes a few pages of his major works to a consideration of legal and political institutions; he has two short essays on human rights; and he makes a number of brief claims in his interviews, the latter being the most important source for the present argument. The essays are "The Rights of Man and the Rights of the Other" and "The Rights of Man and Good Will." For our purposes, the most important interviews are contained in Jill Robbins, ed., *Is It Righteous to Be?: Interviews with Emmanuel Levinas* (Stanford, CA: Stanford University Press, 2001). Nevertheless, the scattered remarks found in these texts involve substantive conceptual commitments, the implications of which I discuss here.

25. Robbins, *Is it Righteous to Be?*, 67. This claim is repeated throughout the interviews contained in *Is it Righteous to Be?* One finds a more concrete discussion of this necessity in Levinas, "Ethics and Politics," in *The Levinas Reader*, ed. Sean Hand (Oxford: Blackwell, 1989).

26. Robbins, *Is it Righteous to Be?*, 51.

27. Levinas, "The Rights of Man and the Rights of the Other," 116.

28. Levinas, *Otherwise than Being, or Beyond Essence*, 124.

29. For the purposes of this chapter, I will assume that the institution of punishment is capable of legitimacy. This view has not gone unchallenged. David Boonin and Angela Davis provide two detailed arguments for the abolition of punishment and incarceration. See David Boonin, *The Problem of Punishment* (Cambridge: Cambridge University Press, 2008), and Angela Davis, *Are Prisons Obsolete?* (New York: Seven Stories Press, 2003). Although I am sympathetic to Boonin and Davis, I do not think that Levinas would side

with them, as he seems to endorse a roughly retributive justification of punishment in his cryptic essay "An Eye for an Eye," in *Difficult Freedom: Essays on Judaism* (Baltimore: Johns Hopkins University Press, 1990).

30. Robbins, *Is it Righteous to Be?*, 230.

31. Ibid., 167.

32. These considerations generate the surprising conclusion that Levinas is, in some sense, more concerned with equality than are mainstream liberals.

33. Debates about inequality in punishment of morally severe crimes are often centered on inequalities in capital sentencing, as that has been the focus of social science research. The proposed remedy to inequality in capital sentencing is to bar execution and replace it with a life sentence, with or without parole. While life in prison is quite clearly a severe punishment, this handy solution may not be available for other crimes. For example, reducing the sentence of a kidnapper belonging to an underpunished group does not seem to give the offender what she deserves in the same way.

34. Of course, it is not enough to attach two ordinal scales to each other. There must be some substantive correspondence (which philosophers of punishment call "commensurability") between the two scales of severity. If a jurisdiction's most severe punishment were ten days in prison, we would probably consider this an inappropriate punishment for the worst type of crime.

35. This does not mean that murderers merit the most severe punishments conceivable, or that they deserve to die. I develop a Levinasian argument against capital punishment in "Responsibility and Revision." I should also note that in jurisdictions with a felony-murder rule, the state can convict someone of first-degree murder when, in the process of committing certain classes of felonies, they do something that leads to someone else's death without intending to cause it. Felony murder is controversial because it violates proportionality, enabling the state to impose the most severe punishment on someone who lacks any intent to kill.

36. An example of the former is murder; an example of the latter is operating a hair salon without a permit.

37. Emmanuel Levinas, *Nine Talmudic Readings* (Bloomington: Indiana University Press, 1990), 133.

38. Emmanuel Levinas, *Totality and Infinity: An Essay on Exteriority* (Pittsburgh: Duquesne University Press, 1969), 201. I am here appealing to one of Levinas's metaethical statements. However, given the previous considerations, this statement can be read as a description of our normative situation.

39. Jill Stauffer drew my attention to the Levinasian overtones of Uncle Ben's saying in *Spider-Man*. Pursuing this, I discovered that the phrase is

traceable to Voltaire, and, even earlier, to the Gospel of Luke (12:48): "For unto whomsoever much is given, of him shall be much required."

40. Immanuel Kant, *Metaphysics of Morals, in Practical Philosophy*, ed. Mary Gregor (Cambridge: Cambridge University Press), 387–388.

41. I do not mean to suggest that as currently defined and employed, aggravators actually *do* capture blameworthiness. There is much to criticize about the way aggravators are employed; see Jonathan Simon and Christina Spaulding, "Tokens of Our Esteem: Aggravating Factors in the Era of Deregulated Death Penalties," in *The Killing State: Capital Punishment in Law, Politics, and Culture*, ed. Austin Sarat (Oxford: Oxford University Press, 1999), 81–113. My point is just that there are mechanisms at law that could be used to capture the aspect of blameworthiness under discussion.

42. Of course, in the second essay of *On the Genealogy of Morals*, Nietzsche claims that a strong, vital society would not resort to punishment at all (§10). I want to reiterate that I am not convinced that punishment is ever justified. But if punishment in general is capable of justification, our current practices of punishment are not.

PRISONS AND PALLIATIVE POLITICS
Ami Harbin

I write this piece in memory of my dad, Walt Hovey, who worked for many years as a correctional officer and crisis negotiator in maximum- and medium-security prisons in Canada. Our conversations about the realities, constraints, and relationships he witnessed in prisons shaped my thinking. The care and support he received from prisoners and co-workers meant a great deal to him, and to me. For helpful feedback at multiple stages, I also thank Lisa Guenther, Scott Zeman, Geoffrey Adelsberg, Alexis Shotwell, Michael Doan, Phyllis Rooney, and Mark Navin.

1. See, for example, *Serving Life*, Dir. Lisa Cohen. Oprah Winfrey Network Documentary Club, 2011. Outside, filmmaker Edgar Barens has been working with the hospice volunteers at Iowa State Fort Madison to produce a documentary, "Prison Terminal," about their experiences and work there (due for release 2013, see http://www.prisonterminal.com).

2. See, for example, Lori Waselchuk and Lawrence N. Powell, *Grace Before Dying* (Brooklyn: Umbrage Editions, 2011).

3. See Felicia Cohn, "The Ethics of End-of-Life Care for Prison Inmates," *Journal of Law, Medicine and Ethics* 27 (1999): 252–259; E. Craig and M. Ratcliff, "Controversies in Correctional End-of-Life Care," *Journal of Correctional Health Care* 9 (2002): 149–157; N. N. Dubler, "The Collision of Confinement and Care: End-of-Life Care in Prisons and Jails," *Journal of*

Law, Medicine & Ethics 26, no. 2 (1998): 149–156; Fleet Maull, "The Prison Hospice Movement," *Explore* 1, no. 6 (2005): 477–479; M. Ratcliff, "Dying Inside the Walls," *Journal of Palliative Medicine* 3, no. 4 (2000): 509–511; and A. Siobhan Thompson, "Caring for Prisoner Inmates the Hospice Way," *Illness, Crisis and Loss* 17, no. 4 (2009): 363–378.

4. To be clear, "palliative care" by definition is care aimed at reducing pain and suffering at any point in an illness (not only at end of life), and "hospice care" is one branch of palliative care, aiming to reduce pain and suffering at end of life specifically, after curative care is no longer being given. Throughout the chapter, I am referring to prison hospice programs that for the most part aim to relieve suffering at end of life (though given the limits of prison health care, there are cases where patients enter hospice well before end of life, or just when very ill or old). Although hospice is the main context I discuss here, the title reflects my interest in the broader politics of reducing pain and suffering in prison at all stages of life.

5. Angela Davis, *The Meaning of Freedom and Other Difficult Dialogues* (San Francisco: City Lights Books, 2012), 124–125, 47. Davis cites Ruth Gilmore's definition of racism as "the state-sanctioned and/or legal production and exploitation of group-differentiated vulnerabilities to premature death, in distinct yet densely interconnected political geographies." Ruth Wilson Gilmore, "Race and Globalization," in *Geographies of Global Change*, ed. P. J. Taylor, R. L. Johnston, and M. J. Watts, 2nd edition (Oxford: Basil Blackwell, 2002), 261.

6. As Angola hospice volunteer Justin Granier says: "Whether I'm in the dorm, or seeing dudes on the urinal, I'm watching dudes die here daily. Nobody is going home who has life sentences. This is death" (*Serving Life*). In another example from the film, as he is dying in prison hospice, Hollingsworth is permitted a visit from his brother, Roy, who is also a prisoner at Angola. Roy says to Kevin, "Me and you been together since you was born, so we both know we lived the life of a dead man. . . . When we hit the streets, we knew we was dead" (*Serving Life*).

7. I have in mind the work of many feminist bioethicists, including Susan Sherwin, Francoise Baylis, Hilde Lindemann, Rosemarie Tong, Anne Donchin, Margrit Shildrick, and many others.

8. Sadhbh Walshe, "When Prison Illness Becomes a Death Sentence," *The Guardian* February 16, 2012. http://www.guardian.co.uk/commentisfree/cifamerica/2012/feb/16/when-prison-illness-becomes-death-sentence (accessed January 29, 2013).

9. I am rephrasing Francoise Baylis here, as she has said in arguing for the importance of medical research involving pregnant women, who are

vastly excluded from participation in trials: sick women get pregnant and
pregnant women get sick. For more information on this research, see http://
www.mcmaster.ca/research/sciencecity/baylis.htm.

   10. Linder and colleagues explain: "Significant overlap exists between
the populations at greatest risk of long-term incarceration and many groups
at elevated risk of human immunodeficiency virus (HIV) infection, tubercu-
losis, liver disease, and other chronic or life-threatening conditions. AIDS
and hepatitis B and C disproportionately affect persons with substance abuse
histories, particularly injection drug users. One-third of state and federal
inmates participate in drug-treatment programs; a considerably larger number report substance use or abuse. Sex-industry workers of both genders are
more likely to be incarcerated and are at elevated risk of HIV seropositivity;
many also have a history of substance abuse. Men who have sex with men
are at elevated risk, whether that risk behavior is a result of sexual preference or environmental circumstance. Finally, women and men of color are
disproportionately overrepresented in the incarcerated population and the
HIV population. Some populations of men and women of color are also at
elevated risk of diabetes and hypertension compared to the general population." John F. Linder, Sheila R. Enders, Elizabeth Craig, Joan Richardson,
and Frederick J. Meyers, "Hospice Care for the Incarcerated in the United
States: An Introduction," *Journal of Palliative Medicine* 5, no. 4 (2002): 550.
See also Marc Mauer and Ryan S. King, "Uneven Justice: State Rates of
Incarceration by Race and Ethnicity," The Sentencing Project, 2007. http://
www.sentencingproject.org/detail/publication.cfm?publication_id=167
(accessed January 29, 2013).

   11. James Ridgeway reports: "As of 2010, state and federal prisons housed
more than 26,000 inmates 65 and older and nearly five times that number
55 and up, according to a recent Human Rights Watch report. (Both numbers are significant, since long-term incarceration is said to add 10 years to a
person's physical age; in prison, 55 is old.) From 1995 to 2010, as America's
prison population grew 42 percent, the number of inmates over 55 grew at
nearly seven times that rate. Today, roughly 1 in 12 state and federal prison
inmates is 55 or older. The trend is worsening. A new report from the American Civil Liberties Union estimates that, by 2030, the over-55 group will
number more than 400,000—about a third of the overall prison population"
(Ridgeway, "The Other Death Sentence"). As bioethicists John Linder and
colleagues report: "The total number of deaths in prison is also increasing.
In 1987, 1407 inmates died in prisons nationwide. In 1998, that number had
risen to 2991, an increase of 112.6%. During that 11-year period, the high
water mark for deaths per year occurred in 1995, when 3345 inmates died
in custody. . . . Prison deaths from other 'natural causes' (excluding AIDS,

suicide, homicide and execution) are also increasing. In 1994, 52.3% of inmate deaths were because of natural causes; in 1998 the percentage grew to 68.6% of 2991 inmate deaths nationwide" (Linder et al., "Hospice Care for the Incarcerated," 550). See also R. G. Falter, "Selected Predictors of Health Services Needs of Inmates over Age 50," *Journal of Correctional Health Care* 6, no. 2 (1999): 149–175.

12. Linder et al., "Hospice Care for the Incarcerated," 549.

13. Linder and Meyers explain: "Medical parole, or compassionate release, is the procedure for securing a terminally ill inmate's release from prison; the process varies by jurisdiction. Of the 49 agencies surveyed in 2001, 43 offered some form of compassionate release. The average number of annual requests was 18, and the average granted was 8. A final decision is reached only after a long and cumbersome process, usually involving the warden and parole or review board, and even the state's governor. Given that the safety of society is the primary mandate of the corrections system, prison systems consistently err on the side of continued confinement of the inmate, even if this means death behind bars. Inmates granted compassionate release are almost always in the final days of life." John F. Linder and Frederick Meyers, "Palliative Care for Prison Inmates: 'Don't Let Me Die in Prison,'" *Journal of the American Medical Association* 298, no. 8 (2007): 900.

14. Linder et al., "Hospice Care for the Incarcerated," 551; see also the National Prison Hospice Association.

15. Linder et al., "Hospice Care for the Incarcerated," 551–552.

16. Fleury-Steiner describes the case of Ward Anderson, who was HIV positive and suffered from numerous severe health problems. In the final months of his life, "medical staff reportedly consulted with Anderson about DNR issues. But Anderson was unsure about these issues at the time of their initial discussion. Dr. Tabet reports, 'The patient just wanted to think about it at that point, and specifically did not want to be placed on Do Not Attempt to Resuscitate (DNAR) status. . . .' In the remaining months, Anderson's health declined. He received very minimal nursing and no hospice care. Contrary to his wishes not to have DNR status, CPR was not attempted at the time of his death." Benjamin Fleury-Steiner, with Carla Crowder, *Dying Inside: The HIV/AIDS Ward at Limestone Prison* (Ann Arbor: University of Michigan Press, 2008), 137–138.

17. Linder and Meyers, "Palliative Care for Prison Inmates," 898.

18. Ridgeway, "The Other Death Sentence."

19. Ibid.

20. Ibid.

21. Sixty-four-year-old Joe Labriola suffers from chronic breathing problems and lives in the Assisted Daily Living Ward. Labriola sees the need for

hospice, and the willingness among prisoners to make it happen. "I see men coming up for medication and insulin at least three to four times per day," he says. "They come in chairs, Canadian canes, geriatric walkers. In one week alone we had three deaths." The hospital's inpatient facilities consist of a series of five small wards with five beds in each. Men in various stages of bad health or terminal illness lie in bed all day long with nothing to do but watch soap operas" (Ridgeway, "The Other Death Sentence").

22. Bertrum Rene Berkett, "Hospice—Sail to Serenity," May 14, 2006, http://www.prisonterminal.com/essays%20sail%20to%20serenity.html (accessed January 29, 2013). Berkett elsewhere describes the development of formal hospice there: "I have been here for 23 years, and we wonder who is going to be caring for you when you are sick. . . . We realize that we are going to die here. . . . It is best to have it as comfortable as possible and to take care of each other. The one that lasts the longest will be the one who has to take care of everyone else." William Petroski, "Hospice Eases Inmates' Deaths," *Des Moines Register*, 2005, republished on http://www.prisonterminal.com/essays%20 hospice%20eases.html (accessed January 29, 2013.) As Mike Glover, another volunteer in Fort Madison's hospice, explains, "Before [the development of hospice] there were a lot of guys just dying by themselves. This is what the hospice program is all about" (Petroski, "Hospice Eases Inmates' Deaths").

23. In the statistics Linder et al. cite, prisoners who die of AIDS are not considered to have died of natural causes—deaths from AIDS are considered unlike deaths from other chronic, preventable health conditions, placed in a category of other "unnatural" deaths alongside homicide, suicide, and execution.

24. Fleury-Steiner, *Dying Inside*. Fleury-Steiner considers the institutional context that made this number of deaths in these conditions likely and understands the failure to adequately treat prisoners with HIV as a microcosm for the inadequate care for prisoners with chronic illness in U.S. prisons generally.

25. Quoted from interview, Fleury-Steiner, *Dying Inside*, 40.

26. As Linder and Meyers state: "In the prison setting, a hospice program's most readily available supply of volunteers is other inmates. Volunteers in hospice programs provide companionship, emotional support, and practical assistance. In 2001, 26 of 49 jurisdictions indicated that inmate volunteers are used to assist chronically ill inmates; 3 of these indicated that volunteers are only used in their hospice programs" (Linder and Meyers, "Palliative Care for Prison Inmates," 899).

27. Angola is the largest maximum-security prison in the United States, holding five thousand incarcerated men with an average sentence (at the time of filming) of ninety-three years. It is a prison farm, situated on eighteen

thousand acres, and it houses the state of Louisiana's death row for men and the state's execution chamber. The land that Angola Penitentiary was built on, for example, was purchased as four plantations and run in the 1880s and 1890s using convicts leased from the state as slaves. A short time later, in 1901, the facility opened as a prison, and its eighteen-thousand-acre complex is still operated as a working farm. The warden of Angola Prison, Burl Cain, introduced the hospice program to Angola in 1997. For more information on the Angola hospice, see C. Evans, R. Herzog, and T. Tillman, "The Louisiana State Penitentiary: Angola Prison Hospice," *Journal of Palliative Medicine* 5, no. 4 (2002): 553–558.

28. Berkett, "Sail to Serenity."

29. In *Serving Life*, hospice volunteers are shown wearing t-shirts with the acronym "Hospice": "Helping Others Share their Pain Inside Correctional Environment." Volunteer Albert Lavalais says of the patient he is caring for, "I'm sentenced to the same second-degree murder he's sentenced to. It could be me. You do get attached." Volunteer Shaheed (Anthony) Middlebrooks Jr. says: "I was just thinking about his situation, passing away without any loved ones. He has us but it's not the same." Some see their work as setting a good example for other prisons that might introduce hospice programs in the future. As Berkett says, "We pray we can be a real influence on those who watch us as we are given the privilege to witness a man's efforts at the most private time this life has to offer—its end."

30. Fleury-Steiner, *Dying Inside*, 136–137.

31. Iris Marion Young, *Justice and the Politics of Difference* (Princeton, NJ: Princeton University Press, 1990), 53–55.

32. Lisa Guenther, *Social Death and Its Afterlives* (Minneapolis: University of Minnesota Press, 2013).

33. Petroski, "Hospice Eases Inmates' Deaths."

34. Judith Butler, *Undoing Gender* (New York: Routledge, 2004), 17. Butler's conception of politics in *Undoing Gender* focuses largely (though never only) on the lives and vulnerabilities of individuals embodying nonnormative genders and sexualities. I am extending her insights to help conceptualize livability for the many other groups susceptible to the harms of oppressive structures, including those in prison.

35. Ridgeway, "The Other Death Sentence."

36. Ibid.

37. See, for example: http://criticalresistance.org/wp-content/uploads/2012/06/Ab-Toolkit-Part-5.pdf, 43.

38. Butler, *Undoing Gender*, 19.

39. It is possible to evaluate what might improve hospice programs in nonideal circumstances. Some possible improvements in prison hospice

mirror possible improvements on the outside: the transition from acute care to palliative care needs to be planned for and carefully considered, and not merely an afterthought. Where treatment aimed at curing or addressing a serious illness (e.g., chemotherapies or radiation for cancer) stops and where end of life care starts is often not a transition well anticipated; it can be sudden and sometimes one that happens later than it needs to, lengthening strenuous treatments and making it even harder for hospices to manage patients' pain and to ensure the best possible quality of life in their last weeks and days. Decisions about when to stop treatment for serious illnesses, how to conceive of them as terminal, and how to introduce questions of end-of-life decision making to patients are always difficult, and these difficulties are exacerbated when acute care is prolonged and palliative care deprioritized.

40. Butler, *Undoing Gender*, 219.

SOVEREIGNTY, COMMUNITY, AND THE INCARCERATION OF IMMIGRANTS
Matt S. Whitt

1. Lauren Glaze and Erika Parks, *Correctional Populations in the United States, 2011* (Bureau of Justice Statistics, November 2012), http://www.bjs .gov/content/pub/pdf/cpus11.pdf (accessed November 13, 2013).

2. Donna Selman and Paul Leighton, *Punishment for Sale: Private Prisons, Big Business, and the Incarceration Binge* (Lanham, MD: Rowman & Littlefield Publishers, 2010), 123. See Mary Bosworth and Emma Kaufman, "Foreigners in a Carceral Age: Immigration and Imprisonment in the United States," *Stanford Law & Policy Review* 22, no. 2 (2011): 436.

3. Jeffrey S. Passel, D'Vera Cohn, and Ana Gonzalez-Barrera, *Population Decline of Unauthorized Immigrants Stalls, May Have Reversed* (Pew Research Center, September 23, 2013), http://www.pewhispanic.org/files/2013/09/ Unauthorized-Sept-2013-FINAL.pdf (accessed November 8, 2013).

4. In the first part of this volume, James Manos takes a similar approach by outlining what criminalization does for *capitalism*, rather than the state. See Manos, "From Commodity Fetishism to Prison Fetishism: Slavery, Convict-leasing, and the Ideological Productions of Incarceration." Our approaches are compatible and our findings are, in my view, complimentary. Notably, each of us emphasizes that criminalization respatializes or remobilizes individuals in ways that do not always look like segregation or quarantine. Although we emphasize different productive functions, we agree that criminalization works, for capitalism and the capitalist state, by moving criminalized individuals *through society* rather than keeping them out of it.

5. Versions of this argument are made in Rebecca Bohrman and Naomi Murakawa, "Remaking Big Government: Immigration and Crime Control in the United States," in *Global Lockdown: Race, Gender, and the Prison-Industrial*

Complex, ed. Julia Sudbury (New York: Routledge, 2005), 109–125; Mary Bosworth, "Border Control and the Limits of the Sovereign State," *Social & Legal Studies* 17, no. 2 (2008): 199–215; Jennifer M Chacón, "Managing Migration through Crime," *Columbia Law Review Sidebar* 109 (2009): 135–148; Bosworth and Kaufman, "Foreigners in a Carceral Age."

6. The most plausible accounts of sovereignty's decline argue that sovereignty is becoming disconnected from state power; state sovereignty is waning, although sovereignty may relocate to other institutions and actors. See Wendy Brown, *Walled States, Waning Sovereignty* (New York: Zone Books, 2010); and Seyla Benhabib, *Dignity in Adversity: Human Rights in Troubled Times* (Malden, MA: Polity, 2011), chaps. 6–7. My analysis is intended to put pressure on even these nuanced accounts of sovereignty's decline. Once we understand sovereignty as the final authority to decide on questions of membership, we can see that states do retain sovereignty, although the mechanisms through which they exercise it—at least in the United States—are becoming more desperate.

7. See, for example, Hendrik Spruyt, *The Sovereign State and Its Competitors* (Princeton, NJ: Princeton University Press, 1996), 3, 36; Robert Jackson, *Sovereignty* (Malden, MA: Polity, 2007), 6, 10–12; Joanne Pemberton, *Sovereignty: Interpretations* (London: Palgrave Macmillan, 2009).

8. As Étienne Balibar writes, "It is precisely the correlation between inside and outside that makes sovereignty what it is (and, above all, that constitutes a 'political community' submitted to a sovereign authority and in some sense 'created' by it, or creating itself through the institution of sovereignty)." Étienne Balibar, *We, the People of Europe?: Reflections on Transnational Citizenship*, trans. James Swensen (Princeton, NJ: Princeton University Press, 2004), 158.

9. Insofar as these oppositions are essential to sovereignty's constitution of the political community, the community is never truly *not* the thing it opposes; the negated element is built into the identity of the community. Thus, for instance, the "state of nature" imagined by liberal philosophy is never completely left behind in the foundation of the political community, insofar as the community's identity and *raison d'être* depend upon its constant differentiation from this purportedly nonpolitical state. Thus, the state of nature haunts the community's exterior (in the "anarchy" of the international sphere) and also its interior (what Charles Mills calls "a moving bubble of wilderness" born by the community's internal outsiders—nonwhite "bodies impolitic"—against whom the community defines itself). Charles Mills, *The Racial Contract* (Ithaca, NY: Cornell University Press, 1999), 53. The same dynamic characterizes Schmitt's friend/enemy opposition and, more explicitly, Agamben's *bios/zoē* opposition. Carl Schmitt, *The Concept of the Political*,

trans. George Schwab (Chicago: University of Chicago Press, 2007); Giorgio Agamben, *Homo Sacer: Sovereign Power and Bare Life*, trans. Daniel Heller-Roazen (Stanford, CA: Stanford University Press, 1998).

10. Descriptions of globalization are hotly debated. Here, my understanding of globalization derives from Saskia Sassen, *Territory, Authority, Rights: From Medieval to Global Assemblages* (Princeton, NJ: Princeton University Press, 2006); and John Agnew, *Globalization and Sovereignty* (Lanham, MD: Rowman & Littlefield Publishers, 2009).

11. Matt S. Whitt, "Democracy's Sovereign Enclosures: Territory and the All-Affected Principle," *Constellations* (forthcoming, 2014).

12. Jürgen Habermas, *The Inclusion of the Other: Studies in Political Theory*, ed. Ciaran Cronin and Pablo De Greiff (Cambridge, MA: MIT Press, 1999), 115. My work has been influenced by scholars who have challenged this way of looking at political communities. See especially Linda Bosniak, *The Citizen and the Alien: Dilemmas of Contemporary Membership* (Princeton, NJ: Princeton University Press, 2006).

13. Nevzat Soguk, "Transnational/Transborder Bodies: Resistance, Accommodation, and Exile in Refugee and Migration Movements on the U.S.-Mexican Border," in *Challenging Boundaries: Global Flows, Territorial Identities*, ed. Michael Shapiro and Hayward Alker (Minneapolis: University of Minnesota Press, 1996), 298–305; Bohrman and Murakawa, "Remaking Big Government," 112–113.

14. Bridget Anderson, Matthew J. Gibney, and Emanuela Paoletti, "Citizenship, Deportation and the Boundaries of Belonging," *Citizenship Studies* 15, no. 5 (August 2011): 550–551.

15. Many deportees are long-term residents of the United States, and the countries to which they are deported are often foreign to them, even if they are technically citizens. For this reason, the cycle of movement does not usually stop with deportation itself; deportees move on to reconnect with families, find stable homes, and often return to the United States through unsanctioned reentry. See Seth Freed Wessler and Julianne Hing, "Torn Apart: Struggling to Stay Together after Deportation," in *Beyond Walls and Cages: Prisons, Borders, and Global Crisis*, ed. Jenna M. Loyd, Matt Mitchelson, and Andrew Burridge (Athens: University of Georgia Press, 2012), 152–162.

16. As Lisa Cacho notes, undocumented immigrants are not protected against "selective enforcement" such as racial profiling. Lisa Marie Cacho, *Social Death: Racialized Rightlessness and the Criminalization of the Unprotected* (New York: New York University Press, 2012), 103. For specific selection criteria, see Juliet Stumpf, "The Crimmigration Crisis: Immigrants, Crime, and Sovereign Power," *American University Law Review* 56, no. 2 (2006): 415–416; Bosworth and Kaufman, "Foreigners in a Carceral Age," 435; Catherine Dauvergne,

"Globalizing Fragmentation: New Pressures on Women Caught in the Immigration Law-Citizenship Dichotomy," in *Migrations and Mobilities: Citizenship, Borders, and Gender*, ed. Seyla Benhabib and Judith Resnik (New York: New York University Press, 2009), 346–347; Bohrman and Murakawa, "Remaking Big Government," 112–113; Jennifer M. Chacón, "Overcriminalizing Immigration," *Journal of Criminal Law and Criminology* 102, no. 3 (2012): 646.

17. "The criteria that immigration laws enshrine read as a code of national values, determining who some 'we' group will accept as potential future members." Dauvergne, "Globalizing Fragmentation," 336.

18. This is not to say that disciplining fully determines the ways that undocumented immigrants participate in the community, or that they necessarily make marginal contributions to it.

19. Soguk, "Transnational/Transborder Bodies." More recently, see Victor Talavera, Guillerma Gina Núñez-Mchiri, and Josiah Heyman, "Deportation in the U.S-Mexico Borderlands: Anticipation, Experience, and Memory," in *The Deportation Regime: Sovereignty, Space, and the Freedom of Movement*, ed. Nicholas De Genova and Nathalie Mae Peutz (Durham, NC: Duke University Press, 2010), 166–195.

20. Mai M. Ngai, *Impossible Subjects: Illegal Aliens and the Making of Modern America* (Princeton, NJ: Princeton University Press, 2005), 2; emphasis added.

21. Lisa Cacho introduces the term "status crime" to describe the precarious legal position of undocumented immigrants. "People subjected to laws based on their (il)legal status—'illegal aliens,' 'gang members,' 'terrorist suspects'—are unable to comply with the 'rule of law' because U.S. law targets their being and their bodies, not their behavior. . . . Even though 'illegal alien' is not a legal term and to be undocumented is not crime, to be an 'illegal alien' is to embody a criminalized status." Cacho, *Social Death*, 9, 43.

22. Throughout this section and the next, I use the phrases "prison apparatus" and "carceral apparatus" interchangeably.

23. In the next section, I will discuss the incarceration of noncitizens.

24. David Garland, *The Culture of Control: Crime and Social Order in Contemporary Society* (Chicago: University of Chicago Press, 2001), 178.

25. Consider New York City's controversial "stop and frisk" tactic of preventative policing, which targets certain persons (overwhelmingly African American males of lower economic class) as potential offenders, regardless of whether they have committed a criminal act. On the racialization of preventative policing, see Michelle Alexander, *The New Jim Crow: Mass Incarceration in the Age of Colorblindness* (New York: New Press, 2012), 66–72, 123–126, 134–137 and Cacho, *Social Death*.

26. As I discuss in the following section, this process is highly racialized.

27. Garland, *Culture of Control*, 178.

28. Pamela S. Karlan, "Forum," in *Race, Incarceration, and American Values*, ed. Glenn C. Loury (Cambridge, MA: MIT Press, 2008), 50–51; Alexander, *The New Jim Crow*, 195–196, 232.

29. Pew Center on the States, *State of Recidivism: The Revolving Door of America's Prisons*, April 2011, www.pewtrusts.org/uploadedFiles/www pewtrustsorg/Reports/sentencing_and_corrections/State_Recidivism _Revolving_Door_America_Prisons%20.pdf (accessed November 13, 2013).

30. Alexander, *The New Jim Crow*, 56–57, 94, 148–151.

31. Jean Chung, *Felony Disenfranchisement: A Primer* (The Sentencing Project, June 2013), http://sentencingproject.org/doc/publications/fd_Felony%20 Disenfranchisement%20Primer.pdf (accessed November 13, 2013).

32. Alexander, *The New Jim Crow*, 142.

33. By "normalization," I mean the operations of power that identify, ascribe, and assess deviation from an imaginary or ideological standard of normality, while also working to minimize, control, or counteract that deviance by disciplining individual subjects into sanctioned modes of being, knowing, and doing. In contemporary U.S. prisons, normalization does not take place with the intent to rehabilitate, but to facilitate control and manage risk. The classic account of normalization, with respect to the present topics, is Michel Foucault, *Discipline and Punish: The Birth of the Prison*, 2nd Vintage Books ed. (New York: Vintage Books, 1995). See also David Garland, *Punishment and Modern Society: A Study in Social Theory* (Chicago: University of Chicago Press, 1990), 145–151.

34. For instance, prisoners are sometimes removed to solitary confinement merely for associating with known gang members or reading literature prohibited by prison administrators. Lisa Guenther, *Solitary Confinement: Social Death and Its Afterlives* (Minneapolis: University of Minnesota Press, 2013), 162–163; Shane Bauer, "Solitary in Iran Nearly Broke Me. Then I Went Inside America's Prisons," *Mother Jones* (November 2012), http://www .motherjones.com/politics/2012/10/solitary-confinement-shane-bauer (accessed November 13, 2013).

35. "Those offenders who are released 'into the community' are subject to much tighter control than previously, and frequently find themselves returned to custody for failure to comply with the conditions that continue to restrict their freedom. For many of these parolees and ex-convicts, the 'community' into which they are released is actually a closely monitored terrain, a supervised space, lacking much of the liberty that one associates with 'normal life.'" Garland, *Culture of Control*, 178. See also Loïc Wacquant, "Prisoner Reentry as Myth and Ceremony," *Dialectical Anthropology* 34, no. 4 (December 1, 2010): 616.

36. Alexander, *The New Jim Crow*, 94.

37. See endnote 25.

38. Guenther, *Solitary Confinement*, 162–165, 227–230.

39. Alexander, *The New Jim Crow*, 151.

40. The term "social death" can be misleading, so I have not used it widely. As Orlando Patterson characterizes it in his groundbreaking study, "social death" is a conceptual distillation of the various forms of social, political, and legal depersonalization and domination intrinsic to slavery. Orlando Patterson, *Slavery and Social Death: A Comparative Study* (Cambridge, MA: Harvard University Press, 1982). However, the term is sometimes taken to indicate *total and permanent* domination, which would eradicate the agency of the individuals reduced to social death. As Vincent Brown has argued, even the victims of chattel slavery are not totally stripped of agency; indeed, slaves participate in acts of resistance that would be ruled out by a too-strong interpretation of social death. Vincent Brown, "Social Death and Political Life in the Study of Slavery," *The American Historical Review* 114, no. 5 (2009): 1231–1249. Recent studies have attempted to politicize the concept of social death, with emphasis on the resistance, as well as the alienation, of criminalized and incarcerated individuals. See Dylan Rodriguez, *Forced Passages: Imprisoned Radical Intellectuals and the U.S. Prison Regime* (Minneapolis: University of Minnesota Press, 2006); Colin Dayan, *The Law Is a White Dog: How Legal Rituals Make and Unmake Persons* (Princeton, NJ: Princeton University Press, 2011); Cacho, *Social Death;* Guenther, *Solitary Confinement.*

41. Illegal drug use rates are extremely close among whites, Latino/as, and African Americans, and drug *dealing* rates are higher among whites (particularly white youth) than among people of color. Overall, the majority of drug users and sellers in the United States are white. Nonetheless, three-fourths of all persons incarcerated on drug charges are Latino/a and African American. Michelle Alexander amply documents these disparities with data from the U.S. Department of Health and Human Services and the Department of Justice in *The New Jim Crow*, 98–100.

42. E. Ann Carson and William J. Sabol, *Prisoners in 2011* (Bureau of Justice Statistics, December 2012), http://www.bjs.gov/content/pub/pdf/p11.pdf (accessed November 13, 2013).

43. Alexander, *The New Jim Crow*, 6. See also Becky Pettit and Bruce Western, "Mass Imprisonment and the Life Course: Race and Class Inequality in U.S. Incarceration," *American Sociological Review* 69, no. 2 (April 1, 2004): 151–169; Glenn C. Loury, *Race, Incarceration, and American Values* (Cambridge, MA: MIT Press, 2008).

44. Loïc Wacquant, "Class, Race & Hyperincarceration in Revanchist America," *Daedalus* 139, no. 3 (2010): 78. See also Wacquant, *Punishing the*

Poor: The Neoliberal Government of Social Insecurity (Durham, NC: Duke University Press, 2009).

45. To use Mills's adopted language of the social contract, these internal outsiders function as "bubbles of wilderness" in opposition to which the body politic constitutes itself. Mills, *The Racial Contract*, 53.

46. See, for example, David M. Oshinsky, *Worse than Slavery: Parchment Farm and the Ordeal of Jim Crow Justice* (New York: Free Press, 1996); Wacquant, *Punishing the Poor*; Alexander, *The New Jim Crow*. In this volume, see Manos, "From Commodity Fetishism to Prison Fetishism: Slavery, Convict-leasing, and the Ideological Productions of Incarceration."

47. Rodriguez emphasizes this creative aspect of mass incarceration, linking it to nation-building. See Rodriguez, *Forced Passages*, 12–14.

48. Bosworth and Kaufman, "Foreigners in a Carceral Age," 442–448; Bohrman and Murakawa, "Remaking Big Government," 115–118.

49. On aggravated felonies, see Bosworth and Kaufman, "Foreigners in a Carceral Age," 442–445; Chacón, "Managing Migration through Crime"; Cacho, *Social Death*, 95.

50. Teresa A. Miller, "Citizenship & Severity: Recent Immigration Reforms and the New Penology," *Georgetown Immigration Law Journal* 17 (2003): 656; Chacón, "Overcriminalizing Immigration," 621–622.

51. Bohrman and Murakawa, "Remaking Big Government," 118.

52. Stephen H. Legomsky, "The New Path of Immigration Law: Asymmetric Incorporation of Criminal Justice Norms," *Washington and Lee Law Review* 64, no. 2 (2007): 472.

53. Chacón, "Overcriminalizing Immigration," 616, n13.

54. Bosworth and Kaufman, "Foreigners in a Carceral Age," 439–440.

55. Chacón, "Overcriminalizing Immigration," 633.

56. Legomsky, "The New Path of Immigration Law"; Chacón, "Overcriminalizing Immigration," 616, n13.

57. Human Rights Watch reports, "Most detainees will be loaded at some point during their detention onto a government-contracted car, bus, or airplane and transferred from one detention center to another," with 46 percent of detainees transferred two or more times and each transferred detainee averaging 370 miles in transit. Human Rights Watch, *A Costly Move*, June 14, 2011, http://www.hrw.org/reports/2011/06/14/costly-move (accessed November 13, 2013). Since May 2012, ICE has implemented a directive limiting detainee transfers, but its effect is as yet unknown.

58. Chacón attributes this judgment to Dora Schriro, a former senior Department of Homeland Security official. Chacón, "Overcriminalizing Immigration," 633.

59. See endnote 41.

60. Bohrman and Murakawa, "Remaking Big Government," 115, 118.

61. Jonathan Simon, *Governing through Crime: How the War on Crime Transformed American Democracy and Created a Culture of Fear* (Oxford: Oxford University Press, 2007).

62. Miller, "Citizenship & Severity"; Bosworth, "Border Control"; Chacón, "Managing Migration through Crime." A recent anthology takes this analysis as its organizing theme. Julie Dowling and Jonathan Inda, eds., *Governing Immigration through Crime: A Reader* (Stanford, CA: Stanford University Press, 2013).

63. This does not mean that the state is fully unconstrained in its actions toward undocumented citizens—simply that it is less constrained. Notably, the state can also strip citizenship away from certain individuals, such as those it deems enemy combatants, in order to circumvent the protections that are nominally in place for citizens. The case of José Padilla is exemplary. However, the same technique is at work, less explicitly, when state power reduces vulnerable citizens to subcitizen status or social death.

64. Lisa Cacho argues that the criminalization of undocumented immigrants devalues their lives in ways that reflect value back onto the regime that criminalizes them. My analysis here is partly inspired by her argument but largely based in a more broadly Hegelian understanding of social value. See Cacho, *Social Death: Racialized Rightlessness and the Criminalization of the Unprotected* (New York: New York University Press, 2012), 13–14, 148–149.

65. Bonie Honig argues that naturalization ceremonies play a similar function: they confirm that the regime is choiceworthy by staging liberalism's "fictive foundation in individual acts of uncoerced consent." Honig, *Democracy and the Foreigner* (Princeton, NJ: Princeton University Press, 2003), 75. The criminalization of immigration, and especially deportation procedures, go further: they present the political community as worthy of not only consent but also significant personal risk.

66. By positioning undocumented immigrants as morally inferior to full citizens, the criminalization of immigration works to legitimate itself. Whereas it would be morally unpalatable for ICE to target individuals designated as "foreigners," the status of "criminal alien" is constructed as always already deserving of surveillance, incarceration, and expulsion. The criminalization of other populations—for example, African American lower-class males—is similarly self-legitimating. See Dayan, *The Law Is a White Dog*, 72–73; Cacho, *Social Death*, 5–6.

67. The regulation of "deportability," as the "protracted possibility of being deported—along with the multiple vulnerabilities that this susceptibility for deportation engenders" is itself a technique by which sovereign authority defines the political community. Nicholas De Genova and Nathalie Mae Peutz,

eds., *The Deportation Regime: Sovereignty, Space, and the Freedom of Movement* (Durham, NC: Duke University Press, 2010), 14. See also Anderson, Gibney, and Paoletti, "Citizenship, Deportation and the Boundaries of Belonging," 554.

68. See endnote 6.

69. I focus specifically on the use of incarceration to structure a political community. For a more general argument that unilateral border control is always coercive, see Arash Abizadeh, "Democratic Theory and Border Coercion: No Right to Unilaterally Control Your Own Borders," *Political Theory* 36, no. 1 (February 1, 2008): 37–65.

70. Loury, *Race, Incarceration, and American Values*, 26; emphasis added.

WITHOUT THE RIGHT TO EXIST:
MASS INCARCERATION AND NATIONAL SECURITY
Andrea Smith

1. Epigraphs are from Adrien Katherine Wing, "Civil Rights in the Post 911 World: Critical Race Praxis, Coalition Building, and the War on Terrorism," *Louisiana Law Review* 63 (2003): 717, 734–735; and from Sora Han, "Veiled Threats," unpublished paper 5, presentation at the American Studies Association conference, Houston, 2002. Similar arguments are made by Richard Delgado, "Centennial Reflections on the California Law Review's Scholarship on Race: The Structure of Civil Rights Thought," *California Law Review* 100 (2012): 431, 443–456; Juan F. Perea, "The Black/White Binary Paradigm of Race: The 'Normal Science' of American Racial Thought," *California Law Review* 85 (1997): 1213, 1213–1221; Robert S. Chang and Neil Gotanda, "Afterword: The Race Question in LatCrit Theory and Asian American Jurisprudence," *Nevada Law Journal* 7 (2007): 1012, 1012–1022.

2. See, for instance, Jared Sexton, *Amalgamation Schemes* (Minneapolis: University of Minnesota Press, 2008).

3. Andrea Smith, "Indigeneity, Settler Colonialism, White Supremacy," in *Racial Formations in the 21st Century*, ed. Daniel Martinez et al. (Berkeley: University of California Press, 2012).

4. Peter Margulies, "Judging Terror in the 'Zone of Twilight': Exigency, Institutional Equity, and Procedure after September 11," *Boston University Law Review* 84 (2004): 383, 418–419.

5. Luana Ross, *Inventing the Savage* (Austin: University of Texas Press, 1998), 15.

6. Angela Davis, *Are Prisons Obsolete?* (New York: Seven Stories Press, 2003); Dylan Rodriguez, *Forced Passages* (Minneapolis: University of Minnesota Press, 2005); Ruth Wilson Gilmore, *Golden Gulag* (Berkeley: University of California Press, 2007).

7. Gilmore, *Golden Gulag*, 28.

8. See Eric A. Posner and Adrian Vermeule, *Terror in the Balance: Security, Liberty, and the Courts*, Kindle Version (Oxford: Oxford University Press, 2007), 257–259; and David Cole and James X. Dempsey, *Terrorism and the Constitution: Sacrificing Civil Liberties in the Name of National Security*, Kindle Version (Jackson, TN: Perseus Books Group, 2006), 238–240.

9. See also Richard A. Posner, *Not a Suicide Pact: The Constitution in a Time of National Emergency*, Kindle Edition (Oxford: Oxford University Press, 2006), 358–364.

10. Epigraphs are from Leti Volpp, "The Citizen and the Terrorist," *UCLA Law Review* 49 (2002): 1575, 1599; and from Mario L. Barnes and F. Greg Bowman, "Entering Unprecedented Terrain: Charting a Method to Reduce Madness in Post-9/11 Power and Rights Conflicts," *University of Miami Law Review* 62 (2008): 365, 388.

11. Michel Foucault, *History of Sexuality, Part 1* (New York: Vintage, 1980), 137.

12. Foucault, *History of Sexuality*, 138.

13. Rodriguez, *Forced Passages*, 47.

14. Posner and Vermeule, *Terror in the* Balance, 1581–1585.

15. Jared Sexton, "Racial Profiling and the Societies of Control," in *Warfare in the American Homeland*, ed. Joy James (Durham, NC: Duke University Press, 2007).

16. Derrick Bell, "Racial Realism," in *Critical Race Theory*, ed. Kimberle Crenshaw et al. (New York: The New Press, 1995), 306.

17. Ibid., 308.

18. Ibid., 307.

19. Ibid., 308.

20. Ibid.

21. Posner and Vermeule, *Terror in the* Balance, 1491–1493.

22. Andrea Smith, "The Moral Limits of the Law," *Settler Colonialism Studies* 2, no. 2 (2012), available at http://dx.doi.org/10.7790/scs.v2i2.334.

23. Mari J. Matsuda, "Looking to the Bottom: Critical Legal Studies and Reparations," *Harvard Civil Rights–Civil Liberties Law Review* 22 (1987): 323, 334.

24. Smith, "The Moral Limits of the Law."

25. Epigraphs are from Taiaiake Alfred, *Wasase* (Peterborough, ON: Broadview Press, 2005), 55–56; and from Waziyatawin, *What Does Justice Look Like?* (St. Paul, MN: Living Justice Press, 2008), 169.

26. Andrea Smith, "Indigeneity, Settler Colonialism, White Supremacy."

27. Taiaiake Alfred, *Peace, Power and Righteousness* (Oxford: Oxford University Press, 1999), 25.

28. Anne McClintock, *Imperial Leather* (New York: Routledge, 1995).

29. See, for instance, Audra Simpson and Andrea Smith, eds., *Theorizing Native Studies* (Durham, NC: Duke University Press, 2014); Alexander We-heliye, "After Man," *American Literary History* 20 (2008): 321; Kara Keeling, "Looking for M," *GLQ* 15 (2009): 565; José Esteban Muñoz, *Cruising Utopia* (New York: New York University Press, 2010).

30. Elizabeth Povinelli, *The Cunning of Recognition* (Durham, NC: Duke University Press, 2002).

31. Dean Spade, *Normal Life* (Boston: South End Press, 2011), 29.

32. Denise Da Silva, *Toward a Global Idea of Race* (Minneapolis: University of Minnesota Press, 2007).

33. Rey Chow, *The Protestant Ethnic and the Spirit of Capitalism* (New York: Columbia University Press, 2002).

34. David Cole, "The Poverty of Posner's Pragmatism: Balancing Away Liberty After 9/11," *Stanford Law Review* 59 (2007): 1735–1737.

35. See also Geoffrey Stone, *Perilous Times* (New York: W. W. Norton, 2005), 13: "In each of these times, the nation faced extraordinary pressures—and temptations—to suppress dissent. In some of these eras, national leaders cynically exploited public fears for partisan political gain; in some, they fomented public hysteria in an effort to unite the nation in common cause; and in others, they simply caved in to public demands for the repression of "disloyal" individuals. Although each of these episodes presented a unique challenge, in each the United States went too far in sacrificing civil liberties."

36. John Yoo, Memorandum for William J. Hayes, US Department of Justice 79 (March 14, 2003), available at www.aclu.org/pdfs/safefree/yoo _army_torture_memo.pdf.

37. Posner and Vermeule, *Terror in the* Balance, 1561–1565.

38. Sora Han, "Strict Scrutiny: The Tragedy of Constitutional Law," in *Beyond Biopolitics*, ed. Patricia Clough and Craig Willse (Durham, NC: Duke University Press, 2011), 106, 119.

39. Epigraphs are from Levi Rickert, *Remembering 9/11*, Native News Network (September 11, 2012), available at http://www.nativenewsnetwork .com/remembering-9-11-2012.html; and from Sora Han, "Bonds of Represen-tation," unpublished dissertation (University of California–Santa Cruz, 2006).

40. Bruce Ackerman, "The Emergency Constitution," *Yale Law Journal* 113 (2004): 1029, 1037.

41. Posner, *Not a Suicide Pact*, 1325–1327.

42. Mary L. Dudziak, "Law, War, and the History of Time," *California Law Review* 98 (2010): 1669, 1670.

43. Curtis A. Bradley and Jack L. Goldsmith, "Congressional Authoriza-tion and the War on Terrorism," *Harvard Law Review* 118 (2005): 2047, 2049.

PRISON ABOLITION AND A CULTURE OF SEXUAL DIFFERENCE
Sarah Tyson

Very special thanks to Geoff Adelsberg, Adam Blair, Lisa Guenther, Richard Odom, and Gillian Silverman for reading drafts of this chapter and providing invaluable feedback, skepticism, and support.

1. It was difficult to pick just one organization when there are so many engaged in transformative antiviolence and response to violence work that refuses to rely on the carceral state—I was particularly compelled by the self-theorization that CARA has done. *Color of Violence: The INCITE Anthology*, *The Revolution Will Not Be Funded: Beyond the Non-Profit Industrial Complex*, and *The Revolution Starts at Home: Confronting Intimate Violence within Activist Communities* are excellent resources to begin learning about organizations like Sista II Sista, the Chrysalis Collective, Creative Interventions, Challenging Male Supremacy, the Audre Lorde Project, and the Northwest Network of Bisexual, Trans, Lesbian, and Gay Survivors of Abuse.

2. Marie Gottschalk, *The Prison and the Gallows: The Politics of Mass Incarceration in America* (New York: Cambridge University Press, 2006), 124.

3. Ibid., 131.

4. Alisa Bierria and Communities Against Rape and Abuse (CARA), "Pursuing a Radical Anti-Violence Agenda," in *The Revolution Will Not Be Funded: Beyond the Non-Profit Industrial Complex*, ed. INCITE! Women of Color Against Violence (Cambridge: South End Press, 2007), 151.

5. Ibid., 151.

6. Ibid., 157.

7. Ibid., 162. One striking feature of this description is how a radical organization can use state funds to provide accessibility and thereby, perhaps, suggest another route for rethinking the work of the state.

8. Chloë Taylor, "Foucault, Feminism, and Sex Crimes," *Hypatia* 24, no. 4 (2009): 5.

9. Loïc Wacquant, "From Slavery to Mass Incarceration: Rethinking the 'Race Question' in the US," *New Left Review* 13 (2002): 60.

10. Don Sabo quoted in James W. Messerschmidt, "Masculinities, Crime, and Prison," in *Prison Masculinities*, ed. Don Sabo, Terry A. Kupers, and Willie London (Philadelphia: Temple University Press, 2001), 67–68.

11. Prince Imari A. Obadele, "Killers," in *The New Abolitionists: (Neo)Slave Narratives and Contemporary Prison Writings*, ed. Joy James (Albany: State University of New York Press, 2005), 115.

12. Ibid., 116.

13. Ibid.

14. Don Sabo, Terry A. Kupers, and Willie London, "Gender and the Politics of Punishment," in *Prison Masculinities*, ed. Don Sabo, Terry A. Kupers, and Willie London (Philadelphia: Temple University Press, 2001), 4.

15. And perhaps in unexpected ways: "The suicide rate among prison guards is 39 percent higher than the average for other occupations, an Archives of Suicide Research study found" ("Prison horrors haunt guards' private lives," http://www.denverpost.com/ci_5510659 [accessed August 30, 2012]).

16. Sabo, Kupers, and London, "Gender and the Politics of Punishment," 12.

17. Stephen "Donny" Donaldson, "A Million Jockers, Punks, and Queens," in *Prison Masculinities*, ed. Don Sabo, Terry A. Kupers, and Willie London (Philadelphia: Temple University Press, 2001), 124.

18. "Probation and Parole in the United States, 2010," http://www.bjs.gov/index.cfm?ty=pbdetail&iid=2239 (accessed June 7, 2012).

19. Cindy Struckman-Johnson and David Struckman-Johnson, "Sexual Coercion Reported by Women in Three Midwestern Prisons," *The Journal of Sex Research* 39, no. 3 (2002): 220.

20. Nancy Wolff et al., "Sexual Violence Inside Prisons: Rates of Victimization," *Journal of Urban Health: Bulletin of the New York Academy of Medicine* 83, no. 5 (2006): 841.

21. Allen Beck and Paige Harrison, "Sexual Victimization in State and Federal Prisons Reported by Inmates, 2007," *Bureau of Justice Statistics Special Report* December (2007): 2.

22. Andrea Smith et al., *Introduction to Color of Violence: The INCITE! Anthology*, ed. INCITE! Women of Color Against Violence (Cambridge: South End Press, 2006), 4.

23. "Body Cavity Searches at Michigan's Women's Huron Valley Correctional Facility," http://www.aclu.org/prisoners-rights-womens-rights/body-cavity-searches-michigans-womens-huron-valley-correctional (accessed January 22, 2013).

24. Ibid. Susan Rosenberg captures the unnecessary brutality of vaginal (as well as rectal) searches in *An American Radical*, while also attesting to its long-standing use as a means of controlling those who are incarcerated (2011).

25. Assata Shakur, "Women in Prison: How We Are," in *The New Abolitionists: (Neo)Slave Narratives and Contemporary Prison Writings*, ed. Joy James (Albany: State University of New York Press, 2005), 85.

26. Mary Gilfus, "Women's Experiences of Abuse as a Risk Factor for Incarceration, VAWnet, a Project of the National Resource Center on Domestic Violence/Pennsylvania Coalition Against Domestic Violence," www.vawnet.org (accessed June 8, 2012).

27. "Women of Color and Prisons," http://www.incite-national.org/index.php?s=117 (accessed June 8, 2012).

28. Andrea Smith et al., *Introduction to Color of Violence: The INCITE! Anthology*, ed. INCITE! Women of Color Against Violence (Cambridge: South End Press, 2006), 4.

29. Ruth Wilson Gilmore, *The Golden Gulag: Prisons, Surplus, Crisis, and Opposition in Globalizing California* (Berkeley: University of California Press, 2007), 16.

30. Ibid.

31. See Michelle Alexander, "The Cruel Hand," in *The New Jim Crow: Mass Incarceration in the Age of Colorblindness* (New York: The New Press, 2010), 137–172.

32. Alexander, *The New Jim Crow*, 151.

33. Andrea Smith et al., *Introduction to Color of Violence: The INCITE! Anthology*, ed. INCITE! Women of Color Against Violence (Cambridge: South End Press, 2006), 4.

34. Communities Against Rape and Abuse (CARA), "Taking Risks: Implementing Grassroots Community Accountability Strategies," in *Color of Violence: The INCITE! Anthology*, ed. INCITE! Women of Color Against Violence (Cambridge: South End Press, 2006), 250.

35. Ibid.

36. More recently, CARA has written: "When survivors access CARA for support, we see them less as clients and more as potential comrades in a struggle for social justice" (Bierria and CARA, "Pursuing a Radical Anti-Violence Agenda," 161).

37. CARA, "Taking Risks," 250. With the language of "aggressor" and "survivor," I am following CARA's usage, which they explain the following way: "For the purposes of this article, we use the word 'aggressor' to refer to a person who has committed an act of sexual violence (rape, sexual harassment, coercion, etc.) against another person. Our use of the word 'aggressor' is not an attempt to weaken the severity of rape. In our work of defining accountability outside of the criminal system, we try not to use criminal-based vocabulary such as 'perpetrator,' 'rapist,' or 'sex predator'" (302).

38. Ibid., 251.

39. Ibid.

40. Ibid.

41. Ibid., 260–263.

42. Ibid., 251.

43. See Kathleen Daly and Julie Stubbs, "Feminist Engagement with Restorative Justice," *Theoretical Criminology* 10, no. 1 (2006): 9–28; Critical

Resistance and INCITE! Women of Color Against Violence, "Gender Violence and the Prison-Industrial Complex," in *Color of Violence: The INCITE! Anthology*, ed. INCITE! Women of Color Against Violence (Cambridge: South End Press, 2006), 223–226.

44. Luce Irigaray, *Je, Tu, Nous: Toward a Culture of Difference*, trans. Alison Martin (New York: Routledge, 1993), 86.

45. Tina Chanter, *Ethics of Eros: Irigaray's Re-writing of the Philosophers* (New York: Routledge, 1995), 177.

46. Sabo quoted in Messerschmidt "Masculinities, Crime, and Prison," 67–68. In writing of Irigaray's reworking of the master/slave dialectic, Catherine Malabou and Ewa Plonowska Ziarek write: "In contrast to Hegel's sacrificial logic, Irigaray redefines sexual difference as *the labor of limitation and cultivation.* Such negativity does not produce synthetic unity, but on the contrary contests any sense of immediacy—for example, the immediacy of the sexed body—and emphasizes the incompleteness of nature, the subject, political community or the universal" (Ziarek and Malabou, "Negativity, Unhappiness or Felicity," 15). Irigaray returns to an abandoned thread in Hegel's work, the labor of love, to offer an account of nonsacrificial intersubjectivity that could address the connection Sabo makes between rape and the master/slave relationship.

47. Chanter, *Ethics of Eros*, 175.

48. Luce Irigaray, *This Sex Which Is Not One*, trans. Catherine Porter (Ithaca, NY: Cornell University Press, 1985), 129–130.

49. Anne Caldwell, "Transforming Sacrifice: Irigaray and the Politics of Sexual Difference," *Hypatia* 17, no. 4 (Fall 2002): 18.

50. Ibid., 23.

51. Ibid., 17.

52. Irigaray envisions the creation of a culture of sexual difference as an end of sacrifice that she explicitly links to a transformation of how we conceive of crime:

> To tell someone that he is a criminal, even against his will, is not a punitive act but rather a way to make him conscious of the self and to allow the other to be. Obviously, this changes the economy of consciousness. The masters of the economy no longer have the alibi of helping others because they alone respect the status of some intangible consciousness. The master, or masters, are doubled into two sexes, at least. What is sacrificed is henceforward the all-powerfulness of both one and the other. This new sacrifice opens things up whereas the old immolation habitually led to the creation of a *closed* world through *periodic exclusion.* This new sacrifice, if sacrifice it be rather than a disci-

pline, means that the individual or the social body gives up narcissistic self-sufficiency. (Irigaray, *Sexes and Genealogies*, 87)

The crime that Irigaray identifies in this passage is the garnering of social stability through the sacrifice of those constituted as outside the community. We can read in this passage the current carceral order as one in which the sacrifice of criminals is justified as helping victims, but that is an alibi for reconsolidating the dominance of a single masculine subject.

53. Irigaray writes that the development of feminine subjectivity may allow us to avoid two ethical mistakes, one of which is: "subordinating women to destiny without allowing them any access to mind, or consciousness of self and for self. Offering them only death and violence as their part" (Luce Irigaray, *An Ethics of Sexual Difference*, trans. Carolyn Burke and Gillian C. Gill [Ithaca, NY: Cornell University Press, 1993], 126).

54. Luce Irigaray, "The Question of the Other," trans. Noah Guynn, *Yale French Studies* 87 (1995): 88.

55. CARA, "Taking Risks," 251.

56. Irigaray, *Je, Tu, Nous*, 22.

57. Penelope Deutscher, *A Politics of Impossible Difference: The Later Work of Luce Irigaray* (Ithaca, NY: Cornell University Press, 2002), 61.

58. Ibid.

59. Irigaray, *Je, Tu, Nous*, 87–88. Irigaray's choice of virginity here is meant to be provocative. She uses a term that has been particularly useful for patriarchal control of women. As Deutscher writes, "She has revalued it as a concept in terms of metaphors of integrity. Virginity would signify both a physical and a moral inviolability of women. The virginity to which woman had a right would not only be bodily but also mental or 'spiritual'" (Deutscher, *Politics of Impossible Difference*, 50). By using such a freighted term, Irigaray both proposes a right for women and reminds us of the power of how women have traditionally been represented.

60. An important question arises here: is the person who was raped also part of the injuring party? Victim blaming remains an entrenched and devastating problem. From reading CARA's reflections on its work, it seems that communities that become involved in taking responsibility for how the community as a whole is responsible for the violence that occurs in it become less prone to victim blaming. Perhaps this is because once a community involves itself in taking responsibility, the need to find an individual to sacrifice in reaction to the violence is transformed into a need to redress and reduce the violence in the community. Thus, considering the survivor as part of society and, therefore, part of the injuring party does not have to be a process of blaming the victim for the harm because the process of assigning blame no

longer reaches its culmination in sacrifice. Rather, the community looks for the habits, mores, norms, expectations, desires, and pressures that contribute to violence—all of which a survivor may have participated in or resisted to varying degrees, but through the accountability process she or he can now become involved in transforming with the rest of the community. To include the survivor as part of the injuring party, rather than reducing to victim blaming, can be a process of actively including the survivor in redressing the harm done and resisting a reduction of the survivor to an innocent or guilty victim.

61. The same amendment is needed for the earlier similar quotation from "The Question of the Other," 88.

62. CARA, "Taking Risks," 253.

63. Ibid., 254.

64. Ibid.

65. Ibid.

66. Luce Irigaray, *I Love to You: Sketch of a Possible Felicity in History*, trans. Alison Martin (New York: Routledge, 1996), 36, 40, 41, 62; Ewa Ziarek, *An Ethics of Dissensus: Postmodernity, Feminism, and the Politics of Radical Democracy* (Stanford, CA: Stanford University Press, 2001), 164; Kelly Oliver, "Vision, Recognition, and a Passion for the Elements," in *Returning to Irigaray: Feminist Philosophy, Politics, and the Question of Unity*, ed. Maria C. Cimitile and Elaine P. Miller (Albany: State University of New York Press, 2007), 131.

67. Caldwell, "Transforming Sacrifice," 26.

68. Luce Irigaray, *Democracy Begins between Two*, trans. Kirsteen Anderson (New York: Routledge, 2001), 9.

69. Critical Resistance and INCITE! Women of Color Against Violence, "Gender Violence and the Prison-Industrial Complex," in *Color of Violence: The INCITE! Anthology*, ed. INCITE! Women of Color Against Violence (Cambridge: South End Press, 2006), 225.

70. Ibid., 224.

71. Ibid., 250.

72. For instance, Irigaray writes, "Women and little girls are raped, boys very rarely; the bodies of women and girls are used for involuntary prostitution and pornography, those of men infinitely less so" (Luce Irigaray, *Thinking the Difference: For a Peaceful Revolution*, trans. Karin Montin [New York: Routledge, 1994], 59). Irigaray here ignores the reality of prison rape and forced prostitution in men's prisons, as well as the widespread sexual abuse of boys, which may be rarer than the sexual abuse of girls but can hardly be said to occur very rarely.

73. Relatedly, Ewa Ziarek writes, "What is missing in Irigaray's concept of sexual difference is the analysis of the way the impossible actualization of subjective identities reveals multiple and conflicting identifications along the

lines of gender, race, and class" (Ziarek, *An Ethics of Dissensus*, 180). My reading is meant as a complement to her radicalization of sexual difference.

74. Sharon Marcus, "Fighting Words, Fighting Bodies: A Theory and Politics of Rape Prevention," in *Feminist Theorize the Political*, ed. Judith Butler and Joan W. Scott (New York: Routledge, 1992), 385–403.

75. Christine Helliwell, "'It's Only a Penis': Rape, Feminism, and Difference," *Signs* 25, no. 2 (Spring 2000): 796.

76. Ibid.

77. See Helliwell, "'It's Only a Penis.'"

THE VIOLENCE OF THE SUPERMAX: TOWARD A PHENOMENOLOGICAL
AESTHETICS OF PRISON SPACE
Adrian Switzer

1. Peter Scharff Smith, "The Effects of Solitary Confinement on Prison Inmates," *Crime and Justice* 34, no. 1 (2006): 443.

2. Smith, "The Effects of Solitary Confinement," 443.

3. Lorna Rhodes, *Total Confinement: Madness and Reason in the Maximum Security Prison* (Berkeley: University of California Press, 2004), 27–29.

4. Smith, "The Effects of Solitary Confinement," 443–444.

5. Ibid., 444.

6. John Irwin et al., "America's One Million Nonviolent Prisoners," *Social Justice* 27, no. 2 (2000): 136.

7. Irwin et al., "America's One Million Nonviolent Prisoners," 135–136.

8. Rick Ruddell, *America Behind Bars: Trends in Imprisonment, 1950–2000* (New York: LFB Scholarly Publishing, 2004), 3.

9. Ruddell, *America Behind Bars*, 2.

10. Smith, "The Effects of Solitary Confinement," 444.

11. On the history of the prison-industrial complex in the United States, see Eric Schlosser, "The Prison-Industrial Complex," *The Atlantic Monthly*, December 1998, 55.

12. Michel Foucault, *Discipline and Punish*, trans. A. Sheridan (New York: Vintage Books, 1995), 200.

13. David Gartman, *From Autos to Architecture: Fordism and Architectural Aesthetics in the 20th Century* (Princeton, NJ: Princeton Architectural Press, 2009), 27–28.

14. Edmund Husserl, "Phenomenological Psychology and Transcendental Phenomenology," in *The Essential Husserl*, ed. D. Welton (Bloomington: Indiana University Press, 1999), 326–327.

15. Edmund Husserl, *Ideas Pertaining to a Pure Phenomenology and to a Phenomenological Philosophy: Book One*, trans. F. Kersten (The Hague: Martinus Nijhoff Publishers, 1983), 308.

16. Husserl, *Ideas I*, 323.

17. The aim is to remain neutral on the topic of what ontological status the transcendent object has for Husserl and instead attend only to the possible modes of space as the transcendental condition of transcendent objectivity. In fact, such ontological neutrality complements my interest in transcendental modality. By not specifying transcendental conditions as conditioning only the existence of transcendent objects—with "existence" taken in an empirically real sense—I allow other aspects or features of those conditions to emerge, foremost, for my present concerns, features having to do with the *mode* of their constitution of a horizon or world. For a further discussion of the "constitutive" relationship between transcendental consciousness and transcendent objectivity, see Karl Ameriks, "Husserl's Realism," *The Philosophical Review* 86, no. 4 (October 1977): 509.

18. Edmund Husserl, *The Paris Lectures*, trans. P. Koestenbaum (Dordrecht: Kluwer Academic Publishers, 1998), 30–31.

19. Husserl, *Ideas I*, 313.

20. Ibid., 87–88.

21. Edmund Husserl, *Thing and Space: Lectures 1907*, trans. R. Rojcewicz (Dordrecht: Kluwer Academic Publishers, 1997), 37–38.

22. Edmund Husserl, "A Phenomenology of Internal Time Consciousness," in *The Essential Husserl*, ed. D. Welton (Bloomington: Indiana University Press, 1999), 200.

23. For further discussion of the problems Husserl faces on the topic of space and the actual sidedness of perceivable objects, see Rudolf Benet et al., *An Introduction to Husserlian Phenomenology* (Evanston, IL: Northwestern University Press, 1993), 120–125.

24. Husserl, *Ideas I*, 81.

25. Gaston Bachelard, *The Poetics of Space*, trans. M. Jolas (Boston, MA: Beacon Press, 1994), xxxv.

26. Ibid., xxxvi.

27. Anthony Vidler, "Spatial Violence," *Assemblage*, no. 20 (April 1993): 85.

28. From a different philosophical vantage, Foucault noticed similar spatial effects, which had largely been left unconsidered and undertheorized; and, perhaps unfairly, Foucault counts phenomenology as equally negligent as other intellectual traditions in failing to "think" space. In his lecture "*Des Espace Autres*," Foucault identifies the space of Bachelard's phenomenological study with "internal space" and proposes under the heading of "heterotopias" to study, instead, "external space" (Foucault, "Of Other Spaces" 23). While differing from Foucault on the opinion of phenomenology's access to the problem of space, I share Foucault's sentiment that our contemporary problematic, after an abiding modern interest in time, seems

to be a matter of thinking space (Foucault, "Of Other Spaces," 21). Further, as I will note in conclusion, I share Foucault's idea from the lecture that the thinking-of-space involves appealing beyond experience and philosophy to aesthetics.

29. Keramet Ann Reiter, "The Most Restrictive Alternative: A Litigation History of Solitary Confinement in U.S. Prisons, 1960–2006," *Studies in Law, Politics, and Society* 57 (2012): 101.

30. Atul Gawande, "Annals of Human Rights: Hellhole," *New Yorker*, March 30, 2009.

31. William Blake, "A Sentence Worse than Death," *Yale Law Journal* 122, no. 6 (Spring 2013): 415.

32. Edmund Husserl, *Ideas Pertaining to a Pure Phenomenology and to a Phenomenological Philosophy, Second Book: Studies in the Phenomenology of Constitution*, trans. R. Rojcewicz and A. Schuwer (Dordrecht: Kluwer Academic Publishers, 1989), 61–62.

33. Drew Leder, "Imprisoned Bodies: The Life-World of the Incarcerated," *Social Justice*, 31, no. 1/2 (2004): 57.

34. Drew Leder, *The Soul Knows No Bars: Inmates Reflect on Life, Death and Hope* (Lanham, MD: Rowman & Littlefield, 2001), 57–58.

35. Alyson Brown, "'Doing Time': The Extended Present of the Long-Term Prisoner," *Time & Society* 7, no. 1: 100–101.

36. Maurice Merleau-Ponty, *Phenomenology of Perception*, trans. C. Smith (New York: Routledge, 2002), 293.

37. Ibid., 295.

38. Ibid., 330.

39. Mikel Dufrenne, *The Phenomenology of Aesthetic Experience*, trans. E. Casey (Evanston, IL: Northwestern University Press, 1973), 244.

40. Merleau-Ponty, *Phenomenology of Perception*, 297.

41. Martin Heidegger, "The Origin of the Work of Art," trans. A. Hofstadter, in *The Continental Aesthetics Reader*, ed. C. Cazeaux (New York: Routledge, 2011), 90.

42. Heidegger, "The Origin of the Work of Art," 90.

43. Ibid., 92.

44. Jeff Malpas, "Objectivity and Self-Disclosedness," *Art and Phenomenology*, ed. J. D. Parry (New York: Routledge, 2011), 59.

45. Heidegger, "The Origin of the Work of Art," 93.

46. Maurice Merleau-Ponty, *The Visible and the Invisible*, trans. A. Lingis (Evanston, IL: Northwestern University Press, 1968), 130.

47. Maurice Merleau-Ponty, "Eye and Mind," trans. C. Dallery, in *The Primacy of Perception*, ed. J. Edie (Evanston, IL: Northwestern University Press, 1964), 180.

48. Maurice Merleau-Ponty, "Cézanne's Doubt," trans. H. Dreyfus and P. A. Dreyfus, in *Sense and Non-Sense* (Evanston, IL: Northwestern University Press, 1964), 12–13.

49. Tim Edensor, *Industrial Ruins: Spaces, Aesthetics and Materiality* (New York: Berg, 2005), 21–22.

PRISON AND THE SUBJECT OF RESISTANCE: A LEVINASIAN INQUIRY
Shokoufeh Sakhi

1. As distinct from a "total system," the complete and completely reproducible social object that totally constructs all subjects according to its requirements, a totalizing system is one characterized by a *systematic impetus* toward absorbing the subject as a function of the systemic object. The emphasis in the differentiation here is upon the fact that such systems are never (so far) completely successful; there is a residue, of greater or lesser extent, that resists construction and incorporation. While the history of these systems cannot be entered into here, candidates for this title clearly extend beyond the Nazis and fascists, the totalitarian "communisms" of China and the Soviet Union, the "iron cage" of market capitalism and fundamentalist Judaism, Christianity and Islam. Of course, there are vast differences among these examples, but here we are concerned with their commonalities as totalizing systems.

2. Resistance to totalizing agendas is not a homogenous totality itself. Often enough, it exhibits a tendency to lose its bearings, its human purposes, frequently its humanity, in and through the very processes of resisting its enforcers. Often enough, too, we become, insofar as we were ever otherwise, ethically indistinguishable from them.

3. The responsibility of the "otherwise than being" referred to here, far from indicating any mystical source, is sought in what Levinas takes to be an imminent, phenomenologically accessible experience prior to the formation of "being."

4. While this paideia has been the experience of prisoners under such states as Nazi Germany, China, the Soviet Union, and the Islamic Republic of Iran, the American CIA project MKUltra, with its interrogation manual known as "Kubark," makes as good a representative example as any.

5. Robert J. Lifton, *Thought Reform and the Psychology of Totalism* (New York: Norton & Company, 1961), 36.

6. Ziba Nawak, *Siba-Zinab* (Essen, Germany: Nima Verlag, 2007), 7. My translation from the original Farsi.

7. These techniques have a long heritage: in the eighteenth and nineteenth century, Jeremy Bentham's prison design, the "panopticon," took the form of a pentagon so constructed that prisoners could never see the guards

but could always be seen by them. The blindfold, so effective in the example of Siba-Zainab, and the goggles on the Afghani prisoners in the U.S. war on terror further isolate, removing the visual support of other prisoners, intensifying the sense of being seen without being able to see. By thus accustoming the psyche to a sense of one-way observation, this technique forms an ideal horizon of psychic heteronomy. Such techniques, and others such as solitary confinement and the like, are intended to reduce and *isolate* the person in her survival-ego by removing contact as much as feasible through maximally restricting external stimuli, including all forms of sociality, thus maximizing the sense that the authority's power is absolute and that one is alone under its gaze.

8. See, for example, A. Agah et al., *We Lived to Tell: Political Prison Memoirs of Iranian Women* (Toronto: McGilligan Books, 2007); Shahla Talebi, *Ghosts of Revolution* (Stanford, CA: Stanford University Press, 2011); H. Darvish, *Hanooz ghese bar yad ast* (Berkeley, CA: Noghte Books, 1997; in Farsi); S. Parsippur, *Khaterat-e Zendan* (Stockholm: Baran Press, 1996; in Farsi).

9. CIA, *Kubark Counterintelligence Interrogation*, July 1963, 66. http://www.gwu.edu/~nsarchiv/NSAEBB/NSAEBB122/index.htm#kubark.

10. Ibid., 41.

11. Ibid., 78.

12. See Guantanamo inmate Padilla's case, who sees his captors as his protectors and his own lawyers as part of a continuing interrogation program. Or the following from Mohammad Hashemi's confession: "I would like to plead with my former colleagues and friends who shared my deviant ideas to return to the correct path, relinquish their false notions, reform themselves, unite against imperialism and overcome the carnal instincts that can lead them towards having relations with Satan and his representatives" Ervand Abrahamian, *Tortured Confessions* (Berkeley, CA: University of California Press, 1999), 165.

13. That is, the former subject has been absorbed by, become a component of the system—the "same" as it.

14. See the testimony of the former Iranian political prisoner at the recent International People's Tribunal at the Hague who, sliding to the bottom of the slippery slope, found himself "pressured into collaborating with prison authorities by shooting other prisoners as a member of a firing squad." He described this pressure as "psychological rape," adding "I was not myself, I was a puppet. . . . It was not me who did this." *International People's Tribunal: Judgment*, February 2013, 24: http://www.irantribunal.com/Eng/EnHome .html.

15. Max Horkheimer, *Dawn and Decline* (New York: Seabury Press, 1978), 152.

16. See Isaiah Berlin's liberal critique of Epictetus and St. Augustine in *Four Essays on Liberty* (Oxford University Press, 1969), 135.

17. See Sigmund Freud, *Civilization and Its Discontents* (New York: Norton & Company, 1959), 109. Another indication, of course, is how often totalitarian regimes resort to mass murder; in Iran, for example, tens of thousands of political dissidents and prisoners are known to have been executed, assassinated, or otherwise killed during the 1980s.

18. Emmanuel Levinas, *Totality and Infinity*, trans. Alphonso Lingis (Pittsburgh: Duquesne University Press, 1969), 237.

19. Ibid.

20. Ibid.

21. See, for example, Emmanuel Levinas, *Time and the Other* (Pittsburgh: Duquesne University Press, 1987), 52–55 and *Totality and Infinity*, 9, 238.

22. Ibid.

23. The "instant," where Heidegger seeks a heroic purity, the "instant," the 'cell-form' of Levinas's theory of time, is where, in contrast to Heidegger, he finds the other. For Levinas, we are potentially free, and we are free insofar as we realize this potentiality in every instant. See Levinas, *Time and the Other*, 56, 7. From this point of view, the totalizing system may be recognized as having the goal of reducing one's "instants" to immediacy, to living in the absolute presence of the totalizing system; thus, one loses or maintains one's resistance in an "instant," in each and every instant.

24. Levinas, *Totality and Infinity*, 237.

25. Ibid., 238.

26. Ibid.

27. Ibid., 239.

28. Ibid.

29. Ibid.

30. Ibid.

31. Those who would reduce all meaning to the status of a "defense" are, of course, already defeated.

32. Emmanuel Levinas, "The Bad Conscience and the Inexorable," in *Of God Who Comes To Minds* (Stanford, CA: Stanford University Press, 1998), 174.

33. Emmanuel Levinas, "Notes on Meaning," in *Of God Comes To Minds* (Stanford, CA: Stanford University Press, 1998), 164.

34. Ibid.

35. See Jacob Timerman, *Prisoner Without a Name, Cell Without a Number* (New York: Vantage Books, 1981). In his account of his confinement in a solitary cell in a clandestine army prison in Argentina, Timerman describes the pressures of such conflicting responsibilities and the efforts of the prison

officials to push one into such conflicts: "More than once I was brusquely awakened by someone shouting: 'Think. Don't sleep, think.' But I refused to think. . . . To think meant becoming conscious of what was happening to me, imagining what might be happening to my wife and children; to think meant trying to work out how to relive this situation, how to wedge an opening in my relationship with the jailers" (35). Timerman's quandary is echoed in other prison memoirs. For instance, "if you don't think about yourself, don't you think about your family?" is a familiar question to political prisoners of totalizing systems in general.

36. Levinas, "Notes on Meaning," 170.

37. M. Raha, *Haghigat Sadeh*, Vol. III (Hanover: The International Organization of Democratic Iranian Women, 1992), 22. My translation from the original in Farsi.

38. However much this engagement within disengagement, this resistance beyond resistance, may necessarily seem an unseemly heroism passing itself off as humility, this obstinacy and stubbornness of the for-the-other is more opposed to such heroism than its usual antonym, cowardice; both heroism and cowardice are artifacts of the will, subject to the mechanics of relative quantities available there. The passivity of the prereflective I, in its responsibility, "does not conserve its assurance in the heroism of the being-for-death [of Heidegger] in which consciousness asserts itself as lucidity and thought thinking *to the very end*" (Levinas, "Notes on Meaning," 170), nor is it the fortifying of a courage in the face of the abyss of existentialism facing nothingness. While such motivations clearly exist, to reduce resistance to them is to miss the point.

39. Faraj Sarkoohi, "A Letter from Prison," *Payvand*, February 1, 1997. My translation from the original Farsi.

40. Nasser Mohajer, *The Book of Prison*, Vol. II (Berkeley, CA: Noghteh Books, 1998), 271. My translation from the original in Farsi.

CRITICAL THEORY, QUEER RESISTANCE,
AND THE ENDS OF CAPTURE
Liat Ben-Moshe, Che Gossett, Nick Mitchell, and Eric A. Stanley

1. See Sylvia Rivera, "Queens in Exile," in *GenderQueer: Voices From Beyond the Sexual Binary*, ed. Joan Nestle, Clare Howell, Riki Wilchins (London: Alyson Books, 2002); Reina Gossett, "An Open Letter for Gender Self-Determination in /at OWS," *PPS* 1 (December 2011): http://www.ppspress .info/documents/PPS_lssue_01_Open_Letters_December_2011.pdf.

2. Gay Liberation Front collectives and ACT UP chapters were surveilled by the FBI and often infiltrated throughout the 1970s and 1980s (see FBI files on the Gay Liberation Front as well as ACT UP for both). See also

Brett C. Stockdill, *Activism Against AIDS: At the Intersections of Sexuality, Race, Gender, and Class* (Boulder, CO: Lynne Rienner Press, 2003). Additionally, David W. Dunlap, "F.B.I. Kept Watch on AIDS Group during Protest Years," *The New York Times* (May 16, 1995): http://www.nytimes.com/1995/05/16/nyregion/fbi-kept-watch-on-aids-group-during-protest-years.html.

3. For more on Ortez Alderson's activism against racist and transmisogynistic police violence in Chicago and how he organized the Chicago GLF to protest against the murder of a black drag queen the day after he got out of prison for his antiwar activism, see Ferd Eggan, "Dykes and Fags Want Everything: Dreaming with the Gay Liberation Front," in *That's Revolting: Queer Strategies for Resisting Assimilation*, ed. Mattilda Bernstein Sycamore (Soft Skull Press: Revised edition, May 2008). For further historiographical material on Alderson's AIDS activist, antiwar, and queer liberationist involvement see: Deborah Gould, *Moving Politics: Emotion and ACT UP's Fight Against AIDS* (Chicago: University of Chicago Press, 2009); Liz Highleyman, "Peace Activism and GLBT Rights," *The Gay & Lesbian Review* (September–October 2004): http://www.glreview.com/issues/11.5/11.5_Highleyman.php; Regina Kunzel, *Criminal Intimacy: Prison and the Uneven History of Modern American Sexuality* (Chicago: University of Chicago Press, 2008); Karla Jay, *Out of the Closets: Voices of Gay Liberation* (New York: New York University Press, 1992); and Mark Harrington, *Tactical Biopolitics* (Cambridge, MA: MIT Press, 2008).

4. Hearts on a Wire's collective report, "This Is a Prison: Glitter Is Not Allowed: Experiences of Trans and Gender Variant People in Pennsylvania's Prison Systems," documents penalization of gender nonconformity inside Pennsylvania prisons (e.g., incarcerated trans/gnc people are placed in the hole, max out because of penalization, etc). Pascal Emmer, Adrian Lowe, and R. Barrett Marshall (Hearts on a Wire Collective), "This Is a Prison: Glitter Is Not Allowed: Experiences of Trans and Gender Variant People in Pennsylvania's Prison Systems" (Philadelphia: Hearts on a Wire Collective, 2011): http://www.galaei.org/documents/thisisaprison.pdf. See also Gabriel Arkles, "Correcting Race and Gender: Prison Regulation of Social Hierarchy through Dress," *New York University Law Review* 87, no. 4 (2012): 859–959.

5. Eric A. Stanley and Nat Smith, eds., *Captive Genders: Trans Embodiment and the Prison Industrial Complex* (Oakland, CA: AK Press, 2011).

6. See Russell Robinson, "Masculinity as Prison: Sexual Identity, Race, and Incarceration," California Law Review 99 (2011): 1309, in which he talks about the K6G unit. See also Dean Spade's response, "The Only Way to End Racialized Gender Violence in Prisons Is to End Prisons: A Response to Russell Robinson's 'Masculinity as Prison,'" *California Law Review* (Dec. 2012).

7. W. E. B. Du Bois, *The Souls of Black Folk* (Chicago: A. C. McClurgh & Co., 1909), 9.

8. Cathy J. Cohen, "Punks, Bulldaggers, and Welfare Queens: The Radical Potential of Queer Politics?" *GLQ* 3 (1997): 437–465, 440.

9. Michelle Alexander, *The New Jim Crow: Mass Incarceration in the Age of Colorblindness* (New York: The New Press, 2010).

10. H. McBryde Johnson, "The Disability Gulag," *The New York Times*, November 23, 2003.

11. R. McRuer, *Crip Theory: Cultural Signs of Queerness and Disability* (New York: New York University Press, 2006).

12. Ibid., 31.

13. J. G. Miller, *Last One over the Wall: The Massachusetts Experiment in Closing Reform Schools* (Columbus: Ohio State University Press, 1991).

14. Fay Honey Knopp, "On Radical Feminism and Abolition," *Peace Review: A Journal of Social Justice* 6, no. 2 (1994): 203–208.

15. See Jacques Derrida, "Force of Law: The 'Mythic Foundations of Authority,'" in *Deconstruction and the Possibility of Justice*, ed. Drucilla Cornell, Michel Rosenfeld, and David Carlson (New York: Routledge, 1992).

16. Lauren Berlant, *Cruel Optimism* (Durham, NC: Duke University Press, 2011): 4.

17. Priya Kandeswamy, "State Austerity and the Racial Politics of Same-Sex Marriage in the US," *Sexualities* 11, no. 6 (2008): 706–725, 707.

18. Mumia Abu-Jamal, *Jailhouse Lawyers* (San Francisco: City Light Books, 2009).

19. Wendy Brown, *States of Injury* (Princeton, NJ: Princeton University Press, 1995), 134.

20. For more information, see http://supportcece.wordpress.com.

21. Dean Spade, *Normal Life: Administrative Violence, Critical Trans Politics, and the Limits of Law* (Brooklyn, NY: South End Press, 2001).

22. J. E. Muñoz, *Cruising Utopia: The Then and There of Queer Futurity* (New York: New York University, 2009).

23. Lee Edelman, *No Future: Queer Theory and the Death Drive* (Durham, NC: Duke University Press, 2004).

24. Ruth W. Gilmore, *Golden Gulag: Prisons, Surplus, Crisis, and Opposition in Globalizing California* (Berkeley: University of California Press, 2006).

25. Lauren Berlant, "Slow Death (Sovereignty, Obesity, Lateral Agency)," *Critical Inquiry* 33 (2007): 754–780.

26. Ibid., 754; emphasis added.

27. Justin Piché and Mike Larsen, "The Moving Targets of Penal Abolitionism: ICOPA, Past, Present and Future," *Contemporary Justice Review* 13, no. 4 (2010).

28. Ibid., 399.

29. Gilles Deleuze, "Postscript on the Societies of Control," *October* 59 (Winter 1992): 3–7.

30. Jasbir Puar, "Prognosis Time: Towards a Geopolitics of Affect, Debility and Capacity," *Women and Performance: A Journal of Feminist Theory* 19, no. 2 (2009): 161–172.

31. Here I am thinking about the critiques of multiculturalism and how that would press upon ideas of the biopolitical. For more, see Jared Sexton, *Amalgamation Schemes: Antiblackness and the Critique of Multiracialism* (Minneapolis: University of Minnesota Press, 2008).

32. See *At America's Expense: The Mass Incarceration of the Elderly*, ACLU June 2012: http://www.aclu.org/criminal-law-reform/report-americas -expense-mass-incarceration-elderly.

33. "Israel: Amend 'Anti-Infiltration' Law: Measure Denies Asylum Seekers Protections of Refugee Convention," *Human Rights Watch* press release June 10th, 2012: http://www.hrw.org/news/2012/06/10/israel-amend-anti -infiltration-law

34. For more, see Yasmin Nair, "How to Make Prisons Disappear: Queer Immigrants, the Shackles of Love, and the Invisibility of the Prison Industrial Complex," in *Captive Genders: Trans Embodiment and the Prison Industrial Complex*, ed. Nat Smith and Eric A. Stanley (Oakland, CA: AK Press, 2011).

35. Adriana Garriga Lopez, "Boricuas ACTing UP in New York and San Juan: Diasporic Puerto Rican HIV/AIDS Activism and Anthropology," *New Proposals:* Journal of Marxism and Interdisciplinary Inquiry 2, no. 2 (2009).

36. Kathambi Kinoti, "Sex Work in Southern Africa: Criminalization Provides Screen for other Rights Violations," *The Association for Women's Rights in Development* 20/02/2009: http://secure1.awid.org/eng/Issues-and -Analysis/Library/Sex-work-in-Southern-Africa-Criminalization-provides -screen-for-other-rights-violations.

37. See South African National AIDS Council, *National Strategic Plan on HIV, STIs, and TB, 2012–2016*, Republic of South Africa, http://www.doh .gov.za/docs/stratdocs/2012/NSPfull.pdf (accessed January 30, 2013).

38. For a great meditation on Genet, temporality, and punishment, see Michael Hardt, "Genet: In the Language of the Enemy," *Yale French Studies Journal* 91 (1997): 64–79.

39. Antonio Negri, *Insurgencies: Constituent Power and the Modern State* (Minneapolis: University of Minnesota Press, 1999).

40. Robert Paul Wolff, Barrington Moore Jr., and Herbert Marcuse, *A Critique of Pure Tolerance* (Boston: Beacon Press, 1969), 95–137.

41. For more on pinkwashing, see "Pinkwatching Israel," http://www .pinkwatchingisrael.com/ (accessed February 03, 2013).

42. Erick Fabris, *Tranquil Prisons: Chemical Incarceration under Community Treatment Orders* (Toronto: Toronto University Press, 2011).

43. Angela Y. Davis and Gina Dent, "Prison as a Border: A Conversation on Gender, Globalization, and Punishment," *Signs* 26 (2001): 1235–1241.

44. Quoted in Julianne Hing, "Who Are Those 'Gangbangers' Obama's So Proud of Deporting?" *Color Lines: News for Action* (October 17, 2012), http://colorlines.com/archives/2012/10/who_are_those_gangbangers _obamas_so_proud_of_deporting.html (accessed January 31, 2013). For an excellent collection of conversations and interventions that connect the politics of deportation to contemporary struggles around immigrant and border justice, see Jenna Loyd, Matt Mitchelson, and Andrew Burridge, eds., *Beyond Walls and Cages: Prisons, Borders, and Global Crisis* (Athens: University of Georgia Press, 2012).

45. Sara Ahmed, "Affective Economies," *Social Text* 79 22, no. 2 (2004): 117–239.

46. Julia Sudbury, "Maroon Abolitionists: Black Gender-Oppressed Activists in the Anti-Prison Movement in the U.S. and Canada," *Meridians: Feminism, Race, Transnationalism* 9, no. 1 (2008): 1–29.

47. Beth Richie, *Arrested Justice: Black Women, Violence, and America's Prison Nation* (New York: New York University Press, 2012).

48. Manning Marable and Leith Mullings, *Let Nobody Turn Us Around: Voices of Resistance, Reform and Renewal: An African American Anthology* (Lanham, MD: Rowman & Littlefield, 2009), 468.

49. Sam Roberts, "Rockefeller on the Attica Raid, From Boastful to Subdued," *New York Times*, September 13, 2011: http://www.nytimes.com/ 2011/09/13/nyregion/rockefeller-initially-boasted-to-nixon-about-attica -raid.html?pagewanted=all.

50. Joshua Page, "Eliminating the Enemy: The Import of Denying Prisoners Access to Higher Education in Clinton's America," *Punishment & Society* 6 (2004): 357–378.

51. Chris Hedges, "War Is a Hate Crime," *Truth Dig*, October 26, 2009: http://www.truthdig.com/report/item/20091026_war_is_a_hate_crime/.

52. Sylvia Rivera Law Project, "Gender Identity Disorder and the Prison-Industrial Complex: Reflections from the Sylvia Rivera Law Project," *The Abolitionist* 19 (February 2013).

Abizadeh, Arash. "Democratic Theory and Border Coercion: No Right to Unilaterally Control Your Own Borders." *Political Theory* 36, no. 1 (February 2008): 37–65.

Abrahamian, Ervand. *Tortured Confession*. Berkeley: University of California Press, 1999.

Abu-Jamal, Mumia. *Jailhouse Lawyers*. San Francisco: City Light Books, 2009.

Ackerman, Bruce. "The Emergency Constitution." *Yale Law Journal* 113 (2004).

ACLU. *At America's Expense: The Mass Incarceration of the Elderly* (June 2012): http://www.aclu.org/criminal-law-reform/report-americas-expense -mass-incarceration-elderly.

Adams, Jessica. *Wounds of Returning: Race, Memory, and Property on the Post-slavery Plantation*. Chapel Hill: University of North Carolina Press, 2007.

Adamson, Christopher R. "Punishment After Slavery: Southern State Penal Systems, 1865–1890." *Social Problems* 30, no. 5 (1983).

———. "Toward a Marxian Penology: Captive Criminal Populations as Economic Threats and Resources." *Social Problems* 31, no. 4 (1984): 435–458.

Agamben, Giorgio. *Homo Sacer: Sovereign Power and Bare Life*. Translated by Daniel Heller-Roazen. Stanford, CA: Stanford University Press, 1998.

Agnew, John. *Globalization and Sovereignty*. Lanham, MD: Rowman & Littlefield Publishers, 2009.

Ahmed, Sara. "Affective Economies." *Social Text* 79, 22, no. 2 (2004): 117–239.

Aikin, John G., ed. "Slaves and Free Persons of Color." In *A Digest of the Laws of the State of Alabama: 1833*. Philadelphia: Alexander Towar, 1833. http://www.archives.state.al.us/teacher/slavery/lesson1/doc1.html.

Albert, Michael. *Parecon: Life After Capitalism*. New York: Verso, 2003.

Alexander, Michelle. *The New Jim Crow: Mass Incarceration in the Age of Colorblindness*. New York: The New Press, 2010.

Alfred, Taiaiake. *Peace, Power and Righteousness*. Oxford: Oxford University Press, 1999.

Ameriks, Karl. "Husserl's Realism." *The Philosophical Review* 86, no. 4 (October 1977): 498–519.

Anand, Prerna. *Winners and Losers: Corrections and Higher Education in California.* Los Altos, CA: California Common Sense, 2012. http://www.cacs .org/ca/article/44 (accessed January 19, 2013).

Anderson, Bridget, Matthew J. Gibney, and Emanuela Paoletti. "Citizenship, Deportation and the Boundaries of Belonging." *Citizenship Studies* 15, no. 5 (August 2011): 547–563.

Andrews, William L., and Henry Louis Gates Jr. *Slave Narratives.* New York: The Library of America, 2000.

Anthony, Thalia, and Chris Cunneen. *The Critical Criminology Companion.* Sydney: Hawkins Press, 2008.

Arkles, Gabriel. "Correcting Race and Gender: Prison Regulation of Social Hierarchy through Dress." *New York University Law Review* 87, no. 4 (2012): 859–959.

Arneson, Richard. "Egalitarianism and the Undeserving Poor." *The Journal of Political Philosophy* 5, no. 4 (1997): 327–350.

Austin, James, and Garry Coventry. *Emerging Issues on Privatized Prisons.* Washington, DC: Department of Justice/Office of Justice Programs, 2001, iii. http://www.ncjrs.gov/pdffiles1/bja/181249.pdf (accessed January 4, 2012).

Ayers, Edward L. *Vengeance and Justice: Crime and Punishment in the 19th-Century American South.* New York: Oxford University Press, 1984.

Bachelard, Gaston. *The Poetics of Space.* Translated by M. Jolas. Boston, MA: Beacon Press, 1994.

Badinter, Robert. *Débats À l'Assemblée Nationale Sur L'abolition de La Peine de Mort En France: Intervention de M. Badinter, Garde Des Sceaux, Ministre de La Justice.* Paris: Journal officiel de la république française, 1981. http://www.peinedemort.org/document.php?choix=4738.

Baldus, David, George Woodworth, et al. "Comparative Review of Death Sentences: An Empirical Study of the Georgia Experience." *Journal of Criminal Law and Criminology* 74 (1983): 661–753.

Balibar, Étienne. *We, the People of Europe?: Reflections on Transnational Citizenship.* Translated by James Swensen. Princeton, NJ: Princeton University Press, 2004.

Bauer, Shane. "Solitary in Iran Nearly Broke Me. Then I Went Inside America's Prisons." *Mother Jones* (November 2012). http://www.mother jones.com/politics/2012/10/solitary-confinement-shane-bauer.

Baze v. Rees. Ginsburg, dissenting. 533 (U.S. Supreme Court 2008).

Baze v. Rees. Roberts opinion. 533 (U.S. Supreme Court 2008).

Beaumont, Gustave de, and Alexis de Tocqueville. *On the Penitentiary System in the United States and its Application to France*. Translated by Francis Lieber. Philadelphia: Carey, Lea, and Blanchard, 1833.

Beccaria, Cesare marchese di. "Of Crimes and Punishments." Constitution. org. http://www.constitution.org/cb/crim_pun.htm (accessed December 1, 2011).

———. *"On Crimes and Punishments" and Other Writings*. Edited by Richard Bellamy. Translated by Richard Davies. Cambridge: Cambridge University Press, 1995.

Beck, Allen, and Paige Harrison. "Sexual Victimization in State and Federal Prisons Reported by Inmates, 2007." *Bureau of Justice Statistics Special Report* December, 2007.

Becker, Gary S. "Crime and Punishment: An Economic Approach." *The Journal of Political Economy* 76, no. 2 (1968).

Belknap, Joanne. *The Invisible Woman: Gender, Crime, and Justice*. Belmont, CA: Wadsworth Publishing Company, 1996.

Bell, Derrick. "Racial Realism." In *Critical Race Theory*, edited by Kimberley Crenshaw et al. New York: The New Press, 1995.

Benhabib, Seyla. *Dignity in Adversity: Human Rights in Troubled Times*. Malden, MA: Polity, 2011.

Berk, Christopher. "Investment Talk: Comments on the Use of the Language of Investment in Prison Reform Advocacy." *Carceral Notebooks* 6 (2010).

Berkett, Bertrum Rene. "Hospice—Sail to Serenity." May 14, 2006. http://www.prisonterminal.com/essays%20sail%20to%20serenity.html (accessed January 29, 2013).

Berlant, Lauren. *Cruel Optimism*. Durham, NC: Duke University Press, 2011.

———. "Slow Death (Sovereignty, Obesity, Lateral Agency)." *Critical Inquiry* 33 (2007): 754–780.

Berlin, Isaiah. *Four Essays on Liberty*. Oxford: Oxford University Press, 1969.

Bernet, Rudolf, et al. *An Introduction to Husserlian Phenomenology*. Evanston, IL: Northwestern University Press, 1993.

Berry, Mary Frances. *Black Resistance, White Law: A History of Constitutional Racism in America*. 1971. New York: reprint 1994.

Best, Stephen, and Saidiya Hartman. "Fugitive Justice." *Representations* 92 (2005): 1–15.

Bianchi, Herman. *Justice as Sanctuary*. Bloomington: Indiana University Press, 1994.

Bierria, Alisa, and Communities Against Rape and Abuse (CARA). "Pursuing a Radical Anti-Violence Agenda Inside/Outside a Non-Profit Structure." In *The Revolution Will Not Be Funded: Beyond the Non-Profit Industrial Com-*

plex, edited by INCITE! Women of Color Against Violence, 151–164. Cambridge: South End Press, 2007.

Blackburn, Robin. *The Making of New World Slavery: From the Baroque to the Modern, 1492–1800*. New York: Verso, 1997.

Blackmon, Douglas. *Slavery by Another Name: The Re-Enslavement of Black Americans from the Civil War to World War II*. New York: Random House, 2008.

Blake, William. "A Sentence Worse than Death." *Yale Law Journal* 122, no. 6 (Spring 2013): 410–415.

Bohrman, Rebecca, and Naomi Murakawa. "Remaking Big Government: Immigration and Crime Control in the United States." In *Global Lockdown: Race, Gender, and the Prison-Industrial Complex*, edited by Julia Sudbury, 109–125. New York: Routledge, 2005.

Bonefeld, Werner. "The Permanence of Primitive Accumulation: Commodity Fetishism and Social Constitution." *The Commoner* 2 (2001): 1–15.

Boonin, David. *The Problem of Punishment*. Cambridge: Cambridge University Press, 2008.

Bosniak, Linda. *The Citizen and the Alien: Dilemmas of Contemporary Membership*. Princeton, NJ: Princeton University Press, 2006.

Bosworth, Mary. "Border Control and the Limits of the Sovereign State." *Social & Legal Studies* 17, no. 2 (2008): 199–215.

Bosworth, Mary, and Emma Kaufman. "Foreigners in a Carceral Age: Immigration and Imprisonment in the United States." *Stanford Law & Policy Review* 22, no. 2 (2011): 429–454.

Bradley, Curtis A., and Jack L. Goldsmith. "Congressional Authorization and the War on Terrorism." *Harvard Law Review* 118 (2005).

Brown, Alyson. "'Doing Time': The Extended Present of the Long-Term Prisoner." *Time & Society* 7, no. 1 (1998): 93–103.

Brown, Vincent. "Social Death and Political Life in the Study of Slavery." *The American Historical Review* 114, no. 5 (2009): 1231–1249.

Brown, Wendy. "Neo-Liberalism and the End of Liberal Democracy." *Theory & Event* 7, no. 1 (2003).

———. *States of Injury*. Princeton, NJ: Princeton University Press, 1995.

———. *Walled States, Waning Sovereignty*. New York: Zone Books, 2010.

Burchell, Graham, et al. *The Foucault Effect: Studies in Governmentality*. Chicago: University of Chicago Press, 1991.

Bureau of Justice Statistics. *Prisoners in 2010*. Washington DC: United States Department of Justice, 2011. http://bjs.ojp.usdoj.gov/index.cfm?ty=pb detail&iid=2230 (accessed January 5, 2012).

Butler, Judith. *Frames of War: When Is Life Grievable?* London: Verso, 2010.

———. *Giving an Account of Oneself*. New York: Fordham University Press, 2005.

———. *Undoing Gender*. New York: Routledge, 2004.

Cacho, Lisa Marie. *Social Death: Racialized Rightlessness and the Criminalization of the Unprotected*. New York: New York University Press, 2012.

Caldwell, Anne. "Transforming Sacrifice: Irigaray and the Politics of Sexual Difference." *Hypatia* 17, no. 4 (Fall 2002): 16–38.

"California General Election Official Voter Information Guide." 2012. http://vig.cdn.sos.ca.gov/2012/general/pdf/complete-vig-v2.pdf (accessed January 18, 2013).

Camus, Albert. "Reflections on the Guillotine." In *Resistance, Rebellion, and Death*, trans. Justin O'Brien, 173–234. New York: Vintage International, 1995.

Carson, E. Ann, and William J. Sabol. *Prisoners in 2011*. Bureau of Justice Statistics, December 2012. http://www.bjs.gov/content/pub/pdf/p11.pdf.

Chacón, Jennifer M. "Managing Migration through Crime." *Columbia Law Review Sidebar* 109 (2009): 135–148.

———. "Overcriminalizing Immigration." *Journal of Criminal Law and Criminology* 102, no. 3 (2012): 613–652.

Chang, Robert S., and Neil Gotanda. "Afterword: The Race Question in LatCrit Theory and Asian American Jurisprudence." *Nevada Law Journal* 7 (2007): 1012–1022.

Chanter, Tina. *Ethics of Eros: Irigaray's Re-writing of the Philosophers*. New York: Routledge, 1995.

Chemerinsky, Erwin. "Cruel and Unusual: The Story of Leandro Andrade." *Drake Law Review* 52 (2003): 1–24.

Children's Defense Fund. "The Cradle to Prison Pipeline, Summary Report" (2009). http://www.childrensdefense.org/child-research-data-publications/data/cradle-prison-pipeline-report-2007-full-highres.html.

Chow, Rey. *The Protestant Ethnic and the Spirit of Capitalism*. New York: Columbia University Press, 2002.

Christie, Nils. "Conflicts as Property." *British Journal of Criminology* 17, no. 1 (1977): 1–15.

Chung, Jean. "Felony Disenfranchisement: A Primer." *The Sentencing Project*, June 2013. http://sentencingproject.org/doc/publications/fd_Felony%20Disenfranchisement%20Primer.pdf.

CIA. *Kubark Counterintelligence Interrogation*. July 1963. http://www.gwu.edu/~nsarchiv/NSAEBB/NSAEBB122/index.htm#kubark.

Cohen, Cathy J. "Deviance as Resistance: A New Research Agenda for the Study of Black Politics." *Du Bois Review: Social Science Research on Race* 1, no. 1 (2004).

———. "Punks, Bulldaggers, and Welfare Queens: The Radical Potential of Queer Politics?" *GLQ* 3 (1997): 437–465.

Cohn, Felicia. "The Ethics of End-of-Life Care for Prison Inmates." *Journal of Law, Medicine and Ethics* 27 (1999): 252–259.

Cole, David. "The Poverty of Posner's Pragmatism: Balancing Away Liberty After 9/11." *Stanford Law Review* 59 (2007): 1735–1737.

Cole, David, and James X. Dempsey. *Terrorism and the Constitution: Sacrificing Civil Liberties in the Name of National Security*. Kindle Version. Perseus Books Group, 2006.

Collins, Patricia Hill. *Black Feminist Thought*. New York: Routledge, 2000.

Colvin, Mark. *Penitentiaries, Reformatories, and Chain Gangs: Social Theory and the History of Punishment in Nineteenth-Century America*. New York: St. Martin's Press, 1997.

Communities Against Rape and Abuse (CARA). "Taking Risks: Implementing Grassroots Community Accountability Strategies." In *Color of Violence: The INCITE! Anthology*, edited by INCITE! Women of Color Against Violence, 250–266. Cambridge: South End Press, 2006.

Conrad, Ryan, et al. *Prisons Will Not Protect You*. Lewiston, ME: Against Equality Publishing Collective, 2012.

"The Costs of the Financial Crisis." 2012. http://www.bettermarkets.com/sites/default/files/CBA%20Report%20CoC%205-31.pdf (accessed January 18, 2013).

CR-10 Publications Collective. *Abolition Now!: 10 Years of Strategy and Struggle Against the Prison Industrial Complex*. Oakland, CA: AK Press, 2008.

Craig, Elizabeth, and Margaret Ratcliff. "Controversies in Correctional End-of-Life Care." *Journal of Correctional Health Care* 9, no. 2 (2002): 149–157.

Critical Resistance and INCITE! Women of Color Against Violence. "Gender Violence and the Prison-Industrial Complex." In *Color of Violence: The INCITE! Anthology*, edited by INCITE! Women of Color Against Violence, 223–226. Cambridge: South End Press, 2006.

Culbert, Jennifer. *Dead Certainty: The Death Penalty and the Problem of Judgment*. Stanford, CA: Stanford University Press, 2008.

Currie, Elliot. *Crime and Punishment in America*. New York: Henry Holt and Co., 1998.

Curtin, Mary Ellen. *Black Prisoners and Their World, Alabama, 1865–1900*. Charlottesville: University Press of Virginia, 2000.

Da Silva, Denise. *Toward a Global Idea of Race*. Minneapolis: University of Minnesota Press, 2007.

Daly, Kathleen, and Julie Stubbs. "Feminist Engagement with Restorative Justice." *Theoretical Criminology* 10, no. 1 (2006): 9–28.

Daniel, Pete. *The Shadow of Slavery: Peonage in the South, 1901–1969*. Urbana: University of Illinois Press, reprint 1990.

Dauvergne, Catherine. "Globalizing Fragmentation: New Pressures on Women Caught in the Immigration Law-Citizenship Dichotomy." In *Migrations and Mobilities: Citizenship, Borders, and Gender*, edited by Seyla Benhabib and Judith Resnik, 333–355. New York: New York University Press, 2009.

Davis, Angela Y. *Abolition Democracy: Beyond Empire, Prisons, and Torture*. New York: Seven Stories, 2005.

———. *Are Prisons Obsolete?* New York: Seven Stories Press, 2003.

———. "Incarcerated Women: Transformative Strategies." *Black Renaissance/Renaissance Noir* 1, no. 1 (1996): 21–34.

———. "Masked Racism: Reflections on the Prison Industrial Complex." *ColorLines*, September 10, 1998.

———. *The Meaning of Freedom and Other Difficult Dialogues*. San Francisco: City Lights Books, 2012.

———. "Race and Criminalization: Black Americans and the Punishment Industry." In *The House That Race Built: Black Americas, U.S. Terrain*, edited by Wahneema Lubiano. New York: Pantheon, 1997.

———. "Racialized Punishment and Prison Abolition." In *A Companion to African-American Philosophy*, edited by Tommy Lott and John Pittman. Oxford: Blackwell Publishing, 2003.

———. *Women, Race, and Class*. New York: Vintage, 1981.

Davis, Angela Y., and Gina Dent. "Prison as a Border: A Conversation on Gender, Globalization, and Punishment." *Signs* 26 (2001): 1235–1241.

Davis, Mike. "Hell Factories." *The Nation*, February 20, 1995, 229–234.

Dayan, Colin. *The Law Is a White Dog: How Legal Rituals Make and Unmake Persons*. Princeton, NJ: Princeton University Press, 2011.

———. "Legal Terrors." *Representations* 92 (2005): 42–80.

———. *The Story of Cruel and Unusual*. Cambridge, MA: The MIT Press, 2007.

"Death Row Inmate Executed Using Pentobarbital in Lethal Injection." http://www.cnn.com/2010/CRIME/12/16/oklahoma.execution/ (accessed March 11, 2014).

De Genova, Nicholas, and Nathalie Mae Peutz, eds. *The Deportation Regime: Sovereignty, Space, and the Freedom of Movement*. Durham, NC: Duke University Press, 2010.

de Giorgi, Alessandro. *Rethinking the Political Economy of Punishment: Perspectives on Post-Fordism and Penal Politics*. Burlington, VT: Ashgate Publishing, 2006.

Deleuze, Gilles. "Postscript on the Societies of Control." *October* 59 (Winter 1992): 3–7.

Delgado, Richard. "Centennial Reflections on the California Law Review's Scholarship on Race: The Structure of Civil Rights Thought." *California Law Review* 100 (2012).

Derrida, Jacques. *The Beast and the Sovereign. Volume 2.* Chicago: University of Chicago Press, 2011.

———. *The Death Penalty. Volume I.* Translated by Peggy Kamuf. Chicago: University of Chicago Press, 2013.

———. "Force of Law: The 'Mystical Foundation of Authority.'" *Cardozo Law Review* 11 (1990): 920–1046.

———. *Of Grammatology.* Translated by Gayatri Spivak, corrected edition. Baltimore: Johns Hopkins University Press, 1997.

Derrida, Jacques, and Elisabeth Roudinesco. *For What Tomorrow: A Dialogue.* Stanford, CA: Stanford University Press, 2004.

Deutscher, Penelope. *A Politics of Impossible Difference: The Later Work of Luce Irigaray.* Ithaca, NY: Cornell University Press, 2002.

Dilts, Andrew. "From 'Entrepreneur of the Self' to 'Care of the Self': Neo-Liberal Governmentality and Foucault's Ethics." *Foucault Studies*, no. 12 (2011).

———. "Incurable Blackness: Criminal Disenfranchisement, Mental Disability, and the White Citizen." *Disability Studies Quarterly* 32, no. 3 (2012).

———. "Michel Foucault Meets Gary Becker: Criminality beyond Discipline and Punish." *Carceral Notebooks* 4 (2008).

———. *Punishment and Inclusion: Race, Membership, and the Limits of American Liberalism.* New York: Fordham University Press, 2014.

Donaldson, Stephen "Donny." "A Million Jockers, Punks, and Queens." In *Prison Masculinities*, edited by Don Sabo, Terry A. Kupers, and Willie London, 118–126. Philadelphia: Temple University Press, 2001.

Dowling, Julie, and Jonathan Inda, eds. *Governing Immigration through Crime: A Reader.* Stanford, CA: Stanford University Press, 2013.

Dubler, N. N. "The Collision of Confinement and Care: End-of-Life Care in Prisons and Jails." *Journal of Law, Medicine & Ethics* 26, no. 2 (1998): 149–156.

Du Bois, W. E. B. *Black Reconstruction in America: 1860–1880.* 1935. New York: The Free Press, reprint 1998.

———. *The Souls of Black Folk: Essays and Sketches.* Chicago: A. C. McClurgh & Co., 1909.

———. "The Spawn of Slavery: The Convict Lease System of the South." *Missionary Review of the World* (October 1901): 737–745.

Dudziak, Mary L. "Law, War, and the History of Time." *California Law Review* 98 (2010).

Dufrenne, Mikel. *The Phenomenology of Aesthetic Experience.* Translated by Ed Casey. Evanston, IL: Northwestern University Press, 1973.

Dunlap, David W. "F.B.I. Kept Watch on AIDS Group during Protest Years," *The New York Times,* May 16, 1995. http://www.nytimes.com/1995/05/16/nyregion/fbi-kept-watch-on-aids-group-during-protest-years.html.

Durazo, Ana C. R., Alisa Bierria, and Mimi Kim, eds. "Community Accountability: Emerging Movements to Transform Violence." Special issue of *Social Justice: A Journal of Crime, Conflict & World Order* 37, no. 4 (2011–2012).

Dutoit, Thomas. "Jacques Derrida on Pain of Death." Seminar presentation at Vanderbilt University, September 2011.

———. "Kant's Retreat." *The Southern Journal of Philosophy* 50, no. 1 (2012): 107–135.

Eberhardt, Jennifer, et al. "Seeing Black: Race, Crime, and Visual Processing." *Journal of Personality and Social Psychology* 87, no. 6 (2004): 876–893.

Edelman, Lee. *No Future: Queer Theory and the Death Drive.* Durham, NC: Duke University Press, 2004.

Edensor, Tim. *Industrial Ruins: Spaces, Aesthetics and Materiality.* New York: Berg, 2005.

Eggan, Ferd. "Dykes and Fags Want Everything: Dreaming with the Gay Liberation Front." In *That's Revolting: Queer Strategies for Resisting Assimilation,* edited by Mattilda Bernstein Sycamore. Soft Skull Press: Revised edition, May 2008.

Ehrlich, Isaac. "The Deterrent Effect of Capital Punishment: A Question of Life and Death." *The American Economic Review* 65, no. 3 (1975).

Emmer, Pascal, Adrian Lowe, and R. Barrett Marshall (Hearts on a Wire Collective). "This Is a Prison: Glitter Is Not Allowed: Experiences of Trans and Gender Variant People in Pennsylvania's Prison Systems." Philadelphia: Hearts on a Wire Collective, 2011. http://www.galaei.org/documents/thisisaprison.pdf.

Evans Carol, Ronda Herzog, and Tanya Tillman. "The Louisiana State Penitentiary: Angola Prison Hospice." *Journal of Palliative Medicine* 5, no. 4 (2002): 553–558.

Ewald, Alec C. "'Civil Death': The Ideological Paradox of Criminal Disenfranchisement Laws in the United States." *Wisconsin Law Review* (2002): 1045–1132.

Fabris, Erick. *Tranquil Prisons: Chemical Incarceration under Community Treatment Orders.* Toronto: Toronto University Press, 2011.

Falter, R. G. "Selected Predictors of Health Services Needs of Inmates over Age 50." *Journal of Correctional Health Care* 6, no. 2 (1999): 149–175.

Fanon, Frantz. *Black Skin, White Masks*. Translated by Richard Philcox. New York: Grove, 2008.

———. *The Wretched of the Earth*. Translated by Richard Philcox. New York: Grove Press, 1963.

Feeley, Malcolm M., and Jonathan Simon. "The New Penology: Notes on the Emerging Strategy of Corrections and Its Implications." *Criminology* 30, no. 4 (1992).

Fierce, Milfred. *Slavery Revisited: Blacks and the Southern Convict Lease System, 1865–1933*. New York: Africana Studies Research Center, Brooklyn College, CUNY, 1994.

"The Financial Crisis Response in Charts." 2012. http://www.treasury.gov/resource-center/data-chart-center/Documents/20120413_Financial CrisisResponse.pdf (accessed January 18, 2013).

Fleury-Steiner, Benjamin, with Carla Crowder. *Dying Inside: The HIV/AIDS Ward at Limestone Prison*. Ann Arbor: University of Michigan Press, 2008.

Foner, Phillip. *The Life and Writings of Frederick Douglass, Volume 4: Reconstruction and After*. New York: International Publishers, 1950.

Forman, James Jr. "Racial Critiques of Mass Incarceration: Beyond the New Jim Crow." *New York University Law Review* 87 (2012): 101–146.

Foucault, Michel. "The Anxiety of Judging." In *Foucault Live: Collected Interviews, 1961–1984*. Edited by Sylvére Lotringer. New York: Semiotext(e), 1989.

———. *The Birth of Biopolitics: Lectures at the Collège De France, 1978–79*. Translated by Graham Burchell. New York: Palgrave Macmillan, 2008.

———. "Considerations on Marxism, Phenomenology and Power." *Foucault Studies* 14 (2012): 109.

———. *Discipline and Punish*. Translated by Alan Sheridan. New York: Vintage Books, 1995 [1979].

———. *The History of Sexuality, Volume 1: An Introduction*. New York: Vintage Books, 1990.

———. "Le Grand Enfermentent." In *Dits Et Ecrits, Tome 2: 1976–1988*. Translated by Perry Zurn. Paris: Gallimard, 2001.

———. "Of Other Spaces." Trans. J. Miskowiec. *Diacritics* 16 (Spring 1986): 20–25.

———. "Pompidou's Two Deaths." In *The Essential Works of Michel Foucault, 1954–1984*, edited by James Faubion. New York: The New Press, 2000.

———. *Security, Territory, Population: Lectures at the Collège De France, 1977–1978*. Translated by Graham Burchell. New York: Palgrave Macmillan, 2007.

———. *Society Must Be Defended: Lectures at the Collège De France, 1975–1976.* Translated by David Macey. New York: Picador, 2003.

———. "What Calls for Punishment?" In *Foucault Live: Collected Interviews, 1961–1984.* Edited by Sylvére Lotringer. New York, Semiotext(e), 1989.

Freud, Sigmund. *Civilization and Its Discontents.* New York: Norton & Company, 1959.

Furman v. Georgia, 408: 238 (U.S. Supreme Court 1972).

Gabbidon, Shaun L., and Helen Taylor Greene. *Race, Crime and Justice: A Reader.* New York: Routledge, 2005.

Garland, David. *The Culture of Control: Crime and Social Order in Contemporary Society.* Chicago: University of Chicago Press, 2001.

———. *Peculiar Institution: America's Death Penalty in an Age of Abolition.* Cambridge, MA: Belknap Press, 2010.

———. *Punishment and Modern Society: A Study in Social Theory.* Chicago: University of Chicago Press, 1990.

Gartman, David. *From Autos to Architecture: Fordism and Architectural Aesthetics in the 20th Century.* Princeton, NJ: Princeton Architectural Press, 2009.

Gawande, Atul. "Annals of Human Rights: Hellhole." *New Yorker,* March 30, 2009.

Genovese, Eugene. "Black Maroons in War and Peace." In *From Rebellion to Revolution: Afro-American Slave Revolts in the Making of the Modern World.* Baton Rouge: Louisiana State University Press, 1979.

———. *Roll, Jordan, Roll: The World the Slaves Made.* New York: Vintage, 1974.

Geuss, Raymond. *Morality, Culture, and History: Essays on German Philosophy.* Cambridge: Cambridge University Press, 1999.

Ghandnoosh, Nazgol. *Race and Punishment: Racial Perceptions of Crime and Support for Punitive Policies.* Washington, DC: The Sentencing Project, 2014.

Gilmore, Ruth Wilson. *The Golden Gulag: Prisons, Surplus, Crisis, and Opposition in Globalizing California.* Berkeley: University of California Press, 2007.

———. "Race and Globalization." In *Geographies of Global Change,* 2nd edition, edited by P. J. Taylor, R. L. Johnston, and M. J. Watts, 261–274. Oxford: Basil Blackwell, 2002.

Gould, Deborah. *Moving Politics: Emotion and ACT UP's Fight Against AIDS.* Chicago: University of Chicago Press, 2009.

Glaze, Lauren, and Erika Parks. *Correctional Populations in the United States, 2011.* Bureau of Justice Statistics, November 2012. http://www.bjs.gov/content/pub/pdf/cpus11.pdf.

Gossett, Reina. "An Open Letter for Gender Self-Determination in /at OWS." *PPS* 1
(December 2011): http://www.ppspress.info/documents/PPS_lssue_o1_ Open_Letters_December_2011.pdf.

Golder, Ben, and Peter Fitzpatrick. *Foucault's Law*. London: Routledge, 2009.

Goode, Erica. "After a Prolonged Execution in Ohio, Questions Over 'Cruel and Unusual.'" *The New York Times*, January 17, 2014. http://www .nytimes.com/2014/01/18/us/prolonged-execution-prompts-debate-over -death-penalty-methods.html.

Gorgol, Laura, and Brian Sponsler. *Unlocking Potential: Results of a National Survey of Postsecondary Education in State Prisons*. Washington, DC: Institute for Higher Education Policy, 2011.

Gottschalk, Marie. "The Past, Present, and Future of Mass Incarceration." *Criminology and Public Policy* 10, no. 3 (2011): 483–504.

———. *The Prison and the Gallows: The Politics of Mass Incarceration in America*. New York: Cambridge University Press, 2006.

Graham v. Florida, 560 (U.S. 2010).

Greenberg, David F. *Crime and Punishment: Readings in Marxist Criminology*. Philadelphia: Temple University Press, 1993.

Gregg v. Georgia, 428: 153 (1976).

Guenther, Lisa. *Solitary Confinement: Social Death and Its Afterlives*. Minneapolis: University of Minnesota Press, 2013.

———. "Toward a Critical Phenomenology of Lethal Injection." *New APPS: Art, Politics, Philosophy, Science*, January 27, 2014. http://www.newappsblog .com/2014/01/toward-a-critical-phenomenology-of-lethal-injection.html.

Habermas, Jürgen. *The Inclusion of the Other: Studies in Political Theory*. Edited by Ciaran Cronin and Pablo De Greiff. Cambridge, MA: MIT Press, 1999.

Hallett, Michael. *Private Prisons in America: A Critical Race Perspective*. Chicago: University of Illinois Press, 2006.

———. "Race, Crime, and For-Profit Imprisonment: Social Disorganization as Market Opportunity." *Punishment & Society* 4, no. 3 (2002): 369–393.

Hamann, Trent. "Neoliberalism, Governmentality, and Ethics." *Foucault Studies* (2009).

Han, Sora. "Strict Scrutiny: The Tragedy of Constitutional Law." In *Beyond Biopolitics*, edited by Patricia Clough and Craig Willse. Durham, NC: Duke University Press, 2011.

Hanchard, Michael. "Afro-Modernity: Temporality, Politics, and the African Diaspora." *Public Culture* 11, no. 1 (1999): 245–268.

Harcourt, Bernard E. *Against Prediction: Profiling, Policing, and Punishing in an Actuarial Age*. Chicago: University of Chicago Press, 2007.

———. "Dismantling/Neoliberalism." *Carceral Notebooks* 6 (2010).

———. *The Illusion of Free Markets: Punishment and the Myth of Natural Order*. Cambridge, MA: Harvard University Press, 2011.

Hardt, Michael. "Genet: In the Language of the Enemy." *Yale French Studies Journal* 91 (1997): 64–79.

Harlow, Caroline W. *Education and Correctional Populations*. Washington, DC: U.S. Bureau of Justice Statistics, 2003.

Harrington, Mark. *Tactical Biopolitics*. Cambridge, MA: MIT Press, 2008.

Hartman, Saidiya. *Scenes of Subjection: Terror, Slavery, and Self-Making in Nineteenth-Century America*. New York: Oxford University Press, 1997.

Hartman, Saidiya, and Frank B. Wilderson. "The Position of the Unthought." *Qui Parle* 13, no. 2 (2003): 183–201.

Hedges, Chris. "War is a Hate Crime," *Truth Dig* (October 26, 2009): http://www.truthdig.com/report/item/20091026_war_is_a_hate_crime/.

Heidegger, Martin. *Ontology—The Hermeneutics of Facticity*. Translated by John van Buren. Bloomington: Indiana University Press, 1999.

———. "The Origin of the Work of Art." Translated by A. Hofstadter. In *The Continental Aesthetics Reader*, edited by C. Cazeaux, 79–122. New York: Routledge, 2011.

Heiner, Brady Thomas. "'From the Prison of Slavery to the Slavery of Prison': Angela Y. Davis's *Abolition Democracy*." In *Radical Philosophy Today, Volume 5: Democracy, Racism, Prisons*, edited by Harry van der Linden, 219–227. Philosophy Documentation Center, 2007.

Helliwell, Christine. "'It's Only a Penis': Rape, Feminism, and Difference." *Signs* 25, no. 2 (Spring 2000): 789–816.

Herivel, Tara, and Paul Wright. *Prison Profiteers: Who Makes Money from Mass Incarceration*. New York: The New Press, 2007.

Highleyman, Liz. "Peace Activism and GLBT Rights." *The Gay & Lesbian Review* (September-October 2004): http://www.glreview.com/issues/11.5/11.5_Highleyman.php.

Hing, Julianne. "Who Are Those 'Gangbangers' Obama's So Proud of Deporting?" *Color Lines: News for Action* (October 17, 2012), http://colorlines.com/archives/2012/10/who_are_those_gangbangers_obamas_so_proud_of_deporting.html (accessed January 31, 2013).

Hinsley, F. H. *Sovereignty*. Cambridge: Cambridge University Press, 1986.

Hirsch, Adam Jay. *The Rise of the Penitentiary: Prisons and Punishment in Early America*. New Haven, CT: Yale University Press, 1992.

Hood, Roger, and Carolyn Hoyle. *The Death Penalty: A Worldwide Perspective*, 4th edition. Oxford: Oxford University Press, 2008.

hooks, bell. "Feminism: A Movement to End Sexist Oppression." In *Feminist Theory Reader: Global and Local Perspectives*, edited by Carole R. McCann and Seung Kyung Kim, 51–57. New York: Routledge, 2010.

Horkheimer, Max. *Dawn and Decline.* New York: Seabury Press, 1978.

———. *Eclipse of Reason.* New York: Continuum Press, 2004.

"Hospice and Palliative Care in Prisons." *Special Issues in Corrections.* Long-
mont, CO: National Institute of Corrections Information Center, 1998.

Hugo, Victor. *Écrits sur la peine de mort.* Paris: Éditions Actes/Sud, 1992.

Human Rights Watch. "A Costly Move." June 14, 2011. http://www.hrw.org/
reports/2011/06/14/costly-move.

———. "Israel: Amend 'Anti-Infiltration' Law: Measure Denies Asylum Seekers Protections of Refugee Convention." Press release
(June 10th, 2012): http://www.hrw.org/news/2012/06/10/israel-
amend-anti-infiltration-law.

Husserl, Edmund. *Cartesian Meditations.* Translated by Dorion Cairns. Boston: Kluwer Academic Publishers, 1991.

———. *Crisis of European Sciences and Transcendental Phenomenology.*
Translated by David Carr. Evanston, IL: Northwestern University Press,
1970.

———. *Ideas Pertaining to a Pure Phenomenology and to a Phenomenological Philosophy: Book One.* Translated by F. Kersten. The Hague: Martinus Nijhoff
Publishers, 1983.

———. *Ideas Pertaining to a Pure Phenomenology and to a Phenomenological Philosophy: Book Two.* Translated by R. Rojcewicz and A. Schuwer. Dordrecht:
Kluwer Academic Publishers, 1989.

———. *The Paris Lectures.* Translated by P. Koestenbaum. Dordrecht: Kluwer
Academic Publishers, 1998.

———. "Phenomenological Psychology and Transcendental Phenomenology." In *The Essential Husserl,* edited by D. Welton, 321–336. Bloomington: Indiana University Press, 1999.

———. "A Phenomenology of Internal Time Consciousness." In *The Essential Husserl,* edited by D. Welton, 186–221. Bloomington: Indiana
University Press, 1999.

———. *Thing and Space: Lectures 1907.* Translated by R. Rojcewicz. Dordrecht: Kluwer Academic Publishers, 1997.

Ignatieff, Michael. *A Just Measure of Pain: The Penitentiary and the Industrial
Revolution, 1750–1850.* New York: Pantheon, 1978.

Irigaray, Luce. *Democracy Begins between Two.* Translated by Kirsteen Anderson. New York: Routledge, 2001.

———. *An Ethics of Sexual Difference.* Translated by Carolyn Burke and Gillian C. Gill. Ithaca, NY: Cornell University Press, 1993.

———. *I Love to You: Sketch of a Possible Felicity in History.* Translated by Alison Martin. New York: Routledge, 1996.

———. *Je, Tu, Nous: Toward a Culture of Difference*. Translated by Alison Martin. New York: Routledge, 1993.

———. "The Question of the Other." Translated by Noah Guynn. *Yale French Studies* 87 (1995): 7–19.

———. *Sexes and Genealogies*. Translated by Gillian C. Gill. New York: Columbia University Press, 1993.

———. *Thinking the Difference: For a Peaceful Revolution*. Translated by Karin Montin. New York: Routledge, 1994.

———. *This Sex Which Is Not One*. Translated by Catherine Porter. Ithaca, NY: Cornell University Press, 1985.

Irwin, John. *The Warehouse Prison: Disposal of the New Dangerous Class*. New York: Oxford University Press, 2004.

Irwin, John, et al. "America's One Million Nonviolent Prisoners." *Social Justice* 27, no. 2 (2000): 135–147.

Jackson, George. *Blood in My Eye*. Baltimore: Black Classic Press, 1990.

Jackson, Robert. *Sovereignty*. Malden, MA: Polity, 2007.

James, Joy. *The Angela Y. Davis Reader*. New York: Routledge, 1998.

———. *The New Abolitionists: (Neo)Slave Narratives and Contemporary Prison Writings*. New York: SUNY Press, 2005.

———. *States of Confinement: Policing, Detention, and Prisons*. New York: Palgrave Macmillan, 2002.

———. *Unfinished Liberation: Policing and Imprisonment*. Edited by Joy James. Special issue of *Radical Philosophy Review* 3, no. 1 (2000).

———. *Warfare in the American Homeland*. Durham, NC: Duke University Press, 2007.

Jay, Karla. *Out of the Closets: Voices of Gay Liberation*. New York: New York University Press, 1992.

Johnson, H. McBryde. "The Disability Gulag." *The New York Times*, November 23, 2003.

Kahn, Si, and Elizabeth Minnich. *The Fox in the Henhouse: How Privatization Threatens Democracy*. San Francisco: Berrett-Koehler, 2005.

Kandeswamy, Priya. "State Austerity and the Racial Politics of Same-Sex Marriage in the US." *Sexualities* 11, no. 6 (2008): 706–725.

Kant, Immanuel. *Metaphysics of Morals, in Practical Philosophy*. Edited by Mary Gregor. Cambridge: Cambridge University Press, 1996.

Karlan, Pamela S. "Forum." In *Race, Incarceration, and American Values*, edited by Glenn C. Loury, 41–56. Cambridge, MA: MIT Press, 2008.

Kaufman-Osborn, Timothy. "A Critique of Contemporary Death Penalty Abolitionism." *Punishment & Society* 8, no. 3 (2006).

Keeling, Kara. "Looking for M." *GLQ* 15 (2009).

Kelley, Robin D. G. *Race Rebels: Culture, Politics, and the Black Working Class.* New York: Free Press, 1994.

Kennedy, Randall. *Race, Crime, and the Law.* New York: Random House, 1997.

Kinoti, Kathambi. "Sex Work in Southern Africa: Criminalization Provides Screen for Other Rights Violations." *The Association for Women's Rights in Development:* http://secure1.awid.org/eng/Issues-and-Analysis/Library/Sex-work-in-Southern-Africa-Criminalization-provides-screen-for-other-rights-violations.

Kirchheimer, Otto, and Georg Rusche. *Punishment and Social Structure.* New Brunswick, NJ: Transaction, 2003.

Knopp, Fay Honey. "On Radical Feminism and Abolition." *Peace Review: A Journal of Social Justice* 6, no. 2 (1994): 203–208.

Kolchin, Peter. *American Slavery, 1619–1877.* New York: Hill and Wang, 1993.

Kukorowski, Drew. *The Price to Call Home: State-Sanctioned Monopolization of the Prison Phone Industry.* Northampton, MA: Prison Policy Initiative, 2012.

Kunzel, Regina. *Criminal Intimacy: Prison and the Uneven History of Modern American Sexuality.* Chicago: University of Chicago Press, 2008.

Lattman, Peter. "Former Citigroup Manager Cleared in Mortgage Securities Case." *New York Times,* July 31, 2012.

Leder, Drew. "Imprisoned Bodies: The Life-World of the Incarcerated." *Social Justice* 31, no. 1/2 (2004): 51–66.

———. *The Soul Knows No Bars: Inmates Reflect on Life, Death and Hope.* Lanham, MD: Rowman & Littlefield, 2001.

Legomsky, Stephen H. "The New Path of Immigration Law: Asymmetric Incorporation of Criminal Justice Norms." *Washington and Lee Law Review* 64, no. 2 (2007): 469–528.

Levinas, Emmanuel. "Bad Conscience and the Inexorable." In *Of God Who Comes to Mind.* Translated by Bettina Bergo. Stanford, CA: Stanford University Press, 1998.

———. *Difficult Freedom: Essays on Judaism.* Baltimore: Johns Hopkins University Press, 1990.

———. "Ethics and Politics." In *The Levinas Reader,* edited by Sean Hand. Oxford: Blackwell, 1989.

———. "Notes on Meaning." In *Of God Who Comes to Mind.* Translated by Bettina Bergo. Stanford, CA: Stanford University Press, 1998.

———. *Nine Talmudic Readings.* Bloomington: Indiana University Press, 1990.

———. *Otherwise than Being, or Beyond Essence.* The Hague: Martinus Nijhoff, 1980.

———. "The Rights of Man and the Rights of the Other." In *Outside the Subject*. Stanford, CA: Stanford University Press, 1994.

———. *Time and the Other*. Pittsburgh: Duquesne University Press, 1987.

———. *Totality and Infinity: An Essay on Exteriority*. Pittsburgh: Duquesne University Press, 1969.

Levitt, Ross, and Deborah Feyerick. "Death Penalty States Scramble for Lethal Injection Drugs." *CNN*, November 16, 2013. http://www.cnn.com/2013/11/15/justice/states-lethal-injection-drugs/index.html.

Lichtenstein, Alex. "Good Roads and Chain Gangs in the Progressive South: 'The Negro Convict is a Slave.'" *The Journal of Southern History* 59, no. 1 (1993): 85–110.

———. *Twice the Work of Free Labor: The Political Economy of Convict Labor in the New South*. New York: Verso, 1999.

Lifton, Robert Jay. *Thought Reform and the Psychology of Totalism*. New York: Norton & Company, 1961.

Linder, John F., and Frederick Meyers. "Palliative Care for Prison Inmates: 'Don't Let Me Die in Prison.'" *Journal of the American Medical Association* 298, no. 8 (2007): 894–901.

Linder, John F., Sheila R. Enders, Elizabeth Craig, Joan Richardson, and Frederick J. Meyers. "Hospice Care for the Incarcerated in the United States: An Introduction." *Journal of Palliative Medicine* 5, no. 4 (2002): 549–552.

Linebaugh, Peter. *London Hanged: Crime and Civil Society in the Eighteenth Century*. New York: Verso, 2003.

"A Living Death: Life without Parole for Nonviolent Offences." 2013. https://www.aclu.org/criminal-law-reform/living-death-life-without-parole-nonviolent-offenses-0 (accessed January 24, 2014).

Lockyer v. Andrade, 538: 63 (U.S. 2003).

Lopez, Adriana Garriga. "Boricuas ACTing UP in New York and San Juan: Diasporic Puerto Rican HIV/AIDS Activism and Anthropology." *New Proposals: Journal of Marxism and Interdisciplinary Inquiry* 2, no. 2 (2009).

Loury, Glenn C. *Race, Incarceration, and American Values*. Cambridge, MA: MIT Press, 2008.

Maimonides. *The Commandments*. Translated by Charles B. Chavel. Brooklyn, NY: Soncino Pr Ltd, 1984.

Malpas, Jeff. "Objectivity and Self-Disclosedness." In *Art and Phenomenology*, edited by J. D. Parry, 54–76. New York: Routledge, 2011.

Mancini, Matthew. *One Dies, Get Another: Convict Leasing in the American South, 1866–1928*. Columbia: University of South Carolina Press, 1996.

Manza, Jeff, and Christopher Uggen. *Locked Out: Felon Disenfranchisement and American Democracy*. New York: Oxford University Press, 2007.

Marable, Manning, and Leith Mullings. *Let Nobody Turn Us Around: Voices of Resistance, Reform and Renewal: An African American Anthology*. Lanham, MD: Rowman & Littlefield, 2009.

Marcus, Sharon. "Fighting Words, Fighting Bodies: A Theory and Politics of Rape Prevention." In *Feminist Theorize the Political*, edited by Judith Butler and Joan W. Scott, 385–403. New York: Routledge, 1992.

Margulies, Peter. "Judging Terror in the 'Zone of Twilight': Exigency, Institutional Equity, and Procedure after September 11." *Boston University Law Review* 84 (2004): 418–419.

Martinot, Steve. *The Rule of Racialization: Class, Identity, Governance*. Philadelphia: Temple University Press, 2003.

Marx, Karl. *Capital*, volume 1. Translated by Ben Fowkes. New York: Vintage Books, 1977.

———. *Das Kapital: Band I*. In *Karl Marx und Friedrich Engels Werke*, volume 23 of 42. Berlin: Dietz Verlag, 1962.

———. "Wage Labour and Capital." In *Karl Marx and Frederick Engels Collected Works*, volume 9 of 50. Edited by Philip S. Forner, et al. New York: International Publishers, 1996.

Matsuda, Mari J. "Looking to the Bottom: Critical Legal Studies and Reparations." *Harvard Civil Rights–Civil Liberties Law Review* 22 (1987): 323–400.

Mauer, Marc. "The Changing Racial Dynamics of the War on Drugs." http://sentencingproject.org/doc/dp_raceanddrugs.pdf (accessed January 18, 2013).

———. "Voting Behind Bars: An Argument for Voting by Prisoners." *Howard Law Journal* 54, no. 3 (2011): 549–566.

Mauer, Marc, and Ryan S. King. "Uneven Justice: State Rates of Incarceration by Race and Ethnicity." *The Sentencing Project*, 2007. http://www.sentencingproject.org/detail/publication.cfm?publication_id=167 (accessed January 29, 2013).

Maull, Fleet. "The Prison Hospice Movement." *Explore* 1, no. 6 (2005): 477–479.

McBride, Keally. "California Penality: The End/Price of the Neoliberal Exception." *Carceral Notebooks* 6 (2010).

McCleskey v. Kemp, 481: 279 (U.S. Supreme Court 1987).

McClintock, Anne. *Imperial Leather*. New York: Routledge, 1995.

McLennan, Rebecca M. *The Crisis of Imprisonment: Protest, Politics, and the Making of the American Penal State*. New York: Cambridge University Press, 2008.

McLeod, Owen. "On the Comparative Element of Justice." In *Desert and Justice*, edited by Serena Olsaretti, 123–144. Oxford: Oxford University Press, 2003.

McRuer, R. *Crip Theory: Cultural Signs of Queerness and Disability*. New York: New York University Press, 2006.

McVay, Douglas A. "Prisons and Drug Offenders: Federal-Specific Data." http://www.drugwarfacts.org/cms/Prisons_and_Drugs#Federal-Data (accessed January 18, 2013).

McWhorter, Ladelle. *Racism and Sexual Oppression in Anglo-America: A Genealogy*. Bloomington: Indiana University Press, 2009.

Melossi, Dario. "The Penal Question in 'Capital.'" *Crime and Social Justice*, no. 5 (Spring-Summer 1976): 26–33.

Melossi, Dario, and Massimo Pavarini. *The Prison and the Factory: Origins of the Penitentiary System*. Translated by Glynic Cousin. London: Macmillan, 1981.

Mendieta, Eduardo. "Penalized Spaces: The Ghetto as Prison and the Prison as Ghetto." *City* 10 (2007): 384–390.

———. "Plantations, Ghettos, Prisons: US Racial Geographies." *Philosophy & Geography* 7 (2004): 43–59.

Meranze, Michael. *Laboratories of Virtue: Punishment, Revolution, and Authority in Philadelphia, 1760–1835*. Chapel Hill: University of North Carolina Press, 1996.

Merleau-Ponty, Maurice. "Cézanne's Doubt." Translated by H. Dreyfus and P. A. Dreyfus. In *Sense and Non-Sense*, 9–25. Evanston, IL: Northwestern University Press, 1964.

———. *Phenomenology of Perception*. Translated by C. Smith. New York: Routledge, 2002.

———. *Phenomenology of Perception*. Translated by Donald Landes. New York: Routledge, 2012.

———. *The Primacy of Perception*. Edited by J. Edie. Evanston, IL: Northwestern University Press, 1964.

———. *Sense and Non-Sense*. Translated by H. Dreyfus and P. A. Dreyfus. Evanston, IL: Northwestern University Press, 1964.

———. *The Visible and the Invisible*. Translated by A. Lingis. Evanston, IL: Northwestern University Press, 1968.

Messerschmidt, James W. "Masculinities, Crime, and Prison." In *Prison Masculinities*, edited by Don Sabo, Terry A. Kupers, and Willie London, 67–72. Philadelphia: Temple University Press, 2001.

Miller v. Alabama, 567 (U.S. 2012).

Miller, J. G. *Last One over the Wall: The Massachusetts Experiment in Closing Reform Schools*. Columbus: Ohio State University Press, 1991.

Miller, Teresa A. "Citizenship & Severity: Recent Immigration Reforms and the New Penology." *Georgetown Immigration Law Journal* 17 (2003): 611–666.

Mills, Charles W. *The Racial Contract*. Ithaca, NY: Cornell University Press, 1997.

Mohajer, Nasser, ed. *The Book of Prison Vol. II*. Berkeley: Noghteh Books, 1998.

Mohler, Henry Calvin. "Convict Labor Policies." *Journal of the American Institute of Criminal Law and Criminology* 15, no. 4 (1925): 530–597.

Montesquieu, Charles de Secondat baron de. *The Spirit of the Laws*. Edited by Anne M. Cohler, Basia Carolyn Miller, and Harold Samuel Stone. Cambridge: Cambridge University Press, 1989.

Motluk, Alison. "Execution by Injection Far from Painless." *New Scientist*, April 14, 2005. http://www.newscientist.com/article/dn7269-execution-by-injectionfar-from-painless.html (accessed February 18, 2013).

Muhammad, Khalil Gibran. *The Condemnation of Blackness: Race, Crime, and the Making of Modern Urban America*. Cambridge, MA: Harvard University Press, 2010.

Muñoz, José Esteban. *Cruising Utopia*. New York: New York University Press, 2010.

Nair, Yasmin. "How to Make Prisons Disappear: Queer Immigrants, the Shackles of Love, and the Invisibility of the Prison Industrial Complex." In *Captive Genders: Trans Embodiment and the Prison Industrial Complex*, ed. Eric A. Stanley and Nat Smith. Oakland, CA: AK Press, 2011.

Naas, Michael. "Philosophy and the Death Penalty." Presented at the Derrida Seminar Translation Project, Caen, France, Summer 2011. http://derridaseminars.org/pdfs/2011/2011%20Presentation%20Naas.pdf.

National Prison Hospice Association. http://npha.org.

Navak, Ziba. *Siba-Zainab*. Germany: Nima Verlag, 2007.

Negri, Antonio. *Insurgencies: Constituent Power and the Modern State*. Minneapolis: University of Minnesota Press, 1999.

Nellis, Ashley. "Throwing Away the Key: The Expansion of Life without Parole Sentences in the United States." *Federal Sentencing Reporter* 23 (2010).

Nellis, Ashley, and Ryan S. King. "No Exit: The Expanding Use of Life Sentences in America." Washington, DC: Sentencing Project, 2009.

Neocleous, Mark. "War on Waste: Law, Original Accumulation and the Violence of Capital." *Science & Society* 75 (2011): 506–528.

Ngai, Mai M. *Impossible Subjects: Illegal Aliens and the Making of Modern America*. Princeton, NJ: Princeton University Press, 2005.

Nietzsche, Friedrich. *On the Genealogy of Morality*. Edited by Keith Answell-Pearson. Translated by Carol Dieth. Cambridge: Cambridge University Press, 1994 [1887].

Nye, Robert. "Two Capital Punishment Debates in France: 1908 and 1981." *Historical Reflections / Réflexions Historiques* 29, no. 2 (2003).

Obadele, Prince Imari A. "Killers." In *The New Abolitionists: (Neo)Slave Narratives and Contemporary Prison Writings*, edited by Joy James, 115–116. Albany: State University of New York Press, 2005.

Ocen, Priscilla A. "Punishing Pregnancy: Race, Incarceration, and the Shackling of Pregnant Prisoners." *California Law Review* 100 (2012): 1239–1311.

Ogletree, Charles J. Jr., and Austin Sarat, eds. *Life without Parole: America's New Death Penalty?* New York: New York University Press, 2012.

Oliver, Kelly. *Technologies of Life and Death: From Cloning to Capital Punishment*. New York: Fordham University Press, 2013.

———. "Vision, Recognition, and a Passion for the Elements." In *Returning to Irigaray: Feminist Philosophy, Politics, and the Question of Unity*, edited by Maria C. Cimitile and Elaine P. Miller, 121–135. Albany: State University of New York Press, 2007.

Oshinsky, David M. *Worse Than Slavery: Parchment Farm and the Ordeal of Jim Crow Justice*. New York: Free Press, 1996.

Page, Joshua. "Eliminating the Enemy: The Import of Denying Prisoners Access to Higher Education in Clinton's America." *Punishment & Society* 6 (2004): 357–378.

Passel, Jeffrey S., D'Vera Cohn, and Ana Gonzalez-Barrera. "Population Decline of Unauthorized Immigrants Stalls, May Have Reversed." Pew Research Center, September 23, 2013. http://www.pewhispanic.org/files/2013/09/Unauthorized-Sept-2013-FINAL.pdf.

Pateman, Carol. *The Sexual Contract*. Stanford, CA: Stanford University Press, 1988.

Patterson, Orlando. *Slavery and Social Death: A Comparative Study*. Cambridge, MA: Harvard University Press, 1982.

Pemberton, Joanne. *Sovereignty: Interpretations*. London: Palgrave Macmillan, 2009.

Perea, Juan F. "The Black/White Binary Paradigm of Race: The 'Normal Science' of American Racial Thought." *California Law Review* 85 (1997): 1213–1221.

Perelman, Michael. *The Invention of Capitalism: Classical Political Economy and the Secret History of Primitive Accumulation*. Durham, NC: Duke University Press, 2000.

Petroski, William. "Hospice Eases Inmates' Deaths." *Des Moines Register*, 2005. Republished http://www.prisonterminal.com/essays%20hospice%20eases.html (accessed January 29, 2013).

Petteruti, Amanda, and Paul Ashton. *Gaming the System: How the Political Strategies of Private Prison Companies Promote Ineffective Incarceration Policies*. Washington, DC: Justice Policy Institute, 2011.

Pettit, Becky, and Bruce Western. "Mass Imprisonment and the Life Course: Race and Class Inequality in U.S. Incarceration." *American Sociological Review* 69, no. 2 (April 1, 2004): 151–169.

Pew Center on the States. "State of Recidivism: The Revolving Door of America's Prisons." April 2011. www.pewtrusts.org/uploadedFiles/www pewtrustsorg/Reports/ sentencing_and_corrections/State_Recidivism _Revolving_Door_America_Prisons%20.pdf.

Piché, Justin, and Mike Larsen. "The Moving Targets of Penal Abolitionism: ICOPA, Past, Present and Future." *Contemporary Justice Review* 13, no. 4 (2010).

"Pinkwatching Israel." http://www.pinkwatchingisrael.com/ (accessed February 3, 2013).

Posner, Eric A., and Adrian Vermeule. *Terror in the Balance: Security, Liberty, and the Courts*. Kindle Version. Oxford: Oxford University Press, 2007.

Posner, Richard A. *Not a Suicide Pact: The Constitution in a Time of National Emergency*. Kindle Edition. Oxford: Oxford University Press, 2006.

Povinelli, Elizabeth. *The Cunning of Recognition*. Durham, NC: Duke University Press, 2002.

Prison Radio. "Memories of Maroon by Mumia Abu-Jamal." Creative Commons Licensed. http://www.prisonradio.org/media/audio/memories -maroon-mumia-abu-jamal.

Puar, Jasbir. "Prognosis Time: Towards a Geopolitics of Affect, Debility and Capacity." *Women and Performance: A Journal of Feminist Theory* 19, no. 2 (2009): 161–172.

Rabinowitz, Howard. *Race Relations in the Urban South, 1865–1890*. Urbana: University of Illinois Press, 1980.

Raha, M. *Haghighat Sadeh (Simple Truths): The Memoirs of Women's Prisons in the Islamic Republic of Iran*. Books I, II, and III. Hannover: The Independent Organization of Democratic Iranian Women in Hannover, Germany, 1992.

Ratcliff, Margaret. "Dying Inside the Walls." *Journal of Palliative Medicine* 3, no. 4 (2000): 509–511.

Re, Lucia. "Structural Discrimination and Color-blindness in United States and European Prison Systems." *Jura Gentium: Rivista di filosofia del diritto internazionale e della politica globale* 3, no. 1 (2007). http://www.juragentium .unifi.it/forum/race/en/re.htm (accessed December 10, 2011).

Read, Jason. "A Genealogy of Homo-Economicus: Neoliberalism and the Production of Subjectivity." *Foucault Studies* 6 (2009).

Reiman, Jeffrey, and Paul Leighton. *The Rich get Richer and the Poor get Prison: Ideology, Class, and Criminal Justice*. New York: Wiley Publishing, 1979.

Reiter, Keramet Ann. "The Most Restrictive Alternative: A Litigation History of Solitary Confinement in U.S. Prisons, 1960–2006." *Studies in Law, Politics, and Society* 57 (2012): 71–124.

Rhodes, Lorna. *Total Confinement: Madness and Reason in the Maximum Security Prison*. Berkeley: University of California Press, 2004.

Richie, Beth. *Arrested Justice: Black Women, Violence, and America's Prison Nation*. New York: New York University Press, 2012.

———. *Compelled to Crime: The Gender Entrapment of Battered Black Women*. New York: Routledge, 1996.

Ridgeway, James. "The Other Death Sentence." *Mother Jones*, September 2012. http://www.motherjones.com/politics/2012/09/massachusetts-elderly-prisoners-cost-compassionate-release (accessed January 29, 2013).

Rivera, Sylvia. "Queens in Exile, the Forgotten Ones." In *GenderQueer: Voices From Beyond the Sexual Binary*, edited by Joan Nestle, Clare Howell, and Riki Wilchins, 67–85. London: Alyson Books, 2002.

Roback, Jennifer. "Southern Labor Law in the Jim Crow Era: Exploitative or Competitive?" *University of Chicago Law Review* 51 (1984): 1161–1192.

Robinson, Russell. "Masculinity as Prison: Sexual Identity, Race, and Incarceration." *California Law Review* 99 (2011): 1309–1408.

Robbins, Jill, ed. *Is It Righteous to Be?: Interviews with Emmanuel Levinas*. Stanford, CA: Stanford University Press, 2001.

Roberts, Dorothy E. "Constructing a Criminal Justice System Free of Racial Bias: An Abolitionist Framework." *Columbia Human Rights Law Review* 39 (2007): 261–285.

Roberts, Sam. "Rockefeller on the Attica Raid, From Boastful to Subdued." *The New York Times*, September 13, 2011: http://www.nytimes.com/2011/09/13/nyregion/rockefeller-initially-boasted-to-nixon-about-attica-raid.html?pagewanted=all.

Rodriguez, Dylan. *Forced Passages: Imprisoned Radical Intellectuals and the U.S. Prison Regime*. Minneapolis: University of Minnesota Press, 2006.

Ross, Luana. *Inventing the Savage*. Austin: University of Texas Press, 1998.

Rothman, David J. *The Discovery of the Asylum: Social Order and Disorder in the New Republic*. Boston: Little Brown, 1971.

Ruddell, Rick. *America Behind Bars: Trends in Imprisonment, 1950–2000*. New York: LFB Scholarly Publishing, 2004.

Ruffin v. Commonwealth of Virginia, 62 Va. 790 (1871).

Sabo, Don, Terry A. Kupers, and Willie London. "Gender and the Politics of Punishment." In *Prison Masculinities*, edited by Don Sabo, Terry A. Kupers, and Willie London, 3–18. Philadelphia: Temple University Press, 2001.

Saperstein, Aliya, Andrew M. Penner, and Jessica M. Kizer. "The Criminal
    Justice System and the Racialization of Perceptions." *The Annals of the
    American Academy of Political and Social Science* 651, no. 1 (2014): 104–121.

Sarat, Austin. "Killing Me Softly: Capital Punishment and the Technolo-
    gies for Taking Life." In *Pain, Death, and the Law*, edited by Austin Sarat,
    43–70. Ann Arbor: University of Michigan Press, 2001. http://www.press
    .umich.edu/11377/pain_death_and_the_law.

Sarat, Austin, and Jennifer Culbert. *States of Violence: War, Capital Punishment,
    and Letting Die*. Cambridge: Cambridge University Press, 2009.

Sarat, Austin, and Jürgen Martschukat. *Is the Death Penalty Dying?* Cam-
    bridge: Cambridge University Press, 2011.

Sarat, Austin, and Karl Shoemaker. *Who Deserves to Die?: Constructing the
    Executable Subject*. Amherst: University of Massachusetts Press, 2011.

Sarkoohi, Faraj. "A Letter from Prison." *Payvand*, February 1, 1997.

Sassen, Saskia. *Territory, Authority, Rights: From Medieval to Global Assem-
    blages*. Princeton, NJ: Princeton University Press, 2006.

Schlosser, Eric. "The Prison-Industrial Complex." *The Atlantic Monthly*,
    December 1998, 51–77.

Schmitt, Carl. *The Concept of the Political*. Translated by George Schwab. Chi-
    cago: University of Chicago Press, 2007.

Sellin, J. Thorsten. *Slavery and the Penal System*. New York: Elsevier, 1976.

Selman, Donna, and Paul Leighton. *Punishment for Sale: Private Prisons, Big
    Business, and the Incarceration Binge*. Lanham, MD: Rowman & Littlefield
    Publishers, 2010.

Sentencing Project. *Fact Sheet: Parents in Prison*. Washington, DC: The
    Sentencing Project, 2012. http://www.sentencingproject.org/doc/
    publications/cc_Parents%20in%20Prison_Factsheet_9.24sp.pdf (accessed
    November 27, 2012).

Serving Life. Dir. Lisa Cohen. Oprah Winfrey Network Documentary Club,
    2011.

Sexton, Jared. *Amalgamation Schemes*. Minneapolis: University of Minnesota
    Press, 2008.

Shakur, Assata. "Women in Prison: How We Are." In *The New Abolition-
    ists: (Neo)Slave Narratives and Contemporary Prison Writings*, edited by Joy
    James, 79–90. Albany: State University of New York Press, 2005.

Shoatz, Russell "Maroon." *Maroon the Implacable: The Collected Writings of
    Russell Maroon Shoatz*. Oakland, CA: PM Press, 2013.

Sylvia Rivera Law Project. "Gender Identity Disorder and the Prison-
    Industrial Complex: Reflections from the Sylvia Rivera Law Project."
    The Abolitionist 19 (February 2013).

Simon, Jonathan. *Governing through Crime: How the War on Crime Transformed American Democracy and Created a Culture of Fear.* Oxford: Oxford University Press, 2007.

———. "Janus Faced Leviathan: California's Prisons and the Universities as Two Faces of State Power." *Carceral Notebooks* 6 (2010).

Simon, Jonathan, and Christina Spaulding. "Tokens of Our Esteem: Aggravating Factors in the Era of Deregulated Death Penalties." In *The Killing State: Capital Punishment in Law, Politics, and Culture,* edited by Austin Sarat, 81–113. Oxford: Oxford University Press, 1999.

Simpson, Audra, and Andrea Smith, eds. *Theorizing Native Studies.* Durham, NC: Duke University Press, 2014.

Smith, Andrea. "Indigeneity, Settler Colonialism, White Supremacy." In *Racial Formations in the 21st Century,* edited by Daniel Martinez et al. Berkeley: University of California Press, 2012.

———. "The Moral Limits of the Law." *Settler Colonialism Studies* 2, no. 2 (2012). http://dx.doi.org/10.7790/scs.v2i2.334.

Smith, Andrea, Beth Richie, Julia Sudbury, Janelle White, and the INCITE! Anthology co-editors. *Introduction to Color of Violence: The INCITE! Anthology, edited by INCITE! Women of Color Against Violence,* 1–10. Cambridge: South End Press, 2006.

Smith, Peter Scharff. "The Effects of Solitary Confinement on Prison Inmates." *Crime and Justice* 34, no. 1 (2006): 441–528.

Soguk, Nevzat. "Transnational/Transborder Bodies: Resistance, Accommodation, and Exile in Refugee and Migration Movements on the U.S.-Mexican Border." In *Challenging Boundaries: Global Flows, Territorial Identities,* edited by Michael Shapiro and Hayward Alker, 285–325. Minneapolis: University of Minnesota Press, 1996.

Solinger, Rickie, et al. *Interrupted Life: Experiences of Incarcerated Women in the United States.* Berkeley: University of California Press, 2010.

Soss, Joe, Richard C. Fording, and Sanford Schram. *Disciplining the Poor: Neoliberal Paternalism and the Persistent Power of Race.* Chicago: University of Chicago Press, 2011.

South African National AIDS Council. *National Strategic Plan on HIV, STIs, and TB, 2012–2016,* Republic of South Africa, http://www.doh.gov.za/docs/stratdocs/2012/NSPfull.pdf (accessed January 30, 2013).

Spade, Dean. *Normal Life: Administrative Violence, Critical Trans Politics and the Limits of Law.* Cambridge, MA: South End Press, 2011.

———. "The Only Way to End Racialized Gender Violence in Prisons is to End Prisons: A Response to Russell Robinson's 'Masculinity as Prison.'" *California Law Review* 3 (Dec. 2012).

Spillers, Hortense. "Mama's Baby, Papa's Maybe: An American Grammar Book." *Diacritics* 17, no. 2 (1987).

Spruyt, Hendrik. *The Sovereign State and Its Competitors*. Princeton, NJ: Princeton University Press, 1996.

Stanley, Eric A., and Nat Smith, eds. *Captive Genders: Trans Embodiment and the Prison Industrial Complex*. Oakland, CA: AK Press, 2011.

"State by State Database." *Death Penalty Information Center*. http://www .deathpenaltyinfo.org/state_by_state (accessed January 28, 2014).

Stockdill, Brett C. *Activism Against AIDS: At the Intersections of Sexuality, Race, Gender, and Class*. Boulder, CO: Lynne Rienner Press, 2003.

Steiker, Carol S. "Capital Punishment and Contingency." *Harvard Law Review* 125 (2012): 760–787.

Stone, Alison. "Towards a Genealogical Feminism: A Reading of Judith Butler's Political Thought." *Contemporary Political Theory* 4, no. 1 (2005).

Stone, Geoffrey. *Perilous Times*. New York: W. W. Norton, 2005.

Struckman-Johnson, Cindy, and David Struckman-Johnson. "Sexual Coercion Reported by Women in Three Midwestern Prisons." *The Journal of Sex Research* 39, no. 3 (2002): 217–227.

Stumpf, Juliet. "The Crimmigration Crisis: Immigrants, Crime, and Sovereign Power." *American University Law Review* 56, no. 2 (2006): 367–419.

Sudbury, Julia. *Global Lockdown: Race, Gender, and the Prison-Industrial Complex*. New York: Routledge, 2005.

———. "Maroon Abolitionists: Black Gender-Oppressed Activists in the Anti-Prison Movement in the U.S. and Canada." *Meridians: Feminism, Race, Transnationalism* 9, no. 1 (2008): 1–29.

Sullivan, Laura. "How Corporate Interests Got SB 1070 Passed." *National Public Radio*, November 9, 2010. www.npr.org/2010/11/09/131191523/ how-corporate-interests-got-sb-1070-passed (accessed January 20, 2013).

———. "Prison Economics Help Drive Arizona Immigration Law." *National Public Radio*, October 28, 2010. http://www.npr.org/2010/10/28/ 130833741/prison-economics-help-drive-ariz-immigration-law (accessed January 20, 2013).

Swaaningen, René van, and Herman Bianchi, eds. *Abolitionism: Towards a Non-Repressive Approach to Crime*. Amsterdam: Free University Press, 1985.

Talavera, Victor, Guillerma Gina Núñez-Mchiri, and Josiah Heyman. "Deportation in the U.S-Mexico Borderlands: Anticipation, Experience, and Memory." In *The Deportation Regime: Sovereignty, Space, and the Freedom of Movement*, edited by Nicholas De Genova and Nathalie Mae Peutz, 166–195. Durham, NC: Duke University Press, 2010.

Tarter, Michele L., and Richard Bell, eds. *Buried Lives: Incarcerated in Early America*. Athens: University of Georgia Press, 2012.

Taylor, Chloë. "Foucault, Feminism, and Sex Crimes." *Hypatia* 24, no. 4 (2009): 1–25.

Taylor, Quintard, ed. "Mississippi Black Codes (1866)." *African American History: Primary Documents.* http://www.blackpast.org/?q=primary/1866 -mississippi-black-codes.

Thompson, A. Siobhan. "Caring for Prisoner Inmates the Hospice Way." *Illness, Crisis and Loss* 17, no. 4 (2009): 363–378.

Thompson, E. P. *Customs in Common.* London: Merlin Press, 2009.

Thompson, Heather Ann. "Rethinking Working Class Struggle through the Lens of the Carceral State: Toward a Labor History of Inmates and Guards." *Labor: Studies in Working-Class History of the Americas* 8, no. 3 (2011): 15–45.

———. "Why Mass Incarceration Matters: Rethinking Crisis, Decline, and Transformation in Postwar American History." *Journal of American History* 98, no. 3 (2010): 703–758.

Timerman, Jacob. *Prisoner Without a Name, Cell Without a Number.* New York: Vantage Books, 1981.

Tucker, Robert C., ed. *The Marx-Engels Reader.* New York: Norton, 1978.

Uggen, Christopher, Sarah Shannon, and Jeff Manza. *State-Level Estimates of Felon Disenfranchisement in the United States, 2012.* Washington, DC: The Sentencing Project, 2012. http://sentencingproject.org/doc/publications/ fd_State_Level_Estimates_of_Felon_Disen_2010.pdf (accessed February 7, 2013).

U.S. Bureau of Justice Statistics Bulletin. NCJ 219416. "Prisoners in 2006." December 2007. http://www.bjs.gov/content/pub/pdf/p06.pdf.

"US Rates of Incarceration: A Global Perspective." 2006. http://www .nccdglobal.org/sites/default/files/publication_pdf/factsheet-us -incarceration.pdf (accessed January 18, 2013).

Van den Haag, Ernst. "The Ultimate Punishment: A Defense." *Harvard Law Review* 99, no. 7 (1986): 1662–1669.

Vidler, Anthony. "Spatial Violence." *Assemblage,* no. 20 (April 1993): 84–85.

Vitulli, Elias Walker. "Queering the Carceral: Intersecting Queer/Trans Studies and Critical Prison Studies." *GLQ: A Journal of Lesbian and Gay Studies* 19, no. 1 (2012).

Wacquant, Loïc. "Class, Race & Hyperincarceration in Revanchist America." *Daedalus* 139, no. 3 (2010): 74–90.

———. "Crafting the Neoliberal State: Workfare, Prisonfare, and Social Insecurity." *Sociological Forum* 25 (2010): 197–220.

———. "Deadly Symbiosis: When Ghetto and Prison Meet and Mesh." *Punishment & Society* 3 (2001): 95–134.

———. "From Slavery to Mass Incarceration: Rethinking the 'Race Question' in the US." *New Left Review* 13 (2002): 41–60.

———. "The New 'Peculiar Institution': On the Prison as Surrogate Ghetto." *Theoretical Criminology* 4 (2000): 377–389.

———. "The Penalisation of Poverty and the Rise of Neo-Liberalism." *European Journal on Criminal Policy and Research* 9, no. 4 (2001).

———. "Prisoner Reentry as Myth and Ceremony." *Dialectical Anthropology* 34, no. 4 (December 2010): 605–620.

———. *Punishing the Poor: The Neoliberal Government of Social Insecurity*. Durham, NC: Duke University Press, 2009.

———. "Three Steps to a Historical Anthropology of Actually Existing Neoliberalism." *Social Anthropology* 20, no. 1 (2012).

Walmsley, Roy. *World Prison Population List*, 9th edition. London, UK: International Centre for Prison Studies, King's College, 2010: http://www.idcr.org.uk/wp-content/uploads/2010/09/WPPL-9-22.pdf.

Walshe, Sadhbh. "When Prison Illness Becomes a Death Sentence." *The Guardian*, February 2012. http://www.guardian.co.uk/commentisfree/cifamerica/2012/feb/16/when-prison-illness-becomes-death-sentence (accessed January, 29 2013).

Ward, Geoff. *The Black Child-Savers: Racial Democracy and Juvenile Justice*. Chicago: University of Chicago Press, 2012.

Warren, Jennifer. "One in 100: Behind Bars in America 2008." *Public Safety Performance Project*. Pew Center, 2008.

Waselchuk, Lori, and Lawrence N. Powell. *Grace Before Dying*. Brooklyn, NY: Umbrage Editions, 2011.

Weheliye, Alexander. "After Man." *American Literary History* 20 (2008).

Wells-Barnett, Ida B. *The Reason Why the Colored American is Not in the World's Columbian Exhibition*. Reprinted in *The Selected Works of Ida B. Wells-Barnett*. 1893. Oxford University Press, reprint 1991.

Wessler, Seth Freed, and Julianne Hing. "Torn Apart: Struggling to Stay Together after Deportation." In *Beyond Walls and Cages: Prisons, Borders, and Global Crisis*, edited by Jenna M. Loyd, Matt Mitchelson, and Andrew Burridge, 152–162. Athens: University of Georgia Press, 2012.

West v. Schofield, 380 SW 3d 105 (Court of Appeals 2012).

Western, Bruce. *Punishment and Inequality in America*. New York: Russell Sage, 2006.

Wilderson, Frank B. "The Prison Slave as Hegemony's (Silent) Scandal." *Social Justice* 30, no. 2 (2003): 18–27.

———. *Red, White, and Black: Cinema and the Structure of U.S. Antagonisms*. Durham, NC: Duke University Press, 2010.

Wolff, Nancy, Cynthia L. Blitz, Jing Shi, Ronet Bachman, and Jane A. Siegel. "Sexual Violence Inside Prisons: Rates of Victimization." *Journal of*

Urban Health: Bulletin of the New York Academy of Medicine 83, no. 5 (2006): 835–848.

Wolff, Robert Paul, Barrington Moore Jr., and Herbert Marcuse. *A Critique of Pure Tolerance*. Boston: Beacon Press, 1969.

Wood, Ellen Meiksins. *The Origin of Capital: A Longer View*. New York: Verso, 2002.

Yoo, John. Memorandum for William J. Hayes, US Department of Justice 79 (March 14, 2003). www.aclu.org/pdfs/safefree/yoo_army_torture_memo .pdf.

Yost, Benjamin S. "Responsibility and Revision: A Levinasian Argument for the Abolition of Capital Punishment." *Continental Philosophy Review* 44 (2011): 41–64.

Young, Iris Marion. *Justice and the Politics of Difference*. Princeton, NJ: Princeton University Press, 1990.

Ziarek, Ewa Plonowska. *An Ethics of Dissensus: Postmodernity, Feminism, and the Politics of Radical Democracy*. Stanford, CA: Stanford University Press, 2001.

Ziarek, Ewa Plonowska, and Catherine Malabou. "Negativity, Unhappiness or Felicity: On Irigaray's Dialectical Culture of Sexual Difference." *L'Esprit Créateur* 52, no. 3 (Fall 2012): 11–25.

ABU ALI ABDUR'RAHMAN is a survivor of domestic violence and prolonged sexual abuse in prison. He is of tsa la gi (Cherokee), Irish (Celtic), and Haitian descent. He has been on death row in Tennessee since 1987.

GEOFF ADELSBERG is a graduate student in philosophy at Vanderbilt University writing his dissertation on the intersections of philosophy of race, nonretributive conceptions of justice, and arguments for the abolition of the death penalty. Since 2012, he has been a participant in the REACH Coalition philosophy reading group on death row at Riverbend Prison in Nashville, Tennessee.

LIAT BEN-MOSHE is assistant professor of disability studies at the University of Toledo. Her recent work examines the connections between prison abolition and deinstitutionalization in the fields of intellectual disabilities and mental health in the United States. Ben-Moshe is the co-editor of *Disability Incarcerated: Imprisonment and Disability in the United States and Canada* (Palgrave Macmillan, 2014) as well as special issues of *Women, Gender and Families of Color* on disability (Spring 2014) and *Disability Studies Quarterly* on disability in Israel/Palestine (Summer 2007). She is the author of articles and book chapters on such topics as deinstitutionalization and incarceration; the politics of abolition; disability, anti-capitalism, and anarchism; queerness and disability; inclusive pedagogy; academic repression; representations of disability; and critiques of the occupation of Palestine.

ANDREW DILTS is assistant professor of political theory in the Department of Political Science at Loyola Marymount University. He is the author of *Punishment and Inclusion: Race, Membership, and the Limits of American Liberalism* (Fordham University Press, 2014). He has also published scholarly articles in *Political Theory*, *Foucault Studies*, *Disability Studies Quarterly*, *New Political Science*, *PhiloSOPHIA*, and *The Carceral Notebooks*. He is currently at work on a study of Michel Foucault's thought in relation to neoliberal economic theories of subjectivity, prison abolition, critical race theory, and queer theory.

Che Gossett is a black gender queer and femme fabulous writer and activist. They are a contributor to *Captive Genders: Trans Embodiment and the Prison Industrial Complex* (eds. Nat Smith and Eric Stanley) and *The Transgender Studies Reader v. II* (eds. Aren Azuira and Susan Stryker). This past summer, they had the honor of being part of a phenomenal delegation of archivists and librarians to Palestine. They are currently working on a biography of queer of color AIDS activist Kiyoshi Kuromiya.

Lisa Guenther is associate professor of philosophy at Vanderbilt University and a member of REACH Coalition, an organization for reciprocal education based on Tennessee's death row. She is the author of *Solitary Confinement: Social Death and its Afterlives* (University of Minnesota Press, 2013).

Ami Harbin is assistant professor of philosophy and women and gender studies at Oakland University (Michigan). Her main research interests are in feminist philosophy, bioethics, and moral psychology.

Brady Heiner is assistant professor of philosophy at California State University–Fullerton, specializing in the areas of critical theory and ethics. His work has been published in *States of Confinement*, *Radical Philosophy Review*, *Continental Philosophy Review*, *differences: A Journal of Feminist Cultural Studies*, *City*, and *Social Justice*. He is currently writing a book titled *Mass Incarceration and the Unfinished Project of American Abolition*. Heiner is on the Inside-Out Prison Exchange Program National Steering Committee and the Steering Committee of the National Prison Higher Education Association. He works in various ways to expand higher educational opportunities for currently and formerly incarcerated individuals, particularly in the greater Los Angeles metropolitan area.

Joy James organized the prototype for Critical Resistance in 1998, together with student activists at CU–Boulder. Their conference papers became the collection *States of Confinement* (2000). James is editor of the anthologies *The New Abolitionists* (2005), *Imprisoned Intellectuals*, and *Warfare in the American Homeland*. Her most recent book is *Seeking the Beloved Community* (2013). James is F. C. Oakley 3rd Century Professor at Williams College where she teaches in humanities, Africana studies, and political science.

Julia Kristeva is professor emeritus at the University of Paris Diderot-Paris 7. She is the author of thirty works including, among others, *Revolu-*

tion in Poetic Language, Tales of Love, Black Sun, Hate and Forgiveness, The Incredible Need to Believe, Possessions: A Novel, and *Murder in Byzantium.*

JAMES MANOS received his MA in philosophy from Miami University and his PhD in philosophy from DePaul University. He works on critical theory, ideology, and punishment. Currently, he is an ACLS public fellow researching the "school-to-prison-pipeline" and alternatives to zero tolerance policies.

NICK MITCHELL teaches black feminist studies, critical theory, and Marxist thought in the Department of Ethnic Studies at University of California–Riverside. Nick's current book project, *Disciplinary Matters: Black Studies, Women's Studies, and the Neoliberal University,* develops an archival approach and conceptual framework that considers black studies and women's studies formations since the 1970s as sites where the neoliberal university first learned to do business.

KELLY OLIVER is W. Alton Jones Professor of philosophy at Vanderbilt University. She is the author of over one hundred articles and ten books. Her most recent publications include *Animal Lessons: How They Teach Us to Be Human, Weapon as Weapons of War: Iraq, Sex and the Media, The Colonization of Psychic Space: Toward a Psychoanalytic Social Theory,* and *Witnessing: Beyond Recognition.*

DERRICK QUINTERO is fifty-two years old. He has been on Tennessee's death row since 1991. He had to learn to reach inside in order to reach out. Soon he, an innocent man, will find his freedom again. Soon . . .

SHOKOUFEH SAKHI received her PhD in political science at York University, Canada, with a specialization in political theory and political philosophy. Her work interrogates the phenomenology of resistance and subjectivity. Following her release from Tehran's Evin prison, where she was incarcerated for eight years as a prisoner of conscience, she came to Canada as a political refugee in 1992. She participated in the National Film Board of Canada's *The Tree That Remembers* and chaired the Iran Tribunal Foundation. She also presented at many academic and community events.

RUSSELL "MAROON" SHOATZ is a dedicated community activist, founding member of the Black Unity Council, former member of the Black Panther Party, and soldier in the Black Liberation Army. He is serving multiple life sentences as a U.S.-held prisoner of war. Shoatz spent more than twenty-two consecutive years in solitary confinement before being released into general population in 2014 after a long struggle led by the Shoatz family, the Human Rights Coalition, Abolitionist Law Center, and Scientific Soul Sessions. Shoatz is the author of *Maroon the Implacable: The Collected Writings of Russell Maroon Shoatz* (PM Press, 2013). He turned seventy years old in August 2013.

ANDREA SMITH is associate professor of media and cultural studies at University of California–Riverside. She is the author of *Conquest: Sexual Violence and American Indian Genocide and Native Americans* and *The Christian Right: The Gendered Politics of Unlikely Alliances*. She is also co-founder of Incite! Women of Color Against Violence.

ERIC A. STANLEY is a President's postdoctoral fellow in the Departments of Communication and Critical Gender Studies at the University of California–San Diego. The editor of *Captive Genders: Trans Embodiment and the Prison Industrial Complex*, Eric's other writing can be found in the journals *Social Text*, *American Quarterly*, *Women and Performance*, and *TSQ*.

ADRIAN SWITZER is program coordinator of the Department of Liberal Studies, Honors Academy faculty fellow, and lecturer of philosophy at Park University in Kansas City. Dr. Switzer's research and teaching interests are in the areas of Kantian and post-Kantian European thought. The author—and translator—of various articles and book chapters on such figures as Kant, Nietzsche, Heidegger, Foucault, Deleuze, Jean-Luc Nancy, and Luce Irigaray, Dr. Switzer is currently completing a manuscript on twentieth-century revolutionary politics and contemporary aesthetics.

SARAH TYSON is an assistant professor of philosophy at the University of Colorado–Denver. Her research has focused on questions of authority, history, and exclusion with a particular interest in the historical exclusion of women from philosophy, as reflected in "Reclamation from Absence? Luce Irigaray and Women in the History of Philosophy" (*Hypatia*, 2013). Since taking a class with inmates on death row, her research has focused on mass incarceration as reflected by the forthcoming anthology, edited with Joshua Hall, titled *Philosophy Imprisoned: The Love of Wisdom in the Age of Mass Incarceration* (Lexington, 2014).

LISA WALSH lectured in French studies and critical theory at the University of Nottingham and currently works as an independent scholar in Austin, Texas.

MATT S. WHITT is a postdoctoral fellow in the Thompson Writing Program at Duke University, where he works at the intersections of philosophy and political theory. His main interests are transformations of sovereignty and the acts of exclusion that shape political communities. His writing has been published in *Political Theory*, *Theory & Event*, and *Constellations* (forthcoming), and he has taught a wide variety of courses at Duke, Vanderbilt University, and Warren Wilson College.

BENJAMIN S. YOST is associate professor of philosophy at Providence College. He specializes in Levinas's ethics, Kant's practical philosophy, and normative jurisprudence. His published work, which appears in journals such as *Kantian Review*, *Continental Philosophy Review*, and *Journal of Social Philosophy*, analyzes arguments for and against the death penalty and develops a Levinasian argument for the abolition of capital punishment.

SCOTT ZEMAN works in the Department of Psychology and Neuroscience at the University of Colorado–Boulder. His research interests include psychoanalysis, trauma theory, philosophy of science, and the influence of unconscious structural power on modern forms of social justice and injustice.